Gil Graham 1995

WINGED PROMISES
A History of No 14 Squadron, RAF
1915-1945

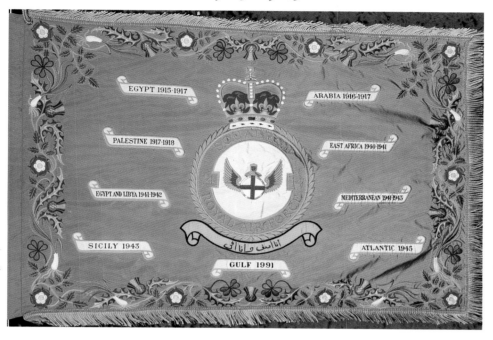

THE SQUADRON'S QUEEN STANDARD

The first Standard with eight Battle honours was presented to the Squadron on 21 August 1954, at RAF Fassberg, Germany, by Air Vice Marshal T C Traill CB OBE DFC. This Standard was laid up in St Clement Danes, London on 22 January 1984. A second Standard with a ninth honour added for the Gulf was presented by Air Chief Marshal Sir Keith Williamson GCB KCB AFC at RAF Bruggen, Germany on 26 November 1992.

Published by The RAF Benevolent Fund Enterprises

Winged Promises

Published by: The Royal Air Force
Benevolent Fund Enterprises,
Building 15, RAF Fairford,
Glos GL7 4DL, England

Publishing Director: Paul A Bowen
Publishing Coordinator: Karen Pell
Typesetting & Design: Sharron Lawrence
Editorial Assistant: Bill Bushell
Cover design: Graham Finch

ISBN 1-899808-45-0

Printed in Hong Kong

FOREWORD FOR No. 14 SQUADRON

by

HIS MAJESTY KING HUSSEIN I

The 'Winged Crusaders' is indeed an appropriate nickname for No 14 Squadron. The Squadron began its distinguished career in the Holy Land at a time of change. Sharif Hussein of Mecca had just launched the Great Arab Revolt to gain Arab independence from Ottoman rule. Operations by No 14 Squadron - in support of General Allenby and Emir Feisal - in Arabia, Transjordan, Palestine and Syria, helped to defeat Turkish opposition and establish the Middle East of today.

Yet, even under the Mandate system, squadrons of the Royal Air Force were called to play a stabilising role in the region following Trenchard's doctrine of 'Control from the Air'. It was during this period that the Squadron strengthened its bond with the Hashemites in Transjordan by using air power to protect and support the independence, freedom and security of Transjordan from the turmoil of the late 1920s and the 1930s culminating in World War II where No 14 Squadron fought hard throughout the Middle East.

Following World War II, the Middle East and the Holy Land continued to be the centre of turmoil and conflict and air power continued to play a pivotal role in the security and defence of regional states. War and conflict took a heavy toll on the region at a time when military might seemed the only way to maintain a sense of security and stability.

During the Gulf War, the Royal Air Force again deployed to the region under the banner of the United Nations to uphold world peace and international security. It was the tragedy of this war that demonstrated the fallacy of the regional arms race and that real security and stability only comes from peaceful co-existence and co-operation and not from the threat of war. For the first time in decades, the Middle East and the Holy Land look set to enjoy the fruits of a just, lasting and comprehensive peace.

However, the prospect of peace in the Middle East has not diminished the threat of conflicts and instability affecting the world. We now live in a new order where all nations should work for international peace and stability. This noble task, rich in the sacrifice and tradition exemplified in the history of No 14 Squadron, must be met with courage and determination. This book is a dedication to all the men of No 14 Squadron, those 'Winged Crusaders' who served, fought and died so that this world can enjoy greater peace and prosperity.

Hussein I
Amman January 1996

CONTENTS
FOREWORD (BY HM KING HUSSEIN OF JORDAN)
PREFACE (BY THE LORD DERAMORE)
ACKNOWLEDGEMENTS

PREFACE

In 1986 some, who had served on No 14 Squadron during the Second World War, suggested a book should be written about its contribution to the Allied Victory. As I had met Professor Vincent Orange in connection with the biography of Air Chief Marshal 'Mary' Coningham which he was then writing, I asked him if he would be willing to undertake this task. He agreed readily and enthusiastically, but suggested the history should cover the years from 1915 to 1945, so as to include the RFC operations in WW1 and the Squadron's association with Lawrence of Arabia.

Professor Orange made a start by collecting documents, photographs and personal reminiscences, which flowed into his office at the University of Canterbury, Christchurch, New Zealand, where he is the senior lecturer in History. They came from this country, Australia, New Zealand and Canada. At the same time his official commitments grew and his growing reputation led to extensive lecture tours in the USA and elsewhere. This and the writing of other biographies denied him the time to devote to the extra-curricular activity of writing our history.

By great good fortune, control of the project passed to the right man at the right time and Air Vice-Marshal Deryck Stapleton has steered the book to publication. He commanded No 14 Squadron in the early days of WW2 and the fact that the history has seen the light of day is due to his tireless and dedicated work.

The book is however the result of co-operation between four authors, each of whom has contributed one or more chapters. Professor Orange has written the first in its entirety and has vetted the others. Inevitably, there may be some diversity in style, but it is hoped that readers will find this of help rather than a hindrance to understanding the realities of life with a squadron, which is unique in having an Arabic motto and has served for most of its (now) 81 years overseas.

There are tales of high endeavour, courage, humour and tragedy. We, who have lived to tell the story, want it to be a worthy tribute to all those who served with No 14 Squadron. They came from the United Kingdom, Australia, Canada, Denmark, Kenya, New Zealand, Palestine, South Africa and South America. A large number of them never returned to their homelands or did so with their health irreparably damaged.

On a personal note, I had the privilege of serving with them in WW2. I shared their comradeship and experienced the wonderful team spirit that imbued the whole Squadron from the CO himself to the humblest 'erk'. For most of the time, we lived a nomadic existence, erecting our tents and moving from place to place. Conditions were often harsh and uncomfortable, luxuries non-existent and rations limited. We were a masculine company, rough in humour, quick in sympathy and stern in loyalty. There were married men separated from their wives and children for years on end and the unmarried distant from their families and loved ones, but we made the best of it and got on with the job. It never occurred to any of us to ask for counselling or claim financial compensation for any stress we suffered!

THE LORD DERAMORE
PRESIDENT OF NO 14 SQUADRON RAF REUNION ASSOCIATION.

ACKNOWLEDGEMENTS

At the start of this project, requests for memoirs and photographs went to past members of the Squadron, these to be channelled to Dr Vincent Orange at the University of Canterbury in Christchurch, New Zealand. The responses were overwhelming - a cellar full - from all over the planet, particularly from the Commonwealth, and of course from the UK. Without them this project would have been impossible. Where appropriate we have acknowledged the origins of material in the chapters, but the grateful thanks of the authors must be recorded, for all those sources were collectively invaluable in contributing to describing the background spirit and structure of the Squadron, yet because of print economies have remained unused in the text. They have been transferred to the archives of the RAF Museum at Hendon.

It is fair and deserving to record the special thanks of the authors for notable contributions towards the genesis of this book. In particular:-

To Mr Sebastian Cox, Deputy Head, Squadron Leader Singleton, and Mrs Donna Walsh of the Air Historical Branch at the Ministry of Defence for their unstinted help and advice in obtaining official records, information and photographs, from their own and Public Records sources. And to the Squadron for the provision of the photograph of their Battle Honours Standard in the frontispiece.

To Lady Patricia Selway for the loan of the unpublished manuscript on the story of the Wellesley, written by her husband the late Air Marshal Sir Anthony Selway KCB DFC, the first No 14 Squadron Commander in WW II.

To the family of the late Colonel Sir Henry Cox KCMG, CMG, DSO, the British Resident in Amman from 1923 to 1939, in particular to his late wife Lady Edith Cox and to his daughter Patricia, and to the daughters Jean and Evelyn of the late Wing Commander S Grant-Dalton DSO, AFC, for their great help over photographs and comments about the early days of the Squadron in WW I, and in Transjordan. Also, to the widow Margaret, son Anthony, and daughter Jennifer of the late Wing Commander John C McGregor Lunn for their helpfulness and consent in using some of their photographs to illustrate events at Amman in the late 1930's.

To Air Vice-Marshal 'Les' Moulton, 'Knocker' Norris, and Flight Lieutenant John Willis for their helpful observations and comments on the contents of chapters 4 and 5. It must also be remarked that several of the amusing 'legends' in the early chapters are recorded from second and third hand sources, no doubt embroidered in the telling and maybe inaccurate in detail, but nevertheless true in theme and happening!

To Dr Michael Crowe, son of Air Commodore H G Crowe, CBE, MC, who provided his father's memoirs and photograph albums and to Ernest G Hardy (Historical Researcher) who did sterling work at the Public Records Office in the beginning and provided Dr Orange with microfilms of the Squadron's Operational Records for WWII.

The author of Chapter 6 wishes to express his thanks to a host of Australians, Britons and others, without whose contributions the chapter could not have been written. Of the Australians especial thanks are due to Group Captain Ken Dee, DFC, RAAF (Ret'd), who corresponded regularly, sent a vast amount of written and photographic material from his countrymen and circulated the first draft of chapter 6 'down under' for correction and amplification. To Jack Canavan, who sadly died before this book was published; Flying Officer Wally Clarke-Hall, DFC, Ron Haley, Squadron Leader R W Lapthorne, DFC, Flying Officer Neil O'Connor, DFC, who contributed so much to the account, and to another Antipodean, Neville Freeman (RNZAF), who also conveyed copies of the complete manuscript to Dr Orange in Christchurch.

A debt of gratitude is owed also to the following Britons:- Group Captain W S G Maydwell, DSO, DFC, RAF (Ret'd), who contributed so much to Chapter 6, which covered the time of his command. He vetted every page for errors and omissions. To Flt Lt Gil Graham DFM RAF (Ret'd), who drew all the maps except one that adorn the book and provided dramatic accounts of operations, during which he flew as Maydwell's rear gunner. The one other map is that agreed for publication by Professor Michael Handel of the Dept of Strategy in the US Naval War Office, Rhode Island, USA. To Ray Ball, Hugh Bates, DFC, whose sense of humour shines through his reminiscences, Harry Lee and two who have died during the long gestation of this book, namely Dr Athol Forbes (Squadron MO) and John Stuart (WOp/ AG), who was the turret gunner in Donovan's Marauder crew. To Mrs Colin Fforde, who kindly translated Walter Honig's account from the German and commented "I'm glad the British behaved like Gentlemen".

Most importantly our thanks to the uncomplaining and hardworking operators of word processors, who miraculously produced impeccably typed manuscript from chaotically typed and scribbled notes. The majority of this work was done at 'Copy Cats' of Axminster by Brenda Burt, Mary Grant and Anne and Michelle Slee. Heroines all. In Watlington Mrs Maria Ranford of 'Perfect Words' recorded and retyped three times the initial drafts of Chapters 7 & 8. By a trick of fate she herself hailed from near Grottaglie! Vicky Taylor of Ryedale Secretarial Services worked wonders in the production of a coherent draft of Chapter 6 in the early stages.

Last, but by no means least, their most grateful thanks from the authors of all the Chapters to their spouses, who bore so nobly with husbands, who must have seemed intolerably obsessed by events of fifty years ago.

D C STAPLETON,
CO-ORDINATING EDITOR, AXMINSTER DEVON.

'The Squadron's WWI Aircraft'

Martin Farman S.7.

Martinsyde G 100.

BE.2c.

'The Squadron's WWI Aircraft'

D.H 1A. (RAF Museum, Hendon, London, NW9 5LL - Ref No. P1367)

RE 8.

Nieuport Scout.

Bristol F26 Fighter ('Brisfit').

CHAPTER ONE

WINGED CRUSADERS

1915-1918

The Palestine campaign, the Last Crusade, can never be divorced from romance, although the tribulations of the desert, added to the exhaustion of the fighting and the labour on the lines of communication necessary to support it, often obscured that romance from the troops engaged.[1]

AN ARABIC CONNECTION

This Squadron is the only one in the Royal Air Force with an Arabic motto. It may be translated as *I spread my wings and keep my promise:* words from The Koran suggested by the Emir Abdullah of Transjordan. The motto was formally approved by King George VI in May 1937 and appears on the Squadron's badge, presented in August of that year by Air Vice-Marshal Cuthbert MacLean, Head of Middle East Command. The badge, showing a winged plate containing a scarlet St George's Cross surmounted by the shoulder-pieces and helmet of a suit of armour, was intended to convey the idea of a crusader. This was an appropriate idea, for No 14 Squadron's earliest operations were in fact directed against the Turk, though not against Islam: just as the wiser crusaders looked for Muslim allies in the Middle East, so did No 14 Squadron assist the Arabs - and the immortal Lawrence - in their fight for independence.

'Each year since its formation,' wrote Abdullah to the Commanding Officer on 7 February 1943, 'I have been pleased to receive greetings from the officers and men of No 14 Squadron. Now, once again, I acknowledge your kind salutation and in return send you my wishes of good fortune for the Squadron in the future.' Abdullah, a son of Sharif Hussein of Mecca, had resided in Amman since 1921, making it the capital of Transjordan, a hard land east of Palestine. Amman had also been the Squadron's home for many years between the wars and several officers and men - who had been brought up on The Bible - found a grim amusement in the fact that King David sent Uriah the Hittite to his death there. The aerodrome at Amman lent point to the joke because it was situated on a little plateau among steep hills with an abrupt drop into a deep wadi at the western end. By 1943, it was practically unusable and even in biplane days had alarmed inexperienced pilots.

TOO CLOSE TO LONDON

The men who would become the first winged crusaders were posted from the headquarters of the Royal Flying Corps' 5th Wing to form a new squadron under the command of Major George Todd at Shoreham, near Brighton in West Sussex, on 3

February 1915.[2] Most squadrons formed hitherto had been sent to the Western Front, but by 1915 it was clear that the army in Egypt needed more air support because Turkey's entry into the war on the side of the Central Powers in October 1914 posed a serious threat to the Suez Canal.

'Sholto' Douglas, soon to become a famous fighter pilot and in the next war a distinguished air commander, was posted to No 14 Squadron on 1 July 1915. By then it was based at Hounslow Heath near Heathrow, now London's principal airport, and was being prepared for service overseas with the latest BE.2c aircraft. "We were a rather wild lot of youngsters," recalled Douglas, "and much too close to London for our own good. One evening, the Squadron ambulance was commandeered and driven to the Piccadilly Hotel where it was brazenly parked outside. That was the last straw, and our Wing Commander moved us out of the reach of temptation by ordering the Squadron down to Gosport, where he had his headquarters." That episode, together with a couple of crashes, persuaded Major Todd that Douglas could be of service to his country in another squadron.[3]

OFF TO EGYPT

The Squadron sailed for Egypt at 1700hrs on 7 November 1915 aboard an Australian Blue Funnel liner, SS Anchises, under the watchful eye of Lieutenant Colonel Geoffrey Salmond, designated commander of a new wing - No 5 - of which No 14 Squadron would form part. At the very outset of its active life, an Australian presence is seen in the Squadron's story - one that will be very important throughout both world wars. Alexandria was reached on the morning of the 17th and everyone remained there for about a week before moving to Heliopolis, near Cairo, where a site for an aerodrome had been selected and prepared. No-one then guessed that later in the war Heliopolis would become, in the words of Captain J C Watson, the Squadron's first historian, 'a huge flying town where all the varied activities that war had forced into the purview of our flying forces would be studied and practiced'.[4]

Shortly after Christmas, No 14 Squadron was relieved at Heliopolis by No 17 Squadron and moved about 65 miles north-east to Ismailia on Lake Timsah, flanking the Suez Canal. These squadrons, together with two others - Nos 30 and 31 - were intended to cover the entire Middle East. Early in January 1916, after the evacuation of Gallipoli, General Sir Archibald Murray had taken command in that theatre. He was charged to preserve order in Egypt and the Nile Valley and prevent invasion either by Senussi tribesmen from the Western Desert or Turkish forces from Palestine and Syria. To help him, 5 Wing HQ moved with Murray's HQ to Ismailia on 9 February.

Ismailia, when No 14 Squadron arrived, was a small French town and the Canal had long been administered from there. 'It was', wrote Watson, 'an oasis of shade and tropical luxuriance in striking contrast with the hard glaring desert that surrounds it, designed and laid out with that happy symmetry in which the French excel, fated to be all that most of the Squadron were to see of civilisation for many a day.' The aerodrome lay about a mile to the north-west of the town and two wooden hangars had already been erected there.

On 20 January 1916, after nearly a year in command of No 14 Squadron, Major Todd was succeeded by a man who went on to become one of the Royal Air Force's most capable and influential officers: Air Chief Marshal Sir Wilfrid Freeman. Unfortunately, his service with the Squadron lasted little more than five months, for he was succeeded on 1 July by Major Edgar Bannatyne.

SINAI

Sinai is a huge triangular waste of shifting sand, traversed by three main routes - northern, middle, and southern - which meet at El Arish, near the north-eastern edge of Sinai, close the Palestine border. The northern route, along the coast from El Arish to Romani (and from there to El Qantara) was exposed to bombardment from the sea and had therefore not been regarded in pre-war days as an enemy's likely line of advance into Egypt. In fact, it was the route chosen by the Turks because the broad shallows off the coast made close bombardment by heavy guns difficult. Water supplies on all three routes were an invader's main problem, though less so on the northern.

Between March and June, sandstorms are frequent in Sinai and sometimes last for days. 'No flying can be done during a bad storm', wrote Peter Drummond (an outstanding Australian airman in both World Wars who reached Air Marshal rank), 'and for many days afterwards there remains in the air a brown haze extending as high as 10,000ft, through which it is difficult to see for any distance, though observation downwards is unaffected. 'This haze', he remarked with characteristic understatement, 'is a serious nuisance when flying over the almost featureless desert stretching from the Canal to the mountain range between El Arish and Agaba.'

Throughout 1916, aeroplanes operating in Sinai would carry out numerous long flights over featureless country. It was impossible to lay down a definite route for pilots to follow and difficult for them if they made a forced landing. All machines therefore carried four days' rations of food and water for the pilot and his observer, a rifle and ammunition for protection against hostile Bedouin or hyenas, a signal pistol, smoke bombs and strips of cloth to lay out on the sand whenever aircraft were heard. Most airmen also had gold coins sewn into their clothing to encourage any Bedouin they met to rescue them and some learned a few appropriate Arabic words. Both sides promised rewards for handing over British airmen unharmed, but Peter Drummond believed the British had a better reputation for prompt payment.[6]

HARD WORK ON THE GROUND

Aeroplane maintenance was a constant problem because huge contrasts between high and low temperatures, both during transit from England and on arrival in Egypt, caused woodwork to shrink and warp. Ground crews - those largely anonymous heroes of all aviation enterprises, civil or military - were plagued, in the words of one historian, by 'the blistering day heat and freezing night temperatures which played havoc with wood, fabric and engines'. Before erecting a new machine, all parts had to be stripped, all nuts and bolts tightened and everything retried. Many parts were found useless before being used and spares were never plentiful. As in the Second World War, the situation was aggravated by the frequent loss of cargo ships to enemy action. Also, a variety of tasks required a variety of aircraft types, and war stimulated rapid changes to those types: all natural enough, but the shortage of spares, tools and manuals kept ground crews on their toes in both wars. As for engines, the main problem was over-heating. The 90hp Royal Aircraft Factory engine gave no trouble, being air-cooled, but the water-cooled Hispano-Suiza and Beardmore engines gave plenty. Desert air remains hot up to 4,000ft in summer and before this height could be reached, many engines had boiled away most of their water. Extra radiators were needed and after much experiment proved successful, though Drummond observed that the extra weight reduced performance. Oil sometimes became so hot that it lost its lubricant qualities and this led to seizures. Again, extra oil tanks proved an adequate answer.

A SCATTERED SQUADRON

The Squadron was soon widely scattered. Headquarters and A Flight remained at Ismailia, where the Flight's major task was to patrol the so-called middle route through Sinai from Egypt to Palestine. B Flight was sent to the Western Desert with troops and armoured cars because Senussi tribesmen were threatening to invade. Two BE.2cs had been transported to El Daba (100 miles west of Alexandria) in December 1915 and from there they were flown a further 80 miles west to Mersa Matruh. Captain F H Jenkins was in command with four officers and an unknown number of other ranks: first of hundreds of 14 Squadron men to serve in the Western Desert - though not in this war.

As for C Flight, it was stationed on the east bank of the Canal and 20 miles north of Ismailia at El Qantara, later to become the great base of the army which invaded and conquered Palestine. At that time, it lay only 30 miles from Turkish lines. C Flight carried out daily reconnaissances between February and June 1916 and frequently raided important oases such as Bir el Abd and Bir el Mazar along the route from Romani to El Arish. Numerous photographs were taken during the spring of that year and when the Turks began to construct defensive positions in the El Arish area, C Flight bombed them - if that is not too impressive a word, here and below, for the almost literally aimless dropping of a few 20lb bombs. These words in no way detract from the bravery and determination shown by Squadron crews, but at this early date they simply lacked the equipment and training necessary to strike heavy blows. As we shall often see in this campaign, ground fire soon became seriously accurate even if bombing did not.[8]

BIR HASSANA: THE PERFECT BOMB DROP

One raid, however, provides a brilliant exception to this rule. From January onwards, regular weekly bombing raids had been made on Turkish strong points, especially three that were quite close together south-west of El Arish: Bir Maghara, Bir Rodh Salem and Bir Hassana. The destruction of enemy water supplies was naturally a prime objective and one attack on Bir Hassana's reservoir has recently been described by an American historian as a 'feat of precision bombing probably unequalled on any front up to that time'.[9] It was carried out by the Squadron's first hero (a man who was, incidentally,

Australian-born though living in New Zealand at the outbreak of the war): Lieutenant Cedric Waters Hill.

Bir Hassana lay about 90 miles south-east of El Qantara and was at that time, as Hill recorded, 'an important Turkish outpost with a large concentration of their army. They had constructed a large concrete reservoir and it was kept filled with water pumped into it from nearby wells'. C Flight, based at El Qantara, was asked to have a crack at it. Because it lay so far away, an extra fuel tank was fitted and on several occasions in January and February pilots flew there solo, carrying three bombs each, but they had no success whatever. Meanwhile, Major Harold Blackburn (C Flight Commander) was at work on a bomb-sight which consisted - in Hill's description - of 'a wooden bracket fitted to the side of the aircraft and on this was fitted a wire running fore and aft, and above that a hinged sighting arm and a spirit level'. The method of using it was to 'fly straight and level dead up wind towards the target so that the target appeared to run along the sighting wire. The sighting arm was adjusted for the height of the aeroplane above the target and the bomb was released as the target reached the sighting point on the wire'.

Hill practiced using the gadget whenever he could, but the Flight had few bombs to spare, so he made his own. "I decided," he said, "to copy a 20lb bomb in shape, size and weight in the form of a bag made of aeroplane fabric and filled with sand. The tail of the bomb could be made of tin sheet." As soon as he had a satisfactory prototype, he moved quickly into mass production. The Flight lacked a bombing range, so once again he made his own amid the many areas of shallow water near the Canal: "by placing an aiming mark on a wet area," he explained, "one had an excellent self-marking target. The splash from the sand bomb hitting the water could clearly be seen by the pilot."

Lt Cedric Hill bombs Turkish Water Tank

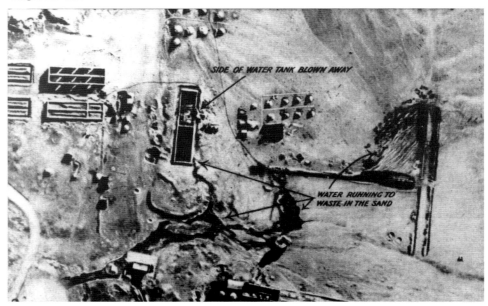

The destroyed Tank and water loss.

Regular practice soon enabled Hill to drop a bomb close to a given spot and on 26
February 1916 he was ordered to make a solo attempt on the Bir Hassana reservoir
early next morning in a BE.2c armed with two 20lb bombs - and the contemporary
blockbuster, a fearful weapon weighing no less than 100lbs. He was also to photograph
results. Apart from the mere detail of actually hitting the target, Hill faced two other
problems. One was to find Bir Hassana (which he had never visited before) and the
other was to avoid the Turkish defenses (thoroughly alerted by previous attacks). He
had, however, seen photographs of the reservoir and spotted it easily from about two
miles away at 13,000ft. As for the defenses, the anti-aircraft guns were not terribly
accurate at first, but their efforts were supplemented by rifle fire and occasionally a
rifle bullet could be heard hitting the plane.

Hill dropped one of his 20-pounders, but it missed by some yards. Still under fire, he
bravely flew round for a second attempt, adjusting his bomb sight, and tried again - this
time with his blockbuster. Not only did he actually land it in the reservoir from 3,000ft,
he even managed to take a photograph of it exploding and sending a huge plume of
water spurting high into the sky. He then returned safely to El Qantara, completing a
round trip of over 180 miles. A reconnaissance flight next day took another picture
which showed the reservoir only half full and a vast stain on the ground nearby. On
the night of his triumph, Hill recalled, "We had a party in the Mess during which all
drink except Creme de Menthe ran out and I finished up by getting as drunk as an owl
on that. I have never been able to touch the awful green stuff since."

Two months later, on 3 May 1916, this gallant airman failed to return from a
reconnaissance over El Arish. Ground fire had damaged his BE.2c, obliging him to land
near an Arab village on the coast close to a big sand dune known as Mount Carsius,

about 40 miles east of Romani. The Arabs greeted him with rifle fire, so he got behind his machine, detached the Lewis gun, gathered together some ammunition, food and a couple of water bottles and then set fire to the aircraft. He took advantage of the flames, smoke and explosions (as the rest of his ammunition went up) to bolt for the shelter of some thorn bushes near the sand dune and dig himself in. Firing single shots, he managed to keep the Arabs at bay for more than two hours until both he and his ammunition were exhausted. Having captured him, some of the Arabs favoured killing him immediately; others wanted their women to have the pleasure of mutilating him first; and a few advised selling him to the British at Romani. Eventually, they handed him over - undamaged - to a Turkish camel patrol. Thus ended Cedric Hill's memorable service with No 14 Squadron, but his wartime adventures were far from over. The fact that he was never decorated lends weight to the opinion of many Servicemen in all wars that gallantry awards seem to be rather a lottery; certainly the reasons for recognising some actions and not others can be hard to fathom.[10]

AUSTRALIAN ARRIVAL

A Middle East Brigade was formed under Geoffrey Salmond (now promoted to Brigadier General) on 1 April 1916 and Lieutenant Colonel Philip Joubert de la Ferte succeeded him as head of 5 Wing. During that month, a squadron formed in Australia arrived at Suez: No 67 (Australian) Squadron, later to be known as No 1 Squadron, Australian Flying Corps. Several pilots and all the observers were promptly sent on to England for further training; the rest were divided into five parties for local training. One party, under Captain Richard Williams (later to become an Air Marshal and one of Australia's most influential airmen) went to No 14 Squadron HQ at Ismailia. Another, under Captain D V J Blake, went to that Squadron's C Flight at El Qantara. Two parties went to No 17 Squadron at Heliopolis, near Cairo, and the fifth to an aircraft park at Abbassia, also near Cairo. These arrangements benefited the Australian fitters and riggers, who were found plenty of work to do, but at first the pilots were given little opportunity to fly. Nevertheless, as L W Sutherland (an Australian observer) pointed out: "The best pilot, the prince of observers, would not have been worth a burial service unless he had the right kind of backing on the ground."[11]

EL ARISH: A SUCCESSFUL AIR RAID

It was also in April 1916 that German aircraft - Rumpler C1 bomber/reconnaissance two-seater machines and Pfalz E II single-seat escorts - first appeared on the Sinai front at an airfield near El Arish. By June, their activities were becoming serious enough to warrant a major attempt to eliminate them on the ground because the BE.2c, in the opinion of Oliver Stewart (a pilot highly regarded by later historians), was utterly incapable in combat, 'the most defenceless thing in the sky'. Nevertheless, this raid, mounted on 18 June by eleven of these machines (eight from No 14 Squadron, three from No 17 Squadron) proved to be - in Watson's opinion - one of the most successful in the Squadron's Great War career. Two BE.s, each carrying an observer, were ordered to fly over El Arish at 7,000ft to protect the other nine (all flown as single-seaters) and record results. Encouraged by Cedric Hill's success with a 100lb bomb, two of the BE.s carried one of these heavies each; the rest carried eight 20-pounders. In addition, the Royal Navy sent trawlers to patrol off the coast and rescue any pilots forced to land in the sea.[12]

The first BE. to arrive (flown by Second Lieutenant Archie MacLaren of No 14 Squadron) dropped its blockbuster from no more than 100ft, 'blowing an enemy aeroplane and its attendant personnel on the ground to pieces', according to Watson. For this feat, MacLaren would be awarded the Military Cross. A second German machine was also hit on the ground and a third, which had just taken off, was destroyed by a small bomb. Six of the ten hangars were hit and two or three burned. Once they had dropped all their bombs, the BE.s strafed the aerodrome with machine-gun fire before making off. The enemy was taken completely by surprise because the British machines, while still within friendly territory, had flown ten miles out to sea and then headed towards the Palestine coast before approaching El Arish from the north-east. Enemy posts in Sinai were therefore unable to provide their usual early warning.

Nevertheless, three of the eleven aircraft failed to return. Captain R J Tipton of No 14 Squadron was shot down over El Arish and captured, though he later escaped. Captain H A van Ryneveld of No 17 Squadron (a South African who would make the first flight from London to Cape Town in 1920) was forced to land on the Sinai coast because a bullet had penetrated the engine sump. Captain Stewart Grant-Dalton of No 14 Squadron (with Second Lieutenant D R Paris as observer) landed beside him and an unsuccessful attempt was made to take off from soft sand with three men aboard. The machine was then dragged to firmer sand and took off safely, the damaged BE. having first been destroyed. Grant-Dalton, who would serve as head of the New Zealand Permanent Air Force from 1929 to 1931, was awarded the first of his two DSOs for this feat and Paris received the MC. The third casualty of the raid, Second Lieutenant M Minter, landed in the sea, but was rescued by one of the providential trawlers.

HOW TO CO-OPERATE WITH THE ARMY

A less spectacular but equally valuable operation was carried out in co-operation with ground forces during the summer of 1916. These troops were sent along Sinai's middle route to destroy wells in the Wadi Muksheib - some 40 miles south-east of Ismailia - and so render any Turkish use of this route virtually impossible. Aircraft of No 14 Squadron patrolled ahead of the troops, reporting regularly to the commander via wireless operators travelling with him. They also dropped messages and covered the withdrawal, once the wells had been destroyed.

As a rule, airmen and soldiers were already working well together. For example, Brigadier General H E Street of the Anzac Mounted Division approved some sensible general rules for air-ground co-operation on 31 July 1916. "In order to spare both crews and machines," he ordered, "the normal average to be expected of a sub-unit of two machines is three hours' reconnaissance in two days." "Moreover," he said, "it is essential that aeroplanes should be adequately protected from the sun, and arrangements will be made by Section Headquarters for transport for tent sheds to accompany columns to which a RFC unit is attached."

The RFC's functions, according to Street, were 'tactical reconnaissance, direction and observation of artillery fire, fighting against other aircraft, special missions' (long reconnaissance, bombing and incendiary raids) 'and offensive action against ground troops'. In common with other protective troops, the RFC was responsible for 'the protection of the force against surprise by day, weather permitting. An enemy once located should never be allowed to get away so long as he is within reach of aeroplane reconnaissance.'

Wireless messages giving tactical information were to be confirmed when possible by a dropped message. The signal K (message received) was always looked for on the ground, Street emphasised, and airmen must never assume that their message has been received until they see that signal. 'Verey lights,' wrote Street, 'or some form of smoke signal made by lighting a fire or burning a bush should be used to attract the attention of an aeroplane.' During an action, if a reconnaissance was required in a certain direction and no other means of communication was available, ground smoke or Verey lights should be used and a man carrying a white flag should run or canter 200 yards in the direction the reconnaissance is required. This procedure, Street pointed out, 'called for careful previous preparation'. To avoid confusion with enemy troops, British troops operating at a distance from the main force should carry with them blue or white flags to wave parallel to the ground when a friendly aircraft approached.

In conclusion, General Street required a pilot or observer to accompany Divisional HQ whenever it moved and establish a report centre there or at an advanced landing ground. This airman would advise the divisional commander as to RFC possibilities; send and receive messages, reconnoitre and lay out landing grounds; supervise any available RFC ground wireless station and, not least, ensure that the signal X was laid out on the ground near the report centre whenever an aircraft approached and arrange acknowledgement with the signal K.[13]

According to Peter Drummond, the development of aircraft co-operation with artillery during the Sinai-Palestine campaigns was handicapped partly by the slowness of Army commanders to realise the possibilities and partly by a shortage of aeroplanes, wireless operators and necessary equipment. The available maps were incomplete and inaccurate and there are few obvious landmarks in the Sinai desert. Numerous photographs were therefore taken. "Before an advance was attempted," recalled Drummond, "the whole of the enemy country to a depth of 30 to 40 miles had to be photographed." Most aircraft crossing the lines for any purposes also took photographs.[14]

Several Army officers were attached to No 14 Squadron during 1916 for training as observers. Having been given the latest information about the present position and possible lines of advance of both friendly and enemy forces, they were instructed in methods of reconnaissance and co-operation with artillery, using wireless as well as message bags and coloured signals. They were given a good trial in the air under the supervision of experienced pilots. Some found themselves at home in the air, others did not and returned to their units. Of those retained, Watson wrote, 'the most useful had the special dash yet caution which aerial work requires in that there could be no reference to higher authority for guidance in work carried out by air and well over enemy lines'. In this way, he concluded, 'the peculiar attributes which make a man suitable for aerial military duty were recruited for the Flying Corps in days when formal schools of instruction, apart from those concerned with the art of flying, were unknown'.

THE DANGERS OF ROUTINE RECONNAISSANCE

Richard Williams had assembled his flight at Heliopolis and taken delivery of his first BE.2c when, on the night of 19/20 July 1916, an urgent message arrived requiring all available pilots and aircraft to report immediately to No 14 Squadron at El Qantara, via Ismailia. Coming in to land at Ismailia next morning, Williams noticed a large crowd assembled in front of the hangars and learned later that they had come to see the Australian land, or perhaps crash. As it happened, he got down safely.

On arriving at El Qantara, Williams was told that the Squadron usually carried out a reconnaissance over the desert early each morning. Following the reconnaissance on 19 July, Brigadier General E W C Chaytor of the New Zealand Mounted Rifles had asked to see the country over which he might soon be fighting. The flight took place that afternoon and to everyone's surprise, Turkish troops were observed on the move and digging in at places much closer to the Canal than had been previously reported. By sending out a regular flight so early and then doing nothing for the rest of the day, No 14 Squadron now realised that it had been making life easy for the Turks, who only had to remain under cover for a few minutes each day. However, the practice of making an early morning reconnaissance was influenced by desert flying conditions. "Soon after sunrise," explained Williams, "the air above the sand became turbulent. In fact, by about 1100hrs it could be said to be violent," and flying above turbulence was difficult because the BE.2c had nothing like the power of even the de Havilland Tiger Moth of later days: it climbed very slowly to 2,000ft and thereafter could manage, at best 100ft per minute.[15]

THE BATTLE OF ROMANI

El Qantara, meanwhile, was growing rapidly from a small native village into a large military base and both railway lines and water pipes - without which no advance was possible - were being laid along the northern route towards Romani. The Turks, aware of this activity, planned an attack and No 14 Squadron had reported as early as 20 June 1916 a marked increase in enemy strength at Bir el Mazar, 25 miles west of El Arish. A month later, on 19 July, the Squadron reported the advance of a force estimated at 8-9,000 men, of whom about half were in Bir el Abd (only eight miles east of Romani) and the rest in Bir Jameil and Bir Bayud, two oases a few miles farther south. By the 22nd, it was clear that a major attack on the Canal was intended. British ground forces were therefore reinforced and every available aircraft - never more than 17 at any one time - was brought into the area.

On the night of 3/4 August, the Turks attempted to outflank Romani on the seaward side, but Major General H G Chauvel (commanding the Anzac Mounted Division) had foreseen the move and placed the 1st Light Horse Brigade there. The two forces met at midnight. The Turks, in greatly superior numbers, forced the Brigade to give ground, but its line remained unbroken. At dawn on 4 August, the 2nd Light Horse Brigade came up in support and though the Turks continued to advance, they suffered heavy casualties. British and Australian airmen were active all day, directing artillery fire, bombing and strafing. At the end of the day, the New Zealand Mounted Rifles Brigade and a Brigade of Yeomanry fell on the Turkish landward flank and at dawn on the 5th the enemy broke under a bayonet attack all along the line. The ground forces were not equipped for pursuit in the desert and lost touch with the retreating Turks, but the airmen harassed them all the way to El Arish. The Turks had committed over 18,000 men to this attack and lost almost a quarter of them, killed or captured, as well as large stocks of food and ammunition.[16]

Capt Stewart Grant-Dalton.

AERIAL COMBATS

Aerial combats were now becoming an intermittent hazard and the Squadron would eventually be equipped with as many as six D.H.1As to enable it to cope with enemy aircraft. This machine was a two-seater pusher (that is, a machine with its engine mounted behind the pilot). The observer, seated in front of the pilot, operated a moveable Lewis gun through a large field of fire and on 5 August an unnamed crew shot down a Rumpler C1 near Bir Salmana. But Second Lieutenants Leonard Hursthouse and George McDiarmid were wounded in a BE.2c on the 10th and next day another BE. was hit by ground fire and then attacked by two Rumplers, although its crew managed to reach British territory before making a forced landing. The pilot, Second Lieutenant E W Edwards, had been hit several times and his observer, Second Lieutenant J Brown, shot through the chest. An ambulance arrived, but Brown refused to have his wounds dressed before making his report, fearing that if he were moved he would faint from the pain. General Chaytor witnessed the incident: "The observer," he said, "very gallantly held himself together till he had dictated his report and verified it; then, his duty done, fainted and died two hours later." Brown had actually been at Port Said, about to embark for pilot training in England, when news of the Turkish offensive came through. He immediately telephoned the Squadron, seeking permission to return and take part in the defence.[17]

In 1952, Mr J F W Golding of Sidcup in Kent recalled these exciting days.[18] He served in No 14 Squadron throughout the Great War, became Flight Sergeant and was awarded the Meritorious Service Medal on 1 January 1918. In July 1916, wrote Mr Golding, 'I was detailed to proceed to Romani, where there was an advanced landing ground within a very short distance of the Turkish lines. Stationed with me were six men of the Australian Light Horse Regiment, acting as spotters for hostile aircraft. If one was seen, it was our duty to telephone to base and a BE.2c would soon see him off.' On 6 August, he reported the arrival of some enemy aircraft: 'Two or three fighters came out, but one of them, piloted by Captain Grant-Dalton, had the worst of a dogfight, forced-landed a few hundred yards from our little camp and stuck fast in some sand dunes. We were dashing forward towards it when we saw the pilot climb out and begin to hop his way towards us, so we ran back to our tent for a stretcher. He was badly shot up, with one finger off, a bullet through his knee and another in his foot. His machine was riddled.' This action earned Grant-Dalton his second DSO, gazetted on 26 November 1916, for conspicuous gallantry in action. According to the citation, 'he attacked two hostile aeroplanes, although quite unsupported. Later, after being attacked by another enemy machine and wounded in three places, be brought his machine back and landed safely.'

MORE AND BETTER TRAINING

By the summer of 1916, it was clear that the RFC in Egypt needed to improve the skill level of its ground and air crews locally. One of No 14 Squadron's most influential officers, Captain John Dixon-Spain, would play a leading part in setting up what had become, by the war's end, a huge training organisation. A technical training class began at Aboukir, ten miles east of Alexandria, on 21 August 1916 when Dixon-Spain arrived from No 14 Squadron and collected round him two or three mechanics under an experienced NCO and began instruction in engines, rigging and general flying subjects.

The class was renamed No 3 School of Aeronautics on 25 November and during the next ten months nearly 1,500 men attended the school, of whom 800 qualified. In June 1917 the School was placed directly under Middle East Brigade HQ and instruction expanded to include wireless use, machine gunnery, artillery observation, formation flying, reconnaissance, bomb sights and photography. In October the School moved again - to the Heliopolis Palace Hotel, near Cairo - where Dixon-Spain, now a major presided until he returned to England in May 1918.[19]

THE FIRST FORWARD LANDING GROUNDS

The British continued to lay rail lines and water pipes along the northern route, reaching a point 50 miles east of the Canal by October 1916. Ground forces accompanied this advance and required No 14 Squadron to find its first forward landing ground: in this war and the next, one of the strongest memories that many Squadron members carried away with them from the desert would be the seemingly endless quest for suitable sites - and the hard labour that followed, once such sites were found. The first of many was found three miles east of Bir Salmana and an aerodrome laid out that was, for a time, ahead of the Army's most forward positions. By November, A Flight was operating from there and bombed both the German aerodrome and the railway station at Beersheba in Palestine on the 11th. Turkish camps at Bir Magdhaba (20 miles south of El Arish) were also bombed. On the 24th, A Flight moved forward another 15 miles to a new landing ground at Mustabeg and B Flight then went to Ismailia to replace A Flight. As for C Flight, its fortunes are recounted below.

THE CAPTURE OF EL ARISH

At this time, No 14 Squadron received some new aircraft: Martinsyde G.100 Elephants. Why they were given that name, Oliver Stewart could not imagine. 'Although the aeroplane did have an appearance of great solidity and strength, it had little else to connect it with an elephant. We noted its only serious fault, was the poor view. The pilot sat just behind the trailing edge of the top plane with the trailing edge of the lower plane almost immediately below him. Forwards and upwards a big arc of view was blanked out by the top plane and downwards and forwards there was another big arc of view blanked out.' These large single-seaters, fitted with 160hp Beardmore engines, were the fastest machines yet operated by the British in the Middle East even though their top speed was a sedate 103mph. More important than sheer speed, however, were good flying characteristics, enabling the Elephants to carry heavy loads over long distances and thus to serve both as bombers and fighters.[20]

A and B Flights joined forces at Mustabeg to carry out many bombing and machine-gun raids, using the new Elephants as well as the old BE.2cs. Then, on 22 December 1916, aerial reconnaissance revealed that the Turks had abandoned their positions at El Arish and were retiring 20 miles down the wadi towards Bir Magdhaba, where trenches were being dug. Mounted troops were hastily sent in pursuit and after riding all night were in position to attack at dawn on the 23rd. Shortage of water made it imperative that Bir Magdhaba be captured before nightfall and as there was no possibility of infantry support, aircraft were used to the full extent of their power. Every machine that could be got to fly had already attacked the Turks on the 22nd and kept at it throughout the critical 23rd. Peter Drummond thought that this was the 'first occasion on which organised machine-gun attack from the air on trenches was attempted, and its effect on the enemy was considerable,' not least in distracting attention from charging horsemen. But most of the aircraft employed were BE.2cs - not an ideal machine for trench strafing - and few Turks were killed or even injured, despite the airmen's best efforts. On the other hand, German airmen did nothing whatever on either day. They had certainly been obliged to leave their aerodrome at short notice when the Turks suddenly decided to abandon El Arish, but Drummond was adamant that there was a 'hole-proof plan for continuance of air work during a squadron's movement'. This principle would be emphasised in desert fighting during the next world war by the RAF's great desert airmen: Tedder, Coningham and Drummond himself.[21]

A FUTILE EXPEDITION

Meanwhile, the Turkish occupation of Nekhl (85 miles south of El Arish) was said to threaten the British right flank in the event of an advance into Palestine. A small village with two wells and a Napoleonic fort, Nekhl had been the residence of the British Governor of Sinai before the Turkish invasion and so, said Drummond - somewhat cynically - "It is probable that the decision to re-occupy Nekhl was influenced more by political considerations than from any real fears for the safety of our flanks." Two columns of troops, setting out simultaneously from Ismailia and Suez, arranged to arrive at Nekhl on the morning of the fifth day. Two aeroplanes based at Ismailia provided reconnaissance en route and kept the two columns in touch with each by dropping message bags. An RFC officer travelled with the column from Ismailia, taking a supply of bombs and petrol loaded on camels. He was to select a landing ground as near as possible to Nekhl on which aeroplanes were to land on the night of Zero-minus-1 and take part in the attack next morning.

In order to take the enemy garrison by surprise, no reconnaissance flights were made to discover its strength, dispositions or equipment, and aeroplanes were forbidden to fly within sight of Nekhl before the actual attack. Unfortunately, the garrison had learned from Arabs that the columns were approaching and withdrew, unobserved and unmolested, two days before they arrived. If the mere sight of aeroplanes was thought likely to cause the garrison to withdraw, Drummond argued that they should have been sent to display themselves freely and so save the expense of sending out two columns - whose progress was certain to be observed and reported anyway. The evacuation by the Turks of the last piece of captured British territory would have sounded no less impressive to the British and Egyptian public had it been brought about by air action, and there would have been the possibility of inflicting at least a few casualties upon the enemy. In the event, the British garrison was soon withdrawn and the Turks then returned.[22]

C FLIGHT IN ARABIA

In October 1916, C Flight was sent on a journey of more than 700 miles from El Qantara south to Rabegh, a major port on the eastern coast of the Red Sea, to assist the Sharif of Mecca in his revolt against the Turks. Major A J Ross commanded the Flight and took with him five pilots and six observers, all officers.[23] The Flight was provided with five new BE.2cs, Crossley tenders specially designed for desert and mountain work and a detachment of soldiers to guard its landing ground. Mecca and Jeddah had quickly fallen to the Arabs and by September they had also taken Taif (the Turkish summer headquarters), but Medina - supplied by rail from Damascus in Syria over a distance of some 700 miles - held out against them. The Arabs feared a Turkish breakout from Medina and an advance on Rabegh. 'The initial difficulty in lending our aid to the Arab rebels,' recorded Captain Watson, 'was that the scene of operations - the Hejaz - was a Holy Land closed with fanatical determination by a tradition as old as the Mahommedan religion to all save Muslims.' For example, when C Flight arrived at Rabegh with an escort of British soldiers, the Sharif raised both political and religious objections to their presence and so the whole party was obliged to return to Suez.

On 13 November, however, a new detachment of six machines and the necessary personnel left Suez for Rabegh - this time without soldiers - and was allowed to land on the 16th. The Royal Navy built a jetty to permit the landing of the aircraft (in packing cases) and the heavy equipment. A site for an aerodrome was quickly found and soon the aircraft were being unpacked and erected, hangars put up and workshops constructed out of the cases. A detachment of Egyptian infantry now formed an aerodrome guard and dug several machine-gun posts around the perimeter.

HUGE, WHIRRING, DRONING BIRDS

'The difficulty and danger of our position as Christians in what hitherto was a forbidden land to all save Muslims and the need of walking warily to avoid all cause of offence was firmly impressed on all ranks,' wrote Watson. Even so, rifles were stacked close to all working places in case 'a sudden fanaticism or the lure of the large monetary award which the Turk at once offered for our destruction when he became aware of our presence' should undo the political preparation which had preceded C Flight's arrival. However, the Hejaz Arabs remained loyal to the Sharif: 'delighting in the new-found joy of modern firearms ... blended with their own curious assortment of battle array - scraps of crusader's armour, curved Arab daggers, scimitars and antiquated but often richly-decorated flintlock pistols.' Moreover, the addition of such a marvellous new weapon as the aeroplane to his army significantly enhanced the Sheriff's prestige. His men were both delighted and alarmed by the sight of 'huge whirring, droning birds' flying wherever they pleased at a breath-taking speed and, consequently, all the Squadron's personnel were treated with respect.

The airmen's first task was to make themselves an accurate map of the entire area of operations. Turkish strong points in the passes at Hamra and El Ghayir, from which troops might deploy onto the coastal plain and then advance via Rabigh to Mecca, were first photographed and then bombed. Regular reconnaissances were made of the passes leading to the plain near Rabegh and also farther north near Yenbo, where Prince Feisal's men held the town and threatened the flank of any Turkish advance southward. However, even the most detailed reports that a particular area showed no sign of an enemy presence did not prevent the circulation of wild rumours - and demands, which were difficult to refuse, for another reconnaissance.

FIRST LINKS WITH LAWRENCE

By the end of 1916, it was clear that a Turkish advance from Medina had no more chance of success than an Arab advance on Medina - and that Mecca's best defence would be to cut the rail link to Medina. Helped by a naval bombardment, Feisal captured Wejh on 24 January 1917 and it became the base for raids on that link. These raids, 'which demoralised the Turk and gave new courage and daring to the Arabs,' in Watson's opinion, 'were in plan and in their more daring execution the work of T E Lawrence'. Eventually, the Turks were forced to retire into Medina, though detachments were pushed north to protect the railway. Medina could neither be relieved nor evacuated and some 12,000 troops were largely immobilised.

During March, Colonel Wilson - in command of the British ground forces - decided to move his base to Yenbo for strategic purposes and Major Ross was ordered to move his flight there as soon as possible in order to attack the railway and Turkish troops. His major worry was sickness (mostly typhoid) among both officers and men, though shipping was available to carry the worst affected to Port Sudan. With the help of soldiers and labour supplied by Prince Feisal, a landing ground 300yds by 300yds was cleared and levelled on high ground north of Wejh by the morning of 17 March. On that day, six officers, seven NCOs and 23 men left Rabegh by sea for Wejh, joined later by others, and all arrived safely on the 19th. A search began at once for additional landing grounds. On 31 March, Ross received heartening news from Lawrence that Turkish deserters reported the destruction by fire of three German aeroplanes in Medina.[24]

C Flight rejoined the rest of No 14 Squadron at Deir el Balah, south of Gaza, early in August 1917. It had spent nine months in an unexplored and torrid land where both men and machines were subjected to exceptional wear and tear. 'It had co-operated effectively,' Watson believed, 'with half-civilised and only partly-disciplined troops in a forbidden land, where religious passion and fanaticism in their most cruel and barbarous forms far exceeded in danger the ordinary risks of war.'

C FLIGHT OVER MA'AN AND ABU EL LISSAN

But the Squadron's connection with the Arab Revolt was by no means at an end. On 26 August, Captain F W Stent - who, among other accomplishments, spoke fluent Arabic - and three of his C Flight pilots flew 100 miles south of Deir el Balah to a landing ground at El Quntilla, carrying with them sufficient food to last four days. From there, they flew a further 65 miles east on the 28th to attack the railway station and troop camps at Ma'an and bombed other camps next day. In Seven Pillars of Wisdom, Lawrence described their remarkable success: 'two bombs into the barracks (at Ma'an) killed thirty-five men and wounded fifty. Eight struck the engine-shed, heavily damaging the plant and stock. A bomb in the General's kitchen finished his cook and his breakfast. Four fell on the aerodrome... .' In the following dawn they were off once more, three of them this time to Abu el Lissan (20 miles south-west of Ma'an), where the sight of the great camp had made Stent's mouth water. They bombed the horse lines and stampeded the animals, visited the tents and scattered the Turks. As on the day before, they flew low and were much hit, but not fatally.[25]

X FLIGHT AT AQABA

Captain Stent and his men flew back to Deir el Balah on 30 August, but only to prepare for a permanent attachment to the Arab forces. They arrived in Aqaba on 9 September 1917 and became a separate unit, known as X Flight, and administered by Air HQ in Egypt. For operations, the flight worked under Lieutenant Colonel P C Joyce, commander of the British section of the Arab Northern Army. It began with three single-seat BE.12s (an ineffective fighter version of its two-seater cousins) and received during October a much superior machine, the single-seat D.H.2 pusher fighter. It also received a pair of two-seater BE.2es. With a single-bay - rather than a two-bay - wing structure, the BE.2e had only four interplane struts to drag through the air as against eight in the 'c' model, but it had the same engine and its maximum speed - under 70 mph - was no better. Working from a landing ground at Aqaba, the flight began a routine of reconnaissances over the Turkish camps along the Hejaz railway, notably those at Ma'an. As a rule, BE.12s were used and the pilots took along a dozen or so 20lb bombs to drop wherever they fancied. [26]

By the end of 1917, Arab forces had advanced 100 miles north of Aqaba to El Tafila, only 15 miles south-east of the Dead Sea, but early in March 1918 they were driven back 20 miles to Esh Shobek by strong Turkish forces concentrated at El Qatrani on the Hejaz railway. Stent had been succeeded in command of X Flight by Captain F H Furness-Williams in January and he was replaced in May by Captain V D Siddons, who retained command until the end of the campaign. From January onwards, the Flight was reinforced by several Martinsydes (G.100s and 102s) and now outnumbered its opponents. According to a captured Turkish pilot, there were only three Rumplers at Ma'an and seven assorted types at Amman.[27]

OPERATIONS AROUND MA'AN

Arab forces under Prince Feisal cut the railway line north and south of Ma'an on 11 April 1918. On the 13th, they captured Jebel Semna, a Turkish post south-west of Ma'an, and next day occupied the station itself. Aeroplanes of X Flight, using an advanced landing ground, bombed Ma'an while the Arabs were attacking and returned on the 17th, ready to drop more bombs, but were warned in time by ground signals that Arabs were in possession. Next day, after they had been driven out, Ma'an was bombed again. Meanwhile, a force under the command of Lieutenant Colonel A G C Dawnay (Hejaz Operations Staff) attacked the railway south of Ma'an. During the afternoon of 19 April, two Martinsydes co-operated in a successful assault by this force of Tel es Sham station, north of Mudawara. As soon as the pilots appeared over the area, strips were laid on the ground asking them to bomb at once, which they did, while the Arabs - supported by armoured cars - charged in. Long sections of the line between Ma'an and Mudawara had now been destroyed and were not repaired.[28]

Throughout the summer, X Flight fought with the Arabs. On 12 May, three pilots, flying from an advanced landing ground - helped in the destruction of the Jordan station, ten miles north of Ma'an. Prince Feisal sent the Flight Commander a message of thanks. 'The attacking infantry,' he wrote, 'were advancing and close to the position. The bombing was most excellent and accurate; nearly all the bombs fell inside the fortifications and the slight casualties sustained by the Sherifian troops is attributed to the skill of your pilots.' The Flight moved nearly 30 miles north from Aqaba to El Quweira in June and was kept busy on photographic and general reconnaissance work, plus occasional bombing raids on Ma'an and Mudawara. German aircraft were rarely seen and attempted little more than tip-and-run raids.[29]

OPERATIONS AROUND DERAA

By September, the Arabs had moved north to Qasr el Azraq, 60 miles east of Amman, and two of X Flight's machines had joined them there in order to reconnoitre the vital rail junction at Deraa, 70 miles to the north-west. A direct attack on Deraa was also contemplated, but the Arabs would undertake it only if the Royal Air Force - into which the old RFC had been transformed since 1 April - promised (in Lawrence's words) 'so heavy a daylight bombing of Deraa station that the effect would be tantamount to artillery bombardment, enabling us to risk an assault against it with our few men'. An attack of such intensity being out of the question, Lawrence decided to concentrate on cutting railway lines all round Deraa. On 15 September, after inspecting the lines north of that junction, X Flight's Bristol Fighter shot down an enemy two-seater, but was itself so badly damaged that it had to be sent to Palestine for repair.[30]

JUNOR'S DEEDS

It was at this time that Lieutenant H R Junor made his name by deeds of great bravery in the air and on the ground. Six D.H.9s of No 14 Squadron bombed Deraa on 16 and 17 September, causing eight German aeroplanes to be sent there from Jenin, 50 miles to the west. They were attacking an Arab force trying to blow up a stretch of railway line when Junor appeared in a BE.12. 'We watched with mixed feelings,' wrote Lawrence, 'for his hopelessly old-fashioned machine made him cold meat for any one of the enemy scouts or two-seaters: but at first he astonished them as he rattled in with his two guns. They scattered for a careful look at this unexpected opponent. He flew westward across the line, and they went after in pursuit, with that amiable weakness of aircraft for a hostile machine, however important the ground target. We were left in perfect peace.' When his petrol was nearly exhausted, Junor landed near the Arabs. His machine was damaged on landing and then destroyed by a bomb from one of his pursuers. There were no spare aeroplanes at Qasr el Azraq and so Junor asked if he could help the Arabs on the ground. He was put in charge of a Ford car in which he ran along the railway towards Deraa and blew up a stretch of track.[31]

THE END OF X FLIGHT

When General Sir Edmund Allenby's final offensive began on 19 September, the Arabs were at El Umtaiye, about 20 miles south-east of Deraa. On the 21st, a Bristol Fighter landed there with dispatches and Lawrence learned of the breakthrough on the coast. He returned in the Bristol to Allenby's HQ, where he and the Arabs were invited to assist in the next major thrust - to Damascus. Lawrence asked for, and received, RAF help against German aircraft around Deraa. Reconnaissance by X Flight from El Quweira reported Ma'an being evacuated on the 22nd as Arab forces moved in. That flight, including a detachment which had operated from Qasr el Azraq, now began to pack up. It left El Quweira for Aqaba on the 26th and early in October went on to Suez, where it was disbanded.[32]

THE SQUADRON MOVES INTO PALESTINE

So much, then, for the deeds of C and X Flights. The rest of No 14 Squadron had meanwhile been fighting hard along the road into Palestine. Having evacuated El Arish on 20 December 1916, about 2,000 Turks withdrew eastward some 30 miles to Rafah (on the border between Egypt and Palestine) and began to prepare new defenses. The main Turkish base - a garrison of about 3,200 men - was at Beersheba and there were small garrisons at El Auja (south-west of Beersheba) and further south at El Kossaima. To hamper the work at Rafah, No 14 Squadron aircraft bombed enemy camps and working parties daily. They also compiled a comprehensive photographic record of these defenses and discovered additional ones ten miles east at Wadi Sheikh Nuran. On the night of 8/9 January 1917, aircraft helped British mounted troops to capture the Rafah positions by bombing, by directing gun fire and by enabling commanders in the rear to keep in touch with their forward troops.[33]

KINGSLEY AND SEWARD

Lieutenant S G Kingsley made his splendid contribution to No 14 Squadron's growing reputation on 11 January 1917. Flying alone in a BE.12 he bravely attacked three enemy aircraft even though he well knew that he was completely outmatched. He was twice wounded and a bullet pierced his petrol tank. Evading his pursuers, Kingsley made for the coast and just reached it before his engine spluttered to a stop. He dropped his bombs en route over enemy encampments - 'waste not, want not' was his thinking - and brought off an excellent landing in the sea north of Rafah. Struggling out of the cockpit, he managed to swim ashore. There he gathered his remaining strength, did what he could about his wounds, and was staggering along the beach in the direction of British lines when some Arabs seized and stripped him. Luckily, a timely Australian cavalry patrol rescued the exhausted, naked pilot - and captured the Arabs.

A few weeks later, on 26 March 1917, Lieutenant W E L Seward would also be rescued by cavalrymen, but only after an even more amazing escape from death or capture. The petrol tank of his Martinsyde Elephant having been holed by AA fire over Ramleh, Seward succeeded in reaching the coast four miles north of Ascalon - and 17 miles behind the enemy lines at Gaza - before being forced to land on the water. He found himself only 200 yards from a Turkish post and hastily swam out to sea to avoid machine-gun fire. After a while, he allowed himself to float and the gunners, believing they had killed him, ceased fire. Seward gradually removed all his clothes and swam southward for four hours until increasing cold and fatigue obliged him to stagger ashore just before dusk. After resting among sandhills, he walked along the beach, past Gaza, to Wadi Guzzeh, a distance of 13 miles. During that walk, he had to take to the water five times to avoid enemy patrols. By dawn, Seward was utterly spent and slept for several hours, buried in sand, before he was rescued.[34]

CLOSE AIR SUPPORT

'Throughout the whole engagement', wrote Captain Watson, 'our machines attacked the enemy everywhere at sight from low heights with bombs and machine-gun fire. Troops on the march were engaged and motor convoys destroyed by bombs. Enemy infantry in their trenches and the crews manning their guns were similarly bombed and machine-gunned from heights of two and three hundred feet.' In order to prevent the enemy from obtaining information about British dispositions and strength, German aircraft were promptly engaged or driven away and their aerodrome at Beersheba was bombed. Rolling stock and the railway station were also bombed, both in daylight and moonlight. As a result, the aerodrome was abandoned and reconnaissance quickly revealed that the Germans had set up a new aerodrome at Ramleh, a place 45 miles to the north, between Jaffa and Jerusalem, that would one day become home to hundreds of men while serving in No 14 Squadron. For those who knew their squadron history, the fact that their predecessors' first action at Ramleh was to bomb it caused much wry amusement - and ready agreement that the old-timers knew what they were doing!

Meanwhile, the railway and water pipeline were being steadily pushed forward, only interrupted when German aircraft attacked the Egyptian labour gangs in retaliation for British air raids on Beersheba. As a result, the RFC was ordered to cease its raids for the time being. To keep pace with the advance, the Squadron moved eastward from Mustabeg on 20 January 1917 to Kilo 143 (a point that many kilometres east of the Canal, near Ujret el Zol, about 80 miles west of El Arish).[35]

From the start of the year, the RFC was operating mainly in new country. During January, the whole of southern Palestine as far north as Ramleh and as far east as the Jordan river was reconnoitred. Practically all reliable information concerning the enemy at this time was obtained by aircraft despite the fact that the enemy was equipped with machines superior in armament, speed and rate of climb. The battle of Rafah, according to a contemporary Australian account, 'was the first occasion on which our aeroplanes co-operated with the artillery in real operations. The method employed was that of the Smoke Ball, and general corrections in reference to specified targets lettered on the plan, no squared maps being available.'[36]

In an attempt to combat low-level bombing and strafing, the Turks ordered their forward patrols and front-line troops to send up smoke signals whenever British aircraft approached. Some Arab nomads helped the Turks in this way - until they too were bombed and strafed. Early in March, the Turks abandoned Wadi Sheikh Nuran and withdrew behind a 30-mile line from Gaza to Beersheba. They were harassed continually by aerial attacks on rolling stock, railway stations, bridges, cavalry, infantry and horse lines in daylight and darkness. German aircraft did little to prevent these attacks and their attempts to re-establish themselves on the aerodrome at Beersheba were ended by persistent bombing. Their other aerodromes at Junction Station (where a branch of the Palestine railway ran eastward to Jerusalem) and Ramleh, eight miles farther north, were also regularly attacked.[37]

GENERAL MURRAY'S NOTORIOUS FORAY

Between 25 February and 3 March 1917, General Sir Archibald Murray made a notorious foray from his headquarters. Air escort, he ordered, must be provided during all daylight hours: from the time of his arrival at El Qantara (as much as 150 miles behind the front line); throughout his journey to El Arish (no more than 30 miles from the nearest Turk); during his stay there; and at all intermediate places along the lines of communication where he stopped to inspect troops and observe tests with tanks on sand. One aeroplane in wireless communication with his train patrolled at 1,000ft above it, ready to report if an enemy aeroplane appeared, while another patrolled at height, poised to plunge into action if summoned.

Owing to the long distances involved and the few aeroplanes available, such a continuous patrol was maintained only with the greatest difficulty and at the cost of several forced landings. These facts further emphasised for Peter Drummond 'the futility of the operation'. Had the enemy been accurately informed of Murray's movements, he would not have seen a single aircraft to attack so far behind the lines, and if he had sent a strong formation the attack could not have been prevented. Such a 'remarkable misuse of air forces is unlikely to occur in the future,' wrote Drummond in 1923, when he was still a naive young air enthusiast. The whole business was foolish, in the opinion of Richard Williams, not only for wasting engine hours but also for drawing attention to the train.[38]

THE BITER BIT

At this time, the Germans copied an effective ploy first used by the British in an aerial attack on El Arish: they flew out to sea for some miles before turning sharply south. By thus approaching their target - the Sinai railway and water pipeline - from an unexpected direction, they achieved the same surprise and caused substantial damage. In retaliation, No 14 Squadron machines mounted major attacks on Ramleh aerodrome, also on camps and dumps elsewhere, attacks that were made easier as the squadron moved forward yet again: first to Rafah (on 25 March 1917) and then a month later to Deir el Balah, ten miles north. Despite these moves, the Squadron camp remained near the coast; everyone was able to enjoy swimming and surfing when off duty and, best of all, casualties remained light.

GERMAN CHIVALRY

The Germans were now showing more enterprise in the air, at least behind their own lines. This was chiefly the inspiration of Oberleutnant G Felmy, who flew an excellent fighter, the Albatross DIII. Some time after forcing down Lieutenants E A Floyer and C B Palmer (flying a D.H.1A on 5 March 1917), Felmy flew low over No 14 Squadron's aerodrome to drop a letter addressed to the CO advising him of their capture - unharmed - and inviting him to drop some clothing and shaving kit over the German aerodrome at Beersheba. Felmy promised that if a British aircraft appeared at a certain time next day to drop these things, it would not be attacked. The Australian observer L W Sutherland devoted a whole chapter of his account of the Palestine Campaign to Felmy, a man for whom he had the highest regard as a chivalrous and skilful opponent.[39]

Captain Frederic Bates, CO of No 14 Squadron's C Flight, recorded in his diary on 11

July 1917 that 'a Hun recco machine escorted by a scout single-seater dropped a message near the aerodrome this morning to say they had buried [Captain Charles Alfred] Brooks [of the Australian Squadron] with military honours. [Second Lieutenant Claude Henry] Vautin [also of the Australian squadron] is a prisoner and they say they like him and are showing him the country. He wanted his kit and would we drop it from a 2c at Huj. They will not attack our machine if it flies a certain course and drops a smoke bomb.' Next day, Vautin's kit was dropped from a very low level over Huj aerodrome by an Australian pilot, Captain Alan Murray Jones, and wrote Bates, 'the Huns waved and the 2c was not fired at going or returning'.[40]

Throughout that campaign, wrote Peter Drummond, 'very sporting relations were maintained between British and German airmen. Partly in the hope of getting information and partly because they had a sort of fellow feeling for Europeans like themselves in a land of barbarians, the German airman showed the greatest hospitality and kindness to any of our officers they captured.' Whenever a machine was lost, a German pilot would drop a message on a British aerodrome, giving news of the crew, indicating where to drop letters or kit for them and promising immunity from attack while doing so. Captives were allowed to send letters to their squadrons, asking for anything they needed. 'By cordially reciprocating these amenities,' added Drummond, 'a feeling of good-fellowship was produced which was of great value. German airmen captured by us and brought to the Squadron felt themselves to be among friends and talked much more freely than they would otherwise have done - thereby giving away a lot of information. It had, of course, to be guarded against that the enemy did not make the same use of that feeling.'[41]

CHETWODE'S FAILURE AT GAZA

The advance of the British railway across northern Sinai and into Palestine now made possible an attack on Gaza, once the home of the mysterious Philistines and later (as an American aviation historian wrote) the place where 'Samson demonstrated his strength after receiving an unsolicited haircut from a girl friend.'[42] Two mounted and three infantry divisions, under the command of Lieutenant General Sir Philip Chetwode, took part in the largest assault mounted in the Middle East up to that time. The attack began on the night of 25/26 March 1917 and by evening on the 26th, after a day of heavy fighting, Gaza was surrounded.

During the assault, the cavalry had been accompanied by a No 14 Squadron flying officer who marked out usable landing grounds and so permitted aircraft crews to report direct to cavalry HQ. Squadron wireless personnel were attached to the chief units engaged in order to receive Morse messages from aircraft, though message bags were also used. Similarly, Chetwode's HQ were kept informed by two specially-attached aircraft about all troop movements, friendly as well as enemy. About twenty aeroplanes had been available to assist the attackers. It was vital that contact patrol and artillery co-operation be uninterrupted (except under extreme pressure from enemy aircraft). Chetwode nevertheless weakened his air strength by demanding hourly reconnaissance reports on certain places, some of which lay as far as 50 miles from the battle area. Obedience to these orders required a flight of three hours to observe what reinforcements, if any, were being sent to Gaza. None were seen - and if any had been, they could not have reached Gaza in time to help.

At Chetwode's HQ, Richard Williams told the Senior Intelligence Officer that Gaza would fall that night. 'He asked if I had seen a column of Turkish infantry coming down from the north-east. I said I had but that it was a very small force and too far away to affect the fate of Gaza.' Nevertheless, Chetwode decided to withdraw, to the astonishment (anger came later) of both the Light Horse commander and the commander of the New Zealand Mounted Rifles. The Turks in Gaza shared their astonishment, for they had been destroying equipment and had intended to surrender at daybreak. Cecil Manson, then an infantry officer, recalled being paraded after the withdrawal 'to listen to a message from the King congratulating us on our resounding victory'. Totally disgusted, he put in an application for transfer to the RFC, was trained as an observer in Alexandria and posted to No 14 Squadron. This disaster, observed Drummond, illustrated the vital need for air forces 'to imbue army and navy commanders with an accurate idea of the capabilities and reliability of air work'.[43]

A SECOND ASSAULT ON GAZA

The Australian airmen followed No 14 Squadron into Rafah, arriving there on 10 April 1917, and during the next few days Williams noticed German aircraft acting for the first time as though they were really annoyed at what we were doing. Normally they did not appear to be very interested in what was happening to the Turkish frontline troops. As for Gaza, it had now become 'a strongly-entrenched modern fortress,' wrote Watson, and in preparation for a second assault, Squadron machines identified its strongpoints for the artillery and the whole area was repeatedly photographed.

On the morning of 17 April, British infantry attacked the trenches west of Gaza, accompanied - for the first time in this campaign - by tanks and supported by artillery; cavalry covered their right, landward, flank. Sadly, the tanks gave off clouds of steam, visible from miles away, and were therefore pounded by heavy artillery fire. Even so, good progress was made - at first. Two days later, on the 19th, No 14 Squadron suffered a rare death in action. Captain Francis Bevan (flying a Martinsyde) shot down an enemy two-seater over Sihan - between Gaza and Abu Hareira - but was himself killed in another combat later that day. According to the diary of Joe Bull, an air mechanic serving with the Australian Squadron, Bevan 'fell out in the air and could not be found, but the Anzac Mounted burnt the machine'. The German aircraft with which Bevan fought was itself destroyed a few minutes later by Captain Wilberforce of No 14 Squadron and the pilot killed.[44]

During these hectic days, an Australian AA battery at Tel el Sheria (behind Abu Hareira, covering the Turkish trench line) was earning itself the respect of both British and Australian airmen. The Australians marked with a rough stone memorial the graves of their victims - eight of them, including Bevan - which was discovered and restored months later, in January 1918. Although the second assault on Gaza failed even more completely than the first, the airmen had worked ceaselessly to support it and managed to set alight the north-west corner of the town.[45]

TRENCH WARFARE

After ten months in command of No 14 Squadron, Major Bannatyne was succeeded by Major A C Boddham Whetham on 6 May 1917. A month later, the Australians joined No 14 Squadron at Deir el Balah, setting up their tents in a fig garden: 'the first time we were able to get any sort of cover or shade for our living quarters,' recalled the ever-grumpy Williams. The summer months were devoted to training: to cope with a change from a war of movement to one of trench warfare on the left of the Gaza front. Systematic, detailed study of that front was made from photographs and direct observation until 'every little peculiarity' (in Watson's words) of the Turkish defenses was understood. Wireless training - especially in artillery co-operation - was directed by the Squadron's wireless officer, Lieutenant A T Thompson. On the right, there was a wide no-man's land offering opportunities for contact work during minor operations. The most important of these came between 21-23 May when aircraft co-operated with troops sent to destroy the railway line and bridges over a distance of 25 miles between El Auja (on the Egypt-Palestine border, 30 miles south of Rafah) and Bir Asluj (15 miles south of Beersheba). Visits by Squadron observers to artillery units helped both airmen and gunners to a better understanding of each other's difficulties and, they hoped, a better combination of their efforts in future.[46]

AN EXCEPTIONAL RAID - AN EXCEPTIONAL VIEW

On 24 June, Captain R H Freeman and Lieutenant S K Muir attempted to cut the Damascus-Medina railway line by destroying a bridge four miles south of Qal'at el Hasa. The flight, in two Martinsyde Elephants, was an exceptional one, lasting five hours and covering a distance of nearly 350 miles: from Deir el Balah south-east to El Khelasa, east to the southern tip of the Dead Sea and then south-east again to the target. Although the bridge was not destroyed, some lengths of track were displaced. At one point in the flight, recorded Watson, Freeman and Muir had 'in simultaneous view the Dead Sea, the River Jordan, the Mediterranean and the Red Sea'. Apart from providing two pilots with a memorable experience, the attack had two objects: firstly, to demonstrate to those Arabs who had not yet joined the revolt the wide range of British power, and secondly, to help those Arabs who had revolted by cutting the only supply line to the Turkish garrison in Medina.

THE ARRIVAL OF ALLENBY

General Sir Edmund Allenby replaced Murray as Commander-in-Chief, Egyptian Expeditionary Force, on 28 June 1917. Allenby, wrote Richard Williams, was 'a bit of a whirlwind' who quickly visited all his units, something Murray never did. He was said to have told the War Office that 'he would not move until supplied with either two more squadrons of the Flying Corps or an infantry division'. This was the first time Williams had heard any army commander express such a high opinion of the value of air power.

In response to Allenby's demand, two new squadrons (Nos 111 and 113) were forming in August to reinforce the British and Australian squadrons. Captain Cuthbert Fellowes and A Flight were transferred out of No 14 Squadron to help form No 111 Squadron under the command of Major Alexander Shekleton. All four would comprise the Palestine Brigade, which was divided into two wings: 5 (Corps) Wing and 40 (Army) Wing. The two corps squadrons - Nos 14 and 113 - were to work in direct co-operation with units of the Army corps to which they were attached, spending most of their time close to the front lines. The two Army squadrons - Nos 67 and 111 - were responsible for strategic reconnaissance, photography, bombing and air fighting.

The Turks were still holding a very strong position from Gaza to Beersheba and British troops were extended over more than 20 miles of front, but except near Gaza a chronic water shortage made close contact impossible. The tactical area for which No 14 Squadron became responsible included Gaza and it was therefore detailed to co-operate with XXI Corps, commanded by Lieutenant General Bulfin. During August, as we have seen, C Flight rejoined the Squadron from Arabia, but on 9 September a Special Service Flight - X Flight - was detached for Aqaba. Also in September, the Australians left Deir el Balah and moved ten miles south to Wadi Sheikh Nuran, a move that reduced pressure on water resources.

Cecil Manson, formerly an infantry officer in front of Gaza, was now to become an aerial observer over Gaza. His first flight was with Captain Frederic Bates, CO of C Flight. "It was a hot assignment", recalled Manson, "as we had to fly low and the AA gunfire was intense. In those days the pilot took the photographs, I acting simply as gunner. Bates did the job thoroughly and finally, when it was time to go home, deceived the AA gunners by pretending to have been hit and out of control. He put the machine into a spin and only pulled out of it a few hundred feet above the Turk trenches...... When we got back we found that our machine was holed by shrapnel in several places. I asked Bates if that was good, normal or bad AA fire we'd had. 'Oh, pretty wild,' he said. But in fact I never again had anything like such a plastering."[49]

One task which agitated Manson was leaflet-dropping. 'Our busy back-room boys in Cairo', as he described them, 'suddenly supplied us with sheaves of leaflets printed in Turkish, encouraging Turk soldiers to desert.' These were supposed to be scattered far and wide over enemy lines, but Manson thoughtlessly decided to get rid of his bundle in one job lot. 'In the BE. machines, the observer's cockpit was in front of the pilot's. As my leaflets left my hand, the rush of air caught them, separated them, and carried them back. When I looked behind, I saw not only the pilot's face covered in paper: he was struggling with one hand to uncover his eyes, while mouthing curses at me; but the tail of the machine and rudder and elevator controls, and the pilot's camera, were all draped in fluttering paper. When we landed, he and I were not on speaking terms.' We may presume, however, that Manson modified his dropping technique on subsequent flights.[50]

'On our tactical recco jaunts,' recorded Captain Bates in his diary, 'we drop literature in Turkish and Arabic, enlightening the enemy about the Great War. We are even kind enough to present him with illustrated papers, specially designed to impress him with the might of the Allies and other things such as the happy lot of Turkish prisoners. He generally expresses his thanks for our kindness by turning on his machine-guns.'[51]

The whole of southern Palestine was steadily mapped by aerial photography;

wireless co-operation with the artillery was increased; and contact patrol techniques were improved. But BE.s could rarely climb as high as 5,000ft in such a hot climate when fully loaded - and, as Henry Hanmer feelingly recalled, "it would often take nearly an hour to get there. At such a height the worst Archie gunners would be disturbing but these gunners, who I believe were German or Austrian, were very good shots .... Their fire was particularly accurate against artillery reconnaissance aeroplanes. These aeroplanes having of necessity to hang about over or near their targets were restricted in their manoeuvrability to the horizontal plane owing to the difficulty of regaining height .... Pilots coming to the Palestine front from France used to say frequently it was the worst anti-aircraft fire they had experienced." Add to this the threat of aerial attack and one understands why the arrival of six Bristol Fighters for No 111 Squadron in October delighted everyone in the corps squadrons: these excellent machines ensured aerial superiority thereafter. Hanmer also noted that pilots with Western Front experience taught them that it was not only safer, but it was also quicker, for the pilot to do the shoot while the observer watched for hostile aircraft.[52]

Soldiers soon felt the benefit. For example, Private Alec McNeur (Canterbury Mounted Rifles) wrote to his sister Mary one Sunday in October about the 'Taubes', a generic term for German aeroplanes: 'we don't like the Taubes a bit and our planes usually keep out of the road, as the German planes are faster and better in every way, but I expect that there are planes somewhere that can beat them.' Next day he added: 'yes, there are planes at last that can beat the Taubes and they have kept our part of the sky clear for two days and I believe they destroyed a German machine ..... I would like to see these new planes come along with us when we go out into the desert.' Alec would get his wish.[53]

THE FALL OF BEERSHEBA AND GAZA

On 4 October 1917, after only five months in command of No 14 Squadron, Major Boddham Whetham was relieved by Major Charles Medhurst, who retained command until the end of the war. This stability at the top no doubt proved beneficial, for Medhurst was the Squadron's fourth CO in the 32 months of its existence. At the Australian Squadron's farewell dinner after the Armistice, Medhurst had been among the guests: 'the only Englishman to command the Squadron', noted Sutherland, 'that was when our CO had a spot of leave. Very much a man, that chap.' Like Wilfrid Freeman, Titch Medhurst would enjoy a distinguished career, reaching Air Marshal rank, in the post-war Royal Air Force.[54]

General Allenby decided to make his main attack at Abu Hareira, midway between Gaza and Beersheba, but first it was necessary to capture Beersheba. The defensive works there were less formidable than those in front of Gaza and the capture of Beersheba would permit Allenby's cavalry to operate freely in the enemy rear. A heavy bombardment of Gaza, in which Squadron machines were to direct the fire of both the artillery and the navy, began on 27 October to prevent the Turks from reinforcing their left, seaward, flank.

By that date, all known or suspected enemy gun positions - and even likely alternative positions - had been carefully registered from the air, as well as every trench, access roads and assembly place. From dawn till dusk, No 14 Squadron aircraft were constantly in the air, watching every enemy movement, reporting active gun batteries and guiding by careful corrections the massed fire of heavy guns on enemy HQ, command posts, reserve billets, ammunition dumps, water supply areas, telephone and signal positions. The Squadron's aircraft also directed flanking fire from ships at sea into Gaza and onto railway and land routes. At night, aircraft bombed known targets and watched for the flash of enemy guns that had remained silent by day, reporting their positions to British gunners.

Arthur Hopkins, a Squadron observer (and a Methodist minister before the war), recorded his experiences at this time. 'Over Gaza,' he wrote, 'we were heavily shelled by Archie, or rather by a heavier type of gun firing a large high explosive shell. I don't quite know how to describe the burst of the shell, except to say that it is like a gigantic matchbox being crushed. If one goes off near the machine, she shakes like anything. One will be sailing along quite nicely, when there will be that sickening 'crunch' and a big ball of black smoke, with a flash in the middle. Then, of course, one dodges, or tries to do so. I'm afraid I haven't much of the heroic spirit, for I'm always jolly glad to get on the ground again. I always imagined Archie fire as rather a joke. On this front it is a very serious proposition indeed.'

Even so, Hopkins enjoyed observing for the artillery. 'It makes one feel good,' he recalled, 'to see the shell bursts getting closer and closer in, and finally, with luck, getting right there.' He also enjoyed reconnaissance work. 'For instance, I was up yesterday scouting ahead of our advancing cavalry, when I spotted two big clouds of dust. What was it? Enemy retiring or some of ours? The method of finding out is as follows: come down low over suspected area, and if you get fired on, it's them!'

Beersheba fell on 31 October, but the bombardment in the west continued until 2 November, when an infantry attack was launched on a three-mile front from the sea to a place known as Umbrella Hill. Steady progress was made, despite heavy going across sand dunes liberally strewn with barbed wire, until a blinding sandstorm erupted. Despite appalling conditions - as well as persistent ground fire - a No 14 Squadron machine remained aloft at no more than 1,000ft for over four hours, directing the artillery. Arthur Hopkins was the observer and would be awarded the Military Cross in part for the work he did that day. Though proud of his award, Hopkins' comment on it reflected an opinion common among those airmen decorated in both world wars: 'every man in the Infantry deserves it as much as I do.'

By the 7th, the Turks had evacuated Gaza. British cavalry had pushed more than 30 miles north to Junction Station to cut rail communication with Jerusalem. And the infantry had advanced ten miles along the coast beyond Gaza to the wadi Hesi. Arthur Hopkins visited Umbrella Hill after its capture and described his impressions in a letter home: 'it is, or was, the nearest enemy point to our lines. Umbrella Hill has had the most strenuous time, believe me. The Turkish trenches are knocked endways - how the poor fellows there stood it all I don't know ...... After Umbrella, we went into Gaza proper. On the way, we examined a vacated gun position under a tree, where the enemy had left 1,000 rounds of perfectly good ammunition....... Poor old Gaza! Samson didn't make the mess there our guns did. The place is a complete ruin, and reminds one of the pictures one sees of an earthquake-shaken city. Every street is piled with ruin. When one thinks of the quiet, peaceful life the city must have led at one time, and looks at the ruins of what once was Gaza, one feels more and more fed up with war.'

Like so many of those who served in No 14 Squadron - and indeed, in all squadrons and all branches of the services - in both world wars, Hopkins did not lose faith in the cause for which he fought and welcomed the close friendships he made. But he gradually came to hate the death and destruction war caused and to reflect on his own likely fate more acutely than young men usually do. 'One can't face death quietly and knowing its risk, without some sort of philosophy about it all. Personally I'm not afraid of death, though I should be very annoyed to be killed, it's so unpleasant. One only thinks about the people left behind. I am looking forward to the end of the war; I hate it, but I wouldn't have missed it for worlds.'55

'It has been a busy time for the RFC,' recorded Frederic Bates. 'At first, during the preliminary bombardment and actual assaults, there was a great deal of artillery observation to be done, directing fire into trenches, wire, gun positions, enemy HQ and so on. Then, when the move came and the heavy guns were temporarily left behind, contact patrol work took the place of work with the artillery. The task has now changed to tactical and strategical recco followed by organised bombing attacks in force on columns of infantry, transport, stations, bridges, junctions and aerodromes.'

'One of my most exciting flights,' continued Bates, 'came following an urgent call to observe an enemy counter-attack at Sheik Hassan. Flying low, we attracted a lot of fire but did some good work as I had wireless to direct our guns..... On another occasion, I left the ground before daylight on a similar job as a dawn attack was expected. One enemy battery gave me some fun. Our guns were slow in getting on to it so I tried the effect of my machine-gun, driving at it from its rear. This thoroughly frightened it and the battery stopped firing for quite a long time. On 7 November about a ton and a quarter of bombs were dropped by the squadron on different objectives.' Captain Bates went into Gaza on the 10th with a couple of friends: 'we took our lunch and a Ford car just like Cook's tourists and inspected the Turk trenches and Hun positions we have gazed upon so often during the past few months. The strafed trenches would make quite a respectable show in France!'56

One morning early in November, Lieutenant Henry Hanmer - flying a BE.2c - came upon a Turkish heavy battery and dived on it, dropping two bombs. As he pulled out, his engine suddenly stopped and for several seconds he thought he would have no choice but to land close beside men whom he had just tried to kill. Then, when only a few feet from the ground, he discovered that while releasing the second bomb he had knocked the engine switch off contact. Switching on again, the engine started. As a result, all switches in the Squadron were thereafter fitted with guards.

Fresh from this shock, Hanmer was ordered to lead an attack upon the bridge at Junction Station, 'for by its destruction,' he later wrote, 'the two branch lines to Jerusalem and Beersheba would be cut off from the railway centre at Ludd'. As well as the bridge, 'a single-span cantilever construction' over the wadi Surar, there was a large stores depot nearby and many Turks were known to be headed in that direction. Lieutenant Hugh McConnell volunteered to accompany Hanmer in making the attack at no more than 500ft with two 100lb bombs each. But no aeroplane in the Squadron was fitted to carry bombs of such weight, nor was there anyone competent to fuse them: 'a young observer who had been in the artillery thought he knew', Hanmer recalled, 'and was allowed to carry on'.

'Our plan of attack,' continued Hanmer, 'was that we should each have two runs at the target, dropping a single bomb each time, and I was to make the first attack. Junction Station was 50 miles north of our line at Gaza and consequently all the country was new to us both and the bridge was not easily located .... None of the bombs exploded. McConnell was brought down a quarter of a mile from the bridge, was taken prisoner and eventually died in Damascus of his wounds, and I was hit while making my second approach. I had a fortunate escape for the bullet, after piercing a longeron and twisting my flying belt buckle in two, embedded itself in a corner of my cigarette case causing a jagged end to be driven into my ribs.' Hanmer spent a night in hospital for anti-tetanus treatment and then returned to the Squadron.[57]

AIRCRAFT: FEWER TYPES; BETTER QUALITY

During November, the Squadron began to be supplied with R.E.8 aircraft (a roomy two-seater fitted with a 140hp air-cooled Royal Aircraft Factory engine) which would remain its standard equipment for the rest of the war. 'No other aeroplanes, I suppose,' wrote Oliver Stewart, 'were subjected during their war service to such continuous and such heavy anti-aircraft fire as the BE.2s and the R.E.8, but the latter was not a good flying machine, and its performance was meagre.' Stewart thought the authorities had made a bad choice in standardising on this aeroplane for artillery work. Captain Watson, however, compared it favourably to the lamentable BE types. These sturdy machines, he wrote, 'had a more effective range, greater power of climb and speed than the old BE machines' and better armament. They carried up to three machine-guns: one Vickers for the pilot (now sensibly placed in the front seat) and for the observer one or two Lewis guns, mounted on a revolving Scarf ring which he could swirl in all directions.

Henry Hanmer also liked his new mount. "We had soon found", he said, "that they were held in considerable respect by the enemy pilots. I remember on one occasion, getting to close quarters with six Scouts. They fired a few rounds and then sheered off, leaving me to continue my reconnaissance." On the other hand, he added, the German machines were "too fast to be taken on by an R.E.8." According to Cecil Manson, crashes were common at first, almost certainly due to the fact that our pilots had no training whatsoever in flying these machines which were larger and heavier than BEs. The pilots were also, slightly nervous of the R.E.8 because of its long extension of the upper wing. They were warned that this extension probably would not stand the strain of a manoeuvre like, say, a loop. [58]

By late 1917, there were a variety of more or less effective fighters that No 14 Squadron could call upon for protection duties. As well as its own Martinsyde Elephants and BE.2s, it could turn to No 111 Squadron, equipped with all sorts: some D.H.2s, a few Bristol 'M.1C' monoplanes, Vickers F.B.19 Bullets (a somewhat optimistic name) and, best of all, a whole flight of Bristol Fighters, appropriately known as *King of the Two-Seaters*. As aircraft supply improved in the New Year, No 111 Squadron reduced its mixed bag to these latter to the excellent S.E.5a, which might well have been styled King of the Single-Seaters. Some twenty or so French-built, second-hand Nieuport Scouts were sent out to Egypt early in 1918. Though inferior to the S.E.5a's, they were adequate for this theatre, bearing in mind the fact that there were probably not more than 60 German fighters to oppose them. A number of Nieuports found their way to No 111 Squadron, which kept them, passing on its Bristol Fighters to the Australians, who happily flew them for the rest of the war. At about the same time, No 14 Squadron also acquired a few Nieuports and was equally happy to use these instead of its own obsolete escorts.[59]

JERUSALEM CAPTURED AT THE GAZA

Although a new railway was being pushed forward at a rate of more than a mile a day ever since the advance began on 27 October, it was decided to repair the Turkish railway as well and make as much use as possible of the rough roads of Palestine for motor transport. Even so, the army's problems of supply and communication remained acute. Contact between the front-line units and rear HQ was in fact maintained by a flight of squadron aircraft sent forward to Julis (20 miles north of Gaza) where machines had to be pegged out in the open each night until the advance caught up with it.

By 16 November, Jaffa had been captured and the Turkish Army split in two: one part retreating along the coast northward, the other eastward through the mountains to Jerusalem. The squadron now found itself yet another home on the 30th. A camp was pitched about two miles east of Junction Station on a hill overlooking a broad, flat belt of land on the right bank of the wadi Surar. It made an ideal aerodrome in the dry heat of summer - but any steady rain soon turned most of the flat land into soggy marsh.

'From the flying point of view,' wrote Henry Hanmer, 'it was not an agreeable change to work over hills rising to 2,000ft when our BE.s, in spite of cooler weather conditions, were not getting to much more than 4,000ft maximum. Moreover, at first there appeared to be nowhere to make a forced landing, but as time went on a few flatter spots were found and pilots gained confidence through some astonishing experiences enforced landings in what appeared impossible places. From the observer's point of view, the retirement of the Turks into the hills was like rabbits going to ground. Even in the open they were difficult to see in their grey uniform, but once in those broken hills they disappeared entirely and the observer could only trace them by their earthworks or their firing.'

At this point in his recollections, Hanmer touched lightly on the ever-present wartime problem of troops suffering from friendly fire. On one occasion, he admitted, good luck played its part in saving them: 'our troops had been held up and not being in their pre-supposed positions, no untoward casualties resulted.' Even with the most experienced pilots, Hamner thought it was a dangerous practice to support a local attack by air-bombing unless the pilots were entirely familiar with the locality and even then enough of the enemy had to be visible to enable the pilot to discriminate between the opposing troops. However, as Cecil Manson recorded, airmen were sometimes on the receiving end of friendly fire. His own Flight Commander, Stephen

Pettit, was one such victim, 'brought down over the enemy lines by, of all things, an Australian field gun tipped upwards' in July 1918. But at least he survived - and not altogether in misery. He had spent some time as a guest at a German squadron, according to Manson, and so good was the feeling then between the two opposing air forces that the German even offered to let him try out one of their machines for comparison. Later, however, Pettit was imprisoned in Constantinople, where his treatment varied according to whether the Turks received good or bad news from the front.[60]

The Turks attempted to stand west of Jerusalem because the ranges rising steeply from the Palestine coastal plain are penetrated only by narrow, steep and winding passes and by a precipitous road where a small but resolute defending force could long deny passage even to a large and well-equipped attacking force. Nevertheless, the road to the Holy City was forced open and Watson believed it was because the 'ceaseless bombardment, the whirling uncertainty and nervousness our bombing induced completely demoralised the Turks. Jerusalem, in short, was captured at Gaza.'

No fighting could be contemplated close to the Holy City and so Allenby decided that it must be isolated by operations beginning on 8 December. Meanwhile, troops who had been forming the extreme right of the British flank in the advance from Gaza were sent up the road from Hebron to capture Bethlehem and then pass east of Jerusalem to seize the road to Jericho and fords across the river Jordan. These moves, it was hoped, would keep the Turks west of that river. Squadron machines patrolled in advance of the British forces, finding the road north of Hebron clear of Turks and Bethlehem unoccupied - the Turkish garrison having already withdrawn to Jerusalem.

On 8 December, however, heavy rain turned the aerodrome near Junction Station into a swamp. 'Aerodrome is in a state of mud,' wrote Frederic Bates in his diary, 'and it seemed doubtful if it was possible to take off without crashing. I was first up at 6am. Got off the ground, but the propeller was smashed by flying mud. It held together long enough for me to climb to 500ft before it flew to bits and I landed again hurriedly. Another machine tried but failed and four propellers were smashed trying to get off the ground. Our camp is on a dry, stony hill overlooking the aerodrome, so I thought of pulling a machine up the slope with ropes and trying to start from there. I did so and glided perilously down a steep incline, reaching the mud of the aerodrome with just sufficient flying speed to unstick and fly away.' Following Bates' lead, several other machines got airborne at a time when all other squadrons were grounded. 'All sorts of special congratulations have been sent to the Unit by the higher commands,' recorded Bates with pardonable pride, 'even a letter from the C-in-C addressed to the whole Flying Corps - which is somewhat galling to the other squadrons as it applies only to No 14.' Once airborne, unfortunately, little could be seen because of mist and low cloud, but everyone in the Squadron was delighted by this show of initiative and daring and equally delighted by the fact that no other squadron managed anything that day.[61]

Next day, 9 December 1917, the civil authorities surrendered Jerusalem and two days later Captain Frederic Bates of No 14 Squadron landed the first British aeroplane within the Holy City, close to the railway station. As the Turks retreated north towards Nablus or north-east towards Jericho, they were persistently attacked by No 14

Squadron aircraft at negligible cost - one pilot being wounded by ground fire on the 10th. General Allenby made his famous walk through the Jaffa Gate into the Holy City on the 11th at the head of a well-mixed force. As Alec McNeur wrote, it included among many others Sammies from Dixie Land, real Yanks, Kilties frae Scotland, English artillery, Indian officers, Australians, New Zealanders, Froggies, RFC. Land, air and water.[62] Watson wrote: 'our unconscious crusade was finished and the sacred places of Christendom were after the lapse of many centuries once more in Christian hands.'

The Turks, however, remained within artillery range of both Jerusalem and Jaffa and it was necessary to push them further back. On the night of 20/21 December, XXI Corps began an advance on the left flank that had driven the enemy eight miles beyond Jaffa by the 22nd. Meanwhile, on the right, XX Corps - supported by No 14 Squadron - was ready to advance by Christmas Eve, but heavy rain that day and the next delayed it. 'Palestine weather,' wrote Watson with feeling, 'at this time of the year is of the wettest. The country is virtually a bog soaked with the rain which is its only supply for the year. Christmas Eve and Day, he added, were among the stormiest and wettest in our experience. Most of the camp was blown down, though the machines and stores were saved.'

'During Christmas,' wrote Bates (who was at that time Acting Squadron Commander), 'we lived in a sea of mud but Christmas Eve surpassed itself. A great gale, and sheets of rain, woke me at 12.30am. The whole camp was roused and stood by the machines which have to live in the open and are vulnerable to wind and rain. The night was spent getting drenched and constantly re-picketing the aeroplanes. Half the tents, including our mess, were removed bodily. My tent stood up and I made a lot of cocoa in a water-can on my Primus stove for drenched officers and men. You cannot work in pouring rain and mud in pyjamas without getting a bit wet!... However, the storm dampened nobody's spirits - and you should have seen our dinner! Two hundred and fifty men crammed into a large marquee to enjoy turkey, plum pudding and beer. That was at 1800hrs. Our dinner was at eight with much the same menu but with the addition of a champagne ration and sweets of sorts. An officer had been sent on leave to Cairo - on condition he brought back Christmas dinners. How he got all his cases up here is a yarn in itself!' Sadly, this excellent example of No 14 Squadron initiative is now forgotten. Even more sadly, Frederic Bates was badly injured in a flying accident a few days later and obliged to leave the Squadron.[63]

The Turks, meanwhile, had attempted to recover Jerusalem in an attack launched at 01.30hrs on 27 December. The attack was held and XX Corps counter-attacked. By the night of the 30th, the Corps had advanced on a 12-mile front to a depth of two or three miles and Jerusalem - together with the road to Jaffa - was secure and the Squadron, which had closely supported the advance, suffered only a couple of minor injuries, though ceaseless rain during the next two months made any further advance impossible.[64]

SONGS AND FROLICS

Despite the weather, which sorely tried men accustomed to the burning heat of Sinai, the atmosphere in the Squadron remained cheerful. A forward landing ground had been established close to Jerusalem and everyone had the opportunity to visit the Holy Places there and in Bethlehem. To while away some of the long hours in camp, shows were arranged and 'improvised songs were sung,' in Watson's words, which find a ready echo in the next war, 'set to popular tunes in which the humours of our life and peculiarities of individuals were quaintly hit off or parodied. Much ingenuity was expended with the limited means at our disposal in inventing costumes. Improvised dramatisations were given, usually farcical, of the whims and routine of Army administration; the foibles of the supply services, the curious byeways, excuses and causes that meant home leave; no less whimsical were the complaints of the hardship of service in contrast with the cushioned splendour of safe jobs at home.'

'Among our frolics,' Watson continued, 'was one concerning the visit of a certain high chief of the Arabs' - actually a Squadron officer in disguise, whose true identity is apparently nowhere recorded. 'This admirable actor was brought to the Mess and welcomed with a shyness that only broke down when he accepted the proffered hospitality of a short drink - slyly observing that he had learned this evil Frankish practice in his student days at Constantinople and was glad to visit us if only to escape for a while the rigours of the austere Muslim desert life.' This supposedly august Arab was then courteously escorted round the aerodrome with all the appropriate deference and shown the aeroplanes.

Allenby Bridge (over River Jordan).

To the delight of Watson and a few others in the secret, men who had served in Arabia with the Hejaz detachment 'affected to recognise him and told stories of his prowess and wealth - chiefly in wives', thereby displaying, observed Watson, 'more native invention than statistical accuracy'. The deception received unforeseen support from the Squadron mascot, a turkey saved from the pot by some curious sentimentalism about a year earlier. This bird, Egyptian born and bred, had a notorious furious and undiscriminating hate of all Egyptians and Arabs, but a quiet tolerance for white men. It immediately displayed so violent a rage against the supposed Arab chief that it had to be shut up in a tent, where it continued to complain for hours.

In the evening, the visitor was royally entertained and numerous solemn toasts paid tribute to his country's gallant history of struggle against oppression and its glowing prospects of a glorious future. His halting reply, in a mixture of French, English and what to their untutored ears did duty for Arabic, raised him still higher in everyone's esteem. 'The scientific members of the mess gravely discussed his physiognomy, descanting how pre-potent in blendings the Arab type was - like its brother the Jew - giving an Arab and Semitic as cast to types so broadly Georgian, if not Caucasian as their guest undoubtedly was.' Officers and men begged to be allowed the honour of taking his photograph and permission was graciously granted. Sadly, it seems that none of these photographs survive. Only after he had made a ceremonial departure was the jest revealed and, concluded Watson with gusto, 'the chaff that poured on the chief victims', the solemn analysts of racial types and the Hejaz romancers, 'kept all merry for many a day.'

JERICHO CAPTURED

Meanwhile, the war went on. German pilots, operating from aerodromes at El Afule (a key point on the Haifa-Deraa railway line, some 18 miles south-west of the Sea of Galilee) and at Jenin (ten miles south of El Afule, on a branch line to Nablus), were generally held at bay by the Palestine Brigade's fighter squadrons while Allenby prepared an attack intended to capture Jericho, drive the Turks across the Jordan and so make his right flank secure. The attack began on 19 February 1918 in what the Air Ministry historian H A Jones would call 'a wilderness of deep-cut gorges and barren hills, almost devoid of communications'.[65] While the infantry of XX Corps moved forward, No 14 Squadron patrolled the whole area and reported only one concentration of Turkish troops - some 300 of them, marching along the Nablus-Bireh road - which artillery fire promptly scattered. A gale then grounded all aircraft for four days, but Jericho was occupied on the 21st. 'Flying from Jericho', wrote Hanmer, 'was a strange experience at first. To start with, the altimeter at ground level registered some 700ft below sea-level - the bumps in the Valley itself are terrific, especially in the heat of the day - and the heat, so long as one is below the level of the hills, is sometimes intense.'[66]

As the aerodrome near Junction Station was now too far behind the front for immediate response to a call for air assistance, a flight of machines moved up to Jerusalem to co-operate with the artillery and to keep HQ informed about the exact position of forward troops, But low cloud and mist made consistent observation exceedingly difficult - and dangerous, for this was mountainous country. One machine, having lost its bearings during a flight on 21 February, crashed at full speed into a mountain, leaving the bodies of Second Lieutenants W J Beer, H T Thorp and their aircraft in 'an unrecognisable mass' in Watson's words. They were buried in Jerusalem. Cecil Manson described the landing ground there as 'nothing much more than a sloping ploughed field with tracks across it. At the northern edge of this field the ground dropped steeply, practically as a cliff, down into that valley of evil repute, the Biblical Valley of Gehinnom or Gehenna. The original name applied, I believe, to Hell.'[67]

CAVALRY AND AIRMEN WORKING TOGETHER

Major W J Urquart, a staff officer at the Australian 2nd Light Horse Brigade HQ, wrote on 6 March 1918 that co-operation with aeroplanes would be of very great importance in coming operations. The 1st Brigade was therefore to select three officers and nine men, all signallers, to ride next day to 5 Wing HQ, where they would be taken on by car to No 14 Squadron HQ at Junction Station to undergo a three day course. Thereafter, the 2nd Brigade and the New Zealand Mounted Brigade would send similar parties to Junction Station for the same course. In return, one pilot and one observer from that squadron would spend three days with the New Zealanders and then three with the Australians to go into questions of aeroplane co-operation and get to know the brigade. The course was to cover such practical matters as rapid, accurate signalling with lamps, shutters, flares and flags and, of equal importance, offer a rare opportunity for cavalrymen to fly and airmen to ride: no better means existed for them to grasp the advantages and difficulties of each other's war.[68]

A SETBACK AT AMMAN

Although the capture of Jericho had secured Allenby's right flank, he lacked a wide enough frontage - clear of the Dead Sea - for operations east of the Jordan. He therefore planned to push forward 20 miles north-east of Jericho to Es Salt, crossing the Jordan at El Auja ford, and then drive 15 miles south-east to cut the Damascus-Medina railway by destroying, as Henry Hanmer wrote, 'a big viaduct three miles south of Amman station - and so cut the Turkish line of communication to Ma'an'.[69] These moves would also encourage Arab forces coming from the Hejaz. Detachments from both No 14 and No 113 Squadrons were sent to Jericho to cover the advance to Amman which began on the night of 21 March 1918.

Unfortunately, torrential rains had swollen the Jordan and left the country on both banks so sodden that a general advance east of the river was impossible until the morning of the 24th - and even then it had to be made through thick mud in the teeth of driving rain and sleet. A pale sun appeared on the 26th, but by then both men and horses were exhausted and needed rest. An attack on Amman next morning made little progress, though raiding parties cut the railway line to the north and south and four pilots from both squadrons dropped fifty-five 20lb bombs on the station, destroying rolling stock and damaging buildings. Stronger attacks on the 28th and 30th also failed, chiefly for want of artillery support, and the force withdrew.

It is worth emphasising at this point that the aircraft of those days were rarely capable of striking heavy blows. For example, Hanmer recorded his efforts against a train carrying reinforcements to Amman from the north: 'on two consecutive mornings,' he wrote, 'I met this train and bombed it, but beyond causing it to stop, enabling my observer to machine-gun the personnel and causing a certain amount of panic, there was not much damage done, I think.' On the other hand, he later mentioned one aspect of air power that receives little attention. The Australian Mounted Division, Hanmer recalled, 'had great difficulty in extricating itself from Es Salt' and his flight dropped medical supplies to a Casualty Clearing Station that had run short of many essentials 'through the number of unexpected casualties'.[70] It is also worth emphasising here that just as No 14 Squadron's first sight of its future home at Ramleh was as attackers, so too was its first sight of another future home at Amman.

By 2 April, except for a garrison holding a bridgehead on the east bank, everyone had re-crossed the Jordan. The No 14 Squadron crews returned to Junction Station on the 4th and moved on to Jerusalem three weeks later. This failure, coming at a time of heavy losses in France, was the first setback for British forces in Palestine since the second battle of Gaza and did much to restore the confidence of Turkish troops and give them faith in General Liman von Sanders, their new German Commander-in-Chief.[71]

A 'BREAD AND BUTTER' SUMMER

From March onwards, substantial forces of experienced troops had been sent from Palestine to the Western Front to counter a desperate crisis there. They were replaced by Indian units new to the Middle East and in some cases untried in battle. Consequently, Allenby could not contemplate any large-scale operations without intensive prior training and in fact no important actions were fought between May and September. Those months were spent by the Squadron on bread and butter work: co-operation with the artillery to register enemy batteries, assembly places and likely lines of advance; systematic photographing of the whole region to make - and correct - maps; and constant efforts to test and improve methods of air-ground communications. It was at this time that No 14 Squadron developed a new technique for picking up messages from the ground. They were seized by a weighted hook fitted to the underside of the fuselage from a line stretched between two poles about 25yrds apart. Pilots could now receive urgent instructions without landing - if the soldiers erected the poles and line at a place offering a clear approach and departure! - and the method became standard in the RAF between the wars.[72]

Certain basic facts were emphasised in discussions between soldiers and airmen. For example, 'aeroplanes cannot stay in the air much more than three hours without landing to replenish petrol. At an altitude of 1,500ft, an aeroplane is almost certain to be hit by rifle and machine-gunfire from the ground unless the enemy is otherwise engaged. At this height, our own troops cannot be distinguished from the enemy with certainty unless the troops assist by making themselves conspicuous to the aeroplane by signals, either agreed or improvised.'[73]

THE FINAL OFFENSIVE

General Allenby intended to launch a final offensive in the early autumn, to avoid both the extreme heat of summer and the heavy rains of winter. He also chose a time of full moon to permit night riding by his thousands of horsemen. The British were facing the Turks on a 50-mile front: from a point 12 miles north of Jaffa, then south-east across the Plain of Sharon and east over the mountains of Samaria. These mountains rise to a height of 2,000ft before falling away to a depression 1,000ft below sea-level. The Turkish line, divided into three sectors - the Plain of Sharon (15 miles in length),

Samaria (also 15) and the Jordan valley (about 20) - was very strong. It ran through ideal defensive country, rugged and broken, served by good roads and railways.[74]

GROWING AIR POWER AND ITS INFLUENCE

During August 1918, the Palestine Brigade was enlarged to seven squadrons, three in 5 (Corps) Wing under Lieutenant Colonel Charles Burnett and four in 40 (Army) Wing under Lieutenant Colonel Richard Williams, both wings having their HQ at Ramleh. Brigadier General Amyas - Biffy to his friends - Borton commanded the brigade from Bir Salem.[75] Between them, they mustered as many as 105 efficient aircraft. The Corps Wing had 52 of these: at Junction Station, No 14 Squadron had 16 R.E.8s and three Nieuports; at Sarona, near Jaffa, No 113 Squadron had 16 R.E.8s and five Nieuports; and No 142 Squadron had seven Armstrong Whitworth F.K.8s at Sarona and five R.E.8s at Jerusalem. The Army Wing had the other 53: at Ramleh, the Australians had 18 Bristol Fighters and the first heavy bomber to see service in the Middle East, a twin-engined Handley Page 0/400; No 111 Squadron had 15 S.E.5a's, 145 Squadron had six of these fighters and 144 Squadron had 13 D.H.9 two-seater bombers at Junction Station.[76]

By the time Allenby's offensive began, on 19 September 1918, the Palestine Brigade dominated the air - a fact which had a powerful influence on the planning and course of that offensive. The brigade had been intensely busy during the six weeks before it began. In addition to the location and registration of enemy guns, tactical reconnaissance and trench photography carried out by the corps squadrons, the Army squadrons had flown long-distance strategic reconnaissances, photographing huge areas for mapping purposes and bombing aerodromes.

As for the aerial opposition, the Air Ministry historian H A Jones said that 'during the hot months the German pilots and observers had had a sorry time. Ill-equipped, remote from their sources of supply, attached to a neglected Turkish army whose morale was weakening, they had to meet aeroplanes superior in performance and number, piloted by officers imbued almost to the point of recklessness with the offensive spirit.' Such supplies as were sent from Germany to Palestine suffered during the long rail journey from careless handling, pilfering and, not least, sabotage - because the Turks actually employed British prisoners to handle cargoes at Rayaq (between Beirut and Damascus, where the track changed from wide to narrow gauge) and whenever opportunity offered, deliberate damage was done.

The Germans lost 59 pilots and observers between the spring and autumn of 1918, according to General von Sanders, and by September air reconnaissance of British positions had virtually ceased. By contrast, Air HQ in Egypt was able to supply the Palestine Brigade not only with replacement airmen and machines, but also experienced officers for vital liaison duties on the staffs of ground commanders where they were able to make informed suggestions to improve ground-air co-operation.[77]

SUCCESSFUL DECEPTIONS

Allenby's main thrust was to be made on the left by XXI Corps under General Bulfin (supported by No 113 Squadron) and by the Desert Mounted Corps under General

Chauvel (supported by No 142 Squadron, less its C Flight). Meanwhile, General Chetwode's XX Corps, supported by No 14 Squadron, was to advance astride the Nablus road. In the Jordan valley, demonstrations to persuade the Turks to expect an attack east of the river were to be made by General Chaytor, supported by No 142 Squadron's C Flight. At Qasr el Azraq (60 miles east of Amman) the Arabs' advanced column was to raid the vital rail junction at Deraa, 70 miles to the north-west and well out of Allenby's reach.

Allenby wanted the Turks to expect an attack in the east and so deserted camps there were left standing, except for a few horses dragging brushwood about to raise dust. German aircraft were allowed to see these - briefly and from a great height - whereas strong, continuous patrols were flown in the eastern coastal areas to ensure that the Germans saw nothing, especially between 1230 and 1430hrs when thousands of horses were being watered. As many as three mounted divisions, five infantry divisions and most of the available heavy artillery moved westward to the vicinity of Jaffa and Ramleh only by night, without lights, and never after 2.30am. Military police were posted by day to prevent movement, enforce concealment (usually in olive groves) and ensure that enemy aeroplanes were not fired on. All cooking was done by means of solidified alcohol instead of smoke-betraying fires. The advantages of a preliminary bombing offensive against enemy aerodromes, artillery dumps and communications centres were held not to outweigh the certainty of alerting the enemy to an impending offensive. During the three weeks prior to that offensive, only four enemy machines were able to cross the British lines, so the Turks had no detailed information about Allenby's dispositions and therefore his likely intentions.[78]

SUCCESSFUL OPERATIONS

To open Allenby's offensive, carefully-planned raids were made on the main Turkish telegraph and telephone centres, whose positions were known from intelligence sources and aerial photographs. The raids were all successful in cutting enemy communications and the consequent disorder could not be remedied by aerial reconnaissance because British fighter patrols kept the Germans at Jenin grounded throughout the day. Smoke screens were also laid by British aircraft to cover the advancing troops. By 20 September, the Turks were in general retreat and every available aircraft was sent to bomb and strafe them. During the six days from 19 to 24 September, the Palestine Brigade's seven squadrons flew a total of just over 1,450 hours between them, and the most hard-worked was No 14 Squadron, with (in round numbers) 305 hours closely followed by the Australians (300) and No 111 Squadron (271). As for the aircraft employed, the seven squadrons had 121 effective machines between them on 19 September of which 105 were serviceable that day. For the next five days, the serviceable average was 97; a fine tribute to skilful and diligent ground crews.[79]

WADI EL FARA - A TURKISH DISASTER

The Turkish 7th Army had been slow to take alarm and by the evening of the 20th found its lines of retreat northward in British hands and was obliged to flee eastward, hoping to escape across the Jordan. In such rugged country, the routes open to the Turk were few and those places where bombs would have maximum impact upon moving columns had all been carefully noted before the offensive began. The most important route to the Jordan lay down the wadi el Fara to Jisr el Mejamie, a bridge about 25 miles north of the Dead Sea. 'We had come,' as Sutherland put it, 'to a bomber's, a machine-gunner's paradise. A giant, greyish-black snake, nine miles in length, was sprawled beneath us' and unable to move forward or back because aerial attacks had caused blockages at the head and at the tail. Men and beasts caught in such a narrow passage could neither scatter nor find effective cover.[80]

'From 0800hrs until noon,' recorded Captain Watson, 'the enemy was incessantly bombed and machine-gunned. Every two minutes, two machines arrived over the column and every half hour an additional formation of six machines bombed and machine-gunned it.' The major attacks were made by the Australians and the other Army squadrons, but all three corps squadrons took part as well. Throughout the day, more than nine tons of bombs were dropped and 56,000 rounds of machine-gun fire aimed at virtually defenceless Turks in what became a valley of death. According to Sutherland, signals of surrender were simply ignored. Two aeroplanes were shot down by rifle fire from men who had managed to climb the hills overlooking the wadi, one of them was piloted by Lieutenant J Webster of No 14 Squadron, who lost his life.

British troops reached the area next day and counted 87 guns, 55 lorries, 4 motor-cars, 837 four-wheeled wagons, 75 two-wheelers and 20 water-carts and field-kitchens. No-one recorded how many bodies of men and animals were found. 'It was a terrible demonstration of the destructive power of war's latest weapon,' wrote Watson and Major General Geoffrey Salmond (head of RAF Middle East) agreed. He visited the area as soon as the troops had moved on and was so upset that he asked Williams and Burnett to discourage their pilots and observers from going to see what they had done.[81]

AN ARMISTICE

Meanwhile, east of the Jordan, the Turkish 4th Army remained inactive, being unaware - thanks to the Palestine Brigade's vigilance - of the disasters west of that river. General Chaytor's force in the Jordan valley had hitherto been responsible for the defence of Allenby's right flank, but as soon as the 4th Army began to retreat - on hearing at last something of what had happened in the west - Chaytor advanced. During 23 September, as some Turkish columns fled along the road from Es Salt to Amman, while others struggled to reach that town from the south-west, all were subjected to constant aerial attack. Amman was captured on the 25th, Deraa on the 28th and those Turks who did not surrender fled in disorder towards Damascus. On 30 September, No 14 Squadron's aircraft were used to airlift petrol and oil supplies into El Afule aerodrome for the use of aircraft operating against Damascus. Next morning, that city was occupied by Arab and British forces and a week later Beirut also fell. The offer of an armistice was accepted by the Turks on 31 October.[82]

T E Lawrence, writing of the victory of the Arab Revolt in *The Seven Pillars*, explained. 'The co-operation of the air with its unfolding scheme had been so ready and elastic, the liaison so complete and informed and quick. It was the RAF, which had converted the Turkish retreat into rout, which had abolished their telephone and telegraph connections, had blocked their lorry columns, and scattered their infantry units.'

'Brilliant work has been done by the Palestine Brigade, Royal Air Force, and the Australian Flying Corps,' wrote General Allenby in his final report. 'Besides taking an active part in the fighting, the Air Forces provided me with full and accurate information as to the enemy's movements. The Royal Air Force photographed the whole of the enemy trench line and country in the rear of it to a distance of roughly 25 miles. From 1 January 1918 to the cessation of hostilities, 15,690 photographs were taken and the topographical information published in map form. A total of 8,000 gallons of aviation spirit was required daily.' Allenby also pointed out how much his air power had grown between July 1917 and the Armistice: from a wing with four squadrons and a balloon company to a brigade with two wings, seven squadrons and a balloon company.

AN END AND A NEW BEGINNING

Early in November 1918, No 14 Squadron embarked for Salonika in Greece to assist in the final assault on Germany, but another armistice on the 11th ended the Great War. After exactly three years of valuable service overseas, the Squadron left its faithful, hard-worked R.E.8s at Junction Station and most officers and men returned to England, just in time for Christmas. According to Air Ministry records compiled in September 1930, supplemented by a careful study published in 1995, 53 officers and men became casualties while serving on flying duties in the Middle East (one of them - Frederic Bates - twice) 23 were killed or died of wounds or injuries, 25 wounded or injured and 5 captured. No record apparently survives of the number of officers and men who suffered illness or death not directly related to operations or training. Even so, it is a very light 'butcher's bill', in comparison with the record of long-service squadrons on the Western Front, and in comparison with the casualties that would be suffered by No 14 Squadron during the Second World War.[83]

On 4 February 1919, the Squadron was formally disbanded at Tangmere, near Chichester in Sussex, about 25 miles west of its birthplace at Shoreham, four years - and one day - earlier. The Air Ministry, however, soon decided that the honourable number should not disappear from the Royal Air Force's order of battle and so No 111 Squadron - based at Ramleh - found itself re-numbered as No 14 Squadron, with effect from 1 February 1920. The Australians had handed over their Bristol Fighters to No 111 Squadron before sailing home and so an unusual link was forged: the first aircraft flown by Australians in the Middle East had belonged to No 14 Squadron; the first aircraft flown by the new No 14 Squadron there had belonged to Australians. That link would be re-forged twenty years later: No 14 Squadron had some Australian members during the First World War and would have many more during the Second; in both, it would fight beside - and above - Australians.

Most of the young men who served in No 14 Squadron, in this war or in the next, were greatly impressed by fighting, service or leave in the Holy Land, where most of the names were familiar to generations brought up on the Bible. Many still practiced their religion whenever they could and all were struck by the contrasts between sacred and profane, squalor and luxury, barren desert and gorgeous gardens and, most of all, by modern machines of war beside peasants scratching a living as in biblical times. The Holy City itself was often a disappointment. As Arthur Hopkins wrote, 'If one looks for reinforcement to one's faith there, disappointment is certain. I much prefer the life of the streets, with their colour and movement, to the deadness of the traditional sacred places.'[84]

Other contrasts also struck them: intense heat and bitter cold, sand storms and lashing rain. Flies were a constant irritation and some men found them as hard to accept as bad food, diseases, wounds and sudden death. Parcels and letters, to and from home, were a vital part of life, especially for those who had to endure captivity. In compensation, deep and lasting friendships were made. However, the return home at the end of both wars would add a new strain: meeting the parents or wives of men who did not return.

'From the shadow of the Pyramids in Cairo,' concluded Watson, 'to the Temple of Jupiter Heliopolis at Baalbec, we had crusaded through the pilgrim lands of history, traversing in our march the ruins of Rome's ancient civilisation, the lore lands of Christendom and the devastating splendours of Asiatic Greece.' Alec McNeur of the Canterbury Mounted Rifles felt less triumphant on 18 December 1918 in a letter to his brother George. 'We lay on the hills of Bethlehem,' he wrote, 'under the midnight stars and listened not to the song of peace but to the roar of the guns. No angels in the morning sky, but great flights of aeroplanes.' More than half a century later, in 1972, the Anglo-American historian Robin Higham was able to grasp the military context. In his opinion, the campaign in Palestine was 'as perfect an example of the proper application of air power as the German blitzkriegs in 1940 or the Israeli campaigns of 1967'.[85]

THE HASHEMITES
OF THE HEDJAZ
The Squadron Connection

THE EMIR
ABDULLAH OF
TRANSJORDAN
1921-1951

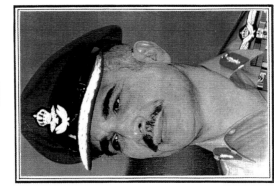

KING
HUSSEIN I OF
JORDAN

THE
EMIR FEISAL OF
SYRIA & IRAQ
1917-1933

CHAPTER TWO

SUPPORT FOR THE FRONTIER STATES

1920 - 1929

While everybody knows what we owed to the Royal Air Force in the Battle of Britain, its services in frontier wars in remote countries have not received adequate recognition. (Sir John Glubb. War in the Desert. Hodder and Stoughton, London, 1960.)

The legacies from World War I (WW1) were profoundly to change the geo-political map of the world, and to introduce a third force into the armed inventory of nations. So it was that, following the collapse of the Ottoman Empire, Britain inherited, amongst other problems, League of Nations mandates for the newly created entities of Palestine, Transjordan, and Iraq, while France acquired the responsibilities for Syria and the Lebanon. So it was also that during and immediately after WWI the rapidity of aeronautical development, and the imperative conclusions drawn from the operations of the Royal Flying Corps of the Army, and of the Royal Naval Air Service, generated the need for a separate organisation, able to develop and conduct its own techniques of control and war from the air. The Royal Air Force was born on 1 April 1918, incorporating the men and aircraft from the RNAS and the RFC into RAF squadrons.

Sir Hugh Trenchard, who had become the RAF's Chief of the Air Staff, propounded a theory that was to win acceptance from a nation drained of money and men by a prolonged period of trench and sea warfare. The threat of, and if necessary attack from the air, should be able, with resulting economies, to control and police populations where previously it had only been thought possible by the deployment of large numbers of troops on the ground.

Accordingly, over the next two decades, even though the theory was in practice to prove its own limitations, a network of air stations and airfields proliferated throughout the Middle East theatre. From the Persian Gulf and Iraq in the east, to the biblical lands of the eastern Mediterranean, and south to the Sudan and Kenya, the air bases heralded not only control but presaged the explosion of air travel and communication by air.

Into this matrix of political and technological developments a new No 14 Squadron, under the command of Squadron Leader William Welsh (later to become an Air Marshal), took over the aircraft and accoutrements of No 111 Squadron at Ramleh in Palestine on 1 February 1920. There it was to stay, equipped with its Bristol Fighters for nearly five years, but until the uncertainties of the mandate responsibilities and boundaries had settled down, detachments for action were deployed to Damascus, Aleppo and Amman to Mafraq, and to Beersheba in Palestine.

The uncertainties were considerable. Britain jockeyed with the French over protection for the Suez Canal. For the Arab fighters, successful with the Emir Feisal and T E Lawrence from the Hedjaz, the goal was Syria. The Palestine area scarcely figured in the Arab mental map of the new Arab State. Sharif Hussein of Mecca almost casually agreed to the exclusion of great tracts of land to the west of Damascus, Aleppo, Homs and Hama, and which later became the Lebanon. It was Britain, to limit French influence in the Levant, who secured via a League of Nations mandate, both banks of the Jordan and thus created Palestine and Transjordan.

The genesis of most of the problems in the countries of the Middle East had already been set in 1917 by the Balfour Declaration in which Britain would use her 'best endeavours to facilitate the establishment in Palestine of a national home for the Jewish people'. At the same time it also declared 'nothing can be done which may prejudice the civil and religious rights of existing non-Jewish communities in Palestine'. Rightly or wrongly, Britain believed she had the political skill, as well as the military strength, to implement this contradictory policy. Arab hostility to Zionism provoked fierce riots in 1920 and 1921 and near civil war in 1929.

The overall operational role for the RAF was thus established in the eastern Mediterranean until the outbreak of World War II. The RAF was given responsibility for the security of the new territories of Kuwait, Iraq, Transjordan and Palestine. In practice this role had threefold tasks: support for the Mandated Power, the delineation, supervision and control of borders which had been drawn with scant regard to indigenous Arab populations, and thirdly whatever time and thought could be spared to the development of techniques of air warfare.

In March 1921, Winston Churchill (newly-appointed Colonial Secretary) presided over a conference in Cairo at which Britain's Middle East policy was reviewed and Trenchard's proposals approved. The Emir Abdullah was favoured as head of the new state of Transjordan. Abdullah's brother, The Emir Feisal, leader of the Arab revolt, was soon to be installed, on British insistence, as King of Mesopotamia (later known as Iraq). Abdullah asked for, and got, British military as well as financial support. 'The decision to underwrite Abdullah with aircraft,' wrote the historian David Omissi, 'mirrored the creation of an Arab kingdom, under Feisal, in Mesopotamia. Abdullah came to depend more and more upon the Royal Air Force for his survival.' As the British High Commissioner for Palestine, Herbert Samuel, remarked in April 1924: "British aeroplanes and armoured cars are the chief means of securing the safety and stability of the Emir's Government."

Transjordan was - and remained - a very poor country and Abdullah's fine personal qualities, as well as British soldiers, airmen and subsidies, were essential to its survival. Lawrence of Arabia regarded him highly. 'In manner affectedly open and very charming,' he wrote, 'not standing at all on ceremony, but jesting with the tribesmen like one of their own sheikhs. On serious occasions he judges his words carefully, and shows himself a keen dialectician. Is probably not so much the brains as the spur of his father: he is obviously working to establish the greatness of the family, and has large ideas, which no doubt include his own particular advancement..... The Arabs consider him a most astute politician, and a far-seeing statesman: but he has possibly more of the former than of the latter in his composition.'

Abdullah's government was sorely vexed by tribal conflict. 'Four-fifths of the country was desert,' wrote James Lunt (biographer and colleague of Sir John Glubb) 'inhabited by about 40,000 Bedouins whose entire existence depended on grazing for their camels.' The two principal tribes were the Beni Sakhr and the Howeitat, the latter immortalised in the English-speaking world by Lawrence for their part in the overthrow of the Turkish empire. Both tribes were under constant pressure from the more numerous - and far more fierce - tribes of central Arabia, whom we shall meet presently, because to the Bedouin, 'grazing for his camel is life and soul; he will, and daily does, risk death to secure it'.

The Cairo Conference also proposed that responsibility for the defence of Transjordan (and Iraq) pass from the War Office to the Air Ministry. As for Palestine, the War Office expressed no interest, but both the Admiralty and the Air Ministry feared that air and naval bases in that country might be used by an enemy to attack Egypt and threaten the entire eastern Mediterranean unless occupied by Britain. In December 1921, therefore, it was decided to add Palestine to the Air Ministry's burdens and in the following May an Army officer - Major General Tudor - took command, acting under the Air Ministry as the military agent of the Colonial Office.

After a few initially bumpy years an outstanding administrator, Lieutenant Colonel Sir Henry Cox followed later by Sir Alec Kirkbride, guided the Emirate into calmer waters and as Abdullah recorded in his memoirs 'did good to the Transjordanians even against their will'. Not over generous praise. Abdullah's lack of experience on the world political stage led him to depend heavily on the guidance and support of his British advisers. It is a tribute to the Emir and to the patient and wise Cox that despite the surrounding predators and the often irritating financial constraints imposed from London, both men built up a mutual respect and trust in these early formative years that set roots for the modern Jordan.

Palace, Amman. HRH Emir Abdullah with Major Glubb at left.

COMMANDERS, OFFICERS AND AIRCRAFT

Security for the Emirate started in 1922 and developed in four main areas. First, the Arab Legion was created - virtually the Transjordan Army named by Abdullah after the regulars who fought with Feisal in the Arab revolt. It was to become the Command of Colonel F G Peake, a former Commandant of the Egyptian Camel Corps, and of (later) Sir John Glubb, who developed the desert patrols.

Secondly, No 14 Squadron moved its base to Amman, retaining detachments with some Bristol Fighters at Ramleh. Squadron Leader John Bradley succeeded Welsh in March 1922. The new D.H.9A, a two-seater, with a pilot and observer/gunner, had a greater range, could carry bombs and was much more suited to its likely roles than the Bristol Fighter. Home for the Squadron until 1940 was now to be an undeveloped tract of land two miles east of Amman used by the Turks as a landing ground, and bounded on the north by a spectacular chasm of a wadi. Adjacent to the airfield at its west end and overlooking Amman, was a pleasant stone Turkish-built camp soon to be supplemented by hangars and the accoutrements of RAF life overseas - messes, living quarters, stores, workshops, the inevitable parade ground, sports area, a swimming pool, and ring barbed-wire fence. At above sea level the climate at Amman is pleasant with tolerable summers and rainy - sometimes snowy - winters.

Thirdly, the security of RAF bases led to the provision of armoured cars. No 2 RAF Armoured Car Company was based at Amman from 1922. Each vehicle had a 1913 Rolls Royce engine and chassis, desert tyres and a single armoured turret with a Lewis gun. They were to achieve significant successes in Transjordan, Palestine and incredibly in the war years of the Western Desert. Finally the British budget in 1926 stretched to the creation of the Transjordan Frontier Force. Based at Zerka of about brigade strength, British commanded and officered and (mostly) Circassian manned, it had cavalry and lorried infantry responsible mainly for the patrol of the northern and eastern Transjordan borders with Syria and Iraq. It was used continuously against threatened Arab incursions from neighbouring states and eventually with great effect against the pro-German uprising in Iran of Rashid Ali in 1940.

From 1920-1924, No 14 Squadron was involved in many minor and some major operations with its Bristol Fighters, and latterly with D.H.9s in both Palestine and Transjordan. Not all, however, was riot and unrest.

Theatre and local headquarters were changing with experience. Inter-service and civil co-operation and communications were improving under testing conditions, and the capabilities of the squadrons were extending in the forges of operational and technological improvements.

Squadron Leader John Bradley (who would also enjoy a distinguished career and retire as an Air Marshal) succeeded Welsh in March 1922 and by that time he had under command a significantly larger body of officers: three flight lieutenants, ten flying officers, two pilot officers, a stores officer and a medical officer. Among those who served in No 14 Squadron during these early days was a famous airman of the Great War: Duncan Grinnell-Milne, author of two classic accounts of his experience, one of flying and fighting, the other of escaping from German captivity. Another famous airman-author returned to the Squadron in the early Twenties: Cedric Hill, the perfect bomber, whose remarkable wartime exploits were described in Chapter One.

Some two years later, in May 1924, when Squadron Leader Wilfred Dolphin briefly succeeded Bradley, the squadron had grown still further. The new CO now had under his command four flight lieutenants, ten flying officers, 3 airmen pilots (unnamed), and an accountant as well as a stores officer and a doctor. Two officers with brilliant careers ahead of them - Ralph Sorley and William Elliot - had done time in No 14 Squadron. By August, after only three months in command, Dolphin had been replaced by Squadron Leader Arthur Gallehawk, who enjoyed the immense satisfaction of presiding over the move from Ramleh to Amman. Charles Baker commended the new station:

> You'll like it, some day when you wander that way;
> For the life of Amman is exciting,
> There is always some 'flap' that is right off the map
> When you fully expected some fighting.
> The camels pass by till the end of July
> And they come back again in the spring
> A raid now and then by some bearded old men
> Is considered a natural thing.
> The Sons of the Prophet are hardy and bold,
> They flap for a while every year
> They wink the odd eye at the blokes in the sky
> And at Abdullah, T J Emir
> When tired of Amman you can try El Lisan -
> A seaside resort - rather low -
> If that shouldn't suit try a spot of Beirut
> Where the wild Wanganuis all go.
> Attractions are legion in that sunny region
> That once was a province of Caesar,
> And though you find fault with the birds at Es Salt
> The Bustards are lesser at Ziza.

Although the *Ninak*, like the *Brisfit*, was a Great War design, it revealed rather more capacity for development. Fitted with a reliable Liberty engine - a 400hp 12-cylinder, liquid-cooled power-plant designed and built in the United States - the *Ninak* soldiered on as the standard RAF all-purpose machine throughout the Twenties. It served throughout the Empire 'as a bomber, air ambulance, survey aircraft, air mail transport and, latterly, as a trainer, until phased out of RAF service in 1931'. Those in the South African Air Force continued in service until 1937 and even that did not mark the end of the sturdy *Ninak* for its RAF replacement, the Westland Wapiti, was based on the same airframe and would still be operational in India until as late as 1942.

'Apart from its nominal warload,' wrote Chaz Bowyer (an aviation historian), 'a *Ninak* usually carried a spare wheel bolted onto the fuselage (in some cases, rather illogically, under the fuselage), while necessary equipment such as bedroll, water bag (usually made from an animal skin), emergency rations and crews' personal kit were attached or hung on various points around the fuselage or under the lower wings.'

Consequently, reported one pilot, he found it difficult to overtake or fly above flights of pelicans, cruising comfortably along at about 70mph. Armed with a synchronised Vickers machine-gun for the pilot and a Lewis gun for the observer, the *Ninak* had a top speed slightly below that of the Bristol and took much longer - nearly 16 minutes - to reach 10,000ft, but its normal endurance was markedly better, at a little over five hours, and it could carry a far heavier bomb-load - up to 740lbs - under wings and fuselage. Unfortunately, only a deaf dwarf would find either machine comfortable for any length of time and no airman - in Britain or the Middle East, aircrew or ground crew - who took even a passing interest in European or American aviation developments could fail to be mortified by the continued employment of such inadequate machines for the air control of the British Empire.

Typical at this time were two minor operations occurring at Jaffa in Palestine and at Kerak in Transjordan. In the spring of 1921 trouble broke out between Jews and Arabs. At Jaffa on May Day a labour meeting was interrupted by Jewish communists. Rioting followed and spread, martial law was proclaimed, but a large body of Arabs from Yehudad attacked the Jewish Colony at Petah Tiqva. Despite being driven off by cavalry, armoured cars and a No 14 Squadron Bristol Fighter, a leading Sheikh, having stolen most of the cattle from Petah Tiqva, established himself north of Jaffa with some 700 men. Threatened with air action and low flying attacks, the Sheikh surrendered his loot, and withdrew, but not before 95 lay dead and 350 were wounded.

In April of 1921 air action was also extended to Transjordan and operations there made an RAF responsibility. In January 1922 unrest was evident in Kerak in the mountains of Moab some 12 miles from the south east coast of the Dead Sea.

The inhabitants divided into two factions, indulged in continuous fighting, and refused to pay taxes. Colonel Peake decided on a show of force with the Arab Legion, and asked for air support. Five Bristol Fighters flew from Ramleh and arrived over the town as Peake began deployment to enter the town. Two Bristols took photographs, three flew low over the crowded streets firing Verey pistols. The move caused panic. Crowds fled into houses, and no opposition was offered to Peake. He later said that the whole operation had been a great success, enabling him to make peace that afternoon between the quarrelling factions, without any casualties.

WAHABI RAIDS

The Wahabis, or Ikhwan meaning brotherhood , was the name adopted by various tribes of a particularly puritanical branch of the central Wahabis in Saudi Arabia. The Wahabi raids were much feared by the Bedouin of the desert, as they were not the usual half-friendly affairs of the nomad world, but were savage slaughters by fanatical tribesmen enforcing their beliefs, and condemning everything that made life tolerable in the harsh conditions of desert existence.

A major operation took place on 13 August 1924 against the Wahabis near Ziza, a railway station twenty miles south of Amman. The Wahabi force with some 4-5000 men mounted on camels and 200 horsemen, had started out from Qasom, north of Riyadh, rode up through the Wadi Sirhan to reach Meshalta (NE of Ziza station) and killed a small Arab Legion party taking rations to Kaf, a frontier post 100 miles south of

Amman. The Wahabi force split into three columns towards El Kastel, Umm el Awad, and Yaduda via Teneib, indicating Amman as the objective. Interestingly, according to the Squadron Operations Record, the Arab force Commander had orders that 'no aeroplanes, cars or English were to be attacked; old men, women and children to be spared, young men to be killed'. Their rifles were of very antiquated Arab and European manufacture.

Two reports of the raid were received at Amman. One from an RAF lorry taking petrol to Ziza and stopped near Kisset, the other from Colonel Peake viewing the raid from a hill whilst out riding. Three RAF armoured cars left for Yaduda whilst a D.H.9A left Amman at 0655hrs to confirm the lorry's report a few minutes later.

As permission was received from Air HQ in Jerusalem to take action at 0823hrs, at 0905hrs three D.H.9s commanded by Squadron Leader John D'Albiac left Amman, and were over the raiders seven minutes later. Mr Kirkbride then in the office of Sir Henry Cox, the British Resident, flew in one of the aircraft and confirmed they were Wahabis. Bombs and machine gun fire quickly put the raiders to flight. D'Albiac then found the three armoured cars near Teneib, and dropped a message directing them to pursue and engage the enemy by crossing the railway near Ziza. At 0930hrs the armoured cars went into action, carrying on a running fight for nearly two hours until their ammunition was exhausted. As the armoured cars withdrew with only three bullet hits on themselves, so aircraft refuelled and rearmed, took up the attack, and again at 1430hrs a D.H.9A and four Bristol Fighters, flown in from Ramleh, completed the rout of the Wahabis, fleeing as a rabble some 40 miles east of Ziza.

The Wahabis, who had killed some 150 desert Arabs on their approach to Amman, lost about 500 men killed, about the same number captured, and with most of their camels and horses killed or scattered. The RAF had one pilot and two airmen wounded. It was a sharp defeat, more than well understood by the neighbours of Transjordan. The Palestine and Transjordan Administration Report for 1924, laconically noted 'prompt and energetic action by the RAF averted a serious menace to the peace of Transjordan and the safety of its capital'. Later the Emir Abdullah, himself only just returned from pilgrimage and under intense pressure from Cox to put his budget in order, was quick to realise the message conveyed by the action. He presented three of the seven Wahabi banners captured in the raid to the RAF - one to the RAF HQ at Amman, one to No 14 Squadron, and a third to No 2 Armoured Car Company. The first two banners - always remarked on by the Emir whenever he graced the RAF Mess dining nights - adorned the dining room of the Officers' Mess at Amman. Sadly, during WWII they were transferred to the Officers' Mess in Cyprus where later, they were lost in a fire at Nicosia.

Aside from indigenous unrest, riot and pillage, British civil and military organisational changes continued throughout the Middle East. In Transjordan, H St John Philby, who had succeeded Abrahamson as British Adviser to Abdullah in 1922 engineered an invitation for Abdullah to visit London. He left for London in October 1922 primarily to achieve international recognition for the State of Transjordan with himself as Emir. Problems with borders, financial arrangements, and local security forces under Peake's command, were discussed at length and finally ironed out, and after a hiccup with the French involving their request for the surrender of Sultan el

Atrash a Druze leader who had taken refuge in Transjordan, an announcement was made six months later: 'Subject to the approval of the League of Nations HMG will recognise the existence of an independent Government in Transjordan, under the rule of His Highness the Emir Abdullah ibn Hussein, provided such Government is constitutional and places HMG in a position to fulfil their international obligations in respect of the territory by means of an agreement to be concluded between the two Governments'. Temporarily Abdullah was pleased - he now had recognised international status, as was Philby who had now the goal of a constitution to work for. Nine months later after mounting distrust Philby was replaced, as recorded earlier, in April 1924 by Sir Henry Cox, a district administrator in Palestine. He stepped into a verbal nightmare, with Britain and Abdullah at loggerheads over finance, and disagreements over Abdullah's cabinet advisers.

As a diversion from the ongoing political alarms and civil disorders, an Aerial Manoeuvres Meet was arranged in May of 1923 at Ramleh. Some 30 pilot competitors attended from Transjordan, Palestine and Egypt. The programme listed nine events - a Relay race of three teams of three pilots each flying Avro 504K, Bristol Fighter and D.H.9As;

an exhibition of aerobatics by Flying Officers Bruce and Marsden of No 14 Squadron in Bristol Fighters; a race of 27 miles restricted to No 14 Squadron pilots around a triangular course to Ras el Ain Castle, round the Russian Church (!) at Jaffa, to a final line drawn across the airfield at Ramleh; a spot landing competition nearest a circle, with engines shut off at 2600ft, and a message picking up demonstration; a balloon Hunt - the objective being to fly and destroy with prop or wing all five balloons released from the corners of the airfield and the fastest time won; the Palestinian Aerial Derby - open to all aircraft types under handicap, flying the above triangular course; an exhibition of Crazy Flying by Flight Lieutenant Noakes of No 216 Squadron (Heliopolis-Egypt) and finally, an attack by 3 Bristols flown by Sorley, Culley and Sanderson of No 14 Squadron against 'an enemy Explosive Factory'!

In May 1924 Group Captain L W B Rees VC OBE MC DFC took command of the Air Forces in Palestine and Transjordan amalgamated under a new HQ P&TJ at Amman. Squadron Leader Everidge took command of No 14 Squadron in June 1926 but relinquished it once again to Squadron Leader Gallehawk on 2 December 1926.

1926 and 1927 were relatively calm in Palestine and Transjordan. Not so in Syria, where the Druze warriors inflicted some serious setbacks on French forces. Eventually the Druze began to lose ground and again sought Transjordanian help, this time in setting up a camp for dependents at the oasis of Azrak. They had, a year later, to be expelled as the area became a rearming centre for the Druze.

Located at the northern end of the Wadi Sirhan caravan route, Azrak (meaning blue) Oasis had long been of strategic importance. The fortress, once an imposing Roman or Byzantine structure was on the edge of a lake in the most romantic of sites. O G S Crawford, a renowned archaeologist, described it: 'One motors for sixty miles over rolling desert, mirages everywhere looking exactly like lakes, until one comes to a real lake with bright green reeds growing on the margins. The scenery with palms and a backdrop of purple covered mountains was strange in a desert.' T E Lawrence described it as 'a silky Eden'. As the only permanent fresh water source for 12,000 square miles it attracted a teeming wildlife of duck, and the RAF at Amman were quick to build a lodge for week-end shoots in season under the shadow of a newly erected Arab Legion fort.

'Tours of duty with the RAF overseas,' wrote Harold Crowe, a flight commander with No 14 Squadron, and later to become Air Commodore, 'were, in the 1920s, five years in India, or two in Iraq plus three in Egypt.' Crowe completed one and a half years in Iraq and three with No 14 Squadron at Amman. 'On posting overseas one had to buy tropical kit from one's tailors. This is what was required - with an allowance nowhere near enough to cover it - khaki topee with RAF flash, khaki shirts with spine pads, drill trousers, tunics and shorts, breeches, puttees and stockings, black shoes, white mess kit jacket with blue shoulder straps, gold badges of rank and wings, miniatures of medals, brass buttons, overall trousers, blue cummerbund, white shirts, butterfly collars and mosquito boots. Cold weather blue uniform and mufti were also taken abroad! What the well-dressed young RAF officer had to wear. They had to pass muster with the CO too!'

Crowe continued to record: 'A ROYAL FEAST - this was a unique occasion. The Emir Abdullah of Jordan who often entertained us to Turkish coffee in his Palace at Amman, under the watchful eyes of his Circassian bodyguard, decided to call all his tribal chiefs to a feast to try to get them to 'bury the hatchet' among themselves.'

'He chose a perfect night with a full moon as we assembled on the floor of the old Roman amphitheatre in Amman.'

The seating plan was:

Sheikhs

	Other notables -
RAF	British Resident
Officers	High Commissioner for Palestine
Myself	The Emir
	Group Captain Rees
RAF	Peake Pasha
Officers	Notables -

Sheikhs

Many of the sheiks were named in Lawrence of Arabia's book *Seven Pillars of Wisdom.*

We were seated cross-legged on rich Persian carpets laid on the earth and, in accordance with Arab etiquette, taking care not to show the sole of a foot to anyone, when a great hubub was heard. We looked round to see eight Nubian slaves (yes, there were still slaves in Jordan and very valuable they were) stripped to the waist carrying a huge wooden dish bearing a baby camel (which had been cooking all day) resting on a bed of rice and in a great pool of very hot gravy which splashed over the rim onto the naked shoulders of the slaves, making them howl. They put the great dish down in front of the Emir. Then drawing their daggers they plunged the knives into the camel's

D.H 9A.

D.H 9A's in squadron formation.

Troop and Official Transport - Circa 1930.

Fairey IIIFs at Amman.

Avro 504s at Ramleh, 1923.

Crazy Flying Demo, Avro 504s.

Spot landing, Bristol Fighter.

hump and cut the smoking meat in strips; then opening up the carcass to expose the intestines. The camel meat was, however, only for the important guests, the lesser sheiks received generous portions of sheep, most of which they took away tucked inside their clothing!

Then the ceremony started. The Emir, with his right hand, selected choice parts of the intestines for his honoured guests and then we were allowed to tackle the strips of meat already cut. It was the custom, of course, to use the right hand only. Tear off a portion of meat. Roll it into the rice and chew away. The meat was rather stringy and after a bit one's fingers stuck together. Rough cloths, soaked in lavender, were brought round, when we had eaten our fill, to clean our hands on. Turkish Delight sweetmeats followed with thick sweet coffee.'

(Postscript — I was telling this story to Grandma Jarratt years later and thought she had been taking it in. When I had finished, she said, "Where was this, dear - the Savoy?")

FLYING OFFICER WILLIAM COOKE REMEMBERS

'No pilot who has been stationed at Amman,' wrote William Cook in 1933, 'will ever forget the tediousness of the south-eastern reccos. Leaving Amman at crack of dawn, when the air is cool and calm, the machines fly over a little line of hills and across the plain to Kasr Tuba, an ancient castle outpost beside a wide wadi, and it is not every pilot who finds it. From here can be seen, away to the south, Thlathukwat, the Three Sisters, whose lean clean white peaks on their lofty watershed are a wonderful landmark to pilots whose navigation is not all that it should be, or who are hampered by bad visibility. In fact, so great a value do No 14 Squadron attach to these peaks that after the great earthquake of 1928 a special recco was sent out to ascertain whether they were intact and in the same place.'

'A few miles south of these peaks,' he continued, 'the machines reach the broad Wadi Bair with its wells, castle and landing ground, a favourite camping ground, amid the stumpy tamarisk shrubs, of the famous Howeitat tribe. The recco then turns eastward across the plains of flinty gravel and sandy wadis until Bair Na'am or Imshash is reached. Here, on a large natural landing ground beside the wells, nigh 200 miles from civilisation and only just within the borders of Transjordan, the pilots frequently land for a cooling drink of water, a welcome snack of bully beef and ration biscuits. At least, these are what the crews officially enjoyed, but William revealed that they actually dined off tins of Palethorpe's sausages and Mr Heinz's beans, washed down with delicious wines; save in the direst emergency, bully beef and ration biscuits were best fed to camels and sheep, who actually appreciated them. The evidence of illicit human feasting was plain to see, scattered around the wells, for any senior officer keen enough to discover it.'

'On once more', Cooke resumed, 'climbing into the air, the machines fly south for a few miles until the white-chalked hills of Hausa are in sight; they turn west and make for Ma'an, flying over the vast sandy area of the Jeefer depression. An interesting little town is Ma'an, and one well acquainted with aircraft, for the Turks had a flying school there during the war. The circle of their aerodrome is still visible. The town stands on a plateau, 4,000ft above sea level, open to all the winds from north and east which blow from Central Asia or from the Caucasus mountains, cold and terrible over the desert to the mountains of Edom above Ma'an, against which their first fury is broken. In the heat of the summer, the air at Ma'an is so thin that it is often unwise to attempt a take off in the middle of the day. After a welcome siesta during the afternoon, the pilots return to Amman in the cool of the evening, generally leaving Ma'an at the last possible moment, and a very pleasant flight that return trip can be, the air cool and calm, the country beneath good, and a pleasant feeling of a tedious job successfully accomplished.'

'The Squadron also patrolled to the north of Amman,' added Cooke following the railway to Zerka: 'where repose in the quiet fastness of their camp, the Transjordanian Frontier Force, who occasionally conduct highly-organised expeditions into the surrounding desert in the name of peace and good will. North of Zerka is the large Plain of Mafraq, on which many squadrons could land in formation.... Here the machines turn east along the southern borders of Syria, crossing the Roman road whose stone causeway stretches across the plain, straight and narrow, to Umm el Jemal, once a fair city but now only a mass of blackened ruins.'

East of these ruins, Cooke recalled, 'the brown plain of Mafraq merges into the desert, to the north of which lies basalt country. The machines follow the clear-cut line which divides the two, passing over a succession of long sandy depressions as far as the wonderful lake of Azraq and then home.' These northern reconnaissances, he thought served a dual purpose'. They prevent the Transjordan tribes massing on the borders to carry out raids into Syria, and they can keep a lookout for Central Arabian tribes who may creep up the Wadi Sirhan, also with Syria as their objective, led by way of the Azraq corridor.'

Although policing work was the Squadron's chief duty, Cooke recorded many others. 'Officials require ferrying about, patients are flown to hospital, important dispatches and mails have to be carried across the hills to Ramleh or down to the pleasant land of Egypt. The fleshpots of Cairo are a great attraction after months of Amman's austerity and keen is the competition to carry mail thither, the lucky pilot's brain being filled with messages, commissions, warnings and advice. Occasionally, very occasionally, Imperial Airways desire assistance for forced-landed machines; more frequently, cars coming across the desert track get lost or run out of petrol and No 14 Squadron proceeds to the rescue.'

At this point, Cooke gave free rein to that Service and Squadron pride which was so common among first-generation airmen, laying a foundation to fortify their successors in the thirties and throughout the terrible war which followed. 'More work of a humanitarian nature is done by the Royal Air Force abroad,' he declared, 'than by either of the other two Services. One does hear occasionally of a warship chasing a minute Chinese pirate vessel, but not often. The Royal Air Force may be the junior Service in age, but it is certainly senior in utility. It is doubtful whether there exists another squadron which does more of this work than No 14. In addition to all these varied duties mentioned above the Squadron also has to go through the normal training routine, which includes such subjects as bombing, front and rear gun, photography, etc. So the pilots are not often idle, and No 14 has earned for itself the reputation of being one of the hardest flying squadrons in the Service.'

The British Resident and Lady Cox with the Arab Legion Guards.

Cooke did not overlook the contribution to the Squadron's achievements of No 2 Armoured Car Company, now stationed at Ramleh with detachments at Ma'an and Azraq.'If armoured cars in the desert are ever unable to locate their vicinity,' he wrote, 'out go the machines, and seldom return without accomplishing their aim, and if machines forced-land, out go the cars at a moment's notice, and in any weather, to render assistance. On one occasion when the Wahabis were known to be on the border, intent on raiding, a machine went down not 20 miles from the border and needed a new engine. Within one hour of the news reaching Amman - yes, one hour - a Leyland lorry, with a spare engine on board, escorted by an armoured car, had left and journeying through the night accomplished the odd 200 miles under 12 hours which, considering the nature of the country and the fact that most of the trip was done during hours or darkness, was a truly marvellous performance.'

1928: A BUSY BUT PEACEFUL YEAR

The Squadron flew as many as 630 hours in the single month of April 1928, mostly on thrice-daily flights over northern, eastern and southern Transjordan to look - in vain - for signs of attack by the Wahabis. One flight was detached 120 miles south to Ma'an, but continual sand storms and an absence of hangars were hard on aircraft, to say nothing of pilots and ground crews. During the whole year, two reconnaissances were carried out each week, policing the country, as the Squadron recorder put it, 'and demonstrating to both friendly and unfriendly tribes the mobility and alertness of the Air Force in the country'. Vigilance was rewarded, enabling the recorder to conclude that 'no shots were fired nor bombs dropped during the year 1928 on any enemy'.

Even so, the year was full of incident. In January, for example, three aircraft paid a liaison visit to the French Air Force in Syria, visiting Damascus, Ryaq and Deraa. The visit was returned in February by three French aircraft, one of which crashed on landing at Amman: the occupants were unhurt physically, at least - and Squadron personnel were doubtless instructed to avoid both critical comment and misplaced smiles. A more serious crash occurred in March, when a *Ninak* crashed while on a routine flight, carrying mail from Amman to Ramleh. The pilot and the observer were both killed and their bodies buried next day in the British Cemetery at Ramleh. Until, then, fatal accidents had been few and far between since the end of the war but four more men were killed in two crashes later that year, one in June and the other in August.

The Crown Prince of Italy visited the Squadron on 7 April and thereby provided a literal dress rehearsal for a much more significant visitor two weeks later: His Majesty the Emir Abdullah, of Transjordan, who presented the prizes at the Squadron sports. The occasion, alas, was somewhat interfered with by low-flying clouds of locusts. In June, the High Commissioner of Palestine and Transjordan (Field Marshal Lord Plumer) paid what was described as an 'unofficial' visit to the Station, though it is likely that everything - and everyone- was highly polished regardless. Visitors of a similar order of magnitude appeared at regular intervals. Some, such as Sir Philip Sassoon (Under-Secretary of State for Air) were merely passing through - en route from Heliopolis to Iraq - and stayed for a couple of hours on 10 October. Others, such as Air Vice Marshal Sir Robert Brooke-Popham, caused a major upheaval in domestic routine by bringing with him two escorting aircraft and a D.H. 60 Moth aircraft in which the Vicomte de Sibour and his wife were touring.

THE LLOYD CUP COMPETITION

This competition was the brain-child of Lord Lloyd who was in 1928 High Commissioner in Egypt. It was designed to be a test of the reliability and efficiency of every RAF squadron in the Middle East Command.

This was the narrative included in Cooke's report, written immediately after he returned to Amman.

'First Day 12 D.H.9As left Amman at 0900hrs and all arrived at Abu Sueir for breakfast. Crews had to refuel their own aircraft and the drill was for the pilot to stand on top of the engine while the passenger opened the 4 gallon petrol tins with the special opener and handed the full tins to the pilot. Refuelling was timed by judges. Leaving Abu Sueir two machines jammed throttles, due to two pilots not experienced enough to know how to free them using the doper. This delayed take off. 12 aircraft left 1130hrs for Ramleh. One machine lagged astern near Kantara. It transpired afterwards that the pilot did not try his switches when the engine commenced to run badly. Had he done so the fault would have been discovered and a landing made at Kantara. Near Maddan station this machine landed on a salt pan. A 'T' was put out and the remainder of the Flight landed. The leader then took far too long in deciding whether the forced landed machine should continue. Meanwhile the remaining 8 who had been circling round decided to land as fuel was running short. All 12 machines were now on the salt pan which was so soft that the wheels left deep ruts. It was at last decided to proceed to Ramleh. 8 planes took off but the 9th went on its nose after a tyre burst. The 8 then landed again and stopped engines. Salvage work on the 9th commenced and it was made fit to take off. Starting up by hand was exhausting in the heat. One's mouth dried up by the strong salt air and water would not slake our thirsts. Water was near boiling in our wing tanks. Eventually 11 machines took off for Ramleh hoping to reach there in daylight. All 11 landed O.K. without wing flares or ground lights which was a great piece of luck as we had no navigation lights and so the danger of air collision was extreme! We were all too exhausted to refuel that night and depressed because by the landings on the salt pan we had disqualified ourselves from the competition! We got 6 hours sleep that night and the next day it was a hot 105° when we refuelled.

Second Day Over-revving engines on the first day had caused water leaks and one machine had to remain at Ramleh because there was no time to change cylinders. Each aircraft took in 100 gallons at Ramleh. The 10 machines reached Heliopolis Cairo and later landed at Aboukir about 1600hrs. Two engines were found to need extensive repairs however, and as under the rules of the competition, our crews had to do all repairs. The men had to work all night changing cylinders and soldering other leaks. We did all we could to help but they were very tired next morning.

Third day 10 machines left at 0600hrs and only had to fly to Cairo and back to Aboukir. This was a rest day and we all felt much refreshed by our sea bathing.

Fourth day 10 left at 0700hrs for Heliopolis (Cairo). We flew by compass and near Katatbara one fell out of formation and landed. The rest of that flight landed and after more troubles 9 machines reached Heliopolis. Two unfortunately had to be left at Heliopolis owing to bad cylinder and water leaks thus cutting out all 'A' Flight and leaving 3 of 'B' and all of 'C'. After another spot of bother with 'B' Flight, 6 aircraft arrived back at Amman. I was very pleased that all my aircraft had come through the competition without trouble. This was mainly due to my not keeping aircraft in the flight after their flying times had expired. There were many lessons to be learnt by the competition and it was very well worth while'.

By the time Squadron Leader Edward Hopcraft succeeded Gallehawk in September 1927, No 14 Squadron's peacetime organisation had settled into an officer staff of 17 pilots divided into three flights - and four other officers, responsible for stores, money and medical attention. A number of unnamed sergeant pilots were listed, but the number of NCOs and airmen on strength remains unknown. It is, however, pleasing to observe that a steady trickle of pilots with the equivalent of Field Marshal's batons in their knapsacks continued to pass through the Squadron, the latest including Gerald Gibbs and Horace Wigglesworth, who both held high commands during and after the Second World War.

ARABS VERSUS JEWS

In 1929 there occurred in Palestine a situation tantamount to civil war. Sparked by religious controversy over holy places in Jerusalem, Arab attacks on Jewish settlements erupted throughout Palestine from Haifa in the north, to Beersheba and Gaza in the south. Army and naval reinforcements from Egypt and Malta were urgently sent for, and after a month of action from desperately stretched resources, order was restored.

The consequences for Britain from the Balfour declaration were starting to be painful in both the political and military areas.

Under Turkish rule in Palestine the problem of the custody of a region, within which are the histories of so many forms of religion, had been treated with a broad minded and tolerant spirit. The Jewish community had well defined, if limited privileges. Places sacred to Moslems, were vested in their own religious bodies. When Britain assumed control, it undertook to maintain the status quo in spite of the Jewish influence. The Arabs watched the fulfilment of this promise jealously, and the Jews sought by degrees to acquire rights not included in their former privileges.

Britain from the experience of communal troubles in India realised that the firm and impartial intervention of force, was the sole means of restoring peace, and of preventing the spread of disorder. The danger was recognised and an efficient British Police Force, 750 strong was provided. However the recurring theme of accepting risks under the urge of economy (will our Budget controllers never learn?), changed the Force to locally recruited, under 150 British officers and NCO's. All ground troops were therefore withdrawn, and security transferred to the Air Ministry.

The Royal Air Force, with armoured cars to co-operate, furnished an effective and economical force to patrol and mount action against outside aggression. However in the absence of ground troops, as had been provided in Iraq by the Levies, air action was not up to crowd control and large scale riot containment. Armoured cars in these circumstances also had their limitations.

16 August 1929 was a prayer day for the Arabs, the 17th a Jewish Sabbath. This was, in any case, a dangerous enough juxtaposition, but the Arabs had converted the Wailing Wall into a thoroughfare from a cul de sac, so destroying the privacy of Jewish prayers. The Jews called for protest, with young men persuaded even to incur martyrdom. Demonstration and counter demonstration escalated feelings fanned by the Press. No 2 Armoured Car Company at Amman was brought to Jerusalem, but the efforts of reconciliation by Government were interpreted as weakness. Violence in the following week erupted throughout the country. The SOS was sent out, and all three fighting services rushed to the rescue.

The Cairo Brigade under Brigadier Dobbie on the 24th sent a South Wales Borderers Battalion in four Victoria aircraft troop carriers to Jerusalem. A company of the Green Howards, some Royal Engineers and the rest of the Borderers transport and machine guns reached Lydda by train on the 25th. The Borderers went to Jerusalem, the remainder to relieve a screen of RAF personnel from Ramleh and to police between Tel Aviv and Jaffa, and the Green Howards to Haifa. HMS *Sussex* arrived at Jaffa on the 26th, HMS *Barham* at Haifa on the 27th and HMS *Courageous* from Malta with the South Staffords Battalion on the 28th. The Navy forces from *Sussex* and *Barham* provided 47 officers and 700 men and took over the situation in Jaffa and Haifa releasing troops for work inland.

At first, an airman - Group Captain Patrick Playfair - was in overall command, but later he handed over to Brigadier William Dobbie. The replacement of an airman by a soldier was a blow to Air Ministry pretensions: the substitution of aircraft and armoured cars for a garrison of soldiers had failed to prevent or suppress an outbreak of violence. The airmen, however, were hardly to blame. The worst violence took place in urban areas, where Arabs and Jews lived close together and could not be distinguished, let alone deterred from the air. In open country, whenever a large group of Arabs was spotted, there was no way of telling whether they intended violent action or merely vehement protest. And how could an airman flying over a ruined Jewish settlement be certain that the people he saw were Arabs looking for loot and not Jews trying to salvage their possessions? Nevertheless, the Air Ministry promptly sent an Air Vice-Marshal - Hugh Dowding (of Battle of Britain fame) - to Palestine. Outranking Dobbie, he replaced him in command, but only on 11 September, after the worst of the disturbances were over.

Meanwhile, a dawn patrol from Amman on 29 August reported all quiet around the shores of the Sea of Galilee, but it was during this day that Jews were massacred at Safed. Another patrol next morning reported much looting and many houses on fire. Looters were fired on and two killed; the rest fled. A huge crowd of Arabs assembled for the midday prayer in the Mosque of Omar in Jerusalem on the 30th, and the opportunity was taken to send all available aircraft to fly low over the mosque as the Arabs emerged. They dispersed quietly to their homes. In the face of such force, the heat had been taken out of the crisis by 3 September, but regular patrols in the air and on the ground continued, though in rapidly decreasing strength. By then, some 133 Jews had been killed by Arabs and 116 Arabs were also dead, mostly killed by the security forces while committing obvious acts of violence, arson or theft. This restraint was imposed by the British authorities because Arab hostility was directed not at the British but solely at the Jews and the authorities saw no point in goading the acquiescent majority into active opposition.

Throughout these tragic events, No 14 Squadron performed admirably. Eleven aircraft were available on 23 August and a twelfth was provided from Egypt three days later. Despite the frequency of operations, the roughness of airstrips and the frailty of elderly Ninaks, there were never less that nine machines serviceable during the first ten days of the crisis. This 'impressive display', as David Omissi described it, 'was made possible by the web of air communications' now linking all the RAF's Middle East units. 'A shortage of cylinders for the Liberty engine was overcome by airlifting supplies from Iraq. After a hundred hours in the air, every machine was flown to the Egyptian depot for a change of engine, this service usually requiring less than two days. If the deficiencies of substitution in Palestine were starkly highlighted in August 1929, the wider strategic benefits conferred by air control were perhaps more subtly demonstrated.'

In these weeks No 14 Squadron flew unending reconnaissances attacking when called upon to do so with small bombs and machine guns. It was an exhausting time for pilots, aircrew and ground crew. The latter often called upon also for guard and civil control duties.

Incursions from Transjordan into Palestine were mostly choked off by the TJFF and the River Jordan air patrols by No 14 Squadron. In a desperate two weeks of rushed deployments and local company ad hoc initiatives, sheer bravery abounded. Brigadier Dobbie, with the full co-operation of the other two services, the police and the civil authority took over full command, and finally stabilised the situation. The country was then divided into three areas:-

Northern Palestine: Haifa and the Plain of Esdraelon. Green Howards and one Company South Stafford plus 12th Lancers Armoured Car Squadron.

Mid Palestine: South   Staffords, less one Company.

Jerusalem & Hebron: South Wales Borderers.

Responsibility for security was reassigned to the RAF in September, and Palestine was never until 1940 to have less that two Battalions resident in Country. Later the AOC Palestine and Transjordan was moved from Amman to Jerusalem to be alongside the High Commissioner, and was to have in the next decade such illustrious Commanders as Sir Arthur 'Bomber' Harris and Roderic Hill.

Finally, No 6 Squadron was brought across from Hinaidi (Iraq) to Ramleh in October with its Bristol Fighters. The No 14 Squadron detachment at Ramleh transferred to Amman there to complete the squadron until 1940.

The Twenties, that allegedly carefree decade, ended in style for 14 squadron with its new commander - Squadron Leader Frank Soden - flying out from England to Amman in his own de Havilland Moth to take over from Hopcraft on 3rd December 1929. So ended the Twenties in Biblical Palestine in a welter of turbulence.

The first half of the Thirties, though not without its later incidents, was comparatively calm. No 14 Squadron was to re-equip with the Fairey IIIF aircraft and to extend its roles in support, and co-operation with the internal Jordanian security forces.

Civil Aviation communications saw developments in the Middle East, but in the last half of the decade Arab/Jewish hostility once more involved the Squadron in operations against both factions.

CHAPTER THREE

TRANSJORDAN - THE DEVELOPING YEARS

1930 - 1939

I found a candour, a lack of introspection, and kindliness I have seldom known in a company of men. Perhaps their isolation, with their little group of aircraft and armoured cars, developed these virtues; the relationship between the few officers and the men was unselfconscious and delightful; the humour was frothy and spontaneous and habits of life were as English as they could make them, within a world of Arabs and sand. (Hector Bolitho. 'Angry Neighbours.' Arthur Barker, London, 1957. Page 85).

FROM CAIRO TO THE CAPE AND BACK
PERSONNEL AND AIRCRAFT

Late in 1929, Middle East HQ decided that No 14 Squadron's long record of efficient and sensible handling of numerous difficult tasks in Transjordan and Palestine should be recognised by awarding it what we now call a PR plum: the honour of making the next flight from Egypt to South Africa and back. This would be the fifth successive Cape Flight and was intended, like its predecessors, to display the Royal Air Force's professional qualities - and social graces - to colonial officials, soldiers, settlers and, of course, to loyal natives. Not forgetting the British air-minded public, for its progress was reported weekly in *Flight*, the *Aeroplane* and other journals.

For such a prestigious task, a more impressive machine than the venerable *Ninak* would be required. The sleek, all-metal Fairey IIIF Mark IV, equipped with a 570 hp Napier Lion XIA engine, was chosen and an example sent to Amman in November for the men selected to carry out the flight, to familiarise themselves with it. One of the most successful of Fairey's designs, the III series saw a wide variety of both naval and air force use and the IIIF - which first flew in March 1926 - was produced in greater numbers than any other British military aircraft (except the Hawker Hart variants) between the wars until the Hawker Hurricane was ordered in 1936. It had a maximum speed of 120mph at 10,000ft and was armed with a single Vickers machine-gun for the pilot and a Lewis gun on a Scarff ring for the man in the rear cockpit; it could carry up to 500lbs of bombs under the wings.

The men chosen to fly this attractive new machine were Flight Lieutenant Cyril Greet (in command); Flying Officers John Hutchinson and Alline Wayte; and four NCOs, Flight Sergeant E H McDonald (a fitter) and Sergeants I T Richardson (pilot/carpenter rigger), N G N Davies and R W Timms (both fitters). Skilled navigators were a rarity in the RAF between the wars (a weakness for which it would later pay dearly) and so Flying Officer David Gibbon, of No 216 Squadron, had to be specially attached to assist this flight. Air Commodore Andrew Board, CMG DSO

1937. Arab Legion Liaison. Centre 2nd row Gp Capt D G Harries Stn Cdr Amman. On either side Capt Lash and Flt Lt Selway, Fg Off Bell, WO Lawson.

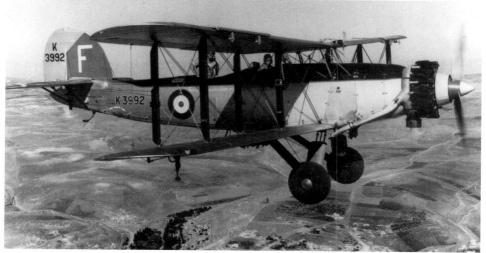

Gordon over Amman.

No 14 Squadron Wellesley over Amman.

Gordons in formation over the Moabite Hills.

was sent along as an officer of sufficient rank to represent the RAF suitably with local officials at civilian or military and social functions en route.

Six weeks before departure, it was represented by many that No 14 Squadron was not up to the task because its pilots and mechanics lacked experience both in general (as compared with men chosen for that flight in previous years) and in particular, of Fairey aircraft. It was also thought that the Mark I should again be used 'as the Mark IV had not been sufficiently tried out.' These objections were considered, but rejected. The selected crews were then sent to Aboukir in Egypt on 9 December 1929 to collect their new aircraft, and to fly them home to Amman a week later. The rest of that month was spent in practice and preparation.

A TRIBUTE TO THE SQUADRON

The Cape Flight of four aircraft set out from Amman for Heliopolis on 6 January 1930. One was forced to land near El Arish and the Flight was therefore obliged to spend a night at Abu Sueir, arriving at Heliopolis next day. It was there joined by Andrew Board. The journey to the Cape began on the 11th and, as the Air Commodore observed, it proved unique in many respects. It was the first time that a Transjordan squadron had been selected and the crews were all post-war trained and had no war experience to assist them. These points were known to many people wherever the Flight stayed and they all remarked on the crews' high standard of efficiency. Whatever the weather conditions, close formation was kept when passing over large towns and on arrival and departure from aerodromes; and there were no bad landings. Except for those in the southern Sudan, landing grounds were good and well maintained. The Shell Company had erected a single pump at many landing grounds, but it was found quicker to re-fuel the aircraft by hand direct from tins.

BUT NOT TO THE AIR MINISTRY

By some remarkable chain of reasoning, the Air Ministry ruled that 3s 6d per day must be deducted from the pay of officers taking part in the Flight. Andrew Board objected strongly (though vainly) both to the obvious injustice of penalising employees for carrying out assigned duties and to the equally obvious injustice of making a flat deduction that would hit the lower paid more severely than the higher paid. In addition, he pointed out that both officers and men had been mindful of their responsibility to return at least some of the hospitality they had enjoyed in the Union to members of the South African Air Force Flight which accompanied them home to Cairo. 'I cannot emphasise sufficiently,' he wrote, 'how generously junior officers and airmen of the Flight did their utmost, within their limited means, to entertain their comrades in Cairo, one of the most expensive cities in the world.'

THE FLIGHT SOUTH

Personnel began to take quinine as soon as they flew south of the Sudan and continued to do so until they returned to Cairo. RAF doctors there held the view that quinine was useless until a person was actually affected by malaria, but Andrew disagreed. Aware that most European residents of lands south of the Sudan took quinine daily as a preventative, the Air Commodore encouraged his men to do likewise. In the event, one officer went down with malaria in Pretoria, but he had suffered from it before the Flight began. Everyone else remained healthy, despite early rising, a long day's flight, recreation and late nights with official dinners, dances and entertainments, and the attendant hospitality displayed by everyone en route.

Many happy hours were spent in the company of former airmen - RFC, RNAS and RAF - who were often able to give good advice about local conditions. This advice was the more valuable because maps supplied by Middle East HQ proved inaccurate and Board recommended that HQ obtain its own copies of the superior maps possessed by District Officials.

AIR COMMODORE BOARD'S REPORT

In May 1930, Board and Greet submitted separate reports on this Flight to Air Vice-Marshal Francis Scarlett, Head of RAF Middle East, in Cairo. When forwarding these reports to the Air Ministry on the 14th, Scarlett noted that the Air Commodore appears to have overlooked the fact that the aircraft employed 'had to proceed at 20 miles per hour under their normal speed owing to the incessant vibration.' Until this problem was rectified, he could not consider the Mark IV model of the Fairey IIIF a satisfactory machine.

It was, however, the first occasion on which this all-metal aircraft had been given a thorough trial. In Board's opinion, it proved an excellent machine, despite many defects in construction (there were none, he thought, in design) and whatever its problems the Flight was unique for punctuality in arriving and departing, despite frequent torrential rains and thick cloud. 'Punctuality', observed Board, 'in the movements of aircraft creates a very great impression on the public mind, especially in a vast continent like Africa where railway communications, if any, are slow and poor, and where large centres are situated many hundreds of miles apart.' Fewer spares were carried - or needed - by this flight than by any of its predecessors. A previous 1925 flight, for example, had required no fewer than three spare aircraft and ten spare engines. Moreover, No 14 Squadron completed the journey in 45 days, far fewer than any predecessor.

'It is difficult for anyone who has not taken part in the Cape Flight to realise the importance of it,' he continued. Despite regular visits during the past five years, interest in the flight was actually increasing, 'and there were many instances at places en route of people travelling over sixty miles by car, and many more by train, to witness our arrival. 'Towns and mining centres actually stopped work,' he reported, to permit men and women to congregate and wave, 'and show their enthusiasm at this visit of British aircraft. The reception from isolated homesteads, engine drivers and from lake and coastal boats was no less remarkable. The Union Jack was frequently displayed. The hearty welcome, profuse hospitality and assistance offered to the flight by every city, town and Dutch dorp from Uganda to the Cape was amazing.' The lack of information between adjoining colonies and protectorates, caused by poor communications everywhere in Africa, struck Andrew as an excellent reason for the rapid development of regular air services.

FLIGHT LIEUTENANT GREET'S REPORT

Greet also recorded his impressions of this flight. By the time it returned to Cairo on 24 February 1930, he noted, 13,200 miles had been flown in exactly 140hrs at an average speed of 94mph. A great many minor defects in the aircraft were experienced, most of them traced to vibration caused by an airscrew which, though efficient, was too heavy. A fractured oil pipe obliged one aircraft (piloted by John Hutchinson with the Air Commodore as his passenger) to make a forced landing 15 miles out of Salisbury on the homeward journey in a field where the grass was up to four feet high and there were many boulders and ant hills. Even so, Hutchinson got down without further damage; the pipe was repaired, a runway cut through the grass and he took off again safely. At several places a considerable amount of fuel had evaporated from the four-gallon tins used to store it, 'but this wastage had been allowed for in laying in the stocks.' It is interesting to note that Greet's observation provoked no measures to replace these inefficient tins and precious fuel would still be wasted in wartime, a decade and more later.

It sometimes proved impossible to report the Flight's arrival at a particular place for two days because, Greet wrote, 'at several towns en route the Flight arrived on a Saturday and the Post Office was shut from midday Saturday until Monday morning. In the schedule laid down, it was arranged that no flying should be carried out on Sundays south of the Sudan, owing to the strong feeling against Sunday flying, especially in North and South Rhodesia and also in the Union of South Africa where it is practically prohibited.' Little difficulty in navigation was experienced, despite heavy rain, low cloud and frequent thunderstorms between

Mongalla and Bulawayo. The maps issued before departure were little help; many road, and even the railways, were simply not marked. David Gibbon the navigator, replaced Hutchinson as a pilot during the homeward journey when the latter was admitted to hospital in Pretoria, suffering from fever.

In Greet's opinion, the schedule laid down was too tight. Only 45 days were allowed for the whole journey, compared with 49 in the previous year (when the Flight terminated at Khartoum) and 59 in 1928. The Flight, he thought, should spend three days in Pretoria on both the outward and homeward legs because no other place en route had adequate facilities for work on airframes or engines. Co-operation exercises were successfully carried out with the 4th Battalion of the King's African Rifles at Entebbe, and with the 2nd Battalion at Tabora, but much more could have been done, with more time and better prior preparation.

PROTECTING AND REFEREEING: POLICING AND CONTROLLING

Meanwhile, the rest of the Squadron soldiered on with its elderly Ninaks, carrying out those tasks which absorbed its energies throughout the inter-war period. It was charged to keep the peace in Transjordan (sometimes in Palestine as well) and did so, to the best of its abilities, as protectors and referees or policemen and controllers.

The fact that map-reading was simple greatly helped operations. The Transjordan desert, as Corporal Henry Barnes (a Squadron fitter) recalled, ' is black, due to its top layer of volcanic ash, through which centuries old caravan routes had worn to reveal the yellow sand below. Thus the tracks stood out clearly like yellow lines on a blackboard and whenever aircraft landed crews were quick to shield their wheels from the fierce sun with canvas covers - and equally quick to remove the covers at dusk to deter scorpions from creeping under them.' A network of emergency landing grounds had been set up throughout the country, all provided with a store of petrol in carefully-buried four-gallon tins. Speaking of petrol; a major on-going task for the Squadron was to protect the oil pipeline running through Transjordan from Kirkuk in Iraq to the port of Haifa.

On 2 February 1930, the largest Ikhwan raid on the Howeitat tribe for some time was reported in the Imshash district. D.H.9s arrived to find the fighting over and many corpses strewn over a large area. A Howeitat sheikh was flown around the area in order to identify and locate the bodies of his people so that they could be collected for burial. This tragic task marked the virtual end of the Ninak's service because a second flight of Fairey IIIFs arrived in Amman on the 22nd and a third flight was delivered in March. By then, the last of the Ninaks had been thankfully waved away. During March, aircraft often had to use a landing ground at Zerqa (12 miles to the north-east) because Amman aerodrome was flooded. One flight was detached to Ma'an (120 miles south of Amman) in the middle of that month.

THE TRANSJORDAN FRONTIER FORCE

Squadron aircraft co-operated with armoured cars and the Transjordan Frontier

Force (TJFF) in a column designated Stracol which left Amman on 14 March via Qasr el Azraq for Landing Ground M on the Cairo-Baghdad air route, a place 170 miles east of Amman on the border with Iraq. Stracol's purpose was to exact a heavy fine in camels from the Ruallah tribes for their part in recent raiding. During this venture, the column was supplied with food and water by air; so too was a detachment of armoured cars guarding the wells at Bair.

Airmen had a warm regard for the TJFF: 'the British equivalent of the French Foreign Legion', Corporal Barnes called it, 'highly-trained and highly-disciplined, multi-national, mainly Circassion, their scout cars always gleaming.' The TJFF consisted of three cavalry squadrons and two mechanised companies, totally 33 British officers, 28 local officers and 835 men, with a further 180 in reserve. Though based in Transjordan, it was an imperial force and would be used in some rural districts of Palestine during disturbances: 'It proved to be loyal and reliable', in the opinion of a British historian, Martin Kolinsky, 'unlike the Arab section of the Palestine Police.'

In May, the desert tribes began their summer raiding 'with unusual vigour', according to the Squadron recorder. Hitherto, armoured cars had operated from bases at Amman and Ma'an and upon report of a raid were promptly despatched towards it usually finding that all the damage had been done and the raiders long gone. This year, therefore, it was decided to place cars on permanent guard at all known watering places used by raiders either of our own tribes or from beyond the border. This decision required careful air co-operation. As well as frequent flying visits to watering places, an aircraft was allotted to and maintained by the cars based there. The pilot carried out dawn and dusk patrols, keeping station over any observed raiders until either cars or a relieving aircraft arrived. In this way, a large party of Transjordan tribesmen, returning from a raid in the Nejed, was found on 9 May and held by aircraft until cars arrived: 22 leaders were arrested and 50 camels confiscated. During that month, the squadron co-operated with as many as six separate columns operating in different parts of the desert.

The Bedouin Control Board then decided to move all tribesmen, for their own protection, to locations west of a line from Azraq through Jafar Fort (30 miles east of Ma'an) to Aqaba, at the head of the Arabian Gulf. Aircraft supported armoured cars in ensuring compliance with this decision. Orders in Arabic and English were dropped on tribal camps and any tribesmen found east of the line after a designated date were guided westward and their chief men arrested.

On the morning of 28 July 1930, a report was received that a Sharakat raiding party was assembling north of Azraq and a Fairey IIIF found it at about 1245hrs. Meanwhile, a mechanised column of the TJFF was travelling eastwards to Azraq from Zerqa, a distance of 45 miles. The raiders began their attempts to evade it about 1715hrs, but the IIIF pinned them down by gunfire until engine trouble forced it to land. Although the pilot gave accurate directions to the column when it reached the landing ground, the raiders had had time to get away. They escaped empty-handed, however, having had no opportunity to cause either damage or injury.

To secure good grazing, the tribes moved eastward at the end of September and, to protect them, ground detachments were established along the frontier with

IIIFs attached from Ma'an to provide dawn and dusk patrols. In a good example of air-air co-operation, a twin-engined Vickers Victoria transport-bomber of 216 Squadron (based at Heliopolis) carried petrol from Ma'an to various outposts. The experiment worked so well that the same pilot, Flight Lieutenant Alan Shipwright, was ordered to repeat it during January 1931. As always, however, the weather gods exacted respect from vulnerable airmen and in that same month of January winds of 70 mph were experienced at Ma'an on the night of the 19th. Aircraft standing in the open were lashed to armoured cars and Morris six-wheelers, these vehicles so positioned that they served as some sort of windbreak. Thanks to these measures, no aircraft were significantly damaged.

THE END OF IKHWAN RAIDING

In May 1932, Sheikh Hamed led his men southward into the Hejaz in an attempt to resist the Ikhwan conquest inspired by Ibn Saud. Semforce, consisting of one flight of IIIFs, a mechanised company of the TJFF, two troops of camels and three armoured cars was assembled at Ma'an, with posts established elsewhere, to prevent supplies and reinforcements from Transjordan reaching the Sheikh. The Ikhwan defeated and killed him in battle near Dhaba (on the Red Sea coast, 150 miles south of Aqaba). They then continued their advance northward, killing every man, woman and child in their path. During August, a handful of survivors from the disaster were making their way back into Transjordan, where they were arrested and disarmed. At the same time, Semforce prevented the merciless Ikhwan from pursuing these survivors across the frontier. Reluctantly, they withdrew and Semforce was disbanded on 2 September. During December, however, reports of a large body of Ikhwan moving towards Transjordan from Arabia resulted in extensive reconnaissance over the southern and eastern frontiers. It was known that they would invade and seize Aqaba, Ma'an and Amman itself if unchecked, but in 1933 the British persuaded the Saudi and Transjordan rivals to sign a treaty of friendship which practically ended frontier hostilities.

A NEW ZEALANDER AT MA'AN

Hector Bolitho, a prolific New Zealand-born author, has left us a rare picture of life at Ma'an, which he visited in May 1932. The bedrooms of the Mess, he wrote, 'look out upon a border of bamboos and spring onions; the hangars and garages are filled with aeroplanes and armoured cars; the surrounding desert is made formidable with wire entanglements and clever traps for rebellious Arabs.' Though isolated, 'the men in the Royal Air Force flourish in character and body. I have never been more contented and amused than I was on the evening I spent with the NCOs of the RAF at Ma'an, drinking beer, telling bawdy stories and talking sentimentally about England. 'Everything is fun when you are sitting in a smoke-filled room in Ma'an, a struggling speck of civilisation in the desert, with eight or ten young Britons.'

'I have never known people more happy,' he continued, 'less selfish, less class-conscious and less irritable. I do not know enough of the services to say how rare this is. But I have never felt the spirit of unsentimental comradeship so pleasantly. Officers and NCOs and men seemed to be as necessary one to the other as limbs growing from one body.... One sees the character of the men growing and blossoming under the warmth of the Transjordan sun'.

There was, wrote Bolitho, 'only one shaking train a week bringing the letters down across the desert, from Jerusalem. Its arrival is the occasion of the week. I was leaving the post office with my letters when an RAF driver, with the good name of Jones, came up and offered to take me back in his lorry. I swung up on the front seat of the enormous vehicle and we rattled over the desert. As we were crossing a dark strip of sand, on the edge of the village, we came upon a lame Arab boy who was going our way. Jones stopped the lorry and asked the boy if he would like a ride. But that was not all. Jones jumped down and lifted the youngster into the back of the lorry. Is it sentimental for me to see some deep influence in these things: Is it foolish for me to feel that the isolation of this life in the desert brings out the positive and yet tender qualities of character in a way that life in England could never do?'

A NEW AIRCRAFT: THE FAIREY GORDON

The first Gordon was received in July 1932 and by September two flights had been re-equipped with the new machine. The Squadron was generally pleased with its performance. Originally designated the Fairey IIIF Mark V, it first flew in March 1931 and was equipped with a 525 hp Armstrong Siddeley Panther engine. Dimensions, armament and bomb load were the same, but its maximum speed was higher - 145mph at 3,000ft and it had a longer range, even though its engine was less powerful. Its appearance, however, was less attractive than that of the IIIF and no-one ever regarded the Gordon, flown for the next six years, as more than a reliable workhorse.

Three Gordons left Amman for Baghdad (a distance of 500 miles) at 1800hrs on 14 October to carry out the first night formation flight to Iraq. Following the oil pipeline track, they reached Rutbah, roughly half way, at 2035hrs and refuelled there, taking off again an hour later. Blowing sand made visibility very poor, but the Gordons reached Hinaidi safely at 0200hrs. The return journey began next night and though one machine had to remain overnight at Rutbah (with a defective magneto) the other two got home without alarm. If suitable beacons were placed at intervals along the route, the crews reported, night air traffic could become a routine matter. Work on landing grounds along the route had been completed by early December and they were described as 'the finest in the Middle East.' The route to Rutbah was by then 'so clearly marked that no further difficulty should be experienced by pilots passing to Iraq.'

The work required of No 14 Squadron in these years usually called for long hours in the air and the Gordon's range was gradually extended until April 1937, when Flight Lieutenants Eric Grace and Michael Aylmer made good use of newly-fitted long-range fuel tanks. They took off from Amman at 0438hrs one morning and flew south to Aqaba, east to Jebel el Tubeik, north to Qasr el Azraq, then home to Amman, landing at 1245hrs. Some 800 miles were covered at an average ground speed of 100 mph. At need, they could have remained aloft for nearly two more hours. Air crews and hangar staffs alike were delighted to know that this excellent range was available. A year later, however, the Gordon would itself be replaced by an aircraft that made a range of 1,000 miles seem very ordinary indeed.

CEREMONIAL INTERLUDES

Throughout the Thirties, the Squadron's peace-keeping, training and rescue duties were interspersed with ceremonial interludes, most of which provoked a round of spit and polish for everything and everyone. On 23 June 1930, for example, a Victoria carrying King Feisal from Iraq was forced to land near Qasr el Azraq. A Fairey IIIF was sent there to carry him on to Amman, where he was received by his brothers, Emir Abdullah and ex-King Ali. All three princes and their attendants were then invited to inspect the aircraft, hangars and other buildings.

Early in April 1931, the Squadron was visited by an even more important prince: the Chief of the Air Staff himself, Sir John Salmond, accompanied by his staff and other luminaries. They were flown east to Qasr el Azraq and then south to Bair for lunch. In the afternoon, they were flown via Imshash and Jafar to Ma'an, where they spent the night. Their tour continued next day, enlivened by a forced landing, but the fault was soon put right, and the great ones disappeared for another year.

There were other early examples of the Squadron performing ceremonial duties. First, a sad day in September 1933 when two flights of three Gordons acted as final escort for a man with whom No 14 Squadron had worked so closely during the war: Lawrence's ally and patron, Feisal, King of Iraq. He had died of a heart attack in Switzerland and his body was carried aboard a Victoria from Haifa on the last stage of its journey home to Baghdad. Secondly, a cheerful day in July 1934 when a formation of nine Gordons escorted Emir Abdullah on the last stage of his return by air to Amman from England; and finally, an important day in May 1935 when nine Gordons flew over Haifa, Jerusalem, Jaffa and Tel Aviv to celebrate the silver jubilee of King George V.

TACTICAL EXERCISES

An interesting tactical exercise took place in the Jordan valley on 15 August 1930. One section of the TJFF, representing raiders, was to attempt an unobserved crossing of the river at Jisr el Mejami, some ten miles south of the Sea of Galilee. Another section, helped by aircraft, was to try to locate and capture them. The Squadron's well-tested technique for picking up messages without landing proved its value yet again. The ground forces hung a message bag on a line stretched between two poles. The aircraft swooped low over the line and snapped up the bag by means of a hook fixed to the fuselage's underside. This rapid method of transmitting information helped the ground forces to capture all the raiders.

Several more exercises were carried out during September by Flying Officer Patrick Halahan, working with outposts of the TJFF in an attempt to clarify and standardise the signals used by aircraft when leading ground patrols towards raiders. The final exercise was held at Ma'an with a troop of TJFF camelry representing the raiders. As the exercise progressed, the raiders broke into two parties, but the two aircraft taking part had no difficulty in leading ground forces to them.

During October 1934, each flight was detached in turn to Ismailia to carry out air firing exercises against towed targets. 'This was the first occasion' noted the recorder, 'on which the Squadron has had an opportunity of firing at air targets since the War': that is, in nearly 16 years.

Almost a year later, in September 1935, an exhibition of dive-bombing was given to officers and men of the TJFF and British troops. Live bombs were used against a target of a hundred men, each one represented by a pillar of three two gallon petrol tins, scattered over an area 120 yrds long by 60 yrds wide. Three Gordons were used and three attacks made, using 20lb bombs. The aircraft started their dives at 4,000ft, pulling out no lower than 1,000ft. 'On inspection of the target', wrote the recorder, 'it was found that a fair number of the pillars were still standing, but all except two or three were hit. Nearly all were pierced many times by splinters or stones.' Naturally enough, he did not point out that real men would not have remained upright and immobile during the attack. They might also have fired back with some success at an aircraft which was no dive-bomber, whatever its other virtues.

RICHARD *(BATCHY)* ATCHERLEY

Squadron Leader Frank Soden flew to Cyprus on leave during September 1930 in his own DH Puss Moth and a few days later, on 13 October, one of the RAF's brilliant pilots - Richard Atcherley, then a Flight Lieutenant - joined the Squadron, having flown from England via Malta and Egypt in his own aircraft, an Avro Avian. 'An aeroplane is awfully useful to one out here' he wrote in a letter home, 'motor cars are practically useless unless you intend to sit in them for about ten hours on end.' Throughout his career, Batchy was made the centre - or butt - of numerous curious or bizarre tales. His identical twin brother, David, also served in the RAF, but never in No 14 Squadron: both of them would have been too much for any unit! Charles Baker recorded one of many anecdotes from these days (which tells us something about standards in air-to-ground firing) and rendered it into verse under the title

'Did it Atcherley Happen?':
The Pilot winged his weary way
Over the Promised Land
Never a soul in sight that day
But miles and miles of sand
When presently he spied a lump
A rock it seemed, or else a stump
So pulling up his C.C. pump
A practice burst he planned
Then having reached the vital spot
He brought his gun to play
He missed it with his opening shot
Which egged him on to stay

72

His bursts the target neatly spanned
With bullets whipping up the sand
The stump began to understand
And quickly ran away.

Whenever leave came round, *Batchy* would be off to London in his Avian or across to the United States, where his aerobatics thrilled spectators at air shows. When not on leave, however, he threw himself into the Squadron's life and work with such enthusiasm and imagination - as he did in all his postings - that critics were disarmed and obliged to admit, even with exasperation, that *Batchy* was different: he floated free while the system broke or subdued other exuberant characters.

Arab Legion desert patrol.

HELPING GLUBB PASHA

During November 1930, three raids were located by Squadron aircraft patrolling from outposts. On the 10th, a dozen or so camelmen were observed and for some time held by gunfire before scattering into the hills - leaving behind seven camels, killed. A few days later, on the 14th, Soden himself spotted about twenty camelmen and horsemen assembling for a raid. He flew over Glubb, then a Captain and Desert (Tribal) Control Officer who was on his way to Imshash by car. Attracting Glubb's attention, Soden directed him towards the raiders and pinned them in one place by gunfire until Glubb and his men arrived to arrest them. Finally, on the 20th, a party of raiders was observed making for the Wadi Sirhan. The pilot checked them by gunfire and then shot several of their riding camels as they split up, abandoning their loot - no fewer than 57 camels. These were then rounded up by members of the TJFF and returned to their owners.

Continuous watch was maintained by IIIFs over tribal movements throughout the country during December and on the two occasions that Glubb chose to fine tribes for looting, aircraft flew over their camps 'to impress them' To impress the

73

Arabs still further, two night reconnaissances were carried out over the area at the end of January 1931. A few days later, on 3 February, Soden made another night patrol over an area east of Azraq because, thought the recorder, 'an aircraft flying at night leaves a great impression on the Arab mind.' Many night reconnaissances followed in April, both to accustom pilots to the look of the country in darkness and also to demonstrate to tribes that, if necessary, night action was as likely as day action.

On five occasions in May, IIIFs carried out night training flights over northern Transjordan and Palestine, landing twice in the Jordan valley. A particular problem was maintaining W/T communication with Amman because of frequent electrical storms. Flights were also made to Aqaba and thence across Sinai to Heliopolis in order to study these routes in the event of night operations being required. A photographic survey of the Aqaba district was also made. During an election period, night flights were made over the more important towns and villages throughout Transjordan.

Tribes had been noticed moving into the Jebel el Tubeiq area (some 90 miles south-east of Ma'an) in December 1930. An area of broken hills with broad stretches of soft sand, it was considered impassable to ground forces. Realising this, the tribes openly defied Glubb. In order to maintain the prestige of the Legion's desert patrols and collect the fines imposed, an operation was organised early in January 1931. A column of Arab Legion camelry set out from Ma'an on the 6th, led by aircraft along the best routes into this rugged area. According to the Squadron's recorder, 'the tribes were very impressed with the show of force' and handed over without demur the number of camels Glubb demanded. Moreover, two places where aircraft could land were located and so 'a new district which at one time was a prohibited flying area has been opened up.

By February 1931, it was Squadron policy to leave tribal control to Glubb, though sufficient aircraft were kept permanently available to help him if and when necessary. At Amman, there were three flights (less a couple of aircraft) and four armoured cars. At Bair (95 miles to the south-east), there were two troops of TJFF personnel with their own motor vehicles as well as two armoured cars. And at Ma'an were two troops of camelry, two cars and two aircraft. All landing grounds were visited during the month and sites located for new ones. Plans were discussed for improving co-operation with ground forces and methods of picking up and dropping messages were practiced. The month proved a quiet one, however, with only the two aircraft at Ma'an employed on active patrols. The rest of the squadron got on with intensive training. Glubb took over full control of the tribes east of the Hejaz railway in March and thereby 'relieved the Imperial Forces from a lot of heavy duties.'

No 14 Squadron was found plenty of heavy duties in Palestine later in the Thirties and so relative calm in Transjordan was all the more welcome. Routine work continued to be punctuated by such major exercises as one named Soucol which took place around Ma'an over two days in January 1938 and involved eleven Gordons. Twenty-two camelmen of the Arab Legion and two armoured cars represented a raiding party of 500 camelmen plus eight vehicles. The enemy were known to be hiding in an area of 1,600 square miles in the Jebel el Tubeiq, which they could reach by trotting through the hours of darkness. It had been intended to maintain a continuous reconnaissance by three aircraft over the area throughout the day, but the enemy were discovered at 1000hrs on the second search. The air striking force attacked the enemy and would in practice have continued to do so until after dark, but in this exercise action ceased after the first attack and one Gordon was left to watch and report enemy movements. Soucol was kept informed by W/T and message-dropping and saw action later in the day. The enemy vehicles were also discovered and attacked from the air.

ACCIDENTS AND ALARMS

On 7 February 1931, Flying Officer Paul Robertson landed his Fairey IIIF some 30 miles south of Hausa Wells with a fractured oil pipe. Sergeant Morris was sent out from Amman to find him, but had no time to do so before dark. By the time he found him next morning, Robertson had managed a temporary repair. A notable feature of this forced landing was that ground wireless sets were used with success by both aircraft.

A year later, on 6 February 1932, everyone in the Squadron was alarmed when only five out of eleven Westland Wapitis (of 55 Squadron, Iraq Command) arrived safely at Amman after a flight from Rutbah. A blizzard prevented searches next day, but five of the missing aircraft were found on the 8th near Imtan in Syria, 60 miles north-east of Amman, and the sixth was found 15 miles further north on the 10th. Though very cold, all crew members were uninjured and their aircraft undamaged. The search had been conducted from Zerqa, Amman aerodrome then being unusable.

During January 1933, regular formation flying was being practiced in preparation for a display at Heliopolis. Unfortunately, a collision between two Gordons resulted in the death of an airman. He baled out, but his parachute opened too late. Twelve aircraft nevertheless went to Heliopolis on the 28th, practiced there, took part in two events (with three other squadrons) on 3 February and returned to Amman on the 7th. These displays, including an item soberly described as a Wing Drill, were a highlight of annual routine in the Thirties and one in which the Squadron never lost another life, either in practice or performance.

But several fatal accidents occurred on duty. For example, while approaching Zerqa en route from Rutbah to Amman with service mail on 27 April 1933, a Gordon struck a very bad bump at 7,000 feet and both passengers were thrown out of the rear cockpit. Flying Officer James Bradley descended safely by parachute, but the wireless operator had not been wearing his parachute pack at the time and was killed. Bradley, alas, did not long survive his good fortune. Only six weeks later, on 12 June, he was killed when a Morris six-wheeler carrying official mail from Amman to Ramleh overturned.

Searches, always prolonged until after all reasonable prospect of success had gone, were an exhausting and frequently distressful aspect of Squadron life. The most tragic occurred on 21 December 1934, when ten Gordons went out to look for a KLM Douglas DC-2 airliner which had been reported missing. The aircraft was found crashed in the Wadi Hauran, 15 miles south-west of Rutbah, and everyone aboard had been killed.

Other searches were exasperating, rather than tragic. An airman pilot of No 14 Squadron with an army officer and an airman as passengers lost himself early in July 1935 and the aircraft was eventually found over 60 miles off course, after involving 46 hours of flying time, eight of them in darkness. All three were unharmed and the aircraft undamaged. The pilot faced a difficult interview with his CO as soon as he had been fed and watered. Even more exasperating, however, was an incident that occurred in May 1937. Information was received that a Chinaman in a civil aircraft had left Gaza for Baghdad and was missing. After searching for more than eight hours, it was learned that he had gone to Damascus instead.

Some alarms had a happy outcome that made up for long hours of anxious searching. One such alarm occurred in October 1935, while members of a touring theatrical group were being entertained in the Officers' Mess in Amman after a performance. A signal was received from Ma'an for urgent medical assistance to a TJFF sergeant. Flight Lieutenant Charles Howes and Dr John Blair took off for Ma'an just after midnight. On examination, the doctor decided that the sergeant must be flown back to Amman on a stretcher. They landed at 4 am and Dr Blair took him to the Italian hospital, where he was successfully treated. According to the Squadron recorder, 'This was the first time that the night-flying equipment recently sent to Ma'an was used.'

There were other occasions when the sight and sound of aircraft was more than welcome. For instance, three armoured cars en route from Ma'an to Amman in February 1938 were caught by a heavy snowfall at Yaduda, eight miles south of Amman, and there they were stuck for three days. As soon as their plight became known through W/T, supplies were flown to them and dropped by parachute. A few days later, on 3 March, three Gordons flew in bad weather to Ramleh, picked up supplies and dropped them on a stranded army unit at Rabah in Palestine. Another Gordon dropped more supplies next day.

AN EXPANDING SQUADRON

Squadron Leader Leonard Cockey succeeded Soden as CO on 29 October 1932. At the end of the following year, he had under his command 14 officer pilots (his three flight commanders, all flight lieutenants, nine flying officers and two pilot officers) and seven NCO pilots. Cockey was promoted to the rank of Wing Commander on 1 July 1935 and replaced as CO by Squadron Leader Thomas Traill, who arrived in Amman on 1 August and took command on the 6th.

By the end of 1935, No 14 Squadron had been temporarily enlarged to include a fourth flight (of six pilots, four of them officers) formed as part of the expansion scheme. The personnel of D Flight arrived from England at short notice in September and their aircraft were supplied by No 6 Squadron (then being re-equipped). The flight carried out extensive training, to fit them for war, in case the crisis with Italy over its conduct in Abyssinia worsened. This training included bombing (dive and level), air firing, night flying, photography, formation flying, searching and reconnaissance. Once training was completed, the flight was equipped with Vickers Vincents and posted on 8 January 1936 to No 45 Squadron at Helwan 'as part of the emergency measures.' Everyone was 'very sorry to see them go' wrote the recorder. Until this time, new faces appeared infrequently and in small numbers, but those days were shortly to end.

The NCO element among the flying personnel continued to grow and by the end of 1936, eight of the 19 pilots were NCOs. By the end of that year as many as ten of the Squadron's 19 pilots were NCOs. Fears of a new war were growing and all pilots and air-gunners had by then practiced take-offs, short flights and landings wearing anti-gas respirators: an ominous sign that war days lay ahead.

The whole Squadron, 1937.

Officers & NCOs. Front row 1st left - FS Crouch (C Flt),
1st right - FS Johns (B Flt), 2nd right - FS King (A Flt).

Officers. Front Row L to R: Flt Lt Fenwick-Wilson, Flt Lt Aylmer, Sqn Ldr Traill (Sqn CO), Flt Lt Gomm, Flt Lt McG Lunn. Back Row L to R: Plt Off Stapleton, Fg Off Cooke, Fg Off Bell, Plt Off Card, Plt Off Robinson. (Sept 1937).

The Squadron's establishment in men and aircraft was nearly doubled in March 1938, from 95 officers and men (17 pilots, of whom six were NCOs, 11 senior NCOs, 55 airmen and 12 civilians) and 14 Gordons, to 175 officers and men and 27 Gordons. Each flight was now to have six aircraft plus two in reserve and there were three more as a Squadron reserve. Strength increased by 80: 11 more pilots (five of them officers), 22 more corporals and 47 more airmen in various trades. The new establishment provided, as before, for one squadron leader in command and three flight lieutenants as his flight commanders. But from now on there were supposed to be 12 flying or pilot officers, 12 NCO pilots, one warrant officer (Armament), three flight sergeants (Fitters I), four sergeants, three sergeant air observers, 20 corporal air observers, 18 corporals, 86 aircraftmen and 12 civilians.

Naturally, this expansion began to change the character of the Squadron. As Corporal Barnes wrote, 'a maintenance unit was formed to deal with major over-hauls and the more serious cause of unserviceability. This added about 30 men to the Station strength, involving the introduction of Fitters Mates unskilled airmen whose purpose was to relieve the technical crews of time-wasting, non-productive chores. Until then, the Squadron's ground crews consisted mainly of ex-Halton apprentices the cream and I must confess that I, like the others, looked down my nose at this unskilled, untrained, uneducated bunch', though he would change his mind about some of them when war came.

The Munich Crisis came to a head at the end of September 1938, and the Squadron was packed up and ready to proceed to its war station in Egypt at a moment's notice. No fewer than ten new pilots arrived from the flying training school in Egypt early that month: six acting pilot officers and four sergeants. After several days standing by, the situation improved and normal work resumed. Including, as so often, hours of flying time spent looking for lost aircraft: in this instance, a Gordon which was later found to have come down in the sea off Gaza whilst flying from Ismailia to Ramleh.

A NEW BADGE

One change which caused lively discussion amongst both officers and men was the design of the Squadron's official badge. No-one who takes an interest in History will be unaware of the power of symbols, especially in newly-formed nations or institutions. After much correspondence with the Chester Herald (the title of the royal official charged with such matters), a new badge - approved by the King - was formally presented to the Squadron by Air Vice-Marshal Cuthbert MacLean, Head of Middle East Command, at a ceremonial parade on 12 August 1937. Since Air Commodore Roderic Hill, AOC Palestine and Transjordan, was also present, one sees at once that this matter of badges was taken seriously indeed by the highest service authorities.

Corporal Barnes was not pleased. 'We lost our splendid Squadron crest', he lamented, 'a crusader's helmet, sword, gauntlets and shield (appropriately winged) of beaten copper on a mahogany base approximately 3/4 of an inches thick. The excuse was that the crest was not registered with the College of Heraldry. The displeasure caused by this loss was intensified by the sight of the new crest - compared crossly with the side of an ambulance - and a transfer at that!' On the day of the presentation parade, Barnes added, 'we were informed that we have been awarded the General Service Medal (Palestine); this award was regarded as a sop to sugar-coat the bitterness engendered by the crest affair.' Not of course true!

The Squadron recorder summed up concisely. 'As our old Badge was one of the oldest in the Royal Air Force we were loath to change it, but in the end we were forced to accept a winged plate in place of the old winged shield '. Another bone of contention was the adoption of an Arabic motto suggested by the Emir Abdullah: but unlike the plate, which never impressed men taught to honour the winged shield, the Arabic motto quickly won enthusiastic approval. It marked in a practical way the Squadron's close association with Abdullah and his country; better still, in Arabic from the Koran it was unique.

MEMORIES

One saving grace of this somewhat remote RAF Station was sport. 'Everyone', wrote Barnes, 'played everything or acted as referee, linesman, umpire or scorer.' The altitude made the climate tolerable for games, even in summer, and the winters, on most days, were no worse than chilly or wet. After Church Parade on Sundays (at which a 50% attendance was required) came the week's big match: usually No 14 Squadron v. Station HQ or officers v. other ranks. After the match, with dusk coming on, long sleeves and trousers were compulsory wear to reduce the risk of sand-fly fever. Or one could spend time in the emergency water supply facility. Permission had been refused by higher authority to build a swimming pool, but it could hardly object to such a facility in a desert country and those responsible for the refusal were not to know that, when built, the facility though surrounded by a high fence bearing the legend in large letters emergency water supply - looked remarkably like a swimming pool, with deep and shallow ends, diving and spring boards and changing cubicles along the sides.

Most evenings were spent in the NAAFI playing darts or dominoes and listening to one or other of the umpteen Bing Crosby records being played on a wind-up gramophone or enjoying a drink and a chat - about anything except religion, politics or women. 'There were few senior NCOs and even fewer officers', wrote Barnes, 'and they all, on the slightest pretext, would spend an evening in the NAAFI with the junior NCOs and airmen. Traditionally, flights or sections sat together and each had its own tables, so the officers and senior NCOs would join the tables of their own men. The atmosphere was relaxed and friendly, but familiarity was unheard of. Occasionally, one of the wealthier young officers would buy the entire stock of beer, ensuring free beer for the airmen until the stocks were exhausted. The programme for such an evening would be a rousing sing-song interspersed with solo turns by the more talented among us.'

Apart from film shows in the Station cinema, recalled as having been unbelievably ancient, the silent entertainment was home-made, plus the occasional revue, straight play and annual pantomime. A peak of artistic achievement, in Barnes' opinion, was reached with a production of Journey's End which had, 'as props, machine guns on the flat roof over the stage, firing into a wired-off piece of desert, in which explosives were buried. The gunners and the airmen detonating (by remote control) the explosives were told to fire and cause explosions at random. Over the stage was stretched a sand-covered piece of fabric with numerous patches to each of which was attached a length of string, causing sand to cascade onto the stage. Every actor, prior to his entrance, smeared himself with mud from barrels in the wings. A carpenter had so built the dugout scenery that a tug on a rope brought it all crashing down. The whole effect was superb.

It was a healthy, stress-free life. 'The Medical Officer and his staff', wrote Barnes, 'had to deal mainly with sports injuries, a few cases of sandfly fever and (fortunately rare among RAF personnel, more common among Arab fishermen in the Gulf of Aqaba) Bell's Paralysis. Cause: a combination of hot sun and a downdraught of cold air from surrounding mountains. Effect: paralysis of the muscles on one or both sides of the face, causing inability to close the eye, smile or show the teeth; highly risible to the onlooker, extremely inconvenient and embarrassing to the sufferer. The RAF cure was three months of radiant heat treatment, the Arab cure a glowing red-hot ember of charcoal on a spot behind the ear; painful, but instant.' As for dental treatment, an elderly Armenian visited from time to time: 'his equipment a foot-operated treadle machine - yet he managed to hold the drill steadily against the tooth even as he pedalled furiously. A gentle man, I have only recently [in 1990] lost the fillings he did for me.'

RAF Amman's hospitality, thought Barnes, was legendary. 'With Palestine and Egypt to the west and Mesopotamia (Iraq) to the east, and given the slow-flying aircraft of that time, it was inevitable that the station would be a 'half-way house' and a re-fuelling stop. Accommodation, with beds made, was prepared; the visitors, according to rank, were entertained in their respective messes; no visitor was allowed to buy a drink their thirsts were quenched "on the house".'

Possibly the most entertaining event of the year was the Autumn Horse Race Meet for Arab owners in the country. VIP tents for the Emir, the British Resident, Senior Officers and their families were set up alongside the airfield. A full printed six race card with entrants limited to ten horses per race, TJFF and Arab Legion restricted races, and Arab owner classes, guaranteed to draw what seemed like half Amman as spectators. Tent pegging by the TJFF and Arab Legion, Cavalry drill and Camel Corps charges made a full day, with the local Arab as near a heavy gambler as the Chinese in Hong Kong. The Accounts section - who else - acted as bookmakers, the Station Warrant officer as starter, and Tote Odds and Race runners on blackboards in English and Arabic. The Emir - with a stable of beautiful pedigree Arab horses - did not win all the races. There was great rivalry from attendant sheikhs.

Another notable annual event was the Boxing Day paper chase. In revenge for the many, long, sun scorched bumpy rides in the back of an open cockpit aircraft, the TJFF provided horses for all aircrew to follow a paper trail laid by them, across wadi, screed, and scrub. To the uninitiated, the military Arab horse has two speeds - flat out and stop. The moment any rider is aboard, and unaware of the right persuasion to select, he is automatically in one or the other modes. A placid but sometimes obdurate donkey was always given to the medical officer to follow. Wastage collection was often high.

There always seemed to be plenty of time on hand at Amman in the Thirties and many took an interest in local history. There was very ancient history, such as the numerous biblical remains - true or false - to be admired in that area: the tomb of Uriah the Hittite, for example, or the spring in the Moab mountains which emerged where Moses struck his rod upon a rock. There was history that was old, represented by a great many Roman remains: most impressive of these, was Philadelphia, the amphitheatre in Amman, but the most striking of course was the 'Rose red' Nabatean, fourth century B.C. city of Petra some 100 miles south of Amman. There were countless ruined crusader castles to visit on local leaves. And there was very recent history: 'the trains that Lawrence of Arabia had derailed', wrote Barnes, 'still lay on their sides, rustless in the dry desert air', while at Ziza, 20 miles south of Amman, lay 'the 'cave of skulls', housing the skeletons of the Wahabi tribes men who died in the battle between their tribe and No 14 Squadron and No 2 Armoured Car Company in 1924.'

Best of all for Barnes, there was plenty of flying. 'These were pre-aircrew days in 14 Squadron', we had officer and senior NCO pilots and, per flight, one air gunner - who wore a winged brass bullet on his sleeve' and Barnes loved 'wadi flying or skimming over the desert at zero feet, both frowned upon but exhilarating.' Inevitably, there were forced landings. 'One, with a dead engine, was at Kolundia, five miles outside Jerusalem. Flying Officer Hugh Cruikshank, with little or no choice, landed the Gordon between a platoon of the Dorset Regiment and a gang of dissident Arabs firing on the kibbutz there. Doubtless discouraged by the Lewis gun on the half-Scarff ring in the rear cockpit, the Arabs crept away. The Tommies, delighted by our intervention, took me to their billet in Ramallah until a new engine could be flown out.'

Barnes' next forced landing came near the Azraq marshes. 'To the utter amazement of Flight Lieutenant Harry Card, (a Canadian) and myself, a young, attractive

Englishwoman came over to greet us. Mrs Jones and her husband were doctors. Their mission was to cure syphilis, so rife among the Arabs (a camel's bite is syphilitic), a futile and unrewarding task because as soon as his external symptoms disappeared, so too did the patient. A charming couple , who fed and housed us in their Arab-type tent until the next day, when spares were flown out with which to replace our engine.'

One day, three Gordons led by Squadron Leader Traill and two of his flight commanders paid a courtesy visit to HMS *Penzance*, a sloop moored at Aqaba. Flying in loose V formation down Wadi Rhum, whose cliffs rise to 7000 feet, the formation ran into dense cloud. Traill indicated to the other two aircraft to fly into tight formation. Suddenly and simultaneously, both flight commanders climbed steeply up and away, quickly lost in the cloud. Traill was first to land at Aqaba. When the other two landed, he sent the passengers out of earshot, then calling the two flight lieutenants to attention, proceeded to tongue-lash them in no uncertain terms. The upshot being that they and the airmen with them had to spend the night on the beach, while Traill enjoyed the sloop's hospitality and a comfortable night's sleep. What the crew of the Penzance made of this - heaven knows! On balance, and military discipline aside, the flight lieutenants were not to blame for getting up and out of the wadi; flying blind down a wadi which bends and narrows is foolhardy to say the least

Then came the visit of Professor Aurel Stein, the renowned Egyptologist, to the Squadron in 1938. He had with him a note from the CAS requesting Traill to give him every facility. There were star-shaped stone formations occurring in the basalt desert between Transjordan and Iraq that had so far defied explanation. As his pilot on most of his exploration flights, Stapleton recalled that, after hours in the sun of the open cockpit of a Gordon, this white-haired seventy year old was only retained in the aircraft by his safety chain as he excitedly pointed to a star shape, shouting at the pilot to land amongst boulders of basalt that would have severed life for ever. It was incredible, said Stapleton later, to accompany this old boy by armoured car to fossick about amongst the stones of these stars and to unearth Roman coins. The stars had been built by the Romans to give safe haven to nomadic sheepdrovers. Stein acknowledged his debt to the Squadron and his enthusiasm certainly encouraged some air crews to examine the ground more clearly during routine patrols.

SQUADRON TREASURES

Not long before the outbreak of the Second World War, the squadron recorder decided to set down in the Operations Record Book a list of the Squadron's silverware and other property. He knew that in the event of war No 14 Squadron would leave Amman and no doubt guessed that even if it remained in the Middle East which was by no means certain - it would once again live out of tents and packing cases, as it had done during the First World War. There would no longer be a stable, comfortable mess and our accumulated mementoes, donated by old boys, visitors and grateful guests, would soon be scattered far and wide. The property was therefore lovingly listed (naming its donors) as a tangible record of years of hard labour and home-made fun and friendship: all dusted, polished, admired and laughed over (in some cases, perhaps, laughed at) by men who would hand on, as best they could, the memories clinging to each item. It is a glimpse into the spirit of that lost world of the inter-war squadrons.

There were silver salvers and cruet sets, single and double, while silver smoking accessories included cigarette boxes, lighters and ashtrays. All these were donated by former members of the Squadron, but presents from soldiers were especially esteemed: a bomb lighter from the Lancashire Fusiliers, 15 ashtrays from the Seaforth Highlanders and a cigarette box from the Central India Horse. Lord Cecil presented a splendidly-carved cigar box. Miscellaneous items of silver work included a card tray, an ink stand, a framed picture of a D.H.9A and a model of a Gordon (donated by Fairey).

L to R: Fg Off Robinson, Flt Lt Selway, Fg Off Stapleton, Sqn Ldr Traill, Mrs Selway, Miss Cox. (Three Sqn COs in picture).

Gordon in Wadi Rhum, 1937.

HRH Abdullah with left Peake Pasha, 2nd right General Wauchope, 3rd right Sir Henry Cox.

AOC's Parade, Amman, 1936.

The Squadron possessed a good many silver cups and tankards (one given by the Iraq Petroleum Company) awarded for sporting prowess - in rugby, boxing and athletics - or success in aerial manoeuvres or, most often, donated simply for those drinking today to recall occasionally those who drank yesterday. There were several pewter tankards. Two rose bowls and (a rarity this) an uninscribed two-handled cup; four cut glass decanters, two silver tea strainers, three menu holders, a match-holder (now broken) and a silver hammer donated by Rupert Pontifex, that splendidly-named Flying Officer of the early Twenties. Other items included a leather visitors' book, a visiting card holder, a pewter salver, a brass firescreen, a globe, a water colour of three Gordons in flight over Transjordan, painted by Roderic Hill, then the AOC Palestine and Transjordan. Overlooking all our treasures from a place of honour above the fireplace in the Officers' Mess was the head of an Oryx with horns of immense length. According to Stapleton, the unlucky beast failed to vacate a landing strip in the wadi Rhum area quickly enough to satisfy an approaching pilot. He therefore shot it and next day the carcass provided steaks

Jackie the Lion.

Flt Lt Lunn and Guts the German Shepherd.

An Armoured Car. (No 2 Armoured Car Co, RAF).

A shooting match with the Fleet Air Arm. (The bag was 52 brace; duck & sand grouse.

Amman Camp Airfield and Village beyond.

for the Sergeants' Mess in Amman. Passing the mess on her way to tea in the garden, the wife of the Ottoman bank manager retrieved the head and skin from a dustbin. She had it cured in Amman, mounted in London and presented the impressive result to the Officers' Mess. It was at that time, the second world record for the length of its horns.

Before leaving the first half of the thirties two incidents must be recorded which have become something of legend in the stay of the Squadron at Amman.

It was the custom at RAF bases overseas for the whole station informally to celebrate Christmas Day. At Amman, after early morning service, every section and flight retired to their own bays - long prepared bars, - usually about nine. Followed at 1030 by the Station Commander's inspection and award for the best atmosphere, decoration, hospitality etc. Followed then, by the sergeants entertaining the officers in their mess, and at last gasp both serving the airmen their always vast and beautifully-arranged Christmas Lunch. Nothing was missing, from the traditional pterodactyl sized turkeys, vegetables and fruit from Egypt and Palestine, and the brandied puddings, mince pies and beer from home.

Dick Atcherley was a flight commander in No 14 one Christmas time. He decided to acquire the Works Department's road roller, to collect the officers from section bars to take them to the Sergeants' Mess. On the way down a steep incline he decided to visit the guard house at the station entrance gate. The roller gathered speed, Dick lost control, and evacuated along with the officers aboard. The juggernaut then rolled majestically through the perimeter wire, gathered speed and neatly severed in half a mud villa near the bottom of the wadi. It was rented by a fellow flight commander, as he and the station commander were the only ones then allowed wives at Amman. The flight commander's wife felt very liberated when her kitchen, Christmas goodies and their bedroom departed onto the road to Amman in a tumble of bricks. The roller, still the right way up, wore half the roof of the villa, when it stopped opposite the prison walls! The retribution for Dick can be passed over, but the total repairs to the house cost him the sum of £5!

Line up. Nos 6, 14, & 216. 1938.

The second incident involved a lion. On one of the route proving flights, necessitating a stay at Nairobi, an enthusiastic game ranger donated an abandoned two week old so-called black lion cub to the flight leader. The carriage of animals in RAF aircraft is prohibited unless properly authorised under rules of safety, care, provisions etc. This particular gift was provided (on advice) with a tea chest, milk-soaked porridge and water. This, as it turned out, was happily accepted at some hygienic cost, as was the journey to Amman. There, some dilemmas, girt with regulations, had to be resolved. Was a lion a pet, who would be minder, what about a cage, what was its menu - apart from people - could it spread or catch diseases? Such are the resources of animal and human beings that solutions were found; enough to turn Jackie into a celebrity.

Some weeks before the arrival of Jackie, an officer had acquired two German Shepherd puppies about three months old from the pedigree kennels of King Fuad of Egypt. He was given the care of Jackie; and the antics of these three became renowned throughout the station. One of the Shepherds was given to the Sergeants' Mess, Guts and Jackie remained together to grow up, and to take on an entertainment role after dinner at the Officers' Mess. The two animals of their own volition decided that centre carpet at the end of dinner was the place to take on mock aggression and exercise. When they were there, each corner of the carpet was lifted, and after the snapping, snarling and delighted tossing the tired duo were ushered into their night quarters.

Tom Traill, the CO, had ideas about introducing new officers into wrestling with the lion. His first demonstration stopped it. Jackie content to play, planted a languid paw on the leg of the CO, dislocating his knee. Jackie was, in fact beginning to show an ominous trend in stalking the food-laden Arab donkeys, traversing near the front exit gate to the Arab village adjacent to the airfield. Jackie had to go. But what to do with a growing, floppy, domesticated yet puppy lion, who would come and go on command?

A throwaway suggestion of a presentation from the RAF to King Fuad of Egypt found a ready acceptance with a publicity-conscious HQ in Cairo. A Victoria transport aircraft was sent up to Amman for the transfer of Jackie and an escorting presentation team. Arrival at Heliopolis and transfer to the Abdin Palace had no effect on Jackie. Neither had the first time wearing of the beautifully-worked leather and chain collar at the gates of the palace. Unfortunately, neck measurements had been determined by someone unaware that the ruff of a lion is not its neck size. Neither were the palace Nubian sentries used to lions on parade. Jackie, with a shake of his head had discarded his collar. Any sudden movement will always alert animals. The Present Arms of welcome from the palace guard, wide eyes focused on Allah, occasioned a sniff of alarmed interest, but Jackie fell in behind his owner, and padded up the steps with the escort.

The glass doors obviously reflected a companion. With a bound, Jackie was through. Chaos in the hall and staircase. Turkish-trousered sofragis opted for cover behind chairs and curtains, attendants on the stairs went over the banisters. Jackie plus escort pounded up the stairs and turned right into the carefully arranged hall of Monarch and side supporters, including a representative of the British Embassy and the RAF Middle East.

Jackie, tired of the strange surroundings, flopped down in front of the majestic chair. Tight smiles from aides to the hurrying escort; 'it had all been arranged, hadn't it?' 'Yes, your Majesty We are pleased to present a gift from the RAF ....' Jackie was led away to a side room by his owner, where he urinated! The palace, a few hours later, transferred him to the Cairo Zoo. No acknowledgement came from HQME, but a brief note of thanks from the palace was received at Amman. Jackie was much visited at the Zoo, and died at a very handsome old age in 1942.

NEW AIRCRAFT : THE VICKERS WELLESLEY

The last half of the decade introduced a marked acceleration into the development of aviation. The final round of the Schneider Trophy in 1929 had indicated a quantum leap in design. Aviation and the increasing sophistication of radio, television and electronics brought both benefit from the spread of information to mankind, and threat from those willing to risk all in the lust for power. Civil aviation spread its services and travel across the globe. Military aviation began the search for techniques in attack and defence unforeseen even five years earlier.

Two examples of a new aircraft had arrived on 19 March 1938, a machine which represented probably as great an advance in design and performance over previous equipment as any with which No 14 Squadron was to be provided down to the 1990s. This was the Wellesley, powered by a single 925hp Bristol Pegasus XX radial engine. First flown in June 1935, its fuselage and wings pioneered the geodetic structure, a system of stressed triangles with curved sides, later used to more famous effect by Barnes Wallis in his twin-engined Wellington bomber. 'The idea was to save weight and also facilitate repair; it also offered an alternative to the modern stressed-skin structure which British companies were reluctant to adopt because of the high tooling costs and their lack of experience.'

A large machine with ample space for fuel, its immense wingspan nearly 75ft gave the Wellesley an exceptional range: it could carry a 2,000lb bomb load at about 180 mph at 15,000ft. With a top speed of 228 mph at 20,000ft, it far outclassed the Gordon, but its armament was no better: a single Vickers machine gun in the right wing and another in the rear cockpit. A third crew member operated the wireless. No other aircraft in the Middle East at that time could carry so heavy a load so fast or at such an altitude. In November 1938, two specially modified Wellesleys (not of No 14 Squadron) flew non-stop from Ismailia to Darwin, in northern Australia: 7,158 miles in just under 48 hours at an average speed of almost 150 mph. The success of these and other long-distance flights, wrote the historians of Vickers aircraft, 'was of equal merit and portent to winning of the Schneider Trophy races by the Supermarine seaplanes which led to the evolution of the Spitfire. The Wellesleys showed the way to the sorties of extreme duration which became part of operation flying in the war.'

Among its many novelties were enclosed cockpits (two of them!), a variable pitch propeller, streamlined bomb-containers mounted on underwing pylons and a retractable undercarriage. On the other hand, as most observed, its cockpit instrumentation was way behind that of civil airliners, with their auto-pilots and radio compasses.

The transition from Gordons to Wellesleys was far from smooth. Due to a defective bracket, the undercarriages of some Wellesleys supplied to the Squadron revealed cracks either before take-off or after landing. Red ink entries from accidents now began to appear in the otherwise unblemished log books of pilots and they were not amused! One Wellesley was lost while firing at a ground target. It went into a dive, fired the front gun - the wing that carried the gun separated and Sergeant Sweeting was killed in the crash. A component attaching the wing to the fuselage had to be replaced in all aircraft by a steel forged substitute sent out urgently from England.

By the end of June, the Squadron was entirely re-equipped. Traill and his flight commanders at once began to practice low-level dive-bombing with fair results, according to the recorder. High-level bombing (from 15,000ft) was also practiced and though the results were bad Traill believed they would improve.

Squadron Leader Anthony Selway succeeded Traill on 5 May 1938. 'When I took over', wrote Selway, 'the last of the Gordons were being taken back to the depot at Aboukir and exchanged for brand new equipment in the shape of the Vickers Wellesley MkI Bomber. Conversion training had not been invented. The most experienced pilots took the Gordons down to Aboukir and were given a little ground instruction on the Wellesley to find to out where all the taps and switches were and then - take off and fly back to Amman again. About a two hour flight.'

Nothing pleases the soldier, sailor or airman more than being issued with a new tank or gun, a new ship or a new plane. Whatever its faults or shortcomings, the new owners - not unlike new car owners - spring to its defence and sing endless praises for their new baby, and what it is going to be able to do for the credit and renown of the Squadron whose badge adorns its side.

The Wellesley was no exception to this rule. It looked streamlined and modern. The pilot shut himself under a perspex sliding hood, which cut out the noise and draught. The propeller had two speeds - changed by a hand switch IN meaning fine pitch for take off and OFF; meaning coarse pitch for everything else. The undercarriage at the touch of a lever wound itself up under the wings. The crew could walk about inside the fuselage with great ease. There were wing flaps operated hydraulically for use when landing and on take off.

All these refinements were quite new to all personnel, but for a time they were woefully misunderstood and mishandled. There were also a number of other pieces of modern equipment designed for the Wellesleys which never reached Amman. And there were a few little tricks which took some getting used to. 'But on the whole', concluded Selway, 'we were pleased with our new babies. We did not then know how good the Wellesley was going to turn out to be.'

There was for a time some doubt in the Squadron over the feasibility of putting Wellesleys down on some of the desert landing grounds it was our duty to look after. It was thought they might be too heavy or clumsy to land safely and take off again, so a Cook's tour was flown with an Arab Legion officer, none other than Major Glubb, and an RAF Staff officer, round a selection of them. First of these were Bair and Jaffar, right out on the Saudi Arabian border, very vaguely marked and hard to find, then Mudawara in the extreme south. Then came the landing ground in Wadi Rumm, one of the most fearsome and impressive looking places to land on, and then back to Ma'an at the end of the Hedjaz railway. The Wellesley had no trouble with any of them.

Selway had under his command 22 pilots, of whom nine were NCOs. On 9 June (birthday of the new King, George VI), he led a squadron formation over 17 parades of troops in Palestine, 'at a time carefully synchronised to coincide with the breaking of the flag.' This was the debut of the Wellesley in Palestine. She [note the feminine!] was well received.'

A flight of three Wellesleys flew in formation around the Sinai Peninsula, landing at Helwan and returning via Aboukir: a distance of 1,040 miles, covered in seven hours' flying time, and this in August 1938. On 21 November, Selway, leading three aircraft, made a practice attack on Baghdad. The distance covered amounted to just over 1,000 miles and took under seven hours. The aircraft would have been able to repeat the 'attack' without re-fuelling. The Squadron registered another first when it was filmed by Movietone News while flying over Amman on the 30th. A signifi-cant achievement on 23 December was the making of R/T contact between two aircraft flying 320 miles apart. Total flying time for 1938 amounted to 4,390 hours, some 500 less than in the previous year, due to re-equipment with a new aircraft and, added the Squadron recorder, excessive unserviceability.

TROUBLE IN PALESTINE

1. MINOR: 1933-1935

'The rise of Adolf Hitler to power in Germany', wrote David Omissi, 'and a sudden resurgence of anti-Semitism in Poland brought thousands of refugees to Palestine. The annual number of recorded Jewish arrivals trebled between 1932 and 1933, and doubled again by 1935. The Arab fear of becoming a minority in their own country seemed likely to materialise, and the nationalist response was swift.'

Nine aircraft of No 14 Squadron and nine of No 6 Squadron made demonstra-tions over several towns in Palestine on 28 October 1933 after anti-Jewish rioting broke out. Messages and food were dropped on an RAF transport convoy making for Jerusalem that had been obliged to halt outside Amman on the 31st because of unrest there. Tension gradually eased, but early in the new year a formation of nine Gordons was invited to carry out an Air Drill over Jerusalem: ostensibly for the delectation of the High Commissioner and the AOC, both of whom sent congratu-latory messages afterwards, but actually as a warning to the city's inhabitants. During 1934, however, aircraft were employed on coastal patrols as what Omissi called 'the visible part' of the government's reply to the Arab charge that it 'did lit-tle to restrain illegal immigration.'

On 16 March 1934, a flight of three Gordons took Sir Arthur Wauchope, High Commissioner for Palestine and Transjordan, from Kolundia to Baghdad. The air-craft remained at Hinaidi until the 24th, when Sir Arthur was flown back to Kolundia. During their time in Iraq, the Gordons visited Ur and Mosul. 'Like India, Palestine fascinated its European rulers', wrote Charles Townshend: none more than Sir Arthur, in office from 1931 to 1938. He ardently believed in consensus, set-ting up municipal councils in 1934 and a legislative council in 1935 with an Arab majority - a council which was rejected by Arabs, Jews and the British government alike.

2. MAJOR: 1936

Two Jews were murdered on 15 April 1936 by Arab bandits (as the recorder called them) on the road between Tulkarm and Nablus. Next day, two Arabs were killed near the Jewish settlement at Petah Tiqvah, east of Tel Aviv. The funeral of the Jews in Tel Aviv on the 17th provoked serious violence. A National Committee of Arabs met in Nablus on the 20th and declared a general strike. On 22 April, two Gordons of No 14 Squadron were sent to Jisr el Mejami (ten miles south of the Sea of Galilee) 'in connection with recent troubles': 50 daytime flights were made, totalling more than 40 hours, but no large movement of Arabs was seen in the Jordan area. One night reconnaissance, lasting 35 minutes, was made to discourage crop-burning. A parachute flare was dropped when a large fire was found, but the culprits had fled.

Meanwhile, the strike call was repeated by committees in other towns and ultimately by a Higher Arab Committee in Jerusalem on 25 April. That committee demanded a cessation of Jewish immigration; prohibition of land sales to Jews; and the establishment of representative government. The port of Jaffa ceased to function, so did road transport, and a tax boycott began. Jewish buildings, crops and plantations were attacked and during May and June armed Arab bands appeared in the hills of Samaria around Nablus.

Zionist leaders as well as British officials were unsure how to respond. Were they faced with a genuine national movement or merely local disturbances, fomented by agitators and criminals? 'Sympathy with Arab fears of Zionist domination', wrote Charles Townshend, 'went along with paternalistic assumptions of Arab incapacity' among many Britons, civilian or military. Sir Arthur Wauchope refused to permit military action even against armed bandits. Troops were called in as guards or to replace the British contingent of the police, who were relieved of ordinary duties so that they could pursue the bandits, but they did so without success.

Throughout May 1936, C Flight operated in Palestine from its base at Jisr el Mejami. Dawn and dusk reconnaissances were carried out on most days with aircraft landing after dark, helped by the headlights of two parked cars. In the squadron recorder's opinion, the usual evening incendiarists were discouraged to some extent.

During that month, the Flight flew some 78 hours (three of them in darkness). It was much busier in the next three months, clocking up 504 hours (including 47 in darkness), mostly over the Jordan valley, before being relieved by B Flight in the last week of August. In September, B Flight added another 110 hours (ten in darkness) to the Squadron's tally. Flares were dropped at night on several occasions and ground forces twice reported that they had been helpful, but it was difficult without two-way radio to drop a flare at the right time and place. In addition to reconnaissances, there was close co-operation with the 13th Infantry Brigade and the TJFF in searching villages and encampments for arms and ammunition and in escorting road convoys. Only rarely did the aircraft actually open fire.

Much of the night flying was intended to help protect Jewish colonies, but reports of heavy firing often turned out to be three snipers at work - and they had long gone by the time a Gordon arrived. It was certain, however, 'that night flying and the dropping of flares has a deterrent effect.' Car headlights were still being used to assist landings, for want of an adequate flare path, and in such circumstances the absence of accidents is a tribute to pilots' skill.

Late in June, the army blasted a way into the old city of Jaffa, centre of the rebellion. Two wide roads were driven through a tangle of narrow streets, once a few snipers had been silenced by heavy gunfire, and thereafter Jaffa remained quiet for months. This Jaffa operation foreshadowed the methods used when the rebellion reached its peak in the autumn of 1938. Even so, Wauchope's aversion to the use of force - with the spectacular exception of Jaffa - prevailed. His standing as High Commissioner was greatly enhanced by the fact that as a Lieutenant General he outranked everyone else in Palestine.

In September 1936, the government in London announced the imminent proclamation of martial law and sent Major General John Dill to enforce it with a division of troops. After the disturbances of 1929, the garrison had been fixed at two battalions; now it was increased to two full divisions. This decision marked the end of a deal whereby the Air Ministry acted as the Colonial Office's agent in exercising direct military control of Palestine, although the arrangement continued in force for Transjordan.

General Dill expected to be appointed military governor of Palestine, but arrived to find that the threat of martial law, coupled with the promise of a royal commission to investigate Arab grievances, had enabled Wauchope to negotiate a compromise: the strike was called off and the armed bands dispersed - but they did not hand over their weapons. Dill and the army authorities in London were furious at what they considered a display of weakness that would make a dangerous situation harder to control in the event of renewed fighting. Between April and September, the security forces suffered 243 casualties: 21 soldiers and 16 policemen killed, 104 soldiers and 102 policemen wounded. Among civilians, 89 Jews and 195 Arabs had been reported killed and some 300 Jews and 800 Arabs wounded.

The 1936 rebellion, concluded David Omissi, was more opportune than that of 1929 for what he calls 'the violently repressive' use of aircraft. In 1929, Arab attacks had usually been aimed at Jews; in 1936, however, the government was the main target. 'In 1936, although the strike was chiefly urban, the armed guerrilla bands usually operated in the steep and boulder-strewn hill country, which slowed the movements of regular foot soldiers. Air power offered an easy method of increasing the geographical reach of the state, even into areas it might not otherwise be able to dispute. The larger numbers of rounds fired, bombs dropped and casualties inflicted reflects both the greater use made of the air force as a policing instrument, and the more prolonged and determined resistance offered by the Arabs.'

Even so, it was the presence of aircraft - rather than their fire power - that usually deterred Arab bands from attacking Jewish settlements or troop convoys and, as Omissi himself says 'the use of the air weapon in Palestine remained, in 1936 at least, subject to the strictest political constraints. Regulations issued in June and re-issued in August forbade the use of bombs heavier than 20 lbs; prohibited all bombing within 500yds of any town, village or building; and even prevented bomb-carrying aircraft from overflying urban areas in case of accident.

CRITICAL: 1937-1939

On 26 September 1937, after a year of relative calm, Lewis Andrews, District Commissioner for Galilee, and his police guard, were murdered in Nazareth. Armed bands reappeared in greater numbers than ever before and began to set up courts, levy taxes and enforce decrees. The British reaction was far more aggressive than in 1936. The Arab Higher Committee and the National Committees were pro-scribed and the Mufti of Jerusalem (widely regarded by the British as a prime trou-blemaker) was dismissed from his official positions. Wauchope's early retirement was announced and the army occupied the old city of Jerusalem. Even so, this clear evidence of determination to rule had limited effect and by 1938 some parts of Jerusalem were out of British control.

John Dill was replaced as GOC Palestine in September 1937 by another General who would play a prominent part in the coming world war, Archibald Wavell, but he too would last only a few months - until April 1938 - when yet another GOC was appointed, Robert Haining. None of these commanders had the strength to destroy the rebel heartland, some 30 miles north of Jerusalem: a triangle between Tulkarm in the west, Nablus in the south and Jenin in the north. A celebrated Iraqi guerrilla leader Fauzi al-Kaukji, who described himself as 'Commander-in-Chief of the Arab Revolutionary Army' - gave a new degree of cohesion to the actions of the armed bands. On the other side, some Jews now began to respond violently to Arab attacks.

Late in 1937, the Palestine Potash Company's convoys from Kallia (on the north-west coast of the Dead Sea) were twice ambushed and so it was decided to pro-vide them with an air escort four times a week. The escort days were to vary and the Gordon was to fly high enough to keep the whole convoy in view, but also low enough to recognise the distress signal - a smoke candle - should it be fired. As this meant flying at about 6,000 feet, any Arabs waiting in ambush could see and hear the Gordon easily and there was little hope of luring them out into the open. Air escorts for the company's convoys nevertheless continued until March 1938.

On 23 and 25 June 1938, a Wellesley was sent to carry out a seaward reconnais-sance of the Palestine coast between Gaza and Netanya (north of Tel Aviv), a dis-tance of 60 miles. Its task was to locate 'foreign steamers suspected of endeavour-ing to land illegal immigrants' (that is, Jews attempting to escape from Nazi oppres-sion in Europe), but nothing was seen on either day. Flights would continue on this dismal task for the rest of that year and the next. Corporal Barnes took part in some of these. 'On one such sweep', he recalled, 'Flight Lieutenant Harry Card, wireless operator Johnny Reeve and myself spotted a Greek ship whose decks were crowded with people vainly trying to hide. The Royal Navy was informed. Subsequently, we three were notified that we were entitled to a share of the prize money - over half a century on, I am still waiting!'

During July, arrangements were made for two routine night reconnaissances a week over a curfew area to the north and south of Lake Hule, ten miles north of the Sea of Galilee, on the Syrian frontier. On the 20th, land forces of the TJFF and the Arab Legion searched for brigands with illegal arms in the Jordan valley. A relay of Wellesleys co-operated throughout the whole day, from 0400 to 1830hrs, successfully maintaining communication with all columns by means of W/T, message dropping and 'Middle East Ground Strip Code'. A photographic mosaic of the whole Jordan valley was completed from a height of over 20,000 feet, necessitating - for the first time in the squadron's history - the use of oxygen equipment. One aircraft was tested up to a height of 28,000 feet: then an undoubted Squadron record.

According to the recorder, 'the situation in Palestine continued to deteriorate' during August. Night reconnaissances of the northern curfew area were carried out on ten occasions and all aircraft dropped flares, but the movement of Arab gangs at night remained practically impossible to detect from the air. This work continued in September, over the northern frontier and elsewhere.

Clashes between the rival factions took on a more serious and vicious significance. Armed mobs and sniping began to increase. Bullet holes started to appear in aircraft. Pilots and aircrew now wore side arms, and rifles were carried with loaded front and rear cockpit machine guns. Events had now become a rebellion. No 6 Squadron lost two Hardy aircraft with their crews killed, and No 14 Squadron had several aircraft, Gordons and later Wellesleys, damaged.

By October 1938, the number of British police had risen from about 700 in 1935 to over 3,000 and some behaved brutally. The Arab police, which had formed the bulk of the force until the rebellion, where transferred to routine duties and 'tactfully' disarmed; meanwhile, the number of Jews employed on security duties steadily increased. A gulf had opened between the opinion of most soldiers that drastic measures (including collective punishment for villages suspected of harbouring guerrillas) were essential if order was to be restored, and the opinion of most civilian officials that such punishments were immoral when the government could not guarantee to protect villagers from intimidation.

On the night of 5/6 October, a request was received from RAF HQ for flare-dropping and desultory bombing in an area some 25 miles north-east of Haifa. Four flights were made between 2100hrs and 0130hrs, dropping between them 16 flares and 14 20lb bombs. Similar operations followed on the 7th and the crews reported no difficulty in dropping bombs with fair accuracy from 600ft on a moon lit night. A report issued by the 16th Infantry Brigade in Haifa declared that their efforts were believed to have had 'great moral effect. Villagers did not realise air action was possible at night. Much wailing, all lights turned out and genuine state of terror set up.'

Two Wellesleys were sent to patrol a triangular area south-east of Haifa on the night of 8/9 October and remained there for more than four hours, dropping 16 flares. HMS *Douglas* in Haifa at the time, added to the illumination by firing star shells over the area. Four nights later, flare and bomb dropping operations were ordered over woods between Haifa and the Sea of Galilee. There was a full moon and one Wellesley was hit in four places by ground fire, though the three crew members were unharmed. Similar operations followed throughout the month and a total of 76 bombs and 53 flares were dropped.

General Wavell came up to say goodbye to the Squadron in October and was given a formal parade and lunch. His remarks to the parade in Amman on that day were remembered: "I suppose you fellows", he said, "think you are doing something unique here up in Amman, something that hasn't been done before. But it has all been done before - without aeroplanes, of course, many years ago. You young men are in a sense the direct descendants of the Roman soldiers who probably sat in the stone seats of the Amphitheatre in this town much as you go to the camp cinema here. You are trained to keep the peace between the people on both sides of the River Jordan, as the Romans tried to do, and I cannot promise that you will have any more of a permanent success than they did. But you ought to be proud of your responsibilities and I want as I say good-bye, to thank you for doing your duty so well. Good Luck to you all!" A man of few words, perhaps the fewer the words the longer are they remembered.

During the early months of 1939, regular patrols were flown in co-operation with the TJFF and the Arab Legion in search of armed bands; the position of vessels approaching the coast suspected of carrying illegal immigrants were reported to the civil and naval authorities; and a number of long-distance flights were also made. Ten Wellesleys operated over Zemal, near Wadi Ziqlab, for the first time on Transjordan territory, from noon until dusk on 11 March. They dropped 75 20lb bombs and fired 2,035 rounds. Later in the afternoon, permission was given by the Emir for heavier bombs to be used and four 250lb bombs were dropped. Twenty casualties were reported.

The armed services had been given a virtually free hand in 1939, though no open avowal of military rule was made. Rough means - as well as paid informers - were used by a large, well equipped force to end open, armed rebellion. 'Under the weight of military pressure', wrote Martin Kolinsky, 'the rebellion increasingly degenerated into an internecine war of frustrated Arab extremists against those willing to accept British authority. During the period 1936-39 the Arabs killed 547 Jews, and almost as many fellow-Arabs - 494.' Striking successes were achieved by Captain Orde Wingate, an unconventional officer, who established Special Night Squads, mixing army volunteers with members of the Jewish Haganah, and occasionally complaining about the RAF flare dropping frustrating his ambushes.

Many civilian observers, however, thought the rebellion died out largely because of political concessions made in a White Paper issued by the British government in May 1939. It set limits on Jewish immigration to Palestine and land purchase and also promised majority - therefore Arab - self-government after five years. Feeling within the Jewish community was naturally bitter about these limits at a time of growing Nazi persecution. Although the outbreak of war made co-operation with Britain imperative, bitter feeling remained. After the war, the device for helping to end the Arab rebellion - the White Paper - became a powerful motive for Jewish determination to end British rule in Palestine.

The work of the Squadron was recognised when both Sergeant L Patey of A Flight and Flying Officer D Stapleton of C Flight were awarded the AFM and AFC respectively, for their outstanding flying in some 25 each anti-insurgency operations over Palestine.

GOODBYE TO AMMAN

'In June', Squadron Leader Selway recorded, 'there began the flow of new young officers to me for training as Wellesley pilots. As we were the first Middle East squadron to get Wellesleys and as I was a qualified flying instructor they sent me quite a lot. They came from all quarters of the Empire. Plunkett, Turtle, Garside, Ferguson, Harrison, Rhodes and Elliot, all from England. Le Cavalier, Soderholm and Matthews from Canada, Mackenzie from New Zealand and Andy Smith from the U S A. All these were given instructions on the Wellesley. As soon as they were able to fly in formation I got 18 aircraft into the air one day in a gigantic armada and we sailed round Palestine to impress the Palestinians! Of course the hard core of the Squadron lay in the old stagers, Harry Card from Canada, Cosme Gomm, from Brazil, Helsby, Robbie Robinson from Jamaica, Kearey from South Africa and Sergeants Patey and Scott, all in A Flight. Whilst in B Flight there were Lunn, Cooke, Godfrey, Greenhill and Sergeants Wimsett, Morrison and Poole. And again Fenwick-Wilson, Stapleton, MacNab also from South Africa, and Sergeants Chick, Broadhurst, Moulton and Norris in C Flight. Alas, many of these good men did not survive the war.'

The British Resident, Mr Alec Kirkbride, witnessed the effect of a practice black-out of Amman in July: an event that alarmed many, European and Arab alike. A few days later, on 20 August 1939, a signal long expected - and long dreaded - was received warning the squadron to be ready to move to its war station. For good or ill, 20 years of protecting and refereeing, policing and oppressing, were at an end. At 0200hrs on the 24th, a phone call from Group Captain Lowe, the Amman Station Commander, ordered a move to Ismailia that day. Four Vickers Valentia transports of No 216 Squadron arrived at Amman from Heliopolis at 0930hrs and left at 1400hrs with an advance party of two officers and 43 airmen; 14 Wellesleys, led by Selway, followed an hour later, The formation landed at Ismailia at 1730hrs to find that it was the first unit to arrive of a new formation, No. 1 Bomber Wing. It was joined next day by two other squadrons from Habbaniyah.

After 15 years in Amman, the rest of No 14 Squadron left that town at 1130hrs on 25 August, arriving at Ismailia early next morning. That day and the next were spent by 30 officers and 146 airmen unpacking and moving into new quarters. Work began on the 28th 'and routine', remarked the recorder - no doubt with massive understatement - 'was as far as possible usual.'

On 30 August the news became worse by the hour. Some said there would be a war, and others said not. The mess was crowded and cheerful but there was an awful lot of office work for everybody. Mediterranean shipping had been suspend-ed and all air mails had stopped. Major Ablitt Bey, the Chief of Suez Canal Police was flown to see the blackout in the Suez Canal area. It was very effective, with Port Said in darkness, but there was a full moon, and the Suez Canal water showed up like a ribbon of silver.

On 1 September, Hitler marched into Poland. There was dead silence in the Mess for the home radio news. Spirits, strangely, were very high, and all were somehow keen to get into action. Britain declared war on Germany on 3 September. Everyone unmoved. The whole mess was present to hear the King's speech on the radio. At the National Anthem all stood. The broadcast that night said that Winston Churchill was First Lord of the Admiralty and that the reasons the Italians were not in the show was that the Germans had said in effect 'thanks very much but we'd rather fight alone.' It was to be months before the Squadron saw action.

On 4 September the BBC announced that British forces had captured the German liner *Bremen*, but to balance this the liner *Athenia*, carrying many women and children, had been sunk. All the Dominions had decided to come in against the Nazis. The CO spoke to the airmen and told them we were now officially on active service though God knew when we would see any. The RAF had been flying over Germany and had dropped 6 million leaflets.

FROM ISMAILIA BACK TO AMMAN

It became clear as all listened to the news broadcasts in the Ismailia Officers' Mess that what came to be called by the British the 'Phoney War' might last indefinitely. Hitler had taken Poland and Czechoslovakia and, during the winter of 1939-40 there was a long pause. Diplomacy was going on behind the scenes but the squadron was to remain poised at war stations against the time when Italy, as Hitler's ally, would come into the war on Hitler's side.

The Squadron continued to train for operations dropping live bombs of heavier weight and firing the guns at ground targets. The Wellesley was very much under-gunned: one fixed Browning firing forward, and one Lewis gun of an antiquated pattern for the air gunner in the open rear cockpit. It seemed very likely that because of slow speed and long endurance, advantage must be taken of the night hours to avoid enemy fighters. Attempts to fly in formation at night were discontinued as even in the clear Egyptian sky it was found too difficult. The countless millions of glittering stars only made the confusion worse between what was a light and what was a star.

A method of silent attack was tried. Cutting the engine right back at 16,000 feet and gliding towards the target at a low speed eventually putting in a low level attack. The idea was to foil the sound detectors, radar not having reached the Mediterranean theatres at this date.

Then the blow fell. The Squadron was to go back to Amman on 19 December. An agonising set-back to a squadron looking forward to a Christmas in the bright lights of the lively Egyptian cities, but who were once again to be faced with the conditions existing in their old home in the Moabite Hills where the view from the Officers' Mess was across the Arab Legion Prison in the wadi, to the little tomb of Uriah the Hittite on the other side. King David, many centuries before, had despatched Uriah - with an ulterior motive - to these hills in order to get rid of him. Was there some similarity? Yes, the supine years were ending.

Bristol Blenheim IV.

Swordfish of 824 Sqn FAA from HMS **Eagle** *1941.*

Wellesley over Iraqi Basalt Desert.

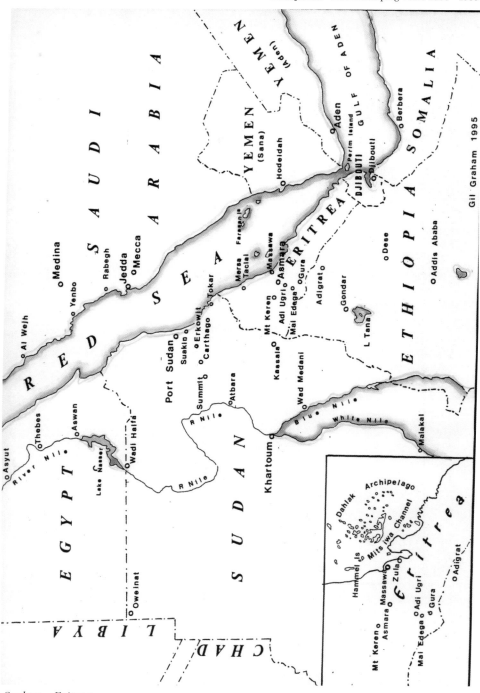

Sudan - Eritrea.

CHAPTER FOUR

THE SUDAN AND ERITREA

1939 - 1941

'So British Sudan and Italian East Africa went to war reluctantly and slowly and with immense misgiving. It was a gentleman's war. There was some undefined but quite real understanding that there would be no bombing of civilians or helpless native settlements... I was to see through the months ahead how this lax but very understandable feeling was to harden into animosity and how in deadly engagements like Keren real hatred was to emerge. But to the end our campaign in East Africa was conducted on lines that never approached the fury and bitterness of Europe, or left scars comparable with even a single week's fighting in the battle of France or Russia.

WAITING FOR THE ITALIANS

Those men who served in No 14 Squadron during the First World War could have told Selway's men ,that war consists of brief periods of frenzied activity or extreme danger and long periods of routine training: boring at best, apparently pointless at worst. These truths began to be taught at Ismailia from September 1939 onwards and had been well learned by the end of the Second World War.

The expectation had been to be fighting Italians in September. Just as the German arm of the Axis rolled over Poland during that month, so would the Italian arm advance upon Egypt. Mussolini's forces threatened the strategically-vital Canal by land from the Italian colonies in Libya, west of Egypt, and from the more recent Italian conquests in Abyssinia, south of Egypt. For years reports and newsreels declared it Duce's unshakeable resolve to extend his already vast African empire at the expense of the effete democracies and thereby, shoulder to shoulder with der Fuhrer, make the world safe for fascists everywhere. But now, when it seemed his hour had come, Mussolini did nothing.

BACK TO AMMAN

Meanwhile, to everyone's surprise and disappointment, orders came to leave Ismailia and return to Amman in October and, as Barnes recalled, 'back to yet another administrative nonsense'. Naturally, mail censorship was in force; the appointed censors for RAF Amman were, incredibly, the station commander's daughters! Understandably, the airmen, senior NCOs and all were furious at this arrangement, but orders being orders there seemed to be nothing anyone could do. A bachelor, Sergeant Bill Townsend, veteran of World War One, a delightful 100% military-minded eccentric, wrote a letter full of four-letter words of a scatological nature to his sister (whether she existed or not we never knew). The station commander sent for Bill and blitzed him for his obscene letter, to which Bill replied that his sister did not mind his language, so why should anyone else? The girls were taken off censorship that day.'

Quite apart from the natural reluctance to retreat still further from the prospect of action, all had been looking forward to enjoying Christmas amid the bright lights of Cairo or Alexandria. Life in Amman had its attractions, but no-one who ever served there regarded it as a centre for fun and frolic; Ma'an even less so. Moreover, hard news as well as letters from home took longer to reach Transjordan than Egypt.

Nevertheless, to Amman the Squadron returned, expecting to pick up again the threads of its traditional policing and protecting routine, 'The food was as well-cooked as ever,' wrote Barnes, 'our huts as cool and spotless; the war a long, long way away, yet the periodical *Aeroplane* with its casualty list of RAF men who had died in action saddened us each time we saw the names of ex-No 14 Squadron personnel. We had forgotten that in wartime squadrons are frequently shunted to and fro, always at short notice, and so it happened now. Early in the New Year, we were back in Egypt, at Abu Sueir, only a few miles from Ismailia.'

Squadron photo September 1939. Ismailia

ANTI-SUBMARINE TRAINING

The air staff at Middle East HQ had concluded that No 14 Squadron should be trained for anti-submarine and convoy protection duties in daylight. Selway pointed out with some emphasis that the Wellesley's defensive armament was negligible and that it had only a single engine. 'Four or more hours out of sight of land', wrote Stapleton, 'relying on one motor was not a very cheerful prospect to contemplate, especially as there had been rumours about being required to do this over the Red Sea, whose denizens were noted for inclinations decidedly carnivorous!' In the event, no Wellesley crew man ever lost his life as a result of engine failure. The Pegasus XX proved a most reliable engine, even in the harsh climatic conditions of north-eastern Africa - though some at least of the credit for that excellent record is due to the Squadron's skilled and conscientious ground crews.

The anti-submarine course proved to be hard but interesting work. It was conducted by Squadron Leader Taylor (Chief Instructor at No 4 Flying Training School and a first-class navigator, a profession, inexplicably rare in the RAF on the outbreak of war) and Flight Lieutenant Manning, one of his ablest assistants. Taylor went with the

Squadron Commander on a trip from the Delta at Damietta, telling him that they would arrive over the end of the breakwater (not just over the breakwater) at Haifa in exactly four hours. They flew north over the Mediterranean at about 1,000 feet, Taylor giving the pilot his courses with occasional corrections, and noting the time carefully, before turning east. Not surprisingly, the CO was immensely impressed to find himself over the position designated within 15 seconds of the navigator's estimate. Clearly, accurate navigation over the sea in a Wellesley was possible.

CHANGING PLACES!

Nevertheless, that aircraft was actually an awkward and ill-equipped one in which to learn about overseas navigation. The pilot, sitting high up in a narrow cockpit close behind the propeller and ahead of the wings, had a poor view downward and to the rear. His instrument panel, primitive by contemporary civilian standards, offered only a compass and drift sight to help him fix his position. The 'observer' (not yet a properly qualified 'navigator') was so placed in the aircraft that he could 'observe' little and, added Stapleton, 'literally nothing through his tiny side windows - placed just above the wing roots so that there was no downward view.' Oil thrown out from the engine came back in a brown, sticky mist obliterating the view from the little window provided for bomb aiming and also made reading the drift sight difficult. As for the third crew member, the rear-gunner, the Wellesley's long, wide wings made it impossible for him to observe more than a small segment of sea.

'The only way the observer could work with the pilot', he wrote, 'was by crawling up the tunnel, poking him on the behind, at which signal the pilot would lower one hand for the observer to put the message into it. There was intercom between all three crew members, of course, and therefore lots of talk, but the lone pilot got very stiff after a few hours. It was possible to change pilots, if they practiced the trick and got it right. The pilot trimmed the aircraft to fly straight and level - if it would - and the second pilot then undid a bolt on the pilot's seat behind his neck, lowering him backwards until he was lying on the floor on his back. The second pilot clambered over him and stood in the seatless cockpit, endeavouring to fly the aircraft while the first pilot regained his feet, pushed the seat up again and locked it. This was all very well, if everything went smoothly, but we did not see how exhausted or wounded crews could perform these acrobatics.'

OFF TO PORT SUDAN

News that the Squadron was to move to Port Sudan, instead of to Ismailia, was received initially with considerable gloom. Why on earth Port Sudan? Why should No 14, the only Squadron of the Middle East Group be banished to a place hardly known? The answers were known only too well. The Squadron was the only one remaining in the North which hadn't been re-equipped with Blenheims. It was to go South to join up with the other Wellesley Squadrons, Nos 47 and 223 to form No 254 Bomber Wing for operations against Eritrea and Abyssinia. Some thought that it could possibly be a little private war, but no wars are nice private ones.

As the situation in France became more desperate the notice to move shortened to four hours. The Squadron was fully ready. Personal kit already stowed in each aircraft, blankets, mosquito nets and kit bags tied onto the bomb racks, and many yards of kite cord expended to make these secure. Air support transport was scarce and everything that could be taken was loaded in the Wellesleys. In the fuselage of each were stacked a mountain of tool boxes, trestles, spare guns, trunks and suitcases of all sizes. The space left for the observer and gunner dwindled until it seemed that one would have to sit on the knees of the other.

The Squadron silver and trophies were listed and packed away in the equipment section at Amman, never, unhappily, to be seen again. In all, 23 aircraft were to go, each containing a pilot and two crew, and this number of men with 4 Bombay transports would enable the Squadron to settle in before the main party arrived by sea. An advance party was sent down to Port Sudan on the 11th May, consisting of 6 Wellesleys and 1 Bombay, Flight Lieutenant Stapleton leading with Flight Lieutenant John Manning from Aboukir to prepare the base, and to escort the arrival of an early Australian contingent on 14 May. 7 patrols were flown and practiced around the progress of their ships to Port Sudan.

The main ground support party followed, first by bus to the Railway at Lydda, then train to the Suez Canal, and then embarked in a commandeered pilgrim ship for the voyage to Port Sudan. The journey took four days. It was lovely weather in Transjordan, and Spring in that country is a season not to be forgotten. The harsh brown hills lose their stony austerity and become the palest green. The roaring water in the wadi below the airfield slowly ceases and becomes a trickle: the clouds thin out and vanish and yet the sun for all its brilliance somehow does not yet scorch the tenderest skin. The Squadron would regret leaving. There were no bright lights in Amman, no cabaret, no bars, no club, and Jerusalem and Tel Aviv were a hundred miles away. But as a result of its location, the Squadron had gathered to its bosom a collection of sturdy and independent characters who were accustomed to meet each and every problem with a good deal of fun, and it was going to find that attribute very much needed in the coming months.

A BALEFUL PLACE

One's first sight of Port Sudan from the air is deceptive, nestling like a jewel in an inlet of an azure sea, it looks most attractive. The port buildings clustered round a natural creek, breaking a broad expanse of scrub and desert. A railway line ran away into a range of purple hills some 15 miles inland. The moment one landed, however, the magic evaporated in a layer of hot air, suffocatingly humid, rising to 500 feet. Off came tunics and on went bush shirts and shorts, only to be soaked in sweat in ten minutes.

Prickly heat, Selway records, is a rash of red spots which develops around the waist like a pink cummerbund. One can attempt to banish it by using various balms, powders and so on, but from practical experience there is no cure - except to move to a drier climate. The humidity at Port Sudan at that time of year was always 100-plus. 'The torments of 'prickly heat' were bad enough for everyone', commented Barnes, but 'the cooks, poor devils, were afflicted from head to toe due to the additional heat from their field kitchens.' The Squadron's officers took up residence in 'The Red Sea Hotel': run by Sudan Railways, it offered the best - and only - public accommodation. The port's residents did all they could to make their unexpected guests welcome, even putting on a cocktail party for all ranks around the swimming pool. Such parties had been rare in Amman, 'They're flat out for us,' wrote Stapleton in a letter home, 'and nothing's too much trouble.'

Officers and senior NCOs were quickly accommodated, but 'Corporals and below were out of luck,' Barnes recalled, 'our billets would not be ready for several days, the dining hall and NAAFI not even started. Thus we - I was a Corporal by now - had our meals seated at tables in the open. The temperature ranged between 110-130F degrees; margarine melted to the consistency of olive oil in which flies galore drowned. Anyone moving near the tables caused clouds of powdery dust to float upwards; this covered the tables and their contents (especially jam, marmalade and the corpse-laden margarine) in an off-putting film which had to be scraped aside to allow access to the food beneath - or, in the case of bread, blown off. Off-putting too, as we queued for breakfast, the sight of the cooks scraping mildew from the tinned bacon. Rice replaced potatoes, which were unobtainable through RAF sources (ironically, every evening we could get away, dozens of us went to a Greek cafe in Port Sudan for egg and chips!). Until our billets (of rush matting) were ready, we slept rough, on the airfield. The discomfort and ridiculous messing arrangements were accepted as war conditions.'

In addition to the mind-numbing heat and humidity, Selway vividly remembered the dust blowing up from the Great Rift Valley and into the Red Sea just south of Port Sudan.' It is the most appalling red, sandy dust, sometimes rising to well over 10,000ft. The District Officer at Trinkitat used to have a rope fixed between his house and his office so that he could get to and fro in the sand storms, which were so thick that he dared not go out for fear of getting lost... This unfortunate man, had to eat his meals out of a drawer in his office, shutting it tight between mouthfuls because of the dust, which had the consistency of red-brown talcum powder.'

Alan Moorehead, an Australian war correspondent, visited Port Sudan in July and remarked that 'the water in the pool at the front of the Red Sea Hotel was so warm that it was a slight relief in the evening to emerge from it into the less warm air. In the hotel it was wise to fill your bath in the evening so that by the morning the standing water would have dropped a degree or two below the temperature of the flat hot fluid that steamed out of the tap.'

PREPARATIONS FOR WAR

At that time, the Squadron's total strength amounted to 232 men (including 22 officers and 37 senior NCOs) and they all had plenty to do - and it had to be done in a hurry, despite the dreadful climate, because war with Italy was imminent. After months of hesitation, Mussolini was at last ready to leap into Hitler's war - just before it ended, he hoped - in order to profit from Hitler's peace-making at the cost of a few thousand dead Italians. Countless tins of petrol had to be safely stacked and carefully camouflaged (more about these wretched tins later); aircraft had to be dispersed, pushed well into the camel scrub and were so well hidden there, wrote Barnes, that pilots reported them 'undetectable even as low as 2,000 feet.' Tents were erected, slit trenches and latrines dug, telephone and power lines laid, defence posts planned, sick quarters set up and equipped, messing for everyone organised as well as possible and, not least, arrangements made for despatch and receipt of mail.

These last, sadly, failed dismally. In Barnes' words, 'No potatoes, no beer, but as the Sudanese weeks lengthened into months, a far more serious lack began to make itself felt - no mail! When I arrived in Cairo in March 1941, en route for Blighty, I was told that all incoming and outgoing mail for the Sudan (and the Western Desert) was being burned for lack of transport! Why in heaven's name did not someone tell us? Firstly, we need not have written (not easy when dripping with perspiration); secondly, and far more importantly, much worry and morale-damaging misery would have been avoided. Not unnaturally, we associated the absence of letters with the *Luftwaffe* bombing raids on Britain and the obvious, dreadful doubt assailed our minds and few cracked up under the strain. Not, let me hasten to add, ex-Amman stalwarts'.

FORMING A MILITARY-CIVILIAN TEAM

As soon as all Squadron personnel were assembled in Port Sudan and set to work, Selway called on the High Commissioner: 'Springfield by name, a man of enormous energy, he had been in the Sudan Civil Service all his life. His residence, was a large stone building of two stories guarded by spotlessly white-clad Sudanese policemen of the blue-black complexion which contrasted with the brown visages of the coastal-bred inhabitants: the Fuzzy Wuzzies of Kitchener's time. The Commissioner was charm itself, and one of the most efficient men I have ever met. Years of service in such a thinly populated country seemed to give all the Sudan Government officers an authority and control which I had certainly not seen before in other British colonies. The keys of the town were metaphorically handed to us, with a mass of useful information.' Port Sudan, Selway learned, had only recently been developed. It was the colony's only outlet by sea for its cotton crop, apart from an ancient port at Suakin, some 30 miles farther south, now virtually closed by silt. 'It was going to be difficult to refuse a seat in one of the Wellesleys to Springers when we flew off to bomb the Italians.'

Selway then visited his opposite numbers, the senior Naval and Army officers. The former, he wrote, 'sat under the white ensign in his quayside office, having been called back from retirement to do his job. One of our reasons for being in Port Sudan was for naval co-operation, and in particular to escort and protect the large troop convoys which were expected to arrive from India shortly'. The latter, Major Knight, 'was a genial Major in the Worcestershires and he became a firm friend.'

'BLACK MAC'

Selway then made contact with No 254 Wing HQ at Erkowit, about 3,000 feet up in the Red Sea hills, some 60 miles south of Port Sudan. According to Alan Moorehead, Erkowit 'had a rest-house to which the overheated white people of the Sudan used to go to relax and cool off a little.... There was nothing to see, nothing to do, but the

Governor General of the Sudan and members of his staff had built themselves houses round about, and it was enough just to be cool.'

Selway met the other two squadron commanders there. Squadron Leader Elton commanded No 47 Squadron, recently based in Khartoum, and Squadron Leader Larking commanded No 223 Squadron, which had come north from Nairobi. Both of them were now at a landing ground named Summit, a few miles west of Erkowit. The Wing was commanded by Group Captain S D Macdonald, known to everyone as 'Black Mac', to distinguish him from two other Macdonalds, one red-haired and the other brown.

'Now *Black Mac*, thank God, as well as being an old friend of the three of us', Selway recalled, 'was blessed with considerable wisdom and knew the difference between Orders and Instructions. All too often, in the early part of Hitler's war, squadron commanders had been given strict orders on how they were to attack their targets - the height, the time, bomb load and so on, which left little to the initiative of the leader himself. Such orders were often given by senior officers who had not had the opportunity of flying the aircraft in question or on operations and were not really qualified to give orders based on their own personal experience.'

Black Mac told his squadron commanders on 10 June that he would be issuing no precise orders, merely instructions to hammer their allotted targets as hard as possible once war was declared. Larking was to attack the fighter airfield at Gura, Elton that at Asmara and Selway was to have first crack at the Massawa naval base, some 300 miles south of Port Sudan. 'We returned to our Squadrons armed with what target maps Mac's staff could give us. I descended into the muggy heat of Port Sudan before dark and broke the news to my flight commanders in the Red Sea Hotel mess.'

THE UMBRIA SCUTTLES

Mr Springfield took Selway onto the roof of his office that same afternoon to look at an Italian ship, the *Umbria*, anchored off the port entrance. She was loaded with aircraft bombs and had been making for Massawa. The Royal Navy inspected her at Suez, but having at that time no legal grounds for detaining her, signalled the senior naval officer at Port Sudan to instruct him to call her in, examine her papers and generally delay her departure for Massawa. War being imminent, the officer went further and placed a prize crew aboard the vessel. Springfield, however, had noticed that she appeared to be settling in the water. 'If she has been scuttled', he told Selway, 'it means that war will be declared within a few hours.' Selway returned to the roof an hour later and by then it was clear that the *Umbria* was sinking, despite the presence aboard of a prize crew.

He dined that night with Mr Thomas, the local head of Sudan Railways, to thank him for all the work his engineers had done for the Squadron. As they sat on the lawn after dinner, the long-expected declaration of war came over the radio. Before he sped away to his headquarters, Mr Thomas and his guests solemnly shook hands with Selway, wishing him good luck. He would need it.

At that time, according to the historian Patricia Wright, 'In the whole of the Sudan, with a frontier of 1,250 miles facing Italian East Africa there were 2,500 British troops and about 4,000 semi-military policemen of the Sudan Defence Force. If one added the small group of Naval personnel at Port Sudan, and a few airmen flying aircraft long since junked by the home-based RAF, the total British force might be increased to something over 7,000 men, totally unsupported by armour or artillery.' Kenya and British Somaliland mustered a further 16,000 men between them to oppose some 260,000 Italians, 60 tanks, about 450 guns and 270 aircraft of various sorts. Another historian, John Terraine, thought the disparity even greater: only 19,000 men under British command, provided with 163 aircraft ('items' from a 'museum catalogue') to oppose 350,000 men under Italian command, provided with 325 aircraft (142 in reserve or under repair). Terraine accepts the figure of 350,000 given by Mussolini to Hitler on 30 May 1940. [2]

In the Red Sea, the Royal Navy usually had six destroyers, an anti-aircraft cruiser and a few sloops and minesweepers. The Italians, based at Massawa and Mogadishu, had eight submarines, nine destroyers, an armed merchant cruiser and various light craft. Luckily for the British, Mussolini had long been convinced, wrote Patricia Wright, that 'armed forces were an extension of the fascist spectacle rather than a utilitarian matter of nuts, bolts and hard training. He was mesmerised by numbers, and quality was sacrificed to achieve quantity.'

THE WELLESLEY GUN BUS

Selway had in the past week been giving much thought to the vulnerability of the Wellesleys to fighter attack. Luckily the Italian Fiat CR32 and 42 fighters, although much faster, had not so far come right close in and kept their fingers hard on the triggers. Selway thought they would soon appreciate that the Wellesley was appallingly poor in defensive guns, having one Lewis gun only in the back (with an extra one underneath it pointing down) and a fixed gun facing forward for the pilot to fire should an enemy aircraft actually fly into his sights. As soon as they twigged how really defenceless was the Wellesley they would close in. What was needed was a lot more fire power from behind and particularly tracer ammunition, which the fighters could see coming at them. It makes all the difference to one's nerves and aim if the evidence is there to see that one is being shot at! The technical team of Warrant Officer Edwin Crouch (later Wing Commander), Selway's air gunner Sergeant Mildren (later Flight Lieutenant) and two stalwarts, Sergeants Farrell and d'Arcy were consulted on the parameters.

In the middle of the Wellesley fuselage, just above the wings there is a small window in each side. These are just wide enough to miss the geodetic structures and are not more than 3 feet wide and 1 foot deep. They are hinged at the top and opened inward and upward to lock open. They were meant originally for using sextant sights. The team was asked to design a removable mounting-for each window on which a Lewis gun could be bolted, capable of being fired by a third man, carried in the fuselage. Each gun would cover a horizontal arc from tailplane to propeller above the wing only, and a vertical arc upwards and as far as about 20 degrees off the vertical. It was essential to have special stops made to prevent the gunner from hitting any parts of his own aircraft and, when in formation to fly in such a way as to leave these gunners a free space in which to loose off their guns. It was important that tracer should be used so that with a formation of five there would be no less than 20 guns firing up, down and sideways when attacked - like a gigantic watering pot!

The aircrews were enthusiastic and various rewards were hinted at for those who could get themselves an enemy fighter! However, there were no extra gunners of any sort, over and above the allowance of one per aircraft, but Crouch, Killington, King and Johns, all senior non-commissioned officers in charge of the various Flights, arranged for lists of volunteers to be opened, and soon full of names from the cookhouse, orderly room, and all the administrative trades. They were given instructions on how to aim and pull the trigger of a Lewis gun, how to change the ammunition drum (often difficult) and to recognise the Italian fighters. The railway workshops of Sudan Railways made the mountings at no charge, so within a short time the Wellesleys of the Squadron were bristling with guns!

MASSAWA: THE ATTACK PLAN

'The interesting thing about the first day of any war', wrote Selway later, is that no-body knows the form. Not unlike the first race for two year olds at the beginning of the flat racing season. A week later a good deal more is known, sometimes to advantage and sometimes not. In the case of the Italian forces in Eritrea most felt able to cope very well, and as the Italians were about to be cut off from contact with their homeland, this would not improve their morale much. Although we were unaware of what it was like to attack a Naval Base, on the other hand their gunners did not know what it was like to defend one.

There was not a great deal of information about Massawa except outline maps of the airfield, the port, the oil refinery and tanks, and the location of aviation fuel storage. It was also known that there were about 6 Anti Aircraft batteries round the base, and the AA fire to be expected from 9 destroyers in the harbour plus searchlights. Eight submarines were based there.

No fighters were based at Massawa. They would have to come from Gura or Asmara from their bases some 50 miles away. 254 Wing staff had briefed that the most damaging thing to the Italian war effort in Eritrea and Abyssinia would be to destroy, as soon as possible, the petrol and oil essential to any modern form of war on land, sea or air. As further supplies could not be obtained from Italy, attacks were to concentrate on the destruction of dumps of petrol or oil before they were concealed or dispersed. The Squadron's first target was to be a complex of oil tanks, hangers, railway yards and port installations in and around Massawa.

Selway pondered - 'The first consideration was the height of the attack. We could bomb if necessary from 10,000 feet after a bit of a struggle to get there, but I knew perfectly well from our efforts on the Zerka (near Amman) bombing ranges that even from 10,000ft and with only 250 lb G.P. bombs we would hit literally nothing as the Wellesley was a poor bombing platform. We shouldn't be troubled with fighters much, and the AA on the first day at any rate, would be unlikely to bother us. But why go all that way and do no damage? So I considered a medium level attack. But even here whilst the accuracy of the bombing would be a little better, we should get a lot more flak and the fighters would hang in the air a little better. And so I came to the third and last method. As low as possible. By arming the Wellesleys with a mixture of 20 lb and 40 lb high fragmentation bombs, and mixing with them some 4 lb incendiaries, and then dropping this load on static fuel tanks from a very low level I believed we could achieve what we were after.

But of course the possible price we would have to pay might be very high. Perhaps half the force might be shot down. And as this would be below parachute height it wasn't to be a very cheerful affair for the aircrew. Moreover, we had all the aircraft we were ever likely to have, and neither we nor the Italians could afford wastage.

Turning this matter over in my mind I had to reject attacking at night for obvious reasons. We had tried night formation flying at Ismailia. It had entailed special lighting, and was too great a strain on the pilots to be of any value. At night over a blacked out Naval Base, our chance of hitting what we wanted to was no better than by doing it from 20,000 feet by day.

By good fortune a solution suggested itself. Port Sudan is in a similar position to Massawa on a roughly equivalent longitude, and both facing East. Massawa was only some 300 miles from us. So dusk would fall on both ports at about the same time. There is not much twilight in these latitudes and I had noticed that at about 1825 hrs each evening I could see Deryck Stapleton's C Flight aircraft coming in from over the sea finishing their convoy patrols, but at 1830 hrs only 5 minutes later dusk had suddenly become near night. Looking towards the East, aircraft were quite invisible. I flew several times round Port Sudan myself at this hour the following week, and found that at 1830 hrs, coming in from East to West, buildings, port installations and so on were clearly visible from the air, and yet I was invisible in the heat and humidity haze from the ground. The plan took shape'

So much for timing, what about height? One of the factors which now had to be considered was the hitting power of the bombs to be used, and how best to distribute them. Selway drove out to a mud flat and arranged for one of the pilots to drop some specimen loads nearby. Each of the boat shaped nacelles under the wings of the Wellesleys carried two small bomb containers. These were long narrow metal containers like inverted window boxes. The container was loaded with a suitable selection of bombs and hoisted in to the nacelle by a winch. The pressing of a button in the pilots cockpit released the bombs. A second panel contained an alternative button which, when pressed, jettisoned the whole container in an emergency. Inspection of the bomb patterns in the mud showed how far the splinters would travel, and also showed that the aircraft could come down to 400 or 600 feet without any danger of being damaged by its own bombs. Selway was satisfied with the research, but the Chief of Police of Sudan had not been notified and the "C-r-r-ump! C-r-r-rump!" of the bombs had caused the air raid alarm to be sounded and the local population to take cover!

Almost everybody remembers the day on which war was declared. Where he was and what he was doing and so on. On the 10th June, Selway flew up to Erkowit to see No 254 Wing HQs staff. There was a feeling in the headquarters that the targets should be attacked within hours of the declaration of War, but Selway explained that the plan for No 14's attack on the strongly defended Naval Base of Massawa would only be successful if we took off at exactly 1600 hrs, whatever time the Go-signal came. There was some demur, but it was pointed out that the attack was to be at low level in order to destroy the fuel dump before it could be dispersed, and the attack could not be done unless it was exactly at nightfall. *Black Mac* agreed.

ATTACK EXECUTION

If the news of the declaration of war had come a little earlier the attack could have been launched that night but the plan could not now work till 1600 hrs the next day. A proportion of air and ground crew slept under the wings of their aircraft, to make sure that another of Hitler's secret weapons - the Fifth Column - did not, if it existed, in Eritrea or the Sudan, have a chance of sabotaging the Wellesleys.

The next day, the 11th June was busy. Group HQs in Khartoum did not seem too happy that at mid-day, the Squadron were still sitting at Port Sudan. Nos 47 and 223 Squadrons attacked in the early morning. No doubt the Italians in Massawa wondered why they had not been bombed at the same time. They didn't have long to wait. Nine aircraft took off at 1600 hrs and circled round Port Sudan climbing up out of the sticky heat and dust of the sea coast, leaving behind long billows of sand blown up by the heavily laden Wellesleys as they staggered off the airfield. As soon as the ninth aircraft had got off, the CO set course on 141 degrees at 10,500 ft for a position far out to sea off the coast - so as to avoid the listening posts - and from which the formation could descend in a timed approach, to arrive suddenly over Massawa at a low level at 1830 hrs.

Sergeants Patey and Brown as No. 2 and 3 in the formation caught up early on, and flew on either side of the leader, absorbed in their thoughts and in station-keeping. Selway's crew of Sergeants Mildren and LAC Lund, said they could just see the 3 aircraft of 'B' Flight a long way behind. Irvine and the 3rd Flight were following. At 1800 hrs Selway altered course and put the nose of the aircraft gently down, opened the bomb doors, and selected switches, double checking everything with the crew. He wanted to be ready early with everything, leaving only the tasks of heading the aircraft and monitoring the timing exactly as to when to release bombs.

From now on concentration was only on hitting the target, the bulk fuel installation on the edge of Otumlo airfield at Massawa. The intelligence target maps showed these as a number of oblong squares. The plan was to drop a stick of bombs across them in four salvoes. The bomb load in each Wellesley was 12x40 lb bombs, 12x20 lb bombs and 60x4 lb incendiaries. A total load of under 1,000 lbs, about half the weight a Wellesley could carry, but the containers were full, and the attack would be at about 500 ft to avoid any bomb fragments.

Selway believed his second container load hit the target, for on the "C-r-rump" there was an immediate bright flash from under the wings, the glow of a petrol fire starting. The firework display by the AA barrage of all colours was impressive. Either Mildren or Lund had left his microphone 'on' and all to be heard flying through the fireworks was "Ker-ist! Ker-ist!" from behind in a low voice. Suddenly it was all over, and the aircraft climbing out seawards and heading for home.

Some years later Squadron Leader L A J Patey DFM AFM (then a Sergeant pilot) wrote the following to Selway:

112

'The timing of the arrival of the Wellesleys over the airfield turned out to be perfect, and there was no difficulty in locating the target area, the light conditions being just sufficient to see it. On the run in to the target, the height was so low that I was able to see personnel standing in the entrance to the hangers. Our arrival must have caught them by surprise, because I am sure they did not know what was happening until they could see the markings of the aircraft. The first load of bombs was on target because fires immediately started as we broke formation in readiness for the run in.

Our run was to be carried out individually because it was too dark for formation flying. By the time we had started the approach it was quite dark, and it seemed as if all hell had been let loose. Tracer and 'flaming Onions' together with flashes from the heavier calibre guns from the Naval ships in the harbour lit the sky. Being the first experience of this sort of thing it was quite frightening to fly into it, to drop our remaining bombs in the target area, and it seemed as if any aircraft going in at the height we were flying would be shot to pieces. But drop the bombs we did, in the area of the airfield and then set a course North to get out of it.

As soon as we were clear of Massawa it was the moment to relax and to check on fuel remaining in the tanks because it was still a long way back to base and quite a few more miles over enemy territory. Everything was still working, and there was still sufficient fuel to get us home so at least one old Wellesley had come successfully through to fight another day! We landed at Port Sudan at 2105 hrs.'

Squadron Leader A F Wimsett D.F.C., then a Sergeant Pilot, flying in the second flight also wrote:

'I remember watching the flak and the searchlights as our Flight approached Massawa and thinking how pretty the flak looked. It was sufficiently dark to show up in red and green colours. On arrival the flak seemed to be going above our height, probably up to about 5 or 6,000 feet, but we also saw tracers coming up at us from small arms fire from the ground.

As our flight was within sight of the airfield the leading flight must have hit the fuel dump, and when we actually arrived the daylight had gone, but we could see the hangers and airfield clearly illuminated by the dump fire and several smaller fires around the airfield. Our flight went into line astern, opened bomb doors and selected bombs for dropping, - four 250 bombs each. I believe I dropped mine on a hanger at the North side of the airfield and over the harbour with my Air Gunner enjoying himself at the back by firing at items on the ground. The middle guns were not fitted on that first raid. I remember hoping that No. 3 flight had not caught up with us as they were to bomb from above our height.

Coming back up the coast we did not see another aircraft until we crossed Sudan border, when all aircraft had been briefed to switch on navigation lights. It then seemed we were surrounded by aircraft. We were also surrounded after landing, as the remainder of the squadron personnel came out, and closed in on the aircraft which had been out on the raid.

An incident happened soon after, when the aircraft was being re-fuelled in the dark by the use of cans of petrol and funnels. One of the re-fuelling fitters perched on the wing of a Wellesley wondered if the tank was full. He had no torch, and asked his mate down below the wing to pass him up a Hurricane Lamp! He did!

The petrol tank went up in flames, and the fitter was blown off the wing. Some damage was done to the aircraft. A bit ironic to have got all the aircraft back safely and to lose one at friendly hands.

On the way back, flying up the coast in the comforting darkness, the crew reported they could still see the fire we had started after 45 minutes. There was a great reception from the rest of the Squadron as we lobbed down on the sandy surface of the airfield at Port Sudan, and a lot of beer was produced as we helped the Intelligence Officer to fill in his brand new and blank 'raid reports'.'

From the intelligence given by crews afterwards it seemed that there were about 9 Anti-Aircraft batteries at Massawa, added to which were the AA guns from the Italian destroyers. A total of six searchlights on land and more from the ships in the harbour. Three Wellesleys were very slightly hit, but the AA gunners were confused by the approach of 3 flights at varying heights. As aircraft were landing at Port Sudan, there were explosions and flashes from the abandoned old Arab port of Suakin, 15 miles to the South. These were Italian bombers mistaking Suakin for the blacked out Port Sudan. This proved to be a very useful decoy for the future. The Commissioner quickly agreed to a dummy flare path there, which in some measure helped to protect Port Sudan.

Pilot Officer Plunket and his Gunner, Sergeant Trayhurn, did not return that night. One casualty out of nine maybe had to be accepted, but incredibly next morning at dawn, in came a Wellesley from the South which landed and taxied calmly in. It was Plunket. He had followed the coast, and then had doubts as to whether he had passed Port Sudan or not. He took a proper if risky decision, and having found what he thought to be a hard piece of foreshore, dropped a parachute flare and landed on the beach. He and Trayhurn had had a good sleep under the wings until first light. He started up next morning after inspecting the surface, took off and flew home. Affection for the Wellesley as a 'get you home' service began to grow, and this was not the last time in the campaign that Wellesleys were to use the beach as a temporary parking lot. Black Mac was pleased when telephoned that night, and he told the Squadron how Nos 47 and 223 had fared that morning. Some days later he showed the CO a signal which said that night nearly 800 tons of aviation fuel had been destroyed.

Sadly, Plunkett went missing again next day and this time did not survive. He had agreed to go with Flight Lieutenant Irvine, B Flight Commander, on a second and completely harebrained attack on Massawa. The CO heard the two aircraft take off at about 1500 hrs on 12 June and drove to the airfield to find out what was going on. There he found a distressed Flight Sergeant who told him that Irvine believed the Wellesley would make an effective single-seat dive-bomber in broad daylight and that he and Plunkett intended to test this belief. After more than five anxious hours of waiting, Irvine's aircraft returned safely. Both he and Plunkett had dropped their bombs and Irvine last saw Plunkett heading for the coast, apparently undamaged. However, a search next day failed to find him and it is believed that he was in fact shot down by a noted Italian pilot named Viscintini acknowledged to be a leading pilot of the Italian No 412 Squadriglia. Selway was unimpressed by this foolish initiative and got rid of Irvine, who sadly flying with No 211 Squadron failed to return from a raid over Southern Serbia on April 13 1941.

CASTAWAYS

One of the Wellesleys was overdue. In the absence of any sort of homing assistance, flare runway lighting, or talk down aids, the CO had ruled that all flying operations were to be landed by fifteen minutes before sundown. An hour had elapsed and no sign of Flying Officer 'Flash' Mackenzie - a monosyllabic soul from New Zealand - returning from his convoy escort.

In the gathering dark the drone of the Pegasus engine was heard. Relief! Two pick up vans with supplemented headlights were deployed two thousand yards apart, enough to land Mackenzie and bring the crew to the Operations Room.

Debriefing priority was interminable; details about the Convoy, its progress, composition, routes and contact positions next day. All routine, no incidents. Mac was grinning, the CO was not. Why were they late? Mac knew the orders. Explain.

"Well," said Flash, "there looked to be some thirty or forty Italian seamen shipwrecked on Bar Marsa Kebir coral island some thirty five miles south east of Port Sudan." How did they know they were Italian? They looked Italian! Were they really shipwrecked. Most were obviously ill, ragged clothes, Acqua was spelt in the sand. There was maybe a grave or two. Was there a shipwreck? None visible, but a long oil streak originated by the island. Possibly a Submarine. It was later known to be the Macelle.

"Urgent investigations. Check with Navy and Port authorities. Rescue first thing tomorrow morning" said the CO. "Send a Wellesley (Mac) to drop supplies." A platoon of the Worcester Regiment, and a sea-going Tug from the Port harbour were persuaded to get seaborne for Marsa Kebir. The CO would fly the Walrus to circle or land near the stranded sailors, and give cover to the Tug.

The Wellesley was airborne at first light, confirmed the location and plight of the sailors, dropped the supplies, and returned to Port Sudan as the Tug was leaving the harbour. The CO was airborne at 1230hrs, the Walrus stuttering along to arrive at Marsa Kebir at about 1250hrs.

"Is this the right island", said the CO. "Eh! Yes." "Well there are no thirty or forty seamen on this reef".

The debris was there, litter, bottles, some shelters, a grave, but no Italians. Between the return of the early morning Wellesley and the Walrus arrival at Marsa Kebir the quarry had flown. A submarine? Maybe. The Tug could be at risk. The report back at Port Sudan was met with not too much credulity. The CO sent out a Wellesley to cover the Tug. The Worcesters clambered ashore, harvested the island of the remnants of the Subwrecked crew and returned to Port Sudan.

Next day revealed that a Diary of one of the Italian sailors had been found. It was translated by an Officer of the Worcesters. It is reproduced unaltered in Appendix 2. A poignant record of a seaman maybe on his way to one of those graves on Marsa Kebir. The crew had been rescued by an Italian Submarine. Years later Selway met the Captains of both submarines. The latter with the crew had submerged on sighting the Walrus.

GLADIATOR DEFENCE

The authorities in Cairo sent a flight of four Gloster Gladiator biplanes from No 112 Squadron to Port Sudan with nine pilots to protect the port and the airfield. The last and most effective biplane fighter to serve in the RAF, the Gladiator could reach 254 mph at 12,400 feet. Armed with four Colt Browning machine-guns, it was a fair match for the best Italian fighter encountered in that region: this was also a biplane, the faster and more heavily-armed Fiat CR 42 Falco (Falcon). These Gladiators brought with them a 'fighter boy' atmosphere, they shot down a Wellesley and a Blenheim by mistake, and over Port Sudan accounted for one certain and one probable Italian bomber. Later, this record was to be commemorated by the 'Bard of Erkowit', an officer, with a certain poetic bent, on the strength of No 223 Squadron.

> 'Twinkle, twinkle. one one two,
> How I wonder what you'll do.
> What next will your target be?
> Italian foe or little me?'

To help detect the approach of enemy aircraft, and to direct the fighter defence No 251 Mobile Radio Unit was also deployed to Port Sudan, and situated just south of the airfield. As its radar equipment was of the earliest kind it could provide information on the direction of approach, but nothing on height or speed. Nevertheless on two or three occasions it was able to warn and position the fighters to make some interceptions, usually well after the raid had bombed.

CONVOY PROTECTION

The pattern of the Squadron's operations over the next few months resolved itself into three main areas-

Reconnaissance for, and the protection of, the troop and supply convoys sailing up the Red Sea from Aden or down from the Suez Canal until January/February 1941. Bombing attacks on the Italian defence resources in Ethiopia and mostly against Air Force and Naval Targets. And photographic reconnaissance over these targets for damage assessment and Intelligence.

A fourth category of attacks did not really arise in any numbers, until the Army had found its way to Keren from the Sudanese border, when all the Squadron's efforts were switched to their support in early 1941.

'Offensive defence' was the keynote of the Middle East Operational Plan in 1940, to meet the Italian threat to our Red Sea communications, Sudan and Aden. 'Security of our Red Sea communications and of Aden constitute the principal commitment of the British forces in this (Aden Command) theatre of operations. In general, the primary role of our air forces is the neutralisation of the enemy air forces, especially during the actual passage of convoys through the Red Sea and entrances to the Gulf of Aden.' Naval and air forces operating from Italian East Africa were regarded as the greatest threat to the Red Sea lifeline.

Such was the measure of the importance attached to Red Sea security that the Air Officer Commanding Aden was instructed, when considering provision of close support to land forces in an emergency, to be guided by the principle that the maintenance of the security of convoys in the Red Sea and of our bases at Aden must have primary consideration:

'Direct support to Allied troops in critical situations will not be afforded if by doing so the maintenance of the security of the Red Sea communications and of Aden will be seriously jeopardised.'

The Plan stipulated that naval co-operation such as reconnaissance and escort duty in the Red Sea would be provided by Aden Command and No 254 (Sudan) Wing. Aden Command would also carry out bombing operations to counter air, sea and land attacks against Aden, the Sudan and Red Sea communications. The role of the Air Force in Iraq was to include co-operation with naval forces in maintaining security of sea communications through the Persian Gulf.

Detailed plans for R.A.F. action in the Red Sea were formulated at an air and naval conference at Port Sudan on 4 May 1940. 'The need for conservation of resources imposed the policy that in the early stages, at any rate, offensive air operations would not be undertaken against the Italians in Italian East Africa unless they attacked our vital interests. But there would be air attack on Italian air forces during British convoy movements through the Red Sea. As well as convoy escort, sea and port reconnaissance and anti-submarine patrols were necessary, and to undertake these there were No 14 Squadron (Wellesleys), which had been earmarked to operate from Port Sudan, and No 208 Squadron at Aden, composed of long-nosed Blenheims. The conference recommended that the Blenheim squadron should be converted to fighters for convoy protection.'

The need for economy in the use of aircraft led to the Air Officer Commander in Chief, Middle East, on 24 May rejecting a proposal from the Rear-Admiral Fourth Cruiser Squadron for a daily routine air reconnaissance from Port Sudan. The Rear Admiral's request arose from the lack of anti-submarine defences at Port Sudan (except for two 6 inch guns) and the fear that enemy submarines would easily be able to waylay shipping and lay mines in the approaches. Shipping facilities in the Eastern Mediterranean were less important, from the strategical aspect, than those in the Red Sea.

The HQME Operational Summary in the first year of operations continued,

"We waited until the first few days of July, after enemy airfields had been steadily bombed, before risking the first convoys through the Red Sea. They passed in both directions with complete immunity. After that, convoys proceeded at intervals of about three weeks, and during their passage bombing was carried out from Aden and the Sudan to keep the enemy air force quiescent."

In the matter of convoy protection the problem was the force of 4 Italian submarines, 6 destroyers, 3 torpedo ships and 6 MTBs in the port of Massawa, directly threatening the Aden Suez Red Sea route. Convoys BN 1, 2 & 3 bringing two Indian divisions, an Australian Division, and supplies were critical to the defence of the Middle East. These were big convoys of a dozen ships or more including tankers, and there were others of lesser number needing escorts and protection until the fall of Massawa to the Allied Forces in April 1941.

For approximately the 1500 mile Sea route, the Aden Squadrons provided protection to just short of Massawa, from where the No 14 Squadron sea navigation C flight took it on to 180 miles north of Port Sudan. For two days escort work, an average of 70 hours flying was needed mostly at 1000 ft ahead of the convoy, but at 50 feet around it by 5 aircraft and 5 crews. This was often repeated at intervals of only a week, placing a considerable strain on maintenance crews working in the most torrid conditions. The Royal Navy usually mustered some 6 destroyers and a cruiser for each stage of a large convoy journey.

Denis Richards in his *History of the RAF at War 1939-45* vividly describes operations:

"Small in numbers as they were, the Sudan, Kenya, and Aden Squadrons gave an astonishingly effective support to our hard pressed ground forces. Nevertheless the main achievement of these squadrons lay in a different sphere. For it was to them, in conjunction with our unfailing Navy, that we owed our domination of the Red Sea and its approaches. This they had achieved in part by hours of patient search and escort - between June and December the Aden and Sudan Squadrons escorted fifty-four Red Sea convoys, from which only one ship was sunk by bombs and one damaged.

But they achieved it also by their unceasing attacks on the Italian air and naval forces. The offensive against the enemy air force was widespread in its application; that against the enemy Navy found two focal points in Assab and Massawa, the main ports of Eritrea. In particular, from the first day of the Italian war when No 14 Squadron bombed the airfield fuel tanks and sent up 780 tons of fuel in flames, the Sudan Squadrons never took their eyes off Massawa. Oil stores, administration buildings, barracks, airfields, port installations, destroyers, submarines - Massawa could always provide something worthy of their attention."

What these vital operations against the Red Sea ports and airfields meant in human terms has been recorded by a skilled pen. On 16th July Alan Moorehead, an Australian, together with one or two others of that remarkable body of men, the War Correspondents, visited Port Sudan where No 14 was based. The target that day was a concentration of warships in Massawa.

'We watched the Wellesleys take off, great ungainly machines with a single engine and a vast wing spread, but with a record of security that was astonishing. For weeks now they had been pushing their solitary engines across some of the most dangerous country in the world - country where for hours you could not make a landing and where the natives were unfriendly to the point of murder - and they had been coming back. Often their great wings were slashed and torn with flying shrapnel. Sometimes they just managed to struggle back with controls shot away and the undercarriage would collapse, bringing the machine lurching down on the sand on one wing, like some great stricken bird. But always they seemed, somehow, to get back.

Now again on this second day of the attack on Massawa the control room at Port Sudan got signals that some of our aircraft had been sorely hit. We knew how many aircraft had gone out. It was a strain counting them as they came in, knowing always from hour to hour that there were still due, three or two or perhaps just one machine, and the chances of the lost airmen ever getting back were diminishing from minute to minute.

In the late afternoon we first heard then saw, the last flight over the sea. They fired their recognition flares then two of the three aircraft fell behind. The progress of the leading machine was very slow. It was obvious that since this was the most badly hit, it had been sent on ahead to make its landing as quickly and as best it could. It circled twice then settled for the landing. Crack went one wheel, down in the sand went the engine, over on one wing went the whole machine. The ambulance, fire brigade wagons, doctors and ground staff raced across the aerodrome. Out of the machine almost unharmed came the crew.

There were many incidents like that in the days that followed. The old Wellesleys were cracking up and we had no newer aircraft to replace them. They were too slow. Always the Italian fighters would wait over Massawa until one machine more badly hit than the others would lag behind. Then the enemy fighters would come and give it hell.

That happened to a young Squadron Leader (Squadron Leader A Theed of No 254 Wing) who after months of staff work on the ground, had asked to take part in this important raid. He was given the job of rear gunner, and his guns were shot away. The pilot was hit. The airman manning the two makeshift guns that sprouted out of the belly of the machine, was mortally wounded. The Squadron Leader fixed a tourniquet, tightened it with his revolver barrel, and got the dying man to hold it in place. Then he manned the two side guns until the pilot, lacking blood, was failing. Then the Squadron Leader took over the controls. That machine too, came back, though they lifted out of it a dead man still holding the revolver that tightened his tourniquet.

Such was the spirit that was bringing the convoys through the Red Sea and cheating the enemy of victory.'

The Squadron suffered no direct casualties from their escort work around and adjacent to the convoys. 1 Wellesley was lost from engine failure, the aircraft landing 200 yards ahead of the destroyer HMS *Kimberly*. The aircrew of Sergeants Burcher, Farrell and Dickson were picked up so quickly they hardly got their feet wet!

RECONNAISSANCES

The Red Sea is the result of a colossal crack in the surface of the earth many millenniums ago. A rift valley stretches from Mount Hebron in the North, through the Jordan Valley into the Red Sea, and on through Eritrea to the Mountains of Ethiopia which give rise to the White and Blue Niles. The whole length is characterised by heat, wind and humidity. The East Coast and most of Saudi Arabia, the Yemen and Aden swelter for most of the year. To the West, the flatlands of Egypt and the Sudan in the North, give way to a belt of jagged seven to nine thousand feet mountains stretching from the lower Sudan through Eritrea to Abyssinia. This heat sink gives rise to some of the harshest flying conditions in the world. Spectacular thunder and electrical storms, boiling up to 40,000 feet and more, sand, wind and humidity levels could and did conspire in those early days of war to unnerve pilots, and to destroy machinery. Aborted sorties understandably were forced on pilots operating aircraft and instruments unable to overcome the wilder moods of nature.

The requests for reconnaissance from the Squadron were multi-sourced. From HQME in Cairo and No 201 Group in Khartoum, from No 254 Wing in Erkowit, from the Army in the Sudan preparing for its conquest of Ethiopia and Eritrea, and from the Navy at Aden and Suez, the variety and degrees of urgency of information needed was unending. Photo-mosaics from 20-25,000 ft for mapping, medium height coverage for target intelligence, any height photographs for damage assessment, and low level "blow ups" for pin point air attacks and enemy defences, were all tasks to be supplied by aircraft flights, and the Photographic Section.

Neither Wellesley nor Blenheim were ideal photographic platforms, but some remarkable photographs were taken from the available 8, 10 or 20 inch lenses. The Squadron had developed a reputation for excellence with its Photographic Section through its experiences pre-war of photo-mosaics for mapping of the Jordan Valley. A high degree of flying accuracy in both constant heading and height is called for in mosaic photography, and an exacting comparable matching precision in photographic layout for maps.

In the ten months of Operations from Port Sudan, hardly a day passed without a reconnaissance flown. In the early days there was urgency to confirm Italian Air Force and Navy base activities strengths, and to fill in blanks - of which there were many - in the Intelligence spectrum. For the Squadron, most bombing targets were in Eritrea - Asmara, Adi Ugri, Gura, Zola, and Massawa. There was, however, a plurality of islands in the Dahlak Archipeligo spanning the immediate sea roads to Massawa. The Italians used these for early air raid warning (from sound detectors), seaward gun defences, and emergency flying boat and aircraft landing areas. All needed constant surveillance, and it was on one of these flights over Harmil Island that Sergeant Norris and his crew of Sergeant D'Arcy and Leading Aircraftman Lampard were shot down on the 1st December and became Prisoners of War.

Sergeant Norris has recorded,

"I was airborne at 0625 hrs in Wellesley 2689, set course for Harmil Island, climbing to 26,000 feet. We approached the island from the sea - turned and commenced photography. First two legs uneventful. Halfway down the third leg we were attacked by 3 CR42s. The first burst of 20mm cannon fire hit Lampard in the leg and damaged the engine controls and hydraulics. Two more attacks but no further damage (I was no longer flying straight and level!) No engine - nowhere to go except down. Ahead a quite small island, rocky and uneven. Classic forced landing approach, but there was a danger of overshooting into the oggin.

No flaps, we almost stalled over the shore line and I shoved the port wing and bomb carrier into the rocky ground and quickly came to rest.

Before I could undo my straps and chute, the aircraft was surrounded by an unruly and excited mob of Italians, who thought they had won the war. I left the aircraft and tried to reach the rear gunners position, but was prevented from doing so. D'Arcy was unable to escape until Lampard had been lifted out and carried away. His leg was almost severed and bleeding profusely.

(The island was manned by the crew of a Lloyd-Tristino vessel, which was in harbour at Massawa. Its Captain, El Capitano de Martino, was the Commodore of the line and was still wearing the DSC won when serving with the Royal Navy in W.W.I.)

There was no Doctor, only a medical orderly, who did his best without any surgical instruments and with only a first aid kit of limited scope. In spite of his best efforts to save him, Lampard died at 0710 hrs on 2 September and was buried in the north west corner of the island the next day, with as much ceremony as possible in the circumstances.

Sergeant D'Arcy and I were well treated, but were not allowed to approach the aircraft to assess the damage. Two days later we were taken by boat to Massawa. Two P.O.W. Camps and 7 months later we were freed by one armoured car of the Sudan Defence force on 1st April 1941.'

FIRST VICTORY IN AERIAL COMBAT

It had become apparent from previous reconnaissances that Zola, some 30 miles south of Massawa was being prepared and used by the Italians for aircraft attacks on the convoys. Zola had been attacked once on 6 July, as it showed numbers of aircraft and stores on the airfield and loading jetty. On 8 July a British Convoy of tankers and freight ships entered the Squadron escort area. A bombing raid led by Flight Lieutenant Robinson, B Flight Commander, was mounted with five aircraft. The attack was successful, but on the return journey an enemy Saroia-Marchetti SM82 bomber a Pipistrello (or bat) flying south was encountered East of the Dahlak Archipelago, undoubtedly having come from either an attack on, or a second reconnaissance for, the convoy. Robinson and his four aircraft with their single front gun .5 Brownings, rotated during attacks to side shots from the newly created Lewis gun positions centrally in the aircraft, and from the rear gunners cockpits. Whether from damage, or to escape, the SM82 descended rapidly to low flying over the sea, only to crash and sink after another attack from Robinson. This was No 14's first blood of the war.

The Italian aircrew survivors managed to float on a life raft back to the island. However they were without the Captain, Cranchini, who recognising there was not enough room for four on the raft elected to remain with the destroyed aircraft. His disappearance and bravery were remembered in the Italian Naval history of events in the area with the award of the Medaglio d'Oro. Exhausted and living off birds eggs for two weeks the others managed to reach inhabited Dahlak, where three weeks later they were returned to Massawa.

THE GIN AND TONIC RAID

Near the end of August 1940, the Squadron Commander was bidden to Wadi Halfa on the Nile, there to meet a Staff Officer from RAF Headquarters in Cairo. All known there was that C Flight - the specialist overseas navigation flight of the Squadron - might be needed in a day or two. It was; and next day 5 Wellesley aircraft accompanied by a Valencia transport aircraft with the ground crews, flew to Wadi Halfa from Port Sudan.

Wadi Halfa in the Sudan lies just south of the Latitude 22º north parallel that forms the Sudan border with Egypt. This border extends westwards along the parallel for about four to five hundred miles until it reaches a carbuncle of a mountain called Jebel Oweinat, rising some 7,000ft from the surrounding desert, and intersecting the 25 degrees East longitude which forms the north/south border between Libya and Egypt. The claims of Wadi Halfa to fame were that it was the terminal connection for the Sudan Railways to and from Egypt, it had a desert airfield strip, and an Imperial Airways hotel for their staging post on the Nile for the Cairo/Khartoum flying boat service. The Wellesley flight air and ground crews were accommodated in this mosquito-netted fan-cooled dust box with a veranda; in fact, quite prettily situated overlooking the second cataract of the Nile.

The Italians were prolonging their resistance against the British and Commonwealth forces by relying almost solely on an air supply link between Asmara in Eritrea and Tripoli in Libya. This supply route, using big Italian SM82 transport aircraft, brought mail, food, fuel and spares, and to the chagrin of the RAF, DIY kits of CR42 fighter aircraft.

The brief was to attack these Italian aircraft whilst refuelling on the desert airfield strip at Jebel Oweinat. Timing was crucial as the process of landing, refuelling and stretching legs, would not be more than about 90 minutes before they took off again for Asmara.

Headquarters Middle East had devised a code, the receipt of which recorded enemy progress and entailed specific reactions from the detachment:
Cointreau followed by a figure.
(Meaning the number of Italian aircraft that had landed in Tripoli from Italy)
(Our action. Complete briefing, load weapons, and bombs)
Martini followed by a GMT time.
(Meaning, Italian aircraft have taken off from Tripoli for Oweinat at x time)
(Our action. Prepare for take-off. The hotel was 30 minutes away from the airfield).
Gin and Tonic
(Our action. Take off. Reach Oweinat. Destroy the aircraft and return to Wadi Halfa).
All therefore was now set for the operation.

If one ever has reason to consult a one in two million air map of 500 miles or more to the west of Wadi Halfa, surprise needs to be forestalled by a few remarks. The map sheets are uniformly coloured beige or brown indicating a slight difference in desert heights above sea level. There is a grid of longitude and latitude. In the east - as if peeking round a theatre curtain - there is a glimpse of green marking the Nile and Wadi Halfa. Directly west along the 22 degrees latitude parallel after over 400 miles to the junction of the Egyptian and Libyan boundaries occurs Jebel Oweinat. In between, God had taken a rest from creation. Nothing except the world's largest supply of sand and rock. No villages, water, nor vegetation; trackless, barren, harsh and featureless. The cartographer as if in aberration, had traced a red dotted line crossing this route to record the wanderings of a 20th century explorer. At briefing, this arid expanse of desolation soon subdued the questions into silence. (900 miles there and back on the reliability of one Pegasus engine, a drift sight, and an old P.4 compass for navigation, was not the best assistance one could have wished for. There was a great deal of checking of desert survival kit. All was made ready. As Isaiah had said "Make straight, a highway, over the desert".

By lunchtime at the hotel, on the second day, no code signal. No Cointreau nor any other had been received. Unless Martini arrived soon, flight time would intrude into the night for the outward flight and thereby cancel any possible attack on the Italian aircraft. The mission looked as though it was going to thread its way into another wait the next day.

No sooner had the beginnings of postponement set in with some ideas mooted of a walk to the colourful market of Wadi Halfa or to the cataract on the Nile, when right on the limits for a daylight attack Gin and Tonic spelled over the radio. The Italian aircraft had left Tripoli heading south east for Oweinat. A rush to the airfield, and five Wellesleys took off, fuel limited to eight hours flying to accommodate a mixed load of 40 lb fragmentation bombs, incendiaries, front gun ammunition and those vicious tyre-destroying spikes to sow on their desert strip. The pilots, Stapleton, Mackenzie, Rhodes, Moulton and Le Cavalier.

Once at height, speed regulated to fuel economy, and settled on course, the flight was in the hands of the 'flight-office' boys - the navigators.

One of the pilots on the raid had recently visited a sister RAF Squadron in the Sudan. He had returned with this further illumination from their resident Bard (with apologies to Masefield and his Cargoes).

'Snappy little Spitfire with a Rolls Royce Engine,
Streaking through the ether with its guns ablaze
Shooting up Heinkels, Dorniers and Junkers
Rolling and looping with the pilots in a daze.
Stately Lockheed Hudson with cushions in the cockpit.
Sailing o'er England and the nice green grass.
With turrets full of Browning guns and Mark 9 gunsights
K guns, cameras and bullet-proof glass.
Dirty British Wellesley with sand-caked mainplanes
Grinding o'er the desert in the noonday sun,
With a single Peggy engine and an oiled up windscreen,
A one ton bomb load, and one Lewis gun.'

The weather was kind; clear blue skies, visibility good, some ominous streams of sand scuffing the surface. In the last 50 miles the flight dropped to low level to make an approach. At the going down of the sun, the silhouette of the conical mountain came up on cue - a jagged pile of an extinct volcano, sandblasted to a core of dark red and beige vertically cracked rocks. The aircraft slotted into line astern, all safety switches locked to off, and the airfield in the lee of the mountain appeared dead ahead in the centre of the windscreen. The navigators had done their stuff. Now for those loaded, refuelling Italian transport aircraft.

At briefing, intelligence had advised that little or no anti-aircraft defence might be expected except possibly from small-arms fire and a 20mm Breda cannon or two. The Italian aircraft might be in line or in a cluster around the refuelling point. The tactics: to front gun the aircraft at low level, pull up, reverse, and dive releasing fragmentation bombs and incendiary, and on a final run sow spikes on the landing strips exiting low and away, hopefully leaving burning destruction behind.

There was the windsock - a somewhat tattered edition, there the refuelling dumps, there the landing strips, but no aircraft. All this grinding flight and there was nothing - not even a building, or a shed, or any transport on the place, to receive explosive frustration.

A lone speeding truck with its lights on left the base of the mountain on the track to the airfield. Perhaps an organising party for their expected Italian arrivals? They received a burst of front-gun fire, turned about and headed back to base, only to be straddled by two bombs. They disembarked to leave the truck to run its course over a small cliff.

There was nothing for it but to return to Wadi Halfa. Accomplishment nil; most of the weapon load still aboard to be jettisoned, if, ominously, a forced landing or missed destination was to be an outcome.

As the return headed east, day was giving best to night. The dark purple band on the horizon was creeping up the sky switching on the desert stars. Those incredibly bright pin pricks in the dark dome shed no light, and no moon either for the return. Navigation lights were switched on to keep track with the leader. A steady compass course on a guessed wind, and a four hours flying tunnel in the dark. Heavy eyes were blinked to pick up Wadi Halfa. To miss with the limited fuel didn't bear thinking about. There was similar geography to the east of Wadi Halfa. The cocooned cockpit of orange glowing instruments flickered the health of the components in the body Wellesley, enough to concentrate thoughts away from other dire possibilities.

The Squadron Commander at Wadi Halfa had said he would try to persuade the authorities of the town to turn on the town lights ten minutes before the expected time of arrival. In the event they refused, claiming their blackout was to prevent the very aircraft we had been after from bombing them. Not that it had ever happened before but one couldn't be too careful, etc, etc.

Luck held, and the quiet application of Observer Sergeant Smith was rewarded. Ahead and slightly to port were eight tiny pin pricks of light. They were the airfield runway flares, lit by the CO confirmed when overflown, as the Chance Light, a mobile floodlight, switched on. The collective sigh of relief was almost audible. The engine of one aircraft stopped before it reached its parking place. No aircraft had more than 20 gallons left.

Incredulity greeted the debriefing reports. Five Italian aircraft had definitely left Tripoli for Oweinat. Had the flight reached the right place? Were there two desert airfields? Scepticism from the intelligence officers was barely concealed. After 8 hours flying, and the good fortune of having all made it back safely, the staff of Headquarters were suspected of a gamble, based on flimsy evidence. Disappointment all round.

Next day with preparations to return to Port Sudan, explanation and vindication arrived. The Italian aircraft had left Tripoli but had run into sandstorms. Two returned to Tripoli, three had force landed in the desert and were wrecked. Later it was known that the Italian outpost at Oweinat had reported the raid. As the desert strip there was now vulnerable the Italians ceased using it. The Gin and Tonic raid, though not as rewarding as had been hoped, had left a small footnote on the eddies of war.

SUMMARY OF FIRST THREE MONTHS OPERATIONS

It is not possible in this history, without extending its length to unacceptability, to record the daily detail of bombing activity in the first three months of the Squadron in the East Africa Campaign. Three separate operations will illustrate the differences in purpose, the risks, the efforts and the results that characterised not only the demands on the Squadron but on the Allied forces ranged against the Italian forces in greatly superior numbers.

After nearly three months of operations against Italian East Africa, a summary shows a total of 24 bombing raids had been flown involving a total flying time of 627 hours. One of these raids was with 9 aircraft, 12 with 5, and the remainder with 4, 3 and a single aircraft. The average duration of each bombing raid was 6 hours 10 minutes and the average load was the maximum permissible all up weight (11,100 lbs) plus an overload of approximately 1500 lbs. On one occasion each aircraft carried an overload of 2500 lbs in order to reach Kassala with 500 lb bombs, but the Wellesleys were able to take off on not much more than half the aerodrome. During these operations a total of two raids failed to reach their objectives owing to weather conditions, and none failed owing to enemy action.

One airman was killed and two officers, a sergeant pilot and an airman were posted as missing and two airmen wounded. One aircraft force landed in the sea whilst on convoy duties.

Two aircraft were lost over enemy territory, and one in the Red Sea. Damage done to our own aircraft by AA and fighter action amounted to 3 aircraft damaged beyond repair, 9 damaged necessitating major repairs, and 5 damaged necessitating minor repairs. In spite of the vintage of the aircraft and these losses, the average percentage of serviceability for the past quarter had been 76.9%.

Apart from the damage known to have been done to targets by bombs, one SM81 bomber was shot down by a Wellesley over the sea, 5 enemy aircraft are known to have been destroyed on the ground, and one fighter had been shot down (confirmed)

Bombing Raid on Asmara Airfield.

Bombing Raid on Asmara Airfield.

Italian Aircraft Graveyard at Asmara, April 1941.

Asmara after surrender.

whilst two further fighters are believed to have been damaged.

These figures do not include the convoy and general reconnaissance flying by C Flight detailed for this work. C flight escorted the three north and south bound convoys successfully, and flew 267 hours in the quarter. During the passage of each convoy most of their pilots did over 12 hours flying.

The daily average temperature during July and August had been between 110 to 120°F. in the shade.

A NEW AIRCRAFT

Three twin-engined Bristol Blenheim IVs arrived at Port Sudan on 14 September 1940. This famous aircraft replaced the obsolete Wellesley. For airmen brought up on biplanes - which meant everyone then serving in the Squadron - the Blenheim represented as exciting a package of novelties as the later Spitfire. In 1934, the newspaper magnate, Lord Rothermere, had asked the Bristol Aeroplane Company to build him a fast, twin-engined, executive aircraft to carry a pilot and six passengers at 240 mph, appreciably faster than any RAF fighter of that date. The result was the Type 142, the first modern stressed-skin monoplane built in Britain with retractable landing gear, flaps, and variable-pitch propellers (imported from the United States). Its performance staggered even the designer: reaching a top speed of 307 mph in May 1935 that was far beyond anything then flying for the RAF - or likely to do so within the next couple of years. The Air Ministry promptly ordered a military version, named the Blenheim, that served as both a light bomber and a long-range fighter.

Late in 1938, the Mark IV version appeared with two 920 hp Mercury XV engines, self-sealing fuel tanks, some metal protection for the crew and a longer asymmetric nose to offer better accommodation for the observer/bomb-aimer. This version had begun to reach the RAF in March 1939. By the time the Middle East received it, some 18 months later, intense operations in Europe had revealed its many deficiencies - in construction, instrumentation, armour, armament, bomb load capacity and even in speed - only too clearly. In the Middle East, however, in comparison with other British and Italian aircraft, the Blenheim IV was superior to most. Everyone in the Squadron knew this and they were glad to have it.

Changing from the biplane Gordon to the monoplane Wellesley had been a long step up, but the further step up to the Blenheim proved less taxing - once pilots learned, for the first time, to handle two engines. In those days, it was rare for pilots to enjoy the luxury of a dual control model when learning to handle a new type. They managed as best they could by studying Pilots' Notes on the ground and, in the air, either initially riding alongside an instructor in the jump-seat, or having him there to monitor first flights. Engine fitters, already familiar with one Bristol engine, had no problem coping with another of similar design and capacity, and airframe fitters found that eggs fried significantly quicker on the Blenheim's metal skin than on the Wellesley's fabric! The new machine, like the old, had a crew of three and so there was no need for a reorganisation of aircrew personnel. Conversion was completed within six weeks.

Far the most dramatic difference between the two machines was in speed, both cruise and maximum, where the Blenheim IV had an advantage of nearly 20%. Its fully-loaded range, though less than the Wellesley's, was still adequate, but its bomb load was no heavier (1,000 lbs) and its defensive armament was as disappointingly puny (a single machine-gun firing forward and two in a dorsal turret covering the upper rear). However, six of the 18 Blenheims had four 20mm cannons mounted just inside the bomb bay for night fighting, ground or sea strafing.

As Blenheims and their crews became available so Wellesley operations decreased. It was remarkable that in the weeks of conversion 20 Blenheim bombing raids were flown, and 26 by Wellesleys. The first attack by Blenheims occurred on 20 September, when led by Flight Lieutenant Birks (who with Pilot Officer Smith instructed the conversions) they raided Otumlo airfield at Massawa. Birks' aircraft was hit and the port engine caught fire, but a forced landing confirmed by Hedjaz radio revealed that all three crew had become POWs.

A NEW COMMANDER

Whilst the conversion was in progress Squadron Leader Stapleton succeeded Selway on 28 September in Command of No 14 Squadron. Having already served in the squadron for three and a half years, the customary settling-in period for a new commander was avoided. 'The lynch pins holding together the structure of a Squadron', he later wrote, 'were the Adjutant and Flight Sergeants: Split Pin King of A Flight, Johnnie Johns of B Flight and Dad Crouch of C Flight. As with most RAF Squadrons, they were the apostles of technical discipline, the directing masters of their technicians and the high priests of adaptability. The Adjutant, Flying Officer Jock Aitken, was an ex-World War One pilot. and he used as his main executive and disciplinary instrument the Squadron Warrant Officer, Mr Killington. Aitken formed an administrative and sociological triumvirate with the Padre, Flying Officer Martin (who later became Archdeacon of Khartoum) and the Doctor, Flight Lieutenant V A F Martin. For a young squadron commander, aged 22 years, there were not very many problems that couldn't be answered by these wise men.'

Squadron Leader Selway together with Squadron Leaders Elton and Larking - the commanding officers of Nos 47 and 223 Squadrons - were awarded DFCs for their demonstrated leadership in bringing their Squadrons from their peacetime roles into the opening, and outstandingly successful, attacks against the Italian forces in East Africa. Selway (later, after the war, to become Air Marshal Sir Anthony Selway, KCB, DFC, AOC in C Coastal Command) was posted to HQ Middle East in Cairo, where with Elton he injected much valued experience into the operational and planning staffs of the Headquarters.

The Italians in Eritrea made extensive use of the coral islands in the Dahlak Archipelago to provide defences in depth to the port of Massawa, and from which to mount attacks against the allied convoys travelling from Aden to Suez. The islands, flanking the shipping lanes to and from Massawa, contained coastal defence and anti-aircraft guns, sound detectors for air defence, radio transmission stations, and anchorages and wharves for small ships. The islands most noted by reconnaissance were Dohul, Dissie, Harmil, Nefasit and Sheik el Abu, all of which since June had been attacked by the RAF Squadrons in Sudan.

It was over Harmil that Sergeant Norris and his crew were shot down and made POWs, and near Dohul that Flight Lieutenant Robinson and his flight destroyed the Italian transport aircraft an SM81. Nefasit island figured in another incident on the 16 November.

The Squadron Commander led six Blenheims to attack the radio station and storage areas on Nefasit, but just short of the target was attacked by three CR42 fighters. One fighter was shot down but not before it severely damaged an engine of the fifth Blenheim flown by the New Zealander Flying Officer Mackenzie and his crew of Sergeants Hitchin and McConnell. The formation attacked the alternative target of coastal defence guns and a listening post on Sheik el Abu. Meanwhile the Squadron record noted 'Mackenzie later said he knew that his starboard motor would seize so fell out of the formation as he was unable to keep up. The engine eventually stopped, but after jettisoning his bombs and blister gun, he could not maintain height, and at 500 feet decided to land as the aircraft appeared also to be on fire with smoke filling the cockpit.' The remainder of the formation returning to the Sudan along the Eritrean coast noticed Mackenzie's Blenheim about to crash land amongst some scrub about a mile inland and about ten miles north of Massawa.

The Squadron record continues: 'The Squadron Commander split-up the formation who circled overhead while he landed beside the disabled aircraft. After endeavouring to destroy it, he picked up Mackenzie and his crew and took off again reaching base safely'. The CO was given an immediate award of the DFC, but even today neither Stapleton nor McConnell can explain how that Blenheim on take off, thrashing through camel thorn, sand mounds, and dried up water courses, ever made it into the air. Some months later McConnell was to survive an equally traumatic and mystifying incident in which he qualified for the gold caterpillar insignia (life saved by parachute).

THE FALL OF KEREN

By the end of 1940, a remarkable army was building up in the Sudan under the command of Lieutenant General Sir William Platt, consisting mainly of Indian and British units, together with Rhodesians, South, East and West Africans, Sudanese and Free French. Better equipped than its opponent, this army had the inestimable advantage of Ultra information. As John Terraine wrote, quoting the official Intelligence history, 'the Cs-in-C in Cairo were able to read the enemy's plans and appreciation in his own words as soon as he issued them; indeed, they sometimes received the decrypts while the Italian W/T operators were still asking for the signals to be checked and repeated.'

Platt's major offensive began in mid-January 1941, supported by some genuine modern fighters - Hawker Hurricanes of the South African Air Force, which swiftly destroyed or grounded most Italian aircraft - and made rapid progress at first. By the end of February, all three Sudan-based Squadrons - Nos 47, 223 and 14 - were employed on photo-reconnaissance and bombing operations along a mountainous route which the multiracial forces were to follow eastward for about 170 miles from Kassala to Asmara, capital of Eritrea and headquarters of the Italian forces commanded by the

Duke of Aosta. Their principal target was the strong fortress of Keren, 60 miles north-west of Asmara, and key to the survival - or conquest - of Italian power in north-east Africa.

On the coast, a valuable landing strip was captured at Marsa Taclai, 120 miles south of Port Sudan, from which increasing pressure was brought to bear on Keren, Asmara and Massawa. During March, No 14 Squadron's Blenheims flew 235 sorties, an average of nearly eight per day, to meet urgent demands for photo-reconnaissance, to make attacks on Italian airfields and defensive positions and to continue their protection of convoys using the Red Sea. One hundred of these sorties used Marsa Taclai, where ground crews - existing in far worse conditions even than at Port Sudan - slaved to keep the Blenheims serviced, re-fuelled and re-armed.

After many heavy ground and air attacks, Keren was taken on 27 March 1941. 'It was to take 54 days of brutal fighting,' wrote Patricia Wright, 'slogging up exposed slopes against the most concentrated and courageous opposition ever put forward by Italian forces.' This victory signalled the end of the campaign in north-east Africa and Air Commodore Leonard Slatter, head of the Sudan-based air forces, distilled five needs for the future. Above all was the desperate need for transport aircraft and second, the need to devise equipment and learn the techniques required to drop supplies safely and accurately. Third came the need for long-range fighters, 'the real answer to the destruction of enemy aircraft on their aerodromes.' In fourth place Slatter drew attention to the need for ambulance aircraft, which would have saved many lives during the heavy fighting around Keren. And finally, he advocated the production of dive-bombers to attack pin-point targets. None of these could be met until the United States entered the war.

VICTORY IN THE RED SEA

The British Commanders-in-Chief in Cairo at this time were anxious about the position in the Western Desert. Most of the Italian army in Cyrenaica had been destroyed and Benghazi captured, but German reinforcements through Tripoli had pushed the allies back to their starting points on the Egypt/Cyrenaica border. It was thus urgent, with problems also looming in Greece, that forces released by victories in East Africa should be transferred to the Middle East as quickly as possible.

On the day after the fall of Keren the 4th Indian Division, and Nos 13 and 94 RAF Squadrons, were ordered immediately to the Middle East. However on the plea of the Naval Commander-in-Chief East Indies, it was agreed that No 14 Squadron, who had during the whole of March, with the squadrons from Aden maintained dawn and dusk watches over Massawa, should be retained in Port Sudan for a further week. There was some doubt about the reasons for this; it was either to support the army operations in Eritrea, or as a precaution against any possible Italian naval sorties into the Red Sea, - Nos 824 and 813 Fleet Air Arm Swordfish Squadrons, already disembarked in Egypt from their carrier HMS *Eagle* were ordered to Port Sudan. They arrived on the 25th and 28th of March with a total of eighteen aircraft. With hindsight, these were two critical, perhaps fortuitous, decisions directly affecting what was about to happen.

The opponents were now drawn up around the Red Sea area. Under mounting pressure from the oncoming Allied Armies towards Massawa, Admiral Bonetti's eight Destroyer and Torpedo Ships had to get out or surrender in harbour.

The routes and targets chosen for the Italian 5th and 3rd flotillas are shown on the accompanying map. Destination Suez for the 5th flotilla consisting of the 1500 ton 34 knot destroyers Pantera, Tigre and Leone, and Port Sudan the target for the 1,000 ton 32 knot destroyers Battisti, Sauro and Manin of the 3rd flotilla. The torpedo ships Orsini, which had had its armament control damaged beyond repair in a previous air raid on Massawa, and Acerbi with its limited range and 600 ton displacement were unable to take part in these operations. In due course these last two scuttled themselves in Massawa harbour. The principal opposition was to be the three Squadrons at Port Sudan, No 14 Squadron of twelve Blenheims, and Nos 813 and 824 Fleet Air Arm Squadrons of eighteen Swordfish. These were backed up in the Sudan by Nos 47 and 223 Squadron of Wellesleys, and 203 RAF Blenheim Squadron in Aden.

What now follows is a description of the action between the British aircraft and Italian destroyers taken from British and Italian Official Histories, from War Diaries of Commands, and from Squadron Records. There are inconsistencies and inaccuracies, not all of which at this distance in time can be corrected, but none of the discrepancies affect the main conclusions to be drawn from this event. This was previously published in *The Aeroplane* magazine (now Aeroplane Monthly) in August/September 1986.

Apart from the daily Royal Air Force dawn/dusk checks on Massawa during March, action began at 1800 hrs on the 31st March by the exit from Massawa of the 5th Italian destroyer flotilla, with Captain Gasparini in command aboard the *Pantera*. Their instructions read, 'Exit on day X after the last enemy air reconnaissance, and proceed at maximum speed during the night to the Hedjaz coast in order to elude the vigilance of enemy aircraft. Thereafter skirt the Hedjaz coast on days X + 1 and X + 2 and arrive at first light, after the night traverse of the Jebel Strait, at Suez on X + 3.' The exit of the three destroyers of the 5th flotilla was not immediately detected. There was a further instruction sent by the Supermarina H.Q. on the evening of the 31st March which probably had some effect on the subsequent decisions of Gasparini. It read 'Remind all Captains that whilst they must ensure, after their missions have been accomplished, that the ship is completely destroyed. It is their absolute and sacrosanct duty to ensure the safety not only of their crew, but also of themselves.'

The three destroyers at 18 knots were in line astern inverted order led by *Leone* (Captain Scroffa) as this was the only destroyer in the flotilla with all navigation facilities functioning.

At 0030 hrs disaster struck. *Leone* hit two unmarked coral outcrops thirteen miles north of Awali Hutur Island. The other two destroyers slid by on either side of *Leone* without mishap, their depth sounders registering plenty of clearance. Initially damage to *Leone* was thought to be slight, and Scroffa said he would take position astern and continue with the mission. It was not to be. Shortly, further checks revealed that sea water was leaking into the engines and diesel tanks. The port propeller had been bent, and fires started in boiler number 4 and in the engine room. Despite all efforts the fires spread. At 0300 hrs Scroffa ordered abandon ship and opened the sea cocks to sink *Leone*. At sunrise the *Leone* had not yet sunk. Gasparini, anxious about the smoke being

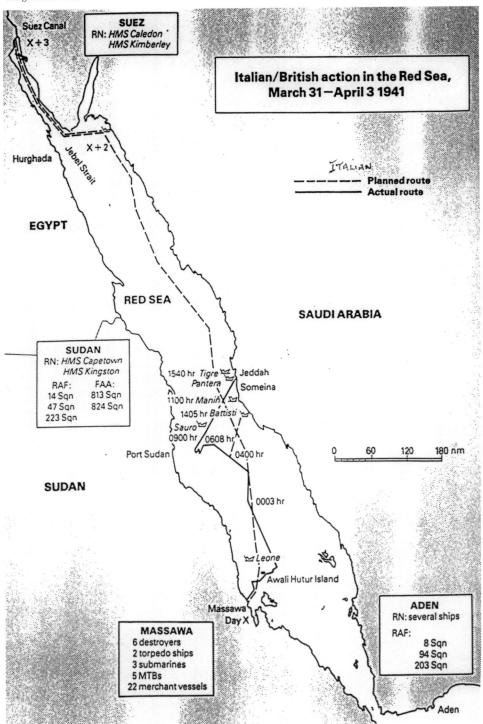

SUEZ
RN: *HMS Caledon*
HMS Kimberley

Suez Canal
X + 3

X + 2

Hurghada

Jebel Strait

EGYPT

RED SEA

**Italian/British action in the Red Sea,
March 31—April 3 1941**

ITALIAN
- - - - - - Planned route
———— Actual route

SAUDI ARABIA

SUDAN
RN: *HMS Capetown*
HMS Kingston

RAF: FAA:
14 Sqn   813 Sqn
47 Sqn   824 Sqn
223 Sqn

1540 hr *Tigre*   Jeddah
        Pantera   Someina
1100 hr *Manin*
1405 hr *Battisti*
Sauro
0900 hr   0608 hr
Port Sudan   0400 hr

SUDAN

0003 hr

0   60   120   180 nm

Leone
Awali Hutur Island

Massawa
Day X

MASSAWA
6 destroyers
2 torpedo ships
3 submarines
5 MTBs
22 merchant vessels

ADEN
RN: several ships

RAF:
8 Sqn
94 Sqn
203 Sqn

Aden

seen by British air reconnaissance ordered the *Pantera* to sink her, which she did by gun-fire. With the *Leone* survivors on board Gasparini decided that *Pantera* and *Tigre* should return to Massawa, decant the *Leone* crew, abandon the Suez plan, and lead the 3rd flotilla into the plan to destroy Port Sudan.

An early Fleet Air Arm reconnaissance on the 1st April had, however, noticed the sinking *Leone*. A strike by three Blenheims of No 14 Squadron at 1100 hrs found the *Leone* already sunk and her life-boats abandoned. Later another Fleet Air Arm reconnaissance saw an Italian destroyer heading at high speed back to Massawa. The British Commands had now decided that the break-out from Massawa was imminent, and the Royal Navy moved the cruiser *Capetown* and the destroyer *Kingston* from the harbour at Port Sudan into the open Red Sea.

By the morning of the 2nd April Gasparini had formed up his two destroyers of the 5th flotilla plus three from 3rd flotilla, and by 1350 hrs was on his way from Massawa to Port Sudan. Both formations of destroyers were noticed by a Blenheim from Aden at 1430 hrs, eight miles outside Massawa heading north. Port Sudan, Suez and Aden were alerted, but another slice of misfortune was to hit Gasparini. The destroyer Battisti, last of the three, in the 3rd flotilla, reported such severe leaking from its boilers that its speed was reduced to a crawl. Captain Peppino sought permission - given at 0315 hrs to turn directly for the Hedjaz coast there to beach Battisti. This was accomplished, and was the end of Battisti at 1405 hrs about 60 miles south of Jeddah.

The Aden Blenheim reports on 2 April, stirred a flurry of armed air reconnaissance at dawn on 3 April, and strike forces at Port Sudan were bombed-up. Six Swordfish of the Fleet Air Arm set off at dawn on a step-aside reconnaissance of the approaches to Port Sudan, plus their Commander flying a sweep of his own. Three Blenheims of No 14 Squadron had left in the early hours to confirm from Massawa at dawn, which they did, that at least four destroyers had departed the harbour. The Blenheims also noticed a motor torpedo boat splashing north at great speed just north of the Dahlak Archipelago. (It was in fact this MTB that scored the only Italian success in the debacle from Massawa. Two days later its torpedoes attacked the Cruiser Capetown and damaged her so badly she had to be towed to port for repairs).

Aden aircraft swept the southern exits of the Red Sea in case the destroyers had turned south. They hadn't. The southern-most Swordfish, and the Commander of the Swordfish force both separately and within some minutes of each other around 0615 hrs, sighted the Italian destroyers some 40/50 miles east of Port Sudan and heading for it at about 30 knots. The Commander called in all the Swordfish to attack, attacked himself but missed with his bombs. He alerted the strike forces at Port Sudan and then returned there. This marked the beginning of the ultimately disastrous end of the Italian destroyer venture.

The sighting alert signal brought a hurried conference in the Port Sudan airfield Operations Room. Amongst other matters, should the town or the vulnerable parts of it be evacuated? If the destroyers came on, shells could be expected within the hour. Other than sounding the sirens when the time came, little could be done. The resident British Commissioner was assured by the 23 year-old Blenheim Squadron Commander, that the problem would be dealt with, and the residents safe! Luckily he was right.

The loss of the *Battisti* now left the 5th and 3rd flotillas with only two destroyers each. At 0630 hrs Gasparini called for the two flotillas to join up for greater protection. He had noted that they were being shadowed constantly by aircraft at low height and out of range of anti-aircraft fire. At 0655 hrs they were attacked by the reconnaissance Swordfish. The latter claimed near misses only. Two strike forces were ready in Port Sudan. The first of seven Swordfish and the second of five Blenheims. At 0718 hrs *Pantera* noticed at 30 degrees off port bow, what it took to be a British Cruiser and two Destroyers, semi hidden by the characteristic grey mass of early morning coastal fog. If a sea fight was to ensue Gasparini had, for reasons of light, to keep to the east of what he judged to be a superior naval force. He issued the signal, 'Enemy in sight.'

Gasparini had two other worries. The initial aircraft attacks had forced destroyer manoeuvres with several changes of direction, and he was expecting further intensive aircraft attacks. Because of his faulty navigation instruments and the poor visibility, Gasparini was not sure of his exact position in the dangerous coral shelves and out-crops to the East of Port Sudan. As he had no air reconnaissance, he was neither sure of the position nor the strength of the enemy naval ships. If there was to be a sea fight he had to change course. In this unenviable position Gasparini took a subsequently much criticised decision to abandon the raid on Port Sudan, and if necessary, to accept a sea fight whilst making for the Hedjaz coast. At 0730 the force of four destroyers initially turned port away from the westward course towards Port Sudan, then on to north, and then shortly afterwards on to 040 degrees for the Hedjaz coast.

Just before 0800 hrs the first strike of Swordfish attacked, but not without a little previous luck. The original finding Swordfish saw the strike force approach the destroyers but turned away not having seen them in the shrouding mists. He chased them and by Aldis and Very light turned them round to lead them back. Armed with 250 lb bombs they attacked singly, and from different directions and height. Gasparini's subsequent report said, 'the aircraft attacks were continuous from about seventy aircraft of every type (in fact fourteen - but it may have seemed like that!). The aircraft of four or five at a time were dropping bombs, going back to base to re-arm, and then continuing the attacks. All the ships fought back strongly with anti-aircraft fire forcing the attackers to stay at high level; but the anti-aircraft guns and the machine guns were overheating and became impossible to use. Then the aerial attacks developed at lower and lower altitudes'.

Just after 0800 hrs two bombs from Sub Lt Struther's RN's Swordfish hit the third in line destroyer, Manin, just forward of the bridge. The splinters wounded several including Captain Fadin who, seriously hit in the legs, continued his command lying on a settee in the chart house. The destroyer for the time being continued. At 0900 hrs Midshipman Sergeant RNVR in a Swordfish attack scored all six of his 250 lb bombs on the stern half of the last in line destroyer, *Sauro*. There was a huge explosion. The destroyer turned over in thirty-five seconds, and sank. Captain Moretti managed to order some life preserving equipment into the sea, before he himself was hurled by an explosion one hundred yards from the bridge into the sea. 95 men were later that day picked up by SS *Velho* from Port Sudan, but 78 men were lost. Ironically Moretti spent his first night ashore in the Officers Mess of No 14 Squadron, before being taken off to the POW Camp. He was bitter about the decision to change course, arguing that a few more minutes would have brought the guns of the destroyers into range of Port Sudan.

Italian Destroyer Flotilla **Pantera,Tigre, Leone.**

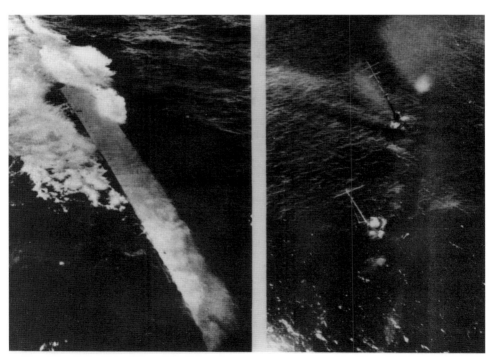

Tigre *& Leone sunk off Saudi Coast.*

Next for destruction was the destroyer Manin. The last remaining destroyer of the 3rd flotilla, despite damage, had continued with *Pantera* and *Tigre* though some fires were still burning below decks. Then the second strike of five Swordfish, followed by five Blenheims, attacked at 0900 hrs and at 1100 hrs. 250 lb bombs from the leading aircraft of both formations hit. They straddled and cracked the hull of the *Manin*. The fires erupted on deck and the destroyer stopped. Captain Fadin ordered abandon ship. The scene according to the report of the leader of the Blenheims was like some disaster in hell. 'Flames, thick black smoke and steam issued under pressure from every wound in the ship. Men were jumping over the side into the sea already littered with broken rafts, ammunition boxes, debris and oil. The sharks of the Red Sea had also arrived. The surrounds of the ship were stained with red and grey swatches from thrashing fish and despairing men. My unofficial passenger, (a fighter pilot from K Flight at Port Sudan) leant across to reach the gun button to fire a burst at the destroyer. "To scare them" he said later, but irrationally I felt a pang at the carnage, and knocked his hand away. *Manin* sank just after 1100 hrs some 110 miles north-east of Port Sudan.'

The surviving destroyers *Pantera* and *Tigre* reportedly still at 27 knots and heading north-east for Jeddah were now out of range of the Swordfish. A third strike of Swordfish ready at Port Sudan was cancelled. Instead a reconnaissance Blenheim and five Wellesleys of No 223 Squadron were despatched at 1130 hrs to continue the battle. Meanwhile Gasparini had decided on a last desperate try from the remnants of his command. At 1350 hrs the two remaining destroyers came to a stop in front of Someina, a small hamlet fifteen miles south of Jeddah, on the Saudi Arabian coast. If he could transfer the diesel, food and medical supplies, and ammunition from *Tigre* to the *Pantera*, sink the *Tigre* and send her crew ashore, then there was a possibility that with *Pantera* he could at least attack the oil wells at Hurgarda and the ships at Aqaba.

It was not to be.

The reconnaissance Blenheim instructed to watch the entrance to Jeddah saw nothing. The five Wellesleys however found the destroyers in the middle of unloading at about 1400 hrs. In the words of Gasparini, "Whilst unloading seven Vickers (the Wellesleys) began a violent attack on the ships with bombs, fragmentation shells and machine guns. With the ships at anchor it was impossible to manoeuvre evasively. The *Tigre* crew were disembarking, and the diesel transfer had to be stopped as being too risky. With the number of Swordfish previously flying it was clear that an aircraft carrier was in the vicinity". (Not so as all came from Port Sudan). At 1445 hrs Gasparini gave orders to the *Tigre* and *Pantera* to disembark their crews, and to sink their ships where they were.

The Wellesleys kept their attacks going against the ships and unloading boats. A lone Blenheim, flown by Lieutenant Forrester, the only one of three sent separately by No 14 Squadron, scored a direct hit with a bomb on *Pantera* and started a fire.

The Wellesleys hit the *Tigre*. Meanwhile one of the Wellesleys developed engine trouble and landed on the Saudi shore. A second Wellesley landed to rescue the crew, but could not take off because of the surface of loose sand. The remaining three Wellesleys then landed on firmer ground, fired the two stranded aircraft, and flew out with the two crews back to their base in the Sudan. In accounting for the four destroyers these two aircraft were the only British casualties during the whole of the episode.

At about 1700 hrs HMS *Kingston* sighted the destroyers reported by the Wellesleys. *Kingston* opened fire (one salvo hit *Pantera's* topside) but as no opposition was experienced ceased fire and closed for inspection. Tigre was down by the bows and sinking, *Pantera*, hit by a bomb and gunfire, was then struck by a torpedo from *Kingston* damaging her bows. *Kingston* sent a boarding party on to the two ships, struck the two ensigns which were still flying (later to give them to HMS *Eagle*), reported the ships as finished and resumed patrol off Jeddah. The following day HMS *Flamingo* was to pick up survivors from Manin, including Captain Fadin who, after release at the end of the war, was to write a long report on the whole action.

Part of Gasparini's final notes were: 'During the night the crews were divided into groups and started their march to Jeddah. I remained on shore with Captain Scroffa, (the ex-Captain of the *Leone* who on return to Massawa had opted to re-embark with Gasparini), the Captain of the *Tigre* (Tortora) and a group of sailors, so that we could do what was needed next morning if the ships had not sunk.

At sunrise I noticed that one destroyer had completely disappeared, and of the second only a small part of the funnel and the forward mast were visible. The latter was the *Pantera*, and the *Tigre* had turned over while sinking. At 10 o'clock having made the boats impossible to use I started towards Jeddah with the group of people who had remained.'

So ended the episode of the aircraft versus the destroyers in the Red Sea in 1941. There were to be further actions during the war before the lessons were really to sink in. There was to be criticism directed at the handling of the destroyers by those, after their imprisonment, who were saved from *Sauro* and *Manin*. There was an Italian Official Committee of Inquiry. Their salient remarks are interesting:

'The fate of the (naval) light units in the Red Sea with the imminent fall of Massawa, and of the other ports of Eritrea, was pretty well decided. It was intended that such fate would be less painful if it could be preceded by an act of war in which the people destined to die could demonstrate the fighting spirit that animated them. Unfortunately the circumstances of such an act of war to damage the enemy were such that it could not be accomplished.

The circumstances first of all forced us to abandon the action against Suez, then against Port Sudan. The acceptance of the possibility of a naval fight was not put to the test, and the last try of Gasparini with the *Pantera* was foiled. The default of the *Battisti*, then the loss of the *Sauro* followed by *Manin* were painful facts that upset the serenity of the mind of the naval commander in charge, all the time oppressed by the anxiety of continuous air attacks. We cannot find any precise fault on his part. His ships were all lost without being able to accomplish that final act of glory. It is from this that bitterness arose, but having examined the circumstances no blame attaches to the people who had to bring to their rather sad end the last Italian ships in the Red Sea.'

A fitting epitaph to those who venture without air cover under hostile skies.

GOODBYE TO PORT SUDAN

Massawa surrendered on 8 April 1941 - together with 10,000 prisoners. After the commander, Admiral Bonetti, had tried unavailingly to break his sword and had been forced instead to throw it in the harbour. Only three days later, President Roosevelt proclaimed that the Red Sea and the Gulf of Aden were open to American shipping. The main aim of the campaign had been achieved, and already so many British troops were being withdrawn for Egypt that the British administration in Eritrea for many months to come had to rely on armed Italian police and civil servants.

Such was one of the more amusing outcomes of this campaign. Another involved Corporal Barnes. Having served overseas for more than six years, he and three other squadron members qualified for repatriation to Britain. En route in March by boat and train to Cairo, they were given the task of escorting Italian officer prisoners: 'immaculate in dashingly smart uniforms, they travelled First Class; we sorry-looking objects went Second Class.' On arrival in Cairo, Henry and his comrades bade the Italians a fond farewell, for 'they had looked after us well on the boat, supplying us with tit-bits from their tables to augment our humbler fare.' However, something deeply satisfying then happened which washed away any cynical feelings our men may have had. They reported to Middle East HQ, 'still in rags and tatters' and were ushered into the office of the Squadron Leader in charge of personnel movements. 'We were amazed when he leapt out of his chair and shook us each by the hand. He went on to say that he was proud to meet anyone from No 14 Squadron as that Squadron had done such a magnificent job against the Italians. Suddenly we were ten feet tall.'

As for the rest of the Squadron, it joyfully departed from Port Sudan for Heliopolis, near Cairo. During ten months of operations from Port Sudan, the aircrews had flown 860 sorties, amounting to 4,500 operational hours. Fifteen men died, twelve of them aircrew, from enemy action, accident or illness and seven became prisoners (released during May). Nine aircraft (five Wellesleys, four Blenheims) were destroyed and the rest kept flying by qualities of skill and devotion beyond those to be expected even in wartime. The Squadron would soon be exposed to much harder fighting in the Western Desert, but no-one expressed the slightest regret at leaving the hot, humid and dusty desolation of the Red Sea coast.

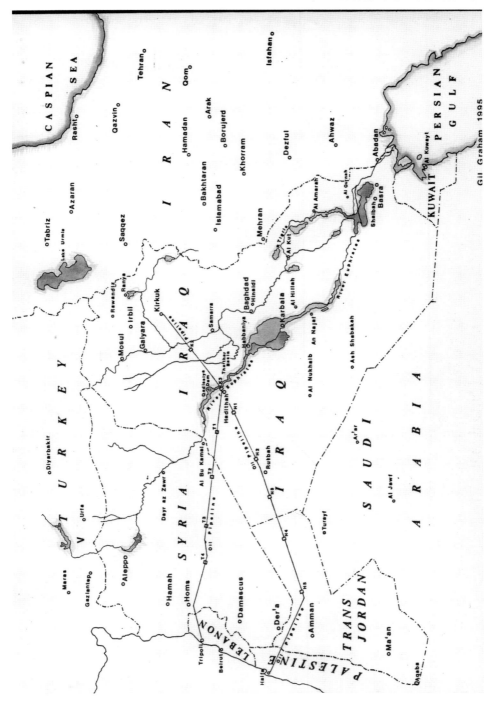

Palestine - Transjordan - Iraq - Iran.

CHAPTER 5

THE WESTERN DESERT, SYRIA, AND IRAQ/PERSIA

MAY 1941 - MAY 1942

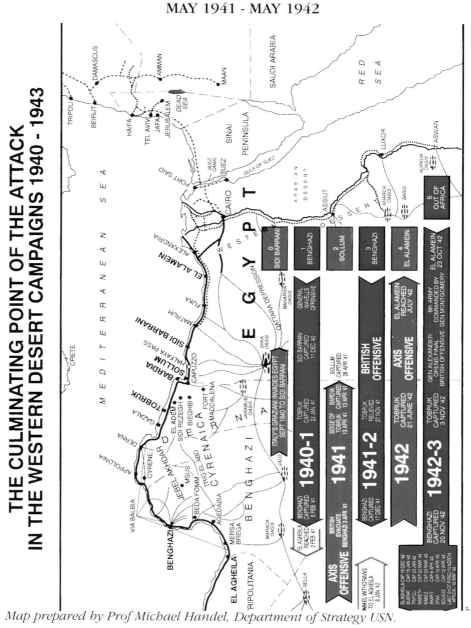

Map prepared by Prof Michael Handel, Department of Strategy USN.

*'Ride on! Ride on! in majesty! The winged squadrons of the sky Look down with
sad and wond'ring eyes To see the approaching sacrifice.'
(Rev.H.H.Milman, 1827. Hymn)*

The Squadron aircraft move to the RAF Station at Heliopolis on the outskirts of
Cairo was complete by 13 April. The ground echelon under Flying Officer J Parker,
the Squadron Equipment Officer, sailed from Port Sudan in the SS *Khedive Ismail*
on 9 April to reach Heliopolis via Port Tewfik also on 13 April.

The move brought relief in three areas to the Squadron. First, freed from relent-
less high humidity and heat of the Red Sea, the spring weather with some leave in
Cairo was doubly welcome. Secondly, for all those who had served more than
three years, (the last, intensely) with the Squadron, a return to the UK was offered.
Most accepted, but it brought a big diminution of experience in both air and
ground crew. The time for training newcomers turned out to be woefully short.
Finally, the Blenheims were given a thorough overhaul with spares reasonably
available instead of the previous long delivery times to the Sudan. However, these
blessings coincided with the need to reorganise the Squadron on to a fully mobile
two-flight and two-tier maintenance structure to conform with the pattern in force
for the Western Desert Squadrons.

The reverses experienced by Italy in Greece, at Taranto, and in the Western
Desert in 1940 precipitated the movement of German forces to the Mediterranean.
By mid-November 1940 Hitler had decided to send *Luftwaffe* units to Italy.
Fliegerkorps X began their move at the end of December. At that time the Italians
had asked for support, and by the middle of January 1941 to prevent an Italian collapse, Hitler agreed to supply a small force of armour to Libya, and two and a half
divisions to Albania. But in February following the British advance to Agheila, Hitler
cancelled the Albanian move, and increased the force for Libya to a complete
Panzer division. The first German troops began arriving in Libya in mid-February -
the 5th Light Division - and General Erwin Rommel on 12 February, followed by
the planned transfer of the 15th Panzer Division by mid-April.

These moves did not change the British Cabinet decision in principle on 24
February to transfer British troops to Greece, and confirmed on 7 March even after
learning of the encounter on 22 February at Agheila with German armoured cars.
On 2 March, the C in C Middle East General Sir Archibald Wavell had estimated that
the Germans might test Agheila, and possibly push on to Agedabia but would not
try to reach Benghazi until about May. Rommel had been to Berlin to seek reinforcements, but was refused, and was told that when the arrival of the 15th Panzer
Division was complete, he should do no more than take Agedabia as a jumping-off
point for an advance into Cyrenaica. British and German estimates of German
capabilities were similar, but it was the uncertainty about the time-table that led
the British Chiefs of Staff to take the risk of sending the code-named Tiger convoy
with armour reinforcements for Wavell through the Mediterranean to Alexandria.

The mistake about subsequent events was not in the estimates of timing of the
German build-up in Libya, but in what Rommel could do with what he already had
in February. Neither the British, nor the Germans had experience of Rommel in
the field in North Africa. On his return from Berlin, Rommel saw things differently.

After taking Agheila on 24 March, he decided on another limited thrust on 30 March, contrary to his instructions and against Italian protests. Realising British weakness, he decided to develop a full-scale offensive.

Rommel's thrust reached Agedabia on 2 April, Benghazi on the 4th, Derna on the 7th and after by-passing Tobruk (which received many of the retreating British) was in the Bardia-Sollum-Sid Omar area by the middle of April, capturing Halfaya pass on the 26th. Here Rommel had to stop, having exhausted his forces, and out-run his fuel, food and ammunition supplies. He sent pleas to Berlin for urgent reinforcements by air, to prevent the loss of Sollum and Bardia and the abandonment of a chance to retake Tobruk. The German High Command in Berlin became alarmed at the risks. The British Commander in the Middle East saw a chance to give Rommel a bloody nose.

General Friedrich von Paulus was sent to Libya on 27 April to make Rommel understand the very limited resources available to help him. On 2 May when the attack on Tobruk failed, Paulus gave Rommel new instructions. The task of the Africa Corps was to retain Cyrenaica with or without Tobruk, Sollum and Bardia. Further attacks on Tobruk were forbidden, priority was the creation of mobile reserves, the establishment of a secure base, and no further advance beyond Sollum, without Berlin's permission until the whole of 15th Panzer division had arrived.

The C-in-C Middle East had received via intercepted radio messages the full text of the instructions to Rommel. Operation Brevity was the planned counter attack against Halfaya and Sollum to be delivered between the 15 and 17 May, as the 15th Panzer Division had not yet arrived in full strength. The British Commanders committed all their available tanks to the attack despite the non-arrival , yet, in Alexandria of the Tiger convoy reinforcements. Initially Halfaya was recaptured, but although the German defensive forces were in a critical state no further progress was made. The most important reason for the failure was the technical superiority of German armour and anti-tank guns. Moreover Junkers Ju88s, Bf109s and Bf110s aircraft were beginning to appear in numbers in the Cyrenaican skies. A similar realisation was to be forced on the Squadron when they began to meet these aircraft instead of the Italian CR42s in Eritrea.

Blenheims of 14 on a desert raid.

DESERT OPERATIONS

It was against this background of urgency, that the preparation of No 14 Squadron accelerated to have them move their 16 Blenheims and 20 mostly newly-recruited air crews to Landing Ground No 21 in the Western Desert on 1 May 1941. There was a 50% turnover in time-expired ground crew including crucially, many senior technicians, and about the same proportion in aircrew.

Operations in the first month in the Desert were to provide a double shock. First, Operation *Brevity*, designed by Wavell to inhibit any further advance by Rommel, who was, in any case in very straightened supply circumstances, brought the stark realisation that German armour and anti tank artillery were far better than their British equivalents. After the Halfaya pass was taken, *Brevity* petered out. Secondly the Blenheim was to prove a good deal more vulnerable to the larger calibre German aircraft machine guns than the Wellesley had been to the Italian fighter aircraft in Eritrea.

During the first half of May, sorties were flown by new aircrew to familiarise them with desert and coastal conditions, and the types of target likely to be attacked. Weather conditions - no matter what season - from Alexandria to Tunis along the North African coast are akin to very misleading moods. Beguiling dawns, the air sparkling and the sky so blue, but from 1000hrs to 1700hrs anything - storm, heat, or the disgust of whipped sand at 50ft above the ground, scarifying food, skin and humour. Then the evening, more often than not, a tranquil conversion to a silent, still night, brightly canopied with almost touchable stars. One could hear a scorpion scuttle at twenty yards: but night-time coastal fogs could and did take their toll of life.

The last half of May brought the Squadron's first operations in the Desert. At the launch of *Brevity* the RAF had readied a sizeable support effort on Standby. Eight aircraft of the Squadron led by the Squadron Commander on 15 May were despatched singly to bomb enemy troops holding up the British at the foot of Halfaya Pass. The comment from the Squadron Commander afterwards was that attacking dispersed transport and tents in the Desert with bombs from 3000ft or higher, appeared very ineffective and virtually impossible accurately to assess damage. The raid claimed some hits and near misses, but ended up strafing vehicles and troops at low level without loss.

Somewhat surprisingly no effort was called for on the two subsequent days. Many years after this operation, analysis of RAF/Army operations in the desert, established that internal communication between units in the Army, the recognition of how the RAF could support, and Army cross-links to RAF formations were entirely inadequate to deal with the on-call needs of Army units in battle. The ALO system (Army Liaison Officer with RAF formations) was soon to be established, but the means and speed of communications still bugged its effectiveness. On the 18 May at the conclusion of Brevity, eight more sorties from the Squadron attacked enemy transport and tented camps on the Sollum-Capuzzo route where Rommel, let off the hook, was preparing to probe the defences of Tobruk. As on the 15th, the Blenheims descended to straff the enemy after bombing with unquantifiable results. All returned, though a 'fair amount' of AA fire was encountered with no damage to aircraft or crews.

On the 21st, seven Blenheim operating singly were ordered to bomb motor transport, encampments and gun positions on the Capuzzo-Tobruk road. All aircraft dropped their bombs on the target areas and reported direct hits on groups of vehicles and tented areas. Five aircraft and crews did not return: Sergeant Johnson with Sergeant Fuller and Morrison, Sergeant Hoskins with Sergeants Eaton and Calver, Flying Officer Metatich with Pilot Officer Sutton and Sergeant Jones, Sergeants Taylor, Parker and Culham, (Taylor and Parker on the 10 May had survived an Italian CR42 attack with Hall, who on this sortie had been replaced by Culham) and Sergeant Gilmour, Wilkie and Riley. Five experienced crews were thus lost out of the seven despatched. No reason for this loss was forthcoming, although it was logical to guess that enemy fighters were the cause.

CRETE

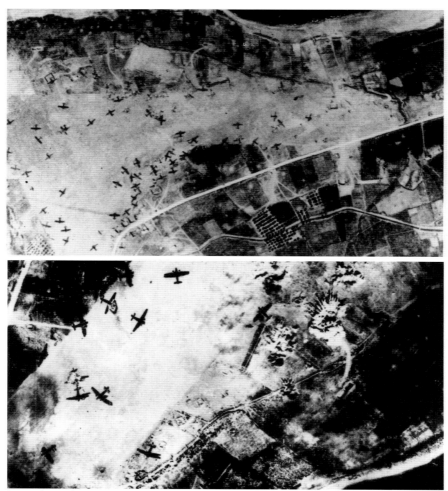

Maleme (Crete) German Para invasion. 14 Sqn's bombs on Maleme.

Four days later, the focus of action was directed against the German airborne invasion of Crete. This was seen to be the first German move to extend their power subsequently through Syria-Iraq-and Iran. On the 25 May the Squadron flew three raids against Maleme airfield, centre point of the German airborne attack. The first raid by six aircraft took off at 0400hrs, led by Stapleton, approached low from the east and bombed from 1900ft, scoring 12 Ju52s destroyed, and an unknown number damaged. Photographs taken during the raid confirmed the destruction and showed over 100 German aircraft on the airfield. All Blenheims returned but Flight Lieutenant Buchanan's Air Gunner, Sergeant Ball sustained a bullet in his foot from small arms fire. The second raid of five aircraft which left at 1046hrs had to turn back when the leaders aircraft developed engine trouble. The third raid of three aircraft in the afternoon mounted against the same target failed to return. Flight Lieutenant Green, Lieutenant Forrester and Sergeant Jeudwine with their crews of Pilot Officer Brown and Sergeants Wilson, Young, Lake, Fretwell and Hall were missing. No report of how, but three more experienced crews lost.

A final raid by the Squadron against Crete had three aircraft piloted by Le Cavalier, Mackenzie and Dickson set out at 0230hrs on the 27 May to bomb enemy troop concentration between Suda Bay and Maleme. Sergeant Dickson's aircraft developed engine trouble, and returned to base. The other two Blenheims completed their bombing and returned to find their base area obliterated by fog.

Le Cavalier's aircraft made its ETA signal to base but shortly after 0740hrs broke radio silence with an SOS. The wreck of the Blenheim was located 30 miles South West of Mersa Matruh with the pilot dead at the controls. The observer, Sergeant Page, and the Air gunner Sergeant Bury had both baled out. Bury was found dead near the aircraft, Page walked across the desert to Mersa Matruh. The remains of Mackenzie's aircraft were found some 60 miles south of El Dhaba. The loss of this crew was of particular concern to the Squadron Commander since it was he who had picked them up after being shot down in enemy territory in Eritrea. Sergeants Fearn, the Air Observer and McConnell the Air Gunner had baled out, and elected to walk north towards the coast. Both were spotted five days later in a swamp near the desert escarpment, - some 45 miles inland from the coast - having lived for five days on snails and berries. Mackenzie had survived the crash, as landing strips (from the emergency desert survival equipment) had been laid out, and the parachute harness, cut free from its silk, hung on a nearby bush. Despite eight days of aircraft and motor bicycle search, Mackenzie was never found.

Apart from two reconnaissances on the 30 May by the Squadron Commander and Flight Lieutenant Illesley - over the desert in the Fort Maddelana/Mechili area looking for possible Rommel moves (negative), and a flight over the Benghazi/Berca/Benina port and airfield complex - photography revealed no build-up of supply activity. The first month in the Western Desert concluded with only three serviceable aircraft and four experienced aircrews.

The operations had exacted a fearful toll on both aircraft and aircrew. From 98 sorties in the month, twelve aircraft had been lost, and 27 aircrew killed or missing. Moreover, if anything, the Squadron had been under-used. This was partially due to the number of fearful dust storms, and to the separate locations of administrative and 2nd Line Servicing, from the aircrews, aircraft and 1st Line Servicing, but mainly in the opinion of the Squadron Commander, to the inefficient direction of the resources of the Squadron by the Desert Headquarters.

On the latter point the Squadron Commander made three observations to the Headquarters. Using Blenheims singly at lower medium heights in daylight against the likelihood of Bf109 interceptions, was to run unnecessary risks. It would have been better to fly them high or very low, or, if medium heights for bombing had to be accepted, in formations of about six where the bomber could rely on cross fire support for defence. If then casualties did occur, at least one knew what had happened. Secondly there was not a cross-fertilisation of ideas and discussions over problems between Headquarters staff and the Squadron. Lastly not enough use was being made of single night attacks, and the provision of an emergency landing strip far enough into the desert to be free of coastal fogs.

The Air Headquarters remedied what they could of these observations which were held also by other Blenheim Commanders.

The Headquarters were under pressure from the Army to provide more reconnaissance over Rommel's positions, and had been from the theatre Headquarters in Cairo over criticism of the RAF for not having done enough in attacking the Germans in Crete. Because our fighters could not reach Crete and return, Wellingtons operations at night from the Egyptian Delta, and the Blenheim operations from the Desert, were used to attack the points of German entry to Crete - Maleme, Suda Bay and Heraklion. Unfortunately to no great effect though the losses sustained by the Ju52s and the German Airborne Division meant that the latter never operated in this role again.

The small force available to General Freyberg Commanding the Allied Forces in the defence of Crete was overwhelmed, and evacuation took place under severe difficulties with at the end of May, many instances of bravery by the Navy and Sunderland Flying Boat crews. Although there was exculpation, the use of the resources available to the RAF for the defence of Crete was criticised by the other Services, and by those who had to undertake the operations.

The month of June for the Squadron saw no operational flying for the first six days, nor between the 13 to 15th, the 18th to 24th, and the 27th to 30th. A total of 19 days used to train four new crews, accept six new aircraft, and bring up the serviceability of the remainder.

There were two events of note. Between the 7th and 12th, eighteen night sorties were directed against German airfields at Gambut, El Adem, Bu Amud, Martuba, Gazala and Derna Satellite.

For the first time the raids used containers with hundreds of spikes (so that when they fell on airfield or tracks one spike of the four always pointed upwards!) and delay action bombs. The latter caused some dislocation to airfield and traffic, but the spikes were discounted by a German captured by the Army. He stated they had little effect on aircraft as the whole German camp was roused early each morning to walk across the airfield and pick them up. Once this was learned they were not used again.

OPERATION BATTLE-AXE

The second event was Operation *Battle-axe*, mounted on 16 June with the object of joining up with the defenders of Tobruk. The initial phase was to drive through the Halfaya Pass, continue on to the Sidi Omar encampment, and from there to develop a push on to the Trigh Capuzzo to Tobruk. 15 sorties - a formation of 6 then 9 - were flown by the Squadron on the 17th to bomb enemy tanks and transport in the Sidi Omar area. The attacks were successful - confirmed by photographs - with an estimated 12 of the 30 tanks destroyed. A further 9 sorties in support were flown on the 18th against similar targets with unquantifiable results. All aircraft returned safely, but the Army was unable to overcome the German armament superiority, and returned to its original positions.

The only other operations during the month were determined attacks against some 50 German aircraft based at Gazala South. On the first occasion six aircraft of the Squadron joined up with six aircraft each from two other Blenheim Squadrons, and six Marylands from a South African Squadron . Unfortunately, because of cloud cover, the lead Squadron failed to locate the target and all returned with their bombs, but the operation was repeated the following day, the target was attacked, and the bombs fell amongst the dispersed aircraft. Several Bf109s were seen to be lining up for take off, but made no contact and all Allied aircraft returned safely.

June recorded only 54 operational sorties. No aircrew or aircraft casualties, but the mainstay of the work had been borne by the experienced crews. Illesley and Buchanan (both Flight Commanders) ten and seven sorties, Sergeant Moulton and Captain Lewis eight each, Dickson four sorties and the Squadron Commander seven.

Wavell was replaced by Auchinlek as Commander in Chief Middle East on 24 June. The Squadron was notified at the end of the month of an impending move to Palestine as a back up to forces intended to secure Syria and Iraq.

It might at this stage be enlightening to look back at some of the technical, administrative and humanitarian factors that affected life in these Middle East Squadrons:

The structure of an RAF Squadron, unlike unit counterparts in the Navy and Army is very much dependent on its base - whether station, airfield or just landing strip. For some 20 years Squadrons had been based on well equipped Stations (Ramleh and Amman) where the supporting services - medical, administrative, technical workshops, equipment stores etc., - were centralised under station direction. The Squadron was confined basically to its aircraft, aircrew and first line servicing, and the station able to support if necessary one or two more Squadrons at the same location. If, however, the Squadron was required to operate from airfields with virtually no buildings, facilities or other amenities, it had to be restructured on a mobile basis, and all the supporting services attached to it to make its operations as self-contained as possible. It became about twice the size it had been on its peacetime base.

The Squadrons in the Middle East, because of the high mobile requirement, were entirely transportable by vehicle - specialist, load and passenger carriers, cars and so on. In an area subject to surprise air attack, and a volatile army front line, it

Plt Offs Keck & Wilson (RAAF) at LG75, December 1941.

Plt Off Ken 'Cobber'
Wilson RAAF, October
1941.

Flt Lt Leon sketches Major Lewis.

was essential to be dispersed, and at the same time to move as rapidly as possible. The Blenheim Squadrons in the Middle East were therefore split. One half contained the aircraft, aircrew and quick-servicing ground crews, the other half the supporting services. The latter, more often than not in the desert were at a different location.

The system had its penalties, both to command and morale. A Squadron Commander's first duties are to fight his aircraft, bring his aircrews to the highest measure of efficiency, and as well, to command the supporting airmen and services. This was more difficult and time consuming when the Squadron was divided. Moreover the 'rear' element is cut off from the flying successes and failures, a fact all disliked.

Food, health and the mail service (both official and private) were critical items affecting morale in the Desert. Most meals were endless varieties of the same two basic ingredients - bully beef or MacConachies M & V (mutton and veal) stewed, fried, hashed or cold. Water was at a premium. A somewhat saline pint per person; half to the Mess and half to wash and shave. The ingenuity and hygiene of the cooks were directly related to Squadron health, and their acquisition from time to time of sundry pigs, rabbits, chickens and other local delectables, whenever the Squadron was on the move, became a marvel of persuasive acquisition.

The Squadron Adjutant is the CO's right hand man in all these matters. He is the conveyor and interpreter of orders, and the counsellor for grumbles. In the Sudan, the Desert, Syria, Iraq and back to the Desert, Flight Lieutenant Jock Aitken fulfilled this post superbly. A pilot himself in World War I, Jock had the understanding of maturity, and used his judgement to encourage the failing and the halt, and to rescue many a miscreant. Three Squadron Commanders relied on Jock, and all endorsed the award of his well deserved OBE.

SYRIA

As preparations were in hand to move to Palestine a tragedy occurred in the death of Flying Officer Harold Parker - the Squadron Equipment Officer. He it was that had brought the main ground support party by sea from Port Sudan to Heliopolis, where he needed to reorganise the administrative and technical stores supplies to meet the new Squadron structure. On returning in his pick-up van from a conference with the CO at the forward landing ground, he was in collision on the night of the 4 July with an Egyptian Ambulance on the coast road near Daba. The CO visited him about an hour later in a wayside first aid centre but his injuries were sufficiently severe for him to die a few minutes later. The whole Squadron mourned a resourceful officer, dedicated to his duties, and the sad loss of a fine man.

The move to Palestine took place in the first week of July. The aircraft and their crews flew directly from LG21 to Petah Tiqva near Tel Aviv. The ground echelon moved by vehicle to Ismaila, and from Kantara on the Canal by train with their vehicles through El Arish and the Gaza strip to Petah Tiqva. The latter was no more than a 1500yrds strip scraped out from a part of an Arab orange grove, with the main camp scattered in tents erected amongst the trees. All day and night continually irrigated: a welcome contrast to the climatic harshness, the water rations, the dreary food, and the bitter results of two months in the Desert.

The Squadron arrived in Petah Tiqva just in time, to witness the signature of the cease-fire with the French in Syria. The British demand for denial of Syrian bases to Axis forces was followed by some token sporadic French opposition to an occupying British Army column. The ceasefire was signed on 14 July. After a plea from the Squadron Commander to the AOC Palestine, Air Commodore 'Bingo' Brown in Jerusalem, the Squadron gathered up 12 aircraft on the 15th to fly a formation demonstration over Beirut, Homs, Aleppo and Damascus. The flight, undertaken at low level proved its point, and was the only participation by the Squadron in the Syrian diversion.

A move to Iraq to repeat the threat against Syria and Persia was the rumour at the Palestine RAF Headquarters. The opportunity was taken to build up the Squadron to a new establishment; to service aircraft, to train new aircrews, and to give much-needed leave to both ground and aircrew. The strength of the Squadron was now to be 21 aircraft and 20 aircrews, and the fully mobile basis meant some 45 vehicles of various specialities, and a total personnel strength of 180 all ranks. squadron commanders and flight commanders were now respectively to be promoted to wing commanders and squadron leaders, ie Squadron Leader Stapleton to Wing Commander, and Buchanan and Illesley to Squadron Leaders. Leave for aircrew also became compulsory at ten days in every three months. Similarly two weeks in every four months were to be taken by ground crew - not as a privilege of course!

PERSIA

Orders for the move to Iraq came through on 2 August. The ground party started their move on the 3rd August. It took six days from Petah Tiqva via Haifa, Mafraq, the Iraq Petroleum Company pipe line pumping stations of H4, H3, then LG5 and so to the RAF Station at Habbaniya; where previously No 4 Flying Training School had been based, having moved there from Abu Sueir in Egypt. Every vehicle reached Habbaniya after some 800 miles of mostly desert travel. Corporal Macleod - a driver on the road convoy - recounts:"That was really a hell of a journey - the tremendous heat, the clouds of mouth clogging sand and dust carried by the lorries. No one wanted to be behind anybody. In open desert it was devil take the hindmost. We started each day at first light to escape the fierce heat, and rested from midday onwards to next first light."

Twelve aircraft followed on the 10 August, the remaining six aircraft four days later.

Two weeks were spent at Habbaniya, the airmen in tents and the aircrew in tents and rooms at the officers and sergeants messes. Two other Blenheim Squadrons (Nos 11 and 45) had arrived, transferred by air to Habbaniya then the largest RAF base overseas. A base which had just come through a traumatic and remarkably brave episode in beating off the attack of a section of the Iraqi Army inspired to revolt by Raschid Ali and his German advisers.

Ray Ball, a member of the previously mentioned catering staff of persuasive acquirers had come up from Petah Tiqva in a Blenheim. His account of Habbaniya follows:

'We couldn't believe our luck being sent to Habb. The kitchens were all electric, the billets air cooled, like staying in a Holiday Inn, but they didn't make us very welcome. They thought we were a scruffy lot. Habb was a peace time station complete with native servants, swimming pools, cinema etc. and real beds. We couldn't understand why the airmen there got a daily overseas allowance of l0d to allow them to live in luxury whilst we, in the desert, got 4d. When we moved to Gaiyara, we could take the beds, so we took as many boards as possible. I also took a large steel cabinet for kitchen or orderly room. There was a bit of an uproar, but on the return journey I remember the Adjutant Flight Lieutenant Jock Aitken, with a twinkle in his eye, reminding me to behave myself. I did, but managed to exchange the cabinet for one with a lock on it!'

At Habbaniya there was a definite frisson between all the members of the Squadron and their hosts. The Squadron and Flight Commanders plus some of the Commonwealth pilots were not slow to contrast the facilities of Habbaniya with those of a mobile tented desert Squadron. A ludicrous episode occurred which led to various harangues in several senior offices.

A cook airman mindful of his future menus had acquired a goose from Petah Tiqva. To build up a later beneficence he used to walk it with a string tied round its neck. At Habb because the Squadron was accommodated in tents on the race track at the edge of a runway, the goose owner inadvertently strolled across the hallowed landing strip one evening when aircraft were on the approach. Ructions followed in the Control Tower, splutterings in charge rooms, and confiscation of goose, but all ended happily with a rescue by Aitken.

As No 14 was the only fully equipped mobile Squadron it moved on 21 August to Gaiyara some 15 miles south of Mosul, adjacent to biblical Nineveh - in Kurd country, and from there it was to operate against Northern Persia.

Gaiyara, like a sizeable area of Iraq north of Kirkuk was flat desert scrub on a sand and oil base. A runway 1800 yards long had been made from a rolled mixture of sand, crushed rock, and tar oil, and it stank of sulphur as only crude can. Three large mud-brick single room blocks served as three messes - of which more later. It was hot, smelly, and a number of men went down with sand fly fever (akin to malaria, but without its long term effects).

The strategic position in Persia was that the ruler, Reza Shah, though originally a British Protégé in a 1921 military coup, had become increasingly hostile to British interests, and had attracted to his own country, a considerable number of German and Italian businessmen, technicians, and 'tourists'. Apart from this, the German invasion of Russia had begun on 21 June 1941, and an Allied supply route through Persia to Russia could compliment the northern sea route to Murmansk, via the railway that ran from the Persian Gulf to the Caspian Sea. Lastly there were the vital British controlled oil supplies from Abadan. On 19 July Britain and the USSR presented a joint démarche to Reza Shah calling for the expulsion of German nationals 'engaged in political activities'. The failure to comply ensured a second démarche giving a further week to comply. It brought no result, so both the USSR and Britain began a joint invasion of Persia on 25 August.

The naval action, commanded by, Commodore Cosmo Graham, included the Aircraft Carrier Hermes. Abadan, the port of Bander Shah, and the railway terminal, were captured by the 8th Indian Division after landing from naval craft.

The ground forces commanded by General Quinan, the General Officer Commanding in Chief in Iraq planned a two-pronged advance. One towards Kermanshah, (via the Pal Tak Pass in the north) and the other to Abadan in the South using the 8th and 10th Indian Divisions.

The first priority for the air forces commanded by Air Vice Marshal D'Albiac was to destroy the Persian Air Force. The second priority was to drop leaflets on the capital, Tehran, and the other main cities, to point out the reasons for the invasion, and to avoid bloodshed by persuading the Persian authorities to comply with Allied demands. The aircraft were not to bomb key points as it was assessed by the

British Embassy in Tehran that most Persians were pro-British.

The Squadrons at Habbaniya and the aircraft from Hermes attacked the Persian Air Force at Ahwaz - near Abadan destroying 50 aircraft, and virtually eliminating the PAF.

Gaiyarah October 1941. Photo of all ranks. Prior to handover by Stapleton on either side of whom Buchanan & Illesly (F/Cdr's).

No 14 Squadron undertook four leaflet dropping operations on 25, 26, 27 and 28 August. The towns of Tehran, Kasvin, Qum, Hamadan, Kermanshah, Senna, Takistan and Zanjan were overflown by formations of 11, 6, 5 and 6 Blenheims dropping a total of 118,000 leaflets. The Squadron Commander led on the first and third raids, and the two Flight Commanders led on the second and fourth sorties. Some opposition was thought possible from fighter aircraft over Tehran, but neither aircraft nor A/A fire was encountered on any of the sorties.

The main difficulty on these operations was the behaviour of the Mercury engines. Tehran was some 400 nautical miles away, and although the theoretical range of the Blenheim was 1450nm, modifications - gun pods, desert camouflage and volkes filters etc. - had reduced this to nearer 1000nm. Consequently the flights to Tehran and other long distant raids, were near marginal. Flights had to be at 10,000ft using the leanest fuel mixture with supplementary oil tanks. These conditions caused three of the first raid to return early to Gaiyara, and engine failure in Illesley's aircraft on the fourth raid caused a crash in the Zagros mountains, luckily without harm to its crew.

Twelve new crews from the UK had joined the Squadron at Petah Tiqva in Palestine, and all were used on the flights over Persia. The target point for leaflet distribution over Tehran had been designated by the Squadron Commander as the British Embassy on Ferdowsi Avenue in the centre of the city! It was rewarding to be told some days later that of the 60,000 leaflets a few had actually fallen in the Embassy garden! The leaflet drop over Kermanshah occurred just prior to its occupation by General Slim with the advance of the Northern Army Column from Iraq.

Operations by all three British services against Persia virtually ceased at the end of August. The Persian authorities had capitulated to all Allied demands, but it took political manoeuvrings, the occupation of designated areas by British and Russian forces, and the abduction of the Shah to South Africa where he died in 1944 - to the end of September, to complete the occupation.

Meanwhile the Squadron had then been designated as non-operative. A training plan was introduced concentrating on formation and night flying practice. The only two practices of note were on 9 September: 12 aircraft from each of the three Blenheim Squadrons flew in a 36 aircraft formation low over the main cities of Persia. Starting on the 25 September, the Squadron contributed 18 sorties over three days to mock bombing, strafing and reconnaissance work with the Army.

Ron Haley, an Australian who joined the Squadron at Port Sudan records his memories of Iraq. From Palestine, he wrote 'We stopped at RAF Habbaniya and had the luxury of beds and good meals. We climbed over the wall to a swimming pool in the moonlight. It's amazing there always seemed to be a full moon in the Middle East. The Mess at Gaiyara consisted of one block and EPI tents. We were supplied with something like Valor stoves. Smelly and smoky in a tent so we moved them outside and used a trench. Once or twice a week I went into the native village and bought chickens. Scraggy, but a change. From what I remember the rations were quite good. We even had bread, but because we were in Indian Command, we received curry powder by the ton, none of it like the curry powder we were used to.'

One evening he and a friend were invited to a meal with the Sheikh of Gaiyara. 'Sitting on carpets and rolling rice balls, then popping them into our mouths with stewed lamb. Later I bought a colourful jacket for the Sheikh's son, and he by return on our departure back to Habb, gave me two daggers the handles ornamented with silver.'

The rumour was that the Squadron was destined for a return to the Western Desert. The news came through on 4 October. On 8 October the Squadron convoy lined up on the Gaiyara runway for a last inspection by the Squadron Commander. They left at 0630hrs to arrive in Habbaniya at 1600hrs the next day. All the aircraft left at 0930hrs to arrive at Habbaniya the same morning.

Wing Commander Stapleton handed over command to John Buchanan, now promoted to Wing Commander on the 10 October. Buchanan was destined to become something of a legend in the Middle East. Stapleton had been continuously with the Squadron since March 1937, as a Pilot Officer then through Flight Commander to Squadron Commander in September 1940. He was awarded an AFC in 1939 for counter insurgency operations in Palestine, and an immediate DFC in 1940 for the rescue of the New Zealander Mackenzie and his crew in Eritrea. He completed over 100 operational missions with the Squadron, and left to join the staff of Air Vice-Marshal Coningham at Air Headquarters Western Desert.

On 12 October the road convoy left Habbaniya for Ramleh in Palestine, night stopping along the same route they had taken from Palestine to Iraq. They arrived on the 16th for a break of three days during which vehicle repairs were completed. They left on the 19th via Gaza and El Arish, reached east of the Suez Canal, then on to the Nile Delta. On the 21st they got to Burg el Arab, on the road just west of Alexandria and finally on the 22nd to LG 116 near Fuka, which was a second road journey of some 800 miles.

THE BEBE INTERLUDE

Not all the journey was unrewarding. Raymond Ball of the entrepreneurial cook's section once again had some comments on life in the Western Desert.

153

'Getting the pig ('Bebe' so called after Bebe Daniels with Ben Lyon, radio come-
dians at the time) on the ration strength started off during a social evening spent
in the house of Baron Von Manesch, a prominent socialite of Alexandrian European
exiles. Manesch or 'George' as we were all allowed to call him, was a very wealthy
Austrian nobleman domiciled in Egypt for many years who used to entertain RAF
personnel every week-end in his large mansion in Alexandria. It was by invitation,
but once you had been there it was easy to gate-crash again. The food was excellent, coffee and ice cream great, and at one of these sessions I happened to mention how I missed 'roast pork'. Of course the chances of pork in a Muslim country
were pretty rare, or so we thought. However 'George' our ever willing host said he
knew a French family some few miles away in the Delta who kept and bred pigs
and he'd arrange for us at least to buy a 6 to 7 week old weaner. So when we
returned to our base we had a whip round and collected £50 and awaited a message to come re picking up our own porker.

This duly arrived via the next weekenders' return and transport was duly organised through a stores trip to Aboukir. On our way back we called in at the farm,
and the French family was much amused and said we were to help ourselves from
a pen of about 20 weaners. In we dived and sorted out the largest one, about 3
score pounds and they refused to take our money. So far so good.

We arrived at Burg-el-Arab only to find we were moving up to Maaten-Bagush,
overtaking those in the advance unit at El Daba (L.G.21) although we called in at
Daba for our kit etc., and introduced Bebe to all and sundry. We also managed to
find a long box to put Bebe in whilst travelling. Rather like a deep coffin. We
arrived in Maaten-Bagush late evening, and were about to get settled in when from
the sea came a very fast 'Blenheim' as we thought. It also fired a flare and we all
said as one "Colour of the Day" but not really knowing, then we saw little black
blobs falling out, and then the black cross on the wings and very soon the crunch
of the bombs. Regrettably they fell in the Transport Section, and very close to the
Photography trailer, and two LAC's of the Photography Section were killed, both
with their knife, fork, mugs and plate in their hands. Bebe was still in her box and
unharmed. It was a near thing because we had intended to make a 'pigsty' for her
out of a ring of 50 gallon petrol drums.

Next day we put her out in the flights and made a sty of bomb boxes and
ammunition boxes and 50 gallon oil drums, and whilst all these objects were
heavy whilst loaded, when they were empty Bebe was able to push them about
and escape into the blue. This happened one morning at about six o'clock and
Bebe ran off down the perimeter of the drome (landing ground) and was spotted
by the Army Bofors Squad. One likely gunner came out from the Post with a .303
and was about to take a pot shot at our 'Bebe'. Fortunately No 14 Squadron stalwarts were in hot pursuit, and managed to thwart the squaddie who insisted he'd
seen it first and thought it was a wild boar. I must say this. All our 'erks' became
potential pig farmers from this introduction to farming whilst on active service.
One thing was certain no lurking Bedouin would pinch our Christmas dinner. We
fed Bebe on soaked Army biscuits, soya sausages and corn beef, oatmeal and yams
(sweet potatoes). She did very well, she was not of course fat but quite firm and
nice and killed out very well.

We had a French Chef's knife and we managed to get it sharpened to a very nice point etc. and the Great Day came. We split open a 50 gallon drum and boiled it clean over a kettle trench and then scalded the pig in it. We had two air frame or wing gantries and with much help managed to crane it in and out of the drum of hot water. Although I say it myself, we made a very good job of it, and for some two or three hours somewhere between Mersa-Matruh and Sidi Barrani, a little bit of English village life was enacted. Some had liver and bacon for breakfast. Some had pork chops for lunch and we all (forward flight) had roast pork for dinner - unfortunately a little early for Christmas, but, all be it, we had a very luscious feed by way of a change.'

The aircraft left Habbaniya on 26 October for a stay of a week at Lydda in Palestine (no one now remembers why), finally arriving on 4 November at LG 15 some five miles north-west of LG 116.

Deployment of the Squadron from the Western Desert to Palestine for the Syrian campaign - virtually over when it arrived - had allowed time for recovery from and replacement of casualties suffered in the Desert and over Crete. The deployment to Iraq however turned out operationally to be something of an anticlimax.

One accepts the logic of the deployment of two operationally-experienced Middle East Squadrons to a Command faced with unknown risks from a country ordered to rid itself of Axis influence. And one also accepts that it was provident initially to attack the Persian Air Force, and to drop leaflets rather than bombs on the capital and major cities of Iran. In the event however there was a sense of overkill since capitulation came very quickly with virtually no casualties to either Army or Air Force operations.

Although drawing the short straw over the nature of its operations, the tasks were understood, yet at no time did the command staff bother to brief the Squadron on the strategic background, or the reasons for the choice of location. So some of the administrative contretemps at the time were not treated with much amusement. There was a whiff of the Pukka Sahib attitude from those still ensconced in the facilities of air-conditioned barrack blocks, beds, swimming pools, and curry, towards those Desert Rats who only recently had left a pint of water a day, bully beef and biscuits and ridge tents dug into the sand. Minor escapades - like the goose on the runway - ended up in charges, and the CO had to face an inquiry when the officers mud block at Gaiayra had its roof destroyed by fire. The contractor was eventually fined, as he had centred the main supporting roof beam through the fire place chimney!

BACK IN THE DESERT

Meanwhile the Squadron was now back in the Desert once more on a split structure basis, after an absence of five months in Syria and Iraq. On 24 July after the failures of Brevity and Battle-axe, General Auckinleck went to London to forestall pressure for an early offensive. Reassured by the promise of reinforcements, he was able to convince the Chiefs of Staff and Churchill to wait until mid-November to launch a full offensive, rather than an earlier limited operation to relieve Tobruk. Operation *Crusader*, intended to drive the Axis from Cyrenaica, was launched by the Allies on 15 November.

Over the next five months the Squadron was continuously engaged in attacks against the Axis Air Force bases including Crete once again, and in support of the Army.

Rommel.

Wg Cdr Buchanan briefing before raid.

R to L: Flt Lt Whittard, Wg Cdr
Buchanan, Major Lewis (SAAF).

Cpl Hanson acquires 2 German
motorcycles 13 January 1942.

The combination of severe winter weather of flash floods and sandstorms,
the short-notice airfield moves by both halves of the Squadron in the gallop west
across Cyrenaica, and the subsequent withdrawal to Egypt, plus the difficulties of
maintaining technically sophisticated aircraft, was to take a noticeable toll of men,
aircraft and equipment.

Two or three improvements were at once apparent in flying operations. The Air
Headquarters under Air Vice-Marshal 'Mary' Coningham (a New Zealander, hence
Maori = Mary!) had acquired three ex-Squadron Commanders on his staff, and the
relationship with squadrons became a welcome two-way exchange. His method of
operating Blenheim Squadrons acknowledged their vulnerabilities. Mostly, but not
always, they went by night singly, or in formations by day often with fighter
escorts. Lastly, there was a much more homogeneous feel between the Squadrons
operating in the desert in different roles, and a far more realistic and closer relationship with the Army.

Asked many months later to record some impressions whilst on the staff of
Coningham, Stapleton wrote:

'On my previous experience of operations in the Desert I had been critical of
the remoteness of the HQ staff from the Squadrons. Coningham had remedied this
by appointing on the operations staff under Group Captain George Beamish - of
Irish Rugby fame - his SASO (senior air staff officer) two general training instructors, one to specialise on fighter requirements, the other for the bombers. Two ex
Squadron Commanders were chosen, Wing Commander Peter Wykeham-Barnes,
(later to become Air Marshal Sir Peter Wykeham) from No 80 Squadron of fighters
and myself from No 14 Squadron. "You- are to be my ears and eyes with the
squadrons" said Coningham "I want to know their successes, their foul-ups, their
problems and their ideas. You will be briefing them on some operations, get to
know them, fly with them and keep me advised through the SASO. There is a staff

car and a Gladiator each to get you around, and I don't want to see much of you in the HQ." Peter and I were delighted, almost no desk-flying involved, and with a pretty free rein for ideas.

For a few weeks Peter shared a tent with me at the HQ with its customary 6 x 5 x 4 feet deep bomb protection hole under the canvas. We were occasionally hosts to visitors from Cairo HQ, from other RAF formations, and from the Army including David Stirling of LRDG fame, soliciting help from Coningham when he couldn't get all he wanted from the Army. One morning both of us returning from dawn flights arrived to find that a flash rain storm had flooded the domestic tent lines. Our hole had two feet of water with most of our belongings including the camp beds floating on the surface. Worst of all was Peter's sodden box of cigars. Rescued, along with other dripping clothes he laid them out singly to dry on a towel in the beaming sunshine. Returning from breakfast, inspection of the precious weeds revealed all had bloomed like brown orchids held firmly to the stalk by the cigar band!

Shortly afterwards Peter was lucky to avoid his curtains when an Bf110 bounced him from cloud when returning in his Gladiator. Beamish listened sympathetically to our argument that it was difficult to fly in company with the Squadrons with a Gladiator when they were operating in Hurricanes and Kittihawks, Blenheims and Marylands. Our slow Gladiators were replaced with Hurricanes, and after the tiring Blenheims I felt like a pilot reborn. It took the bomber squadrons quite some time to find out who was the lone Hurricane that occasionally accompanied them on a raid!'

The pre-Crusader air operations in November were directed against the German Air Force. On the 9th, five aircraft singly attacked by night the air stores area of Gazala North. Some fires were started. A counter attack was made by the German dive-bombers at 1730hrs the following day. One airman (LAC Turner of the Squadron photographic section) was killed, and one of the No 113 Squadron Blenheims was damaged. On the 12th six Blenheims night-attacked the maintenance area, this time of Gazala South. This time leaflets were also dropped, but though the bombs fell in the target area results were unassessable due to ground mist.

WESTWARD HO!

The 14th, 15th and 16th were recorded as quiet days, 'getting ready for the gallop west'. On the 17th, six aircraft were briefed to attack German aircraft and storage areas at Gambut, but as the leaders bombs hung up, due to a faulty accumulator, all returned without bombing to LG 75, where one day later the ground convoy arrived. Meanwhile the flight had been supplemented by all available aircraft from LG 15, and four aircraft attacked Bir el Baheira where 12 German aircraft were bogged down from rainstorms. Bombs landed amongst them.

From 19 November to the end of December intensive activity was directed in support of Army operations. After a slow start from the Allied offensive, Rommel began to withdraw westwards and the retreating German columns came under severe pressure from bombing and strafing attacks. On the 19th, and on every day until the 1st December, some 124 sorties were flown against tank and transport targets on the Tobruk, Bardia, El Adem and Acroma tracks. On the 25th, one of the most active days in the Squadron's history, 32 sorties were despatched against a large concentration of vehicles moving south from Sidi Omran. Rod adapters - designed to explode bombs just above ground level to maximise the shrapnel effect - and leaflets to lower German morale were used extensively during these raids. There was some slight damage to aircraft from AA fire, but no casualties were incurred.

In December, despite deteriorating weather conditions and constant movement, intense flying activity was again maintained, and 146 sorties were flown by 21 aircrew, averaging seven raids per crew in the month. The pressures told, and there were casualties to crews and aircraft. A system of stand down for full servicing was introduced rotating through all the Squadrons in the Wing. More effort was called for on the days of stand by, and remedial administrative and technical matters including vehicle problems were dealt with on stand down days. There were six stand down days in December, and sandstorms prevented operations on three others.

On 1 December the Squadron provided six aircraft, with a further 18 from Nos 45, 84 and the 'Free French' Lorraine Squadrons. These 24 aircraft with a fighter escort, mounted an attack from 7300ft, against some 200 armoured fighting vehicles. Bombs were assessed as on target, anti aircraft as little, and all aircraft returned.

On four days in the first half of December, 27 sorties were flown against armoured fighting vehicles, refuelling points, and soft skin vehicles on roads west of Derna, El Gubbi, and Bir el Gobi. On the 9th, flying independently, using cloud cover, Sergeant Grimsey, attacked a gun emplacement at Bomba, but because of petrol shortage, failed to reach base. He and his crew, Sergeants Spiller and Miller had to make a parachute jump, which they did successfully, and subsequently reached the Squadron after a desert walk.

On the 14th, eight Blenheims flying independently using cloud cover attacked transport on the Derna, Bardia and Capuzzo roads. Little AA fire was encountered, and no fighter opposition, but Flying Officer Dennis and his crew of Sergeants Campbell and Redfern did not return. Between the 17th and 21st, four aircraft were lost, two from engine failure and two from landing and take-off crashes. All aircrew were unhurt, but one of the aircraft on take off crashed through a tent killing the occupants Sergeant Chubb, an air observer, and two air gunners, Sergeants Jenkins and Ellis.

From the 17th to the end of the month, intense operations continued against a variety of targets as the Germans retreated westwards. Targets were not easy to pin down sufficiently long for the bombers to be briefed after reconnaissance, and then to fly to the map reference and identify the target. Attacks were flown against aircraft at Barce Megrun and against Bir el Baheira on the 18th where German aircraft were bogged down on the airfield. It was on this raid that Pilot Officer O'Laughlin and his crew of Pilot Officers Main and Franks were lost. Their grave was later found dug by the Germans and inscribed on a simple cross 'to 3 brave airmen'. Attacks were also mounted against traffic south of Agedabia, but mainly and heavily against a defensive position at Bardia. The latter took 20 bombing raids on the 27th, followed by 20 each on the 29th and 30th. On these days and on the 29th, many additional sorties were flown against traffic south of Msus; 80 in four days. Bombing in the main was successfully scored on the Bardia defensive area, attacks varying from 7,000 down to 2,200ft. Only one aircraft was damaged by AA fire. The Squadron was telephoned by 270 Wing Headquarters on the 27th to say that the Army considered the bombing had been accurate and effective. The Wing also congratulated the Squadron on the photographs taken, confirming several verbal and visual damage assessments.

During these months of Crusader advance, and the start of Rommel's resurgence, Pilot Officer John Willis, who joined the Squadron in the desert as a Sergeant Pilot direct from No 4 FTS at Habbaniya in June 1941, has recorded his impressions of operations and life in the Desert at that time:

'By Christmas 1941 the Squadron had members from nearly every Commonwealth Nation; and while one could say there was a British Command, undoubtedly the strong presence of crews from Australia, Canada, New Zealand and South Africa made an informal approach to command and discipline a natural outcome. If that was coupled with the primitive conditions on the advanced landing grounds where internal communications across 3 square miles relied on Aldis lights and clanging triangles it followed that 'line command' was often non-existent. Some exclusion from this generalisation should apply to the ground crew who had, to my knowledge, at least one Halton Flight Sergeant (George Hedges - a 'King-size' man) and were all virtually from the U.K.

'Stapleton was keen on formation skills. Buchanan was obsessive about them and demanded the highest standards. The early consequence of this was to determine the nature of command and authority on the Squadron. Whatever criticism there must be of Buck's command on the ground, in the air he was a perfect 'gent'. He knew that Blenheims would always be struggling to take station after take-off - one had about 20 knots in hand to catch leading aircraft. He would stooge around on very wide circuits at low speeds to encourage early linkups. On course he was steadiness itself. So, it was possible to formate with one's port or starboard wing right over his complementary wing in complete confidence that he would not budge. So, with his strict adherence to performance, he could always put up a perfect box of 6 and have a sporting go at 9 and 12. He once took 6 of us on cloud-cover raid. I flew in the No 4 position on that occasion, and was quite scared with a stiff neck. The beneficial result of this for the crews was that we always seemed to lead any wing formation raids, and any casualties from fighters were with trailing squadrons. No 14, to my knowledge, was never attacked as a unit in Wing or Squadron formation. Furthermore, at Christmas 1941 when Blenheim Squadrons were sent to the Far East they significantly left No 14 with the Middle East Command.'

The unremitting urge of Buchanan to fly, whether on tests, training, or operations, tended to leave his Flight Commanders short of experience in flight leadership. Squadron Leader Tony Smythe joined No 14 Squadron as a Flight Commander in October 1941, left only two months later to take command of No 11 Blenheim Squadron, yet never was able to lead any of the eighteen bombing operations he completed with the Squadron!

Willis now turned to a famous, near scandalous episode in No 14's desert history. It concerned an American journalist named Morley Lister. 'My recall of Morley Lister was that of a physically imposing woman, bright auburn hair and standing near six feet. Her 'Campaign Trousseau' was a USA bottle-green tailored suit with a press flash. My hunch is that she was from Boston. She came, I guess, officially to see a Bomber Squadron in the heat of battle for we were flying our pants off thereabouts with the Germans still in hasty retreat. My awareness that something was odd came when a semi-official request was put to me to offer my camp bed (unusable in a hole bivouac) for use by Morley. It was returned within 2 days squashed flat!

Morley flew with Buck on perhaps 6 raids. I formated on her beacon-like auburn head on 2 or 3. Certainly Joe Elliott flew No 3 (more difficult) on one of these. Flight Lieutenant Whittard was the Observer. When we were returning from Agedabia I saw Buck's wing tip open up from light flak - so she was courting risks then. When we landed Buck summoned Elliott and myself to his tent where Morley and he faced us with glasses in hand. He commended us most graciously for our discipline in staying 'tight' and then gently rebuked Joe for flying so tight that Buck's aileron control was sloppy from airflow turbulence!'

Stapleton adds that Air Vice-Marshal Coningham asked the American Ambassador in Cairo to invite Morley Lister to return to Cairo as her journalistic accomplishments appeared to have been completed! She left the Squadron with regret, a well admired 'Life' correspondent.

January 1942 was to prove another month of intensive flying. Axis ground and air forces had pulled out to just west of Antelat, but a pocket of resistance had been left at Halfaya Pass.

On New Year's Day 1942 the COs of No 14 and the Lorraine Squadron were ordered by the Group Captain Commanding 270 Wing, to send seven aircraft each to Msus. They were to be armed with 250lb bombs fused instantaneous with rod adapters, and were to be there at first light, where briefing and fighter escort was to be arranged. If both Squadrons were to operate together then No 14 Squadron was to lead the formation.

In fact three aircraft from No 14 Squadron flew to Msus that day where they led the Lorraine Squadron and No 11 Squadron, on a sortie to bomb enemy concentrations of motor transport, south east of Agedabia. Due to low cloud (base at 2500ft) bombing took place at 2000ft. The concentration of transport was reported to have been well dispersed so little damage was done. Most of the flight was hit by AA and one aircraft from No 11 Squadron was shot down.

Another report, which does not give a date for the sortie it describes, states that five aircraft led a Wing Formation one evening to a pin point where they found a concentration of approximately 75 well dispersed Motor Transporters. They bombed from 2000ft because of the low cloud. One direct hit and several near misses were reported, confirmed by photographs. The AA was mainly from Italian Breda AA cannon, both strong and accurate.

On 2 January four aircraft were on standby all day for further sorties at Msus. However, they were not ordered off the ground, primarily because of the appalling state of the landing ground. After a night of heavy rain the sickbay was flooded under a foot of water while the rest of the camp was under six inches or more.

In the early hours of 3 January, five aircraft flew to Msus but returned in the evening without having flown a sortie as no target was found for them. On this day, two other aircraft bombed Halfaya Pass independently.

On 5 January five aircraft bombed Halfaya Pass. The aircraft bombed independently from a height of 5000ft and attacked gun emplacements, fortifications, motor transports in wadis, and a suspected enemy headquarters in the pass. Some flak was experienced in the early part of the day but diminished as the day wore on. A large number of photographs were taken. On the last sortie of the day a small patrol boat was seen, which after some difficulty, identified itself as friendly. One report said that twelve sorties were carried out that day and a great deal of damage was inflicted.

Next day, seven sorties were flown over the Pass. The focus for the attack was once again gun emplacements and motor transport in wadis. Good results were reported. Until midday the target area was seldom clear of aircraft, but at this time a sandstorm blew up and further operations stopped. Very little AA fire was experienced.

John Willis was much involved on these attacks and records one sortie as follows:

'Getting a 'bullseye' at Halfaya Pass. Halfaya though cut off for many weeks held out over Christmas '41 and the New Year '42. German Ju 52 transports were used at night to drop provisions and goodies; they made special efforts for that Christmas. No 14 flying from Gambut, would go over in single daylight raids and keep chivvying them.

'The Germans, both personnel and M.T. were well dug in. So, there were no obvious targets; but equally there seemed to be no AA of any consequence - the nearest being at Bardia where an 88mm 'Bardia Bill' was active and too accurate for comfort. One would stooge around at 3000ft and the observer would release four 250lb bombs to no particular effect. My log book records that on 5/6/7 January we made single aircraft raids each days and this included ground strafing. But even then I did not see the enemy. On 7 January 1942 I told Eric Barr - my observer that I wanted him to hold the 4th Bomb and I would 'dive bomb' and press the 'tit' release myself. There must have been some confusion in my mind because a Blenheim released its bombs by simple gravity where the weight forced open the bomb bay doors secured by heavy caliper thongs. If you couple that with the 9 inch detonating rods, the simple expedient of going into a vertical dive and releasing the selected bomb was not necessarily going to produce greater accuracy: it might even get jammed in the bay and make any return landing at Gambut a moving occasion!

'However, Eric did not reason otherwise and I, relieved that we were not going to have an argument one way or the other, quickly responded on seeing an escarpment where there were six MT of modest size alongside a wooden shack which I took to be some command post where, perhaps, local commanders were meeting. I had settled for flying at 4000ft and diving for no more than 2000ft on the premise that the aircraft might lock-up at whatever speed I might reach after that descent. I had two things going for me: I was very sure that Blenheims were capable of violent manoeuvre around 40 knots (taxying gave one this conviction) and the single .300 Browning gun in the starboard wing was aligned on the wing chord. For good measure the cockpit gunsight gave one the precise alignment that dive bombing would require. The only 'flaw' in this novel theory was the need for an unimpeded gravity bomb release; a requirement that never entered my tiny mind!

'It was all over in a minute or so: having spotted the target immediate below my port wing I throttled right back, pulled the Blenheim up vertically from 160 knots and rapidly slowed to 40 knots kicked savagely to port and keeled over dolphin-like into the vertical dive right over the target - almost spot on as it happened. A very minor adjustment on the rudder and elevators and the target was dead centre in the gun sight. At this point airspeed was still only 190 knots; but then in rapid succession and in no recalled order, I found that I pressed the tit and encountered fierce turbulence which seemed partially to lock the controls. I could not understand this because 190 knots was still well below maximum speed for the Mk IV. Many years later I concluded that the bomb having been freed from its fastenings was 'floundering' in the bay, and perhaps emerged free at the point I pulled out - the pull out was done on trim because I did not like the locking-up that had developed. The closing proximity to the ground at 2000ft was not really a perceived danger. I wheeled away in a recovery dive looked back and saw we had had a direct hit on the wooden building: no flame - just seemingly a massive sand cloud burst where the building had been.

'Two or three months later, when Eric returned from a New Zealand hospital in the Delta suffering a broken ankle from our late February bale-out over Martuba, he told me he met a New Zealander in hospital who had been in a POW pen at Halfaya when we had bombed and saw the direct hit. Unfortunately, he seemed unaware of the command status of the hut and the significance of the MT parked there'.

7 January was described in one report as, 'A much better day and with five serviceable aircraft we carried out 24 sorties against Halfaya. Only the possible shortage of bombs made Wing HQ call us off'. Another report said that, from heights varying from 2000 to 5000ft, the Squadron dropped 92 250lb bombs on gun emplacements, fortifications, buildings and motor transport in Halfaya Pass. Photographs taken show that direct hits were obtained, and considerable damage done. There was very little AA fire and none of No 14 Squadron's aircraft were hit.

On the same day an order was sent to the COs of No 14 and the Lorraine Squadron from No 270 Wing detailing the following day's duties. Lorraine Squadron was to provide two aircraft every hour with the first two reaching the target at 0830hrs. No 14 Squadron was also to provide two aircraft every hour with their first sortie to be over the target at 0900hrs. Targets had the following priority: enemy shipping, Gun emplacements, motor transport (as indicated in photographs) and enemy Headquarters suspected at a point indicated on the map supplied and other motor transport and encampments in wadis.

Briefing was to take place before departure at 0730hrs for Lorraine Squadron, and 0800hrs for No 14 Squadron. The orders directed that a total of 19 sorties were to be flown next day. These were completed but a further 15 sorties were flown against Halfaya Pass. The Squadron gained 'good results'. Clearly one advantage that day was that the AA encountered was so slight and only when the aircraft bombed from 2000ft did they experience any at all. A report recorded that at least six direct hits were scored on enemy positions by bombing individually from heights of 2000 to 5000ft. Two vehicles were seen to overturn and a fire started. AA was slight and confined to Breda cannon, allowing one aircraft to descend to 1000ft, and to machine gun two light AA positions.

Intelligence on 8 January from 270 Wing noted that the enemy was supplying Halfaya by a German Ju 52 early every morning. The Ju 52 was making a landfall north of Halfaya, and following the coast to Sollum where a white and green coloured signal was fired from the aircraft. A circle of flares was then lit at Halfaya, whereupon the Ju 52 descended to about 1000ft and dropped the supplies. An order from 270 Wing intended 'to interfere and upset these supply flights to the maximum, and if possible destroy the enemy aircraft'. The method of operation was to be for two aircraft to be detailed to patrol over Halfaya from 0400 to 0630hrs beginning on the morning of 9 January. A series of details outlining patrol lines and heights, recognition signals, bomb loads and flares were provided with the intention of trapping the Junkers, or at least preventing further supplies from reaching the Germans at the Pass.

On 9 January two aircraft flew the early morning patrols. Weather conditions were bad with little visibility. No flares from the ground were seen, nor any enemy aircraft. The Halfaya targets area was bombed at first light.

The next day two aircraft were again sent to carry out an independent offensive patrol south of Halfaya Pass and had more success than on the previous day. At 0230hrs as the second aircraft approached the pass, a circle of gooseneck flares was observed, and a stick of bombs dropped from south east to north west. The last two bombs dropped near the flares. The first aircraft had left the target area but on seeing the flares returned and bombed twenty minutes later. No enemy aircraft were seen on this occasion although the green/white Very light (the German signal from the air) was spotted. Late in the morning a severe sandstorm blew up, preventing further operations.

One aircraft was ordered to Halfaya Pass on 11 January where, at 0225hrs, it spotted five flares in a circle at the same location as on the 10th. A bombing run was made, and 15 seconds later the flares were dowsed. The enemy aircraft was sighted. but turned out to sea without dropping any supplies once it saw the Blenheim.

Separately from the Halfaya anti-supply operations six aircraft were instructed to proceed to Msus landing ground, to arrive in the afternoon of 9 January so they could be armed with four 250lbs bombs instantaneous fused with rod adapters, in preparation for an operation during 10 January. The aircraft were to operate with No 11 Squadron, but the operation took place that afternoon. The Squadron record gives details of a second sortie on 9 January, which involved six aircraft flying from Gambut, taking off at 0800hrs, and landing at Msus at 1200hrs. After briefing they were escorted by fighters and led four aircraft of No 11 Squadron to bomb a concentration of approximately 75 enemy motor transport east of El Agheila. At least two direct hits were observed and twenty four 250lb bombs were dropped from 6000ft. Intense AA fire came from the target area. Two enemy aircraft were seen, one possibly having been shot down by the fighter escort. Four of the aircraft returned to Gambut, leaving two at Msus.

A sortie on 11 January involved the two aircraft already standing by at Msus joining a formation of No 11 Squadron to bomb motor transport. Pilot Officer Goode and his crew dropped four 250lb bombs, but, Willis and his crew were unable to bomb, due to an electrical release failure. Bombs were seen to hit the target, damaging at least twelve motor transports. No fighter opposition was seen, but on return it was learned that three Kittyhawks of the fighter escort were lost, although all three pilots were safe. The aircraft stayed overnight at Msus, returning to Gambut in the morning.

Another entry in the record of 11 January shows that six aircraft took off in the morning for Msus where, 'provided there are sufficient bombs - they are to spend the night there. This gave a total of eight aircraft at that landing ground.' 12 January was a day of inactivity at No 14's base at Gambut since most of the aircraft were away at Msus on standby. The first sortie of 13 January involved an aircraft flying to LG75, Wing Headquarters gave permission for it to bomb Halfaya Pass en route, and a stick of four 250lb bombs was seen to fall across fortified positions, and may have silenced the one gun which had regularly shown signs of accuracy.

Buchanan led a second sortie of six aircraft on 13 January with four more aircraft from the Lorraine Squadron on a raid on Halfaya pass. Four 250lb were dropped by all aircraft across the German fortified positions seen to be hit. Later in the afternoon Wing Headquarters informed the Squadron they were to 'stand down' completely for four days. Thus, 14 January was the first of the days where both aircraft and motor transport came in for 100% servicing. A considerable amount of catch-up maintenance was done owing to good weather. The armament sections had to fit 500lb bomb racks in preparation for future activity.

Late on the 15th the Squadron received a signal informing them that they were, from 16 January, to be under the command of No 3 South African Wing. The record shows that at 1230hrs on 16 January a break in servicing was caused by Wing calling for three aircraft to bomb Halfaya Pass. The sortie was a formation raid which achieved good results with direct hits on gun positions, and at least one lorry overturned. A small amount of inaccurate AA was encountered, and one aircraft was hit by a bullet in the petrol tank; the crew was uninjured. General servicing continued on the 17th, but at 1400hrs four aircraft joined No 11 Squadron at Bu Amud to 'stand by' for a first light operation next morning. As it turned out, two returned at mid-day without having done anything.

During the afternoon of the 17th word was received that Flight Lieutenant Jock Aitkin, the popular Adjutant, was posted, Flying Officer Robinson added the duties of Adjutant to those of his duties as Intelligence Officer and was rewarded with promotion to Flight Lieutenant.

The Squadron support section, who were about four miles from Gambut moved over to join the operational section, on 18 January once again uniting the whole Squadron.

There was no action next day and the two aircraft with No 11 Squadron returned from Msus without having operated. Six aircraft remained on standby until 1200hrs when they were informed they would not be needed. 20 January was essentially the same as the 19th with six aircraft standing by from 0600hrs until 1200hrs with no operations taking place. All these 'stand bys' with no targets bore out the difficulty of obtaining and acting on requests from Army units in time to be effective.

The record for 21 January begins by noting that, with the disbanding of 270 Wing, it became necessary for the Squadron's Signal Section to begin a double W/T watch, both on aircraft and ground point to point wavelengths. At 1500hrs word was received that all available aircraft were to leave early next morning each loaded with two 500lb Semi Armour Piercing bombs to attack shipping. Twelve aircraft were prepared and crews briefed.

Nine aircraft, re-armed with 250lb bombs, left Gambut at 1020hrs on the 22 January and flew to Msus where they collected fighter escorts. In formation they attacked a large concentration of German motor transport on the El Agheila-Agedabia road. The formation dropped thirty six 250lb bombs, all of which fell slightly wide, the only damage possibly from fragmentation. Some light, accurate AA came from the column itself, striking one aircraft, and while not injuring the crew, damaged the pilots cockpit cover.

Twenty minutes before the target was reached three Messerschmidt 110s were seen to be chasing the formation. As the fighter escort was seen to dive to attack them, the Bf110s turned out to sea. A few moments later, six Bf109s (Es and Fs) attempted to attack the formation but only one succeeded in getting close. His reward was to be fired at, and hit by, three of the Squadron's gunners, although it was not seriously damaged. The report concluded that the Bf110s were intended to act as decoys to the escort. The aircraft landed again at Gambut after more than five hours in the air.

These operations on 21/22 January turned out to be over the beginnings of Rommel's drive to Egypt that was eventually halted at Alamein.

Early next morning nine Blenheims flew to Berka via Benina. They reached Berka at 1045hrs and four of them headed off in search of an Italian convoy believed to be north-west of Benghazi. The area was thoroughly searched until the light failed and nothing was seen of the ships. Two aircraft returned to Gambut that afternoon, and the rest spent the night at Berka. Six aircraft returned from Berka, during the afternoon of the 24th. One aircraft had to be abandoned because it was impossible to repair it before the enemy was expected to arrive.

Seven aircraft flew to Mechili on 25 January where they were briefed to bomb 'anything south of Antelat'. A phrase not normally used by precise RAF target designations and maybe indicating difficult days to come. They left Gambut at 0540hrs and landed at Mechili an hour later. Approximately thirty motor transport were found on the Antelat - Agedabia road. The aircraft flew in formation, and although the target was well dispersed close bomb bursts were seen and two vehicles overturned. During another raid later that morning, 24 250lb bombs were dropped from 6000ft against the same target with unquantifiable results. Shortly after noon they learned that the Squadron was to be split again; the base party to remain at Gambut, while the operational section moved up to Bu Amud. Preparations began

166

for a move at dawn next day, but a sudden sandstorm forced a delay until the next morning.

Seven aircraft flew from Gambut, to Mechili early on the 27th. Four of the aircraft were briefed to locate and bomb enemy concentrations south of Mechili and they were provided with a fighter escort. Unfortunately they failed to find the enemy and had to return to Mechili with their bomb loads, where they spent the night.

Meanwhile, on the evening of the 27th the ground staff began their move to Bu Amud. Due to a lack of transport, a shuttle system was used. Lorries would unload at the new landing ground and immediately return to Gambut for a fresh load. Rain delayed movements but by nightfall the operational party, with the exception of B Section, was established at Bu Amud. where they dug in and erected tents. The main Squadron servicing echelon remained at Gambut.

Surprisingly, over the last few days of January no operational action took place. The aircraft were held in readiness , wrote the Squadron recorder, 'but were not called upon the operate'.

WITHDRAWAL EASTWARDS

The speed of Rommel's recovery from his own retreat caught the Allied forces by surprise. Sustained by modest reinforcements, the Axis had built up during late December and January a mobile striking force that soon probed, then overcame the Allied ground force screens. Stretched to the limits of their supply lines, and now backed mostly by troops inexperienced in desert warfare, there were flashes of disorder as the Allies fell back.

For the Allied air forces, reliant on the ground forces for the security of their bases, the withdrawal eastwards posed problems of technical support and provision that strained the whole RAF organisation of the Middle East. The situation bit deep into the resources needed to have available the fuel, armament, and spares at the right time, when ephemeral forward landing strips were lost almost overnight.

In the first six months of 1942, until the allied defensive line stabilised in July at Alamein, there were as many heroics on the ground as there were in the air. The resourcefulness and endurance of the ground crews were sorely tested yet seldom found wanting, and they suffered their casualties too.

THE STRUCTURE OF A SQUADRON

Perhaps at this point it would be appropriate to outline briefly the organisation of a tactical bomber Squadron thrust into the support of highly mobile land battles in the western desert in 1941/42. Apart from the fighting element of its aircrews and aircraft, the backing for their operations was organised into a series of specialist Sections grouped later into what was to become known as the Technical and Administrative Wings of a Squadron. In the early years of the war this formal top structure did not exist, and Sections took their natural command channels through to the Engineer Officer or to the Adjutant. The characteristics of these Sections follow:

Administrative Section

The Squadron Orderly Room, headed usually by the Adjutant with the Squadron Warrant Officer as his executive, was the hub of the well-being of the Squadron. Through these offices passed all official mail, the endless forms and records of pay, promotions, postings, leave, merits and disciplines. Together with the Accounts Office, most of their equipment was of the trusty typewriters, desks and filing cabinets, frequently the first to suffer in panic moves. About a dozen clerks and orderlies made up the staff. If there was a Padre, he, too, when not in his invariably makeshift and attractive Chapel, centred his hours in these offices.

Technical Staff

This is the power house for the availability of serviceable aircraft for the aircrews. Pride in the standards of maintenance and engineering emanated from the superb training given by the RAF to its apprentice aeroengine and airframe fitters, notably from Halton, and to its students through the Technical Training Schools. Headed by an Engineering Officer and staffed predominantly by senior NCOs, this was the largest Section in the Squadron, frequently split into First and Second line groups. The First a quick-fix element, themselves split into two or three flights to conform with the flying wing organisation, were responsible for refuelling and rearming turn rounds. The Second for the component maintenance, testing, repairs or replacement just in rear of the first line at forward airfields. Careful to husband some of the best tools, diagnostic and repair equipment available, this Section as much as any other, accomplished the seemingly impossible in keeping the aircraft fit to fly, and more than any other promoted the modernisation of its servicing schedules.

Equipment Section

Racks, storage bins, and crates, carried the wherewithal of spares, consumables and replacements for the knife, fork and spoon, through clothing to aeroengine supplies. And when discarded that packaging invariably formed the furniture of the messes and tents of a squadron on the move. Accounting, labelling, and storage was a nightmare, and the staff, usually an Officer and half a dozen equippers, always seemed too small for the inevitable depot scrounging needed to look after the basic luggage of a Squadron.

Transport Section

Next to the Engineers, this was probably the largest unit in the Squadron, with twenty to thirty mechanics and specialist drivers, normally led by a senior NCO. The servicing of all the Squadron vehicles was in their remit, which normally ran some 75 vehicles varying from the heavy load carriers, specialist bowsers for fuel and water, cranes, Chance Lights (for the runway at night), light vans, cars, and trailers. They were the blood in the arterial supply lines to the Squadron, and if anyone ever wanted to know the whereabouts of a unit or a piece of equipment, or even an individual, a member of the MT Section knew the answer.

Catering Section

The cookhouse, trailer or tent, with its operatives of some half-dozen cooks and their assistants, never failed to garner kicks or compliments. Blessed with the most rudimentary heating and cooking equipment - usually supplemented with in-house inventions - rations, though adequate, were uniformly dull, made palatable by the ingenuity and acquisitiveness of a cook, from a local bazaar, market or farm. This urge to vary the diet often meant that this section contributed more to scrapes with the authorities than any of the others!

Medical Section

Headed by a qualified Doctor, the MOs' duties were akin to those of a GP in civilian life, supplemented by the need to tend aeromedical and stress-related symptoms. Mostly adequate, though not lavishly, equipped, surgeries dealt with day to day ailments, precautions against locally-inspired menaces (malaria, sand fly fever and the like) the annual medical checks (critical to aircrew) and, importantly, with the effectiveness and manning of the Ambulance (on standby during all flying) and the standards of hygiene observed throughout the camp. Usually a very busy section, directly involved with casualties. The staff of perhaps less than six nurses and orderlies were seldom underburdened.

Radio, Electrical and Instrument Sections

Generally under the aegis of the Technical Section, and manned by highly qualified technicians, their numbers and their expensive test equipment varied with the degree of sophistication of the aircraft systems. Their responsibilities extended over external (WT), internal (RT & telephone) communications, the power systems used in the operation control rooms and in twenty to thirty aircraft, and the host of instruments needing calibration and testing throughout the Squadron. Certainly as complicated a task as tending a modern naval destroyer.

Armament Section

Handling explosives brings a distinctly serious approach to working methods. Their laden bomb trollies and inscribed messages to the intended recipients so familiar to the media, mask physically demanding tasks where mistakes can be lethal. The spectrum of weapons in this armoury extended to revolvers, rifles, Lewis, K, and Browning machine guns, 20mm cannon, bombs varying from 20 to 500lbs with their attendant fuses and detonators, mines, torpedoes and the miscellany of flares, Very cartridges and shells. There are records of armament failures (guns jamming, unexploded bombs hang-ups etc.) but seldom of any aircraft having to abort from failed armament.

Photographic Section

With a small staff of perhaps three or four photographers, led normally by an NCO, the dark room and layout trailers and the 8, 12, and 20" cameras probably experienced a greater urgency of calls on their work than most others. Asked to provide mosaics for mapping and targeting, as much for the Army as for the Air Force, prints for damage assessment and intelligence, and the action shots for publicity, the section was known for its chemical aura, and for the numerous compliments received from higher formations.

Fire and General Duties Section

The fire engines of the RAF - in keeping with their aircraft - have progressively become more complicated, and though sturdy and tough they were not designed for mobility over deserts. They adapted to foam suppressants - water was a rare bonus. The crews trained for fire and rescue, at stand-by during flying, were usually the first to arrive at accidents and lives depended on their speed and expertise. A very close eye was always focused on their efficiency, and they were seldom found wanting. Unfairly, in some ways, they were often called upon to reinforce the orderly squads directed by the Squadron Warrant Officer with 'nobody else available'. Everybody knew what that meant in parade, fatigue, or escort duties. They deserve an accolade. In the early days of WW2, Police were not normally thought necessary in a squadron, but as security measures increased, so did their numbers to guard sensitive areas.

OPERATIONS

The pattern of daily flying operations throughout February and March settled into opportunist bombing attacks against Rommel's advancing forces. Both sides were much handicapped by severe cold weather, rain and sandstorms, with flooded airfields and rutted desert tracks. Allied army units in retreat found it difficult to provide accurate estimates of enemy size and intentions in the time needed to mount, brief and despatch bomber attacks. Any army requests and targets located by air reconnaissance were best met by having the strike forces and their escorts on stand-by. Frequently, but understandably, only to be stood down after a long wait with nothing accomplished.

In February aircraft were often moved to and from airfields that had previously been their main bases, but which were now vulnerable landing grounds. Bu Amud, Mechili, and Gambut were used mostly with six aircraft on stand-by, with the second line support element withdrawing on 1 February to LG 76. On the 2nd through to the 7th, good bombing results were recorded against enemy transport and columns on the move at Antelat, and on the coast road near Derna, and at night against German aircraft at Martuba, but once more base sections were ordered further eastwards to LG 116.

On 9 February six Ju 88s and He llls attacked Gambut at dawn with bombs and by ground strafing. Two were shot down by fighters from El Adem but not before four of No 14's Blenheims were damaged, two seriously. There were no crew casualties. On 10 and 11 February attempts were again made to attack by night German aircraft at Martuba, and raid by day traffic on the Appolonia-Gazala road, but both ended in abortions due to total cloud cover and unserviceabilities.

Squadron Leader Mills arrived on 12 February at LG 116, to take command of a newly formed C Flight. 14 aircrews, and a few ground crew were posted in between 16 and 22 February, but no further ground equipment, necessitating a great deal of re-allocation of hard protected stores. A strike with good results, confirmed by photographs, was made on 15 February, by six aircraft each from Nos 14 and 11 Squadrons against transport and tanks just south of Gazala. There was no opposition, but on the same day four Bf109s bombed LG 116 causing neither damage nor casualties. Another forward airfield move on the 20th, occurred fortuitously when all aircraft left Gambut for Bir el Baheira, minutes before a German aircraft strike on Gambut caused no casualties or damage to the forward servicing echelon, or to the ground equipment, as these also had left at dawn. The reorganisation into three flights begun on 12 February was complete by the 23rd.

Also on the 23rd, the aircraft were ordered to move from Baheira to their rear base at LG 116. On the way Sergeant Bosworth and his crew of Sergeants Swann,

Hoyle and Curtis crash-landed having been attacked four times by Bf109Fs. Swann died later from head injuries, Hoyle recovered in hospital from chest and arm wounds, but nothing was recorded about Bosworth or Curtis.

The final operation in February on the 25th ended disastrously. Six aircraft led by Buchanan were briefed individually to attack by night different German airfields. Two bombed Martuba in appalling visibility with no observed results. One was hit by AA fire and jettisoned its bombs before the crew had to bale out, Eric Barr was injured on landing but Sgt Philip Tew never got out, and was killed. A fourth aircraft bombed but ran out of fuel and crash landed in the sea, the fifth aborted with an electrical fault, and the sixth, could not attack due to poor visibility, landed at Fuka main some 3 miles west of LG 116.

March opened with three aircraft involved in accidents. Two were repaired from a mid-air collision, and the third (on delivery, flown by Pilot Officer Harvie, RAAF), hit the officers mess tent on approach to land and crashed in flames, killing the pilot. As Rommel thrust his way through Cyrenaica towards the Gazala line, the targets were still predominately against either his air or ground forces, including German aircraft using Heraklion in Crete, and his supply convoys using Benghazi. Against the latter 500lb bombs were specified.

The uncertainties and dislocations in the overall military scenario meant that a total of only 45 sorties were flown against the Axis in March out of some 70 made available. Casualties occurred more from inexperience than from the enemy, and where serviceability ostensibly improved from the centralisation of first and second line resources on one base, when airborne, components were proving to be over their useful life in desert conditions. Of the operations flown, 10 sorties were directed against German aircraft on 7 and 10 March at Tmimi and Martuba, one of which inexplicably crashed on take-off on a clear night killing all the crew of Sergeants Stevenson, Johnson, and Honey of the RCAF. Eighteen sorties were briefed and thirteen flown on the 14th and 20th against Heraklion, where the blackout appeared non-existent. Those that arrived reported good results, but the shortfall saw two more accidents on take off, the first killing all the crew, and the second injuring all members after striking an oil drum. Three sorties were cancelled due to rising mists.

6 aircraft on 14 March, due to a rare timing error, completely overshot an attack on enemy transports at Agheila. Squadron Leader Mills and his crew of Sergeants By and Hunt had to force land from lack of fuel, but after walking for 150 miles behind enemy lines and surviving on aircraft desert rations, were picked up by a British armoured patrol. They were given a short leave!

Seventeen sorties with 500lb bombs were flown against reported convoys off Benghazi and Crete on 17 and 30 March. Nothing was seen, but three crews and their aircraft were lost. Two collided shortly after take off, killing both crews of Sergeants Good, Windmill, Godly, Linley, Humphries and Smail. The third aircraft lost was flown by Flight Lieutenant Keck RAAF, with his crew of Flight Sergeants Hibbert and Rylands sadly shot down in error by South African Hurricanes.

As, towards the end of March, calls for attacks were becoming less frequent, the opportunity was taken to provide much needed night flying practice to new crews, and to institute a navigation programme for 10 crews conducted by the command navigation officer. Both activities were often interrupted by weather which was nevertheless improving, and by air raid warnings, which were lessening.

The position of the Allied ground forces in April and May deteriorated sharply. The battles for the Gazala line and the Knightsbridge Cauldron were imminent. The Squadron was hardly used in connection with these, flying a total of only 28 operational sorties in April, mostly on sweeps for possible submarines (nothing sighted), and night bombing against Maleme and Heraklion in Crete. Four aircraft were lost, two on take off at night, the crew of the first uninjured. The pilot of the second was killed, the Observer and the Air Gunner injured. The third had an engine failure, never got airborne, and sustained severe damage, the crew being shaken but uninjured. The fourth, in transit from an advanced landing ground, crashed in sand haze conditions killing all the crew - Second Lieutenant Chappit, SAAF, and Sergeants Cornwall and Richardson.

On 7 May, it was announced by Wing HQ that Wing Commander Buchanan, Major Lewis, SAAF, Flight Lieutenant Whittard, and Pilot Officer Goode had been awarded DFCs, and Sergeant Chaplin the DFM, all five of whom had completed over 70 operations with the Squadron. For Buchanan it added a Bar to his earlier DFC.

A training programme was instituted on the 13th and continued for the rest of April, until indications were given that the Squadron would soon move near to Ismailia.

The Squadron ground section left LG 116 in a hurry on the 29th, reaching Amriya that evening, and el Forden on the 1st. The majority of the aircraft arrived at the latter on the 2nd, but on the 3rd, four returned to LG 116 with pilots to fly out the remainder, and to bring back as much equipment as possible including tents, of which there was an acute shortage. The early part of May concentrated on maintenance, formation practice, and several exercises in co-operation with the Suez Canal defence guns.

On 15 May there was a change of Command. Wing Commander T K Buchanan, DFC and Bar, was succeeded by Wing Commander W S G Maydwell, DFC. In difficult times Buchanan had become an inspiration to his pilots and to his air and ground crews. A native of Southsea, 'Buck' had joined the RAF on a Short Service Commission on 3 May 1937, and after training at No 8 FTS, Montrose, was posted to No 101 Squadron at Bicester on 27 November 1937 to pilot Boulton Paul Overstrand Bombers. In June 1938 the unit replaced these with Blenheim Is. Buchanan remained a bomber pilot during the following four years and gained a DFC in July 1940. He was posted to No 14 Squadron in September 1940, and remained flying with the Squadron in Egypt, Palestine and Iraq, until be became in October 1941, Commander of the Squadron. By then he had already gained a considerable reputation in Middle East bomber circles as an adventurous, even cavalier pilot, yet never foolhardy. His constant interest in and obvious love of flying were exemplified by his mounting total of operational sorties, apart from seizing every opportunity to be airborne between sorties on training or testing flights, or simply as he said, 'to keep my hand in'.

According to his observer, Flight Lieutenant Geoffrey Whittard, 'Buchanan's appearance was disconcerting. He was slight, immaculately dressed, and quietly spoken with great charm. It was obvious from the first day he joined the Squadron that his main love and interest in life was flying. He would never miss an opportunity to fly on any operational flight. Considering his many achievements he was the most modest of men and never talked of his successes'. (Quoted from *Desert Air Force at War* by Bowyer and Sherer).

In May 1942, with a total of some 200 operational sorties already recorded in his log book, Buchanan was posted to a staff post at HQ Middle East. After he had talked his way out of a staff appointment, he took Command of No 272 Squadron of Beaufighters in Malta where he was awarded the DSO after 11 enemy aircraft were confirmed shot down. Unfortunately his aircraft was shot down by flak during a patrol across the Aegean. 'He and his navigator, a Warrant Officer, were seen to scramble into a dinghy. They reached a small island but were not relocated for some days. Unfortunately by then, Buchanan was dead. He had died from severe internal injuries, and his navigator had been obliged to bury him. On hearing of his death, Air Marshal Sir Keith Park said 'The RAF has lost one of its most illustrious leaders.' Let these words remain as a fitting tribute to a great warrior.'

As far as can be ascertained from records available, Buchanan must be credited as having piloted the RAF record number of over 230. He was on operational Blenheim and Beaufighter flights against the enemy in World War II. An incredible example of sustained and distinguished service, and a sad loss to his country.

CHAPTER 6

FIRST WITH MARAUDERS

MAY 1942 - SEPTEMBER 1943

Wing Commander Dick Maydwell assumed command of No 14 Squadron on 15 May 1942. Rommel's Afrika Korps had just begun its second offensive in the Western Desert, and the Squadron's operations were bombing enemy airfields, giving direct support to our ground troops and, predominantly, attacking the Axis supply routes across the Mediterranean and denying enemy shipping safe crossings from Europe to Africa.

B26-Marauder Dominion Revenge.

By May, the Blenheims had seen long and arduous service in the Middle East under very adverse conditions. Despite the great efforts of the ground crews, serviceability was not satisfactory. One of the new CO's first acts was to have all aircraft cleared of sand and full maintenance carried out. Aircrew replacements and new aircraft were an immediate need. The source for newly trained crews was 70 OTU at Nakuru in Kenya. This station was situated at 6,000ft in very mountainous country. Mt. Kenya and Mt. Elgon were ever present hazards and night flying training was restricted to moonlit nights, so the new crews had very limited night flying; unfortunate, as the Squadron was mainly employed on night intruder operations. Half the new aircrew members arriving from Nakuru were Australians, and when these were added to the Australians already flying with No 14 Squadron they were in a majority over the Britons, South Africans, New Zealanders, Canadians, one Dane and a British Latin American volunteer!

One of the Australians wrote a graphic description of joining No 14 Squadron in June 1942:

'The retreat to El Alamein was on in earnest; after several days in a Western Desert transit camp and wandering around by truck, we eventually found No 14 Squadron. At one stage we were advised by a bearded gaunt army Major heading east that German tanks were not far behind him, and if we proceeded further west we risked being shot up or taken prisoner. We were presented to our new C O, and his Adjutant Flight Lieutenant C Wall (RAAF). The CO, referred to as 'The Boffin', a name earned by his reference to anyone who put up a black as a 'stupid Boffin', made us welcome and quickly advised us of the do's and don'ts. The enemy was to be hammered at every opportunity, we were to accept the harsh conditions. He and his adjutant would be addressed as Sir, other officers and NCOs by their Christians names as many crews were made up of both Officers and NCOs.

'LG97 was a desolate stretch of desert. We were issued with a standard ridgepole tent and soon had it erected, and had an 'L' shaped slit trench dug nearby. The latter was for protection from enemy aircraft bombing and strafing. The existing personnel of No 14, both aircrew and ground crew were a sorry looking lot. Having been forced to retreat by the Nazi armies, only bare essentials had come with them. Many were unshaven and unwashed - water was a very scarce commodity indeed. There were two messes only, one for officers and NCO's and one for other ranks. Our mess was a large canvas marquee, sand floor, trestle tables and wooden benches. Because of the terrible conditions under which the ground crews were forced to work, maintenance of aircraft was a major problem. Our first flights were ferrying semi-serviceable aircraft back to Abu Sueir and Ismalia in the Delta for repairs, and returning with serviceable aircraft. Living conditions were primitive. However, no one complained; we were close to the front line. Water was rationed so we were not required to shave or wash. Food? Well not much variety, bully beef and biscuits being the mainstay. Our cook Fritz - a Palestinian German - did a wonderful job. In my mind's eye I can still see 'Fritz' with a ladle scooping out the flies from the boiling copper of milk tea with a strong flavour of chlorine. "she be right boys, the Doc says if she boil, she be right".

'Flies. From dawn to dusk one was constantly pestered with myriads of them. Part of one's dress was a horse-hair whisk (purchased in the Bazaars in Cairo) which hung on one's wrist. Dust was into everything. When the khamseen (hot southerly wind) swept up out of the desert, visibility was reduced at times to a hundred metres'.

(In explanation of the unkempt appearance of personnel, when O'Connor joined the Squadron, an urgent withdrawal from LG116 had been necessitated by the Army's headlong retreat in the face of Rommel's advance. This withdrawal had been achieved with a high degree of discipline and so successfully that all transport and serviceable aircraft were retrieved without loss.)

The Aussies were never orthodox in their attitude to military discipline and it says an enormous amount for the new CO's leadership qualities that he quickly won their respect and affection by his understanding and lack of pomposity.

Recently, Squadron Leader Lapthorne, RAAF emphasised this and added, 'Decisions he made had a profound influence on the future of the Squadron's Marauder operations.'

Some two weeks were spent in getting the Blenheims fully serviceable, and the new crews trained in night flying before orders were received that the Squadron should leave Kabrit and be based at LG116 in the Western Desert near Mersah Matruh. From there it was to carry our night intruder operations over enemy airfields in Crete, from which the *Luftwaffe* was attacking Allied convoys bringing much-needed supplies to the Army.

The plan was to arrive at an airfield after the Heinkels had left and to create as much havoc as possible to prevent the returning aircraft from landing. If intelligence radioed the crews that the Germans were being diverted to another landing ground, the Blenheims forestalled their arrival.

Shortly before midnight on 7 June 1942 the first of six Blenheims took off for Crete. Its captain was Squadron Leader Moore. The other 5 aircraft were piloted by Slade, Lapthorne, Grimsey, Ellis and Elliott. On the following night, the CO was the first to carry out a similar raid. He wrote 'My crew had the satisfaction of seeing a well-lit flarepath at Heraklion. This was bombed at intervals, which ensured a complete blackout. Meanwhile other Blenheims were on their way to keep up the attack.' The second aircraft flown by Flight Lieutenant Brooks turned back with engine trouble, missed the flarepath, and crash landed in the Desert. These intruder operations were carried out for ten nights and were very successful. The enemy was forced to abandon its Crete airfields and retreat to Greece, where longer range Wellingtons took on the task. Some of the Blenheims carried a crate of empty beer bottles. When falling, the bottles made a noise like falling bombs and added to the anxieties of the enemy!

On 13 June at LG116 there was night flying practice for the less experienced crews. Two aircraft lost contact. The wreckage of one was found but all the crew, Sergeants Highman (Pilot) Lynch (Observer) and Corsegio (Wireless Operator AG) had been killed. That night Pilot Officer Elliot attacked Heraklion aerodrome. He followed an enemy aircraft in, when the flarepath was lit and enemy aircraft were circling with navigation lights on. He dived from 10,000ft to 3,000ft and released the bombs East to West across the flarepath and successfully returned to base. The following night, Squadron Leader Pirie's aircraft was last heard calling for bearings south east of Derna and it was later learned it had crashed, but the crew, Pirie, Observer Ridley and Wireless Operator AG Payne walked away and were picked up on the way home.

These intruder raids were carried out until the 24th, when the Squadron was ordered to bomb enemy motor transport from LG116. This landing ground was attacked by an enemy bomber, which made two bombing runs and strafed. It was shot down in flames by a RAF night fighter, but not before the unfortunate LAC Friel had been killed by a bomb fragment.

On 25 June General Ritchie was relieved of his command and General Auchinleck took direct control of the British 8th Army. On the 28th the Squadron was ordered to withdraw to LG97, east of Alamein. Despite all the many moves around the Desert at this time, there were never any complicated operation orders issued. Every NCO and airman knew his lorry and his load so that when a move was ordered, the CO and Engineering Officer decided on a date, starting time, night stop, route and destination. After that everything worked smoothly. To the great credit of the ground crews, this difficult journey of over 200 miles along sand tracks and scrub, all the motor transport, including the chance light and tractors were saved, despite the fact that on one night the Luftwaffe bombed the convoy. A Corporal Electrician, Harry King, was hit in the right thigh by a bomb splinter and had to be operated on at a casualty clearing station before treatment at Heliopolis hospital. The Blenheims flew ahead, but the CO kept watch on the convoy from his aircraft.

Corporal Ron Haley, a cook on the Squadron, described the retreat:

'We were on our way up to Gambut and pulled up for the night. Just off the coast road things were starting to move, and everyone was a bit on edge, the traffic back towards the Canal was getting heavy. Just before we left the previous LG, the airman who looked after the mess tent had 7 or 8 tankards, engraved with the Squadron Crest and the name of the Sergeant, who donated them. In the morning, there was a panic to get away, back towards Cairo. The road was jammed. I suddenly remembered the tankards and asked what had been done with them. He told me he had buried them in a trench towards the escarpment. We pushed between the Free French, coming back from Bir Hacheim and had their company until we turned off to go up to LG110 or one of the landing grounds in that area.

I remember one Frenchman spoke about the retreat in France and how it was happening all over again. The following morning about fifteen ground staff and myself, plus an officer with about five lorries took off, not to Cairo but back to Gambut. We seemed to amuse the troops going the other way and the remarks, punctuated by the usual grammar, indicated that we were going in the wrong direction. On the way traffic had thinned out and by the time we were through the pass we had the road to ourselves. On arriving, we dispersed the vehicles and kipped down on the ground.

Sometime during the night, we were awakened by the drone of a strange aircraft. It came in and landed, solely by the light of the full moon. It didn't like the look of things, so took off again. It appeared to be a Swordfish. An uneasy morning dawned and we were alone, except for an army demolition party. Petrol etc started to burn.

The officer in charge came across from a hut on the far side, so we moved off quickly towards the coast road. At the top of the escarpment we came to a halt. Apparently Jerry was already on the coast road. We turned, then took off across the Desert. Later we passed through an Indian armoured car unit, which detached one of its units to check us out. That night, we pulled into some sand dunes, brewed up, then got our heads down, but not for long. Suddenly all hell let loose, flares, bombs, light ack-ack. We felt we must have been of great importance for such a show. Needless to say we had very little sleep that night. An early start next morning took us out of the sand dunes, then lo and behold we had arrived at the head of the rail road at Mersah Matruh.'

The Squadron now reverted to its earlier role of supporting the Army by bombing the advancing enemy transport. By 30 June 1942, the strategic situation was becoming serious and orders were received to withdraw to LGY. At LG97, a Kittyhawk landed but struck a Blenheim, overturned and killed the pilot. Corporal Gubbins, who was working on the Blenheim, received fatal injuries and died within half an hour. So within one week, two of the Squadron's ground crew were killed.

During July, a number of night operations against enemy landing grounds, motor transport and Mersah Matruh harbour were undertaken. Squadron Leader Pirie's and Sergeant Russell's crews failed to return. The Observer in Sergeant Meadwell's Blenheim described the raids:

'Single aircraft were sent out at intervals throughout the hours of darkness to drop bombs on Mersah Matruh and other targets. In theory we were supposed to bomb from about 6,000ft, but some of the aircraft were so decrepit they could not climb to that height with a full bomb and fuel load (Four 250lb Bombs and four 25lb incendiaries) before the target was reached. The whole trip lasted between 3 and 4 hours.

Our crew did four of these operations, two to Mersah Matruh and two to Maaten Bagush. I well remember the trauma of flying over a peaceful moonlit Mediterranean, then turning south for the coast and being met by a sudden upsurge of flak on the run-in to the target. The perspex nose of the Blenheim, in which the Observer/Bomb-aimer sat, offered no sense of protection. We observers used to sit on our tin hats to protect those parts of our anatomy we regarded as most important!'

On 4 July, three Australian Sergeants, Russell, Dyson and Nichols were shot down while bombing Maaten Bagush in a Blenheim. They walked back and rejoined the Squadron, three days later. All three were awarded 'The Flying Boot'.

On the 23rd, Lapthorne's Blenheim led a formation of 4 aircraft to bomb shipping in Mersah Matruh harbour. His own aircraft was hit by flak, which wounded his navigator and wireless operator/air gunner, but they returned to base where the injured crewmen were treated and the Blenheim scrapped.

In July came the good news that No 14 was to be re-equipped with Martin B-26A Marauder, which carried a crew of six, so two Blenheim crews were merged and an extra gunner for the tail gun added instead of the now superfluous second navigator.

In August, preparations for conversion to Marauders began and pilots were trained in the use of tricycle undercarriages on Boston aircraft.

On 13 August, General Montgomery assumed command of the 8th Army and General Alexander replaced General Auchinleck.

CONVERSION TO B-26A MARAUDERS

On 26 August 1942 the Squadron moved to Fayid for the conversion. A group of US Army Air Force personnel were attached to No 14 to instruct the pilots and ground staff in the use of the new aircraft. The Americans regarded it with awe, and had nicknamed it 'The Flying Prostitute' because 'it had no visible means of support'. This was an allusion to the very short wing span and its angle of attack. These characteristics resulted in the Marauder, which had a tricycle undercarriage, having a take off speed of around 150mph and a touch-down speed of over 120mph. The tyres therefore had a limited life under desert conditions. It flew in a characteristic tail down attitude and was not happy at higher altitudes. Later B-26s had a modified wing, which improved these matters.

The Americans commanded by Colonel Garrison demonstrated starting drill. Clad in immaculate white overalls, he and his co-pilot took the controls of a stationary B-26. Two US ground staff stood in front of each of the 2,000 hp Pratt & Whitney radials armed with fire extinguishers. "OK Starboard?" called the Colonel "OK Sir" "OK Port?" "OK Sir" "Start the Put-Put!" It came as something of an anticlimax when a small two-stroke engine in the tail burst into life and a wisp of exhaust gas issued from the fuselage. This drove the inverters and enabled the electric starters to turn the engines, which coughed into life with an impressive bellow.

There was a certain amount of antagonism between the American 'enlisted men' and the other ranks of the RAF. The Americans used to sing. "The limeys think they'll win the War by drinking tea from two to four!" Colonel Garrision disciplined his men by depriving them of their beloved Jeep.

Adjusting to the higher landing speed of the B-26As, from the comparatively low speed of the Blenheims was not easy for aircrews or those on the ground. This was illustrated on 20 August when Garrison was landing his Marauder. He had lowered the undercarriage, when four Egyptians in a truck misjudged his speed and drove across the runway directly in the path of the aircraft. They were struck by a wheel and all four in the truck were killed outright. The Marauder's undercarriage was damaged and the aircraft crashed, fortunately without harm to the crew.

During night-flying practice, a Marauder was diverted to a landing ground used by Wellingtons. Given a green light, the pilot touched down on the flarepath and came to a halt. A near apoplectic flying control officer drove up and shouted "What the hell do you think you're playing at, coming in like a bloody lunatic at that sort of speed?" Then he realised the dimly-lit aircraft had a tricycle undercarriage, and two large four-bladed propellers!

On the 27th, a guard caught sight of two Arabs leaving the tent, in which the Squadron armour was kept. Knowing they had no right to be there and suspecting they were stealing weapons or ammunition, he challenged them, and they ran off. He shot one dead and severely wounded the other.

On 1 November, Flying Officer Joe Elliott, who had completed several operations on Blenheims, took his crew on the Squadron's first Marauder operation. In addition to his own Blenheim crew he had Pilot Officer Ted Donovan and his Blenheim Wireless Operator AG plus an extra gunner. It was an unarmed reconnaissance past Crete and up into the Aegean Sea. They saw two ships and an unidentified enemy aircraft and returned to Mariut, the base airfield for Alexandria, after being airborne for 8 hours and 45 minutes.

Donovan with his observer, Pilot Officer Peter Willis and wireless operator AG Sergeant Stuart had flown a Blenheim out from England. He and Willis, like Maydwell, had all been commissioned in the Army before transferring to the RAF.

The CO's crew took off at Fayid at 1150hrs on the 6th and flew north over the Mediterranean at a height of 50ft to avoid enemy radar. North of Crete they found a number of large barges filled with German soldiers heading for Crete. Flying over them, the rear gunner of the Marauder, Sergeant Gil Graham, was able to rake them with cannon shells and had the satisfaction of seeing many soldiers diving overboard.

Maydwell continued flying north, but shortly afterwards, a lone Ju52 was sighted. This was clearly marked with large Red Crosses and was left in peace. Next sighted was an enemy troopship of 2,500 tons, escorted by a He115 seaplane and a naval sloop flying the red and white Swastika battle ensign of the *Kriegsmarin*. It subjected the Marauder to a hail of flak and badly holed the rear of the aircraft, wounding the turret gunner in the leg. A small fire was also started in the overload fuel tank in the bomb bay, which would have proved disastrous had not Sergeant Clarke, the wireless operator, acted with commendable speed and snuffed it out before it spread.

Very shortly afterwards, the Marauder came across a shipping convoy heading south, escorted by two destroyers and seven Ju88s. Three of the enemy aircraft peeled away to attack the British aircraft. With the turret guns out of action, Maydwell took violent evasive action, increased speed and eventually escaped their attentions. By now it was nearly dusk, and the landing was made in the dark after eight hours flying. An ambulance was waiting to take the injured gunner to hospital.

In November a tragic accident occurred during low-level bombing practice at Abu Sueir. Pilot Officer Dickie Bower from Winnipeg in Canada had recently been given his own crew. His navigator was an Englishman called Hepworth, affectionately known as 'Pop', one of the oldest men flying with the Squadron, was on leave in Cairo, Bower decided to get in some bombing practice and borrowed Donovan's navigator, Willis, to take his place. On one bombing run, an aircraft flying nearby saw the Marauder's tail fin snap off and the aircraft crash. The whole crew were killed.

An Inquiry reported in due course and as a result all the Marauders were grounded to have the tail fins strengthened. (The Glenn Martin Aircraft Corporation in the USA flew technicians to Egypt, who completed the necessary modifications to all the aircraft in a few days). Unfortunately this was not done until after two more aircraft had been lost with the loss of 21 lives. Among these, Squadron Leader Peter Goode, a Flight Commander, crashed in the bay of Algiers during the move from Egypt to North Africa. With him in the aircraft was Flying Officer Sieward, the Squadron Intelligence Officer, who had with him the Squadron Records.

In December the Squadron received orders that the Marauder crews were to be trained in torpedo dropping and moved to Shalufa, where messes were shared with No 39 Squadron flying torpedo-carrying Beauforts and doing sterling work at considerable cost in casualties.

Donovan recorded:

No 5 METS Torpedo Course.
Front Row R to L: Flg Off Phillips RAF, Flt Sgt Freeman RNZAF, F/Sgt Wright RAF, F/Sgt Bates RAF.
Back Row R to L: F/O Donovan RAF, Lt Graham SAAF, F/Sgt Russell (RAAF).

Marauder Captains, A Flight.

Top L to R: Flt Sgt Einsaar DFM RAAF (POW), Sqn Ldr Law-Wright DFC RAF (killed in accident), Capt Richardson SAAF (POW), Flt Sgt Rawlins RAF Kenya (killed in action).
Middle L to R: Flt Sgt Dee RAAF, Flt Off Slade RAAF (wounded - repatriated), Flt Lt Goode RAF (killed in accident), W/O Francis BLAF (killed in action).
Bottom L to R: Flt Sgt Bullock RAF (killed in action), Flt Off Brown RAAF, Flt Sgt Hunter RAAF (POW wounded), W/O O'Connor RAAF.

Marauder Captains B Flight

Top L to R: Plt Off Willis DFM RAF (POW), Plt Off Elliott DFC RAAF, Capt Young SAAF (POW), Major Lewis DSO DFC SAAF, Sqn Ldr Lapthorne DFC RAAF.
Middle L to R: Lt Jones SAAF (missing), Wg Cdr Maydwell DSO DFC RAF, Sqn Ldr Grimsey DFC RAF, Flt Lt Phillipps DFC RAAF.
Bottom L to R: Flt Sgt Trueman RAAF (missing), Flt Lt Johnston DFC RAF, Flt Lt Clarke-Hall DFC RAAF, Lt Leech SAAF (returned to S. Africa).

Naval Torpedo hung beneath a Marauder.

'In December we carried on with low-level and torpedo training. The trips were called ALTS, which meant 'Attack Light Torpedo'. They were 18 inch torpedoes provided by the Navy and there was some difficulty in dropping them because we had to have drum control gear. This consisted of wire in the bomb bays to allow the torpedo to drop evenly into the water. At this stage no flying tails had been developed and it was a long drawn out affair as one had to press the button to release the torpedo, then count five while the weapon was guided into the sea. It was a long five seconds! This training went on through most of December and we also developed a method of flying in fluid pairs, that is two aircraft in loose formation each with torpedoes.'

On 19 December 1942 Sergeant Einsaar led a vic of three aircraft to lay mines in Tunis harbour. His crew consisted of Sergeants Dixon (2nd Pilot), Exell (Navigator), Ploskin (Wireless Operator AG), Cockington (Turret Gunner) and Willcocks (Tail Gunner). His aircraft was hit by flak over Tunis, which caused a loss of fuel, but on the way home the B-26s were intercepted by fighters, from Malta. A Spitfire pilot did not recognise the Marauder and attacked Einsaar's aircraft forcing him to ditch. Sergeant Carr in Flying Officer Brown's Marauder returned fire and damaged the Spitfire's undercarriage, forcing it to make a belly-landing at Luqa.

Three of Einsaar's crew managed to get into a dinghy. Einsaar himself was separated from his navigator by a sea of flames, but he dived under them to rescue Exell (another Australian) but he was so badly injured he died in Einsaar's arms shortly afterwards. Einsaar was awarded a DFM for his bravery.

'Len' Einsaar was a magnificent giant of a man. Over 6ft 4 ins in height with a physique hewn out of granite, he had been a policeman in Broken Hill, one of the toughest mining towns in Australia. He had also been an Olympic oarsman and rowed in the Berlin Olympics of 1936. For all his great strength and courage, he was the gentlest and kindest of men.

O'Connor remembers:

'There followed almost three months (to December) of frustration and spasmodic training, due to the problem of obtaining aircraft and spares. By early November, however, I had my own crew, original navigator Sergeant Buckland and wireless operator Gannan; my co-pilot was Long, turret gunner Platt and the rear gunner Hundley, three English lads. My first solo flight in a Marauder was on 5 November

1942.

'At that time my total solo flying time on twin-engined aircraft was a mere 140hrs with a grand total of all flying of just over 300hrs. Our first operational flight on a Marauder was on 19 December 1942. The CO called me up and asked if I thought I could cope with a mine-laying sortie despite the fact I had not yet flown solo at night on a B-26A. The confidence of youth? Naturally my answer was 'yes'.'

The operation was to lay mines in Tunis harbour, so the aircraft required an extra 1,000 gallons of fuel in a bomb-bay tank. The mines were loaded at Shalufa and the Marauder flown to Benghazi, a trip of four hours. After landing for a meal and refuelling, O'Connor's aircraft headed out over the Mediterranean as the sun was setting. In company with two other Marauders, they flew at 1,000ft through numerous rain squalls before sighting the Italian island of Lampedusa, about 480 miles from Benghazi. From there to Cape Bon on the north eastern tip of Tunisia, the weather cleared and the Marauders flew on in clear moonlight. From Cape Bon/ they descended to 200ft and rounded the coast towards Tunis. Half-way there the rear gunner, Platt, called out on the intercom:"Fighter 5 o'clock, 300ft, above, turn right, turn right." After a series of violent turns near the surface of the sea, they lost him. Approaching Tunis Bay, O'Connor cut back on the throttles and started a low level run towards La Goulette Mole and the Tunis Canal. The mines were magnetic and filled with high explosive. The instructions were to drop them at 50ft and at as slow a speed as they dared.

On the first run, O'Connor saw he was too close in, so turned and carried out a second run. Sergeant John Buckland opened the bomb bay doors and, due to an electrical fault the navigation lights came on, but despite heavy flak, they dropped the mines. O'Connor pulled up and turned for Tunis Bay out into the Mediterranean. Leaving Cape Bon behind, he asked the navigator, Buckland, to enter the bomb bay and transfer 200 gallons from the bomb bay tank to each main tank. He reported that this was done, but the cockpit fuel gauges recorded nothing. Sergeant Carl Long, Second Pilot, was sent back to check the pumps and returned with the news that both the mines and the 1,000 gallon extra fuel tank were no longer in the bomb bay. Buckland had used the 'Mickey Mouse' bomb release and had swept all 18 contacts to ensure he had no hang-ups. He had thus released the petrol tank as well as the mines. Now there was only an hour's flying possible, and they were still some 500 miles from Benghazi.

O'Connor handed control to Long and went back to consult the navigator. To land at Malta was the only hope so Sergeant Gerry Gannan sent out an SOS but was advised there was an air raid in progress. Fortunately the raid was over by the time they reached the approach corridor for Luqa airfield, which ran from a point 20 miles due South of Valetta Harbour. By great good fortune, Long had flown Spitfires from Malta for three months, so O'Connor handed over to him to fly the circuit, but carried out the landing himself, once the Marauder was lined up. It was his first solo night landing and on to a flarepath of dim glim lights. The aircraft touched down successfully at 120mph. There were no brake pedals only rudder pedals at the co-pilot's position, and shortly after touch down, Long yelled, "Brakes! Put the brakes on. Put the bloody brakes on!" They ran through the end glim lights and came to a shuddering halt. O'Connor flicked on the landing lights momentarily to see the cause of his co-pilot's anguished cry and saw huge rocks directly ahead! It was the first time an aircraft with a tricycle undercarriage had landed at Luqa.

Next morning, the Marauder was the object of intense interest and O'Connor found it surrounded with people and some had clambered inside, including an officious Squadron Leader, who ordered O'Connor out. The Australian Sergeant Pilot roundly informed him that he was the Captain of the Aircraft and ordered the senior officer out!

After a three hour flight, the Marauder landed back at Benghazi, where they were greeted with astonished relief as no message had been received from Malta to tell of the landing there and they had been posted as missing. Pilot Officer John Willis aircraft had failed to return from the same operation. It had been shot down and Willis was taken prisoner. The rest of the crew were killed.

In accordance with Service custom, the Officers and NCOs waited on the airmen for lunch on Christmas Day 1942. Wing Commander Maydwell was called upon to 'Give us a song or show your ring!' 'The Boffin' stood up and gave a magnificent display of Swiss yodelling, which he had learnt while a student in Switzerland.

The New Year saw the Axis Forces in North Africa in a trap. Allied air and sea units were effectively cutting off supplies to Rommel's army and the Allied armies advancing from both east and west were driving it back to Tunisia, where it was being massively reinforced by both German and Italian forces.

No 14 Squadron played a significant part in depriving the Axis forces of men and material, by attacking shipping, laying mines and maintaining a constant daylight surveillance over the strategic areas of the Mediterranean.

From the humblest AC2 to the CO, the Squadron was in very good heart. Despite physical discomforts and danger morale was high. The unit was remarkable in having so many different nationalities fighting in it. Relationships between officers and the non-commissioned were not marked by rigid divisions of rank. The Squadron was a team and discipline was based on mutual respect rather than King's Regulations. There was pride in being a member of No 14 Squadron and some disregard for military smartness.

Cook Ron Haley, whose memoirs have been quoted earlier, describes this tellingly in his account of an incident at Blida aerodrome in Algeria:

"We did the job on the aircraft and then went over to the hangar. As I remember it was a huge open-sided affair. At the other end were four or five officers, two or three with scrambled egg on their caps, and, possibly because the hangar was empty, we could hear what they were discussing. One officer without gold on his cap glanced in our direction - we were dressed slightly differently to the mob just out from the UK and remarked, "Can't something be done to smarten these airmen up?" An officer with gold all over his cap then answered, "See those aircraft dispersed all over the field, the only ones serviceable belong to No 14 Squadron and as far as I am concerned they can go about in their underwear if they want to!"

On Sunday, 3 January 1943, two Marauders carried out an armed reconnaissance, flying as a fluid pair, in the Aegean and around the Cyclades Islands. The captains were both South Africans. Captain Young and Lieutenant Jones. The former's crew consisted of Sergeant Meadwell, Pilot Officers Foli-Brickley and Bennett, Flight Sergeant Ray and

Sergeant Hunt. The observer from Meadwell's Blenheim crew was not required on this operation as Foli-Brickley navigated. Jones' crew consisted of Sergeants Kelly, Dube, Mack, Ackland and Taylor. In the Cyclades, visibility was very poor, but a ship was sighted and the two aircraft went in to attack it. 3,000ft short of the target, Young turned to starboard to attack from a different angle, while Jones continued his run to drop his torpedo. The ship's crew were taken entirely by surprise. Unfortunately, the torpedo missed the ship. There was an autogyro hovering nearby and several Messerschmitt Bf110's above. One of these aircraft must have shot down Young's Marauder, because his wireless operator, Bennett, managed to send out two messages. One: 'We are being attacked by fighters' and two: 'We are ditching'. Young was the only member of the crew not to perish in the ditching. He was taken prisoner and the rest of the crew were buried on Seriphos Island. Lieutenant Jones' aircraft returned to Fayid from Gambut on the 5th and the crew were able to report details of the loss of Young's aircraft.

On the 9th 1943, the CO led a formation of three Marauders on a mine-laying operation. The intention was to lay the mines in the Burgi Channel, the neck at the southern end of the Gulf of Evvoia, north of Athens at Chalais, deprive the enemy of this route for their shipping, and force them out into the Aegean Sea, where Royal Navy submarines could attack them. Sergeant Gil Graham, tail gunner in the CO's crew described the trip: 'It was important that we did not get involved with enemy shipping or enemy aircraft. Although we made several sightings of both shipping and aircraft, we kept well clear and very low over the water. Weather conditions were very bad in places with frequent heavy rain squalls but we managed to locate the target and dropped the mines in exactly the right place. Rather surprisingly we encountered very little opposition in the target area and the only real danger was a schooner, which opened up at us'.

About a week later, on the 17th Flight Lieutenant Forbes, the new Medical Officer, joined the Squadron. In 1987, he described his impressions on his arrival. 'I joined No 14 Squadron on 17 January 1943 at Fayid, a very isolated part of the desert (sic!) and conditions were very primitive. For example, there were no screens round the lavatories so everything was visible! However, I soon learned in spite of the conditions the morale of the Squadron was extremely high'. The lavatories of which he wrote were urinals formed from used oil or petrol cans and buckets, on which were perched wooden seats with flap covers. Old newspapers were cut up and used as toilet paper.

The urinals were nicknamed 'Desert Lillies'. One day it was announced that an officer from Headquarters would visit the Squadron and give a lecture on 'Desert Survival'. This caused much ribald laughter. In the event, an aircraft landed at a time when several men were sitting on the buckets, exposed for all to see. Out of the aircraft stepped a very pretty WAAF officer and there was much hurried adjustment of dress!

On Wednesday 20 January 1943, the Squadron's Marauders drew their first blood with a torpedo drop. Elliott and Pilot Officer Harry Grimsey captained two aircraft flying as a fluid pair on an offensive reconnaissance up into the Aegean. In Elliott's crew were Donovan (Co-pilot), Flight Sergeant Davies (Navigator) and Sergeants Simmonds (Wireless Operator AG), Stuart (turret gunner) and Clarke (tail gunner).

Sergeant Bullock was Grimsey's co-pilot and Flight Sergeant Teddy Tolman his navigator. Between Crete and the island of Melos, the pair sighted a ship of about 1,500 tons, and went in to attack it. A German Arado floatplane, which was escorting the ship, opened fire with machine guns and cannon. Grimsey broke off and Elliott did a straight and level run to drop a torpedo.

Meanwhile John Stuart, his turret gunner, was returning the Arado's fire to such good effect that the float plane had to land in the sea. The torpedo struck the bow of the ship and blew it away, sinking the ship. Donovan photographed the whole engagement. The ships crew got into lifeboats and the crew of the Arado clambered out on the floats. Stuart did not fire again, saying "We can't shoot sitting ducks". The Marauders then carried on with their patrol before returning to Mariut. The crews received the AOC's congratulations. The Intelligence Officer, who debriefed them, said he knew the ship and it would undoubtedly have been carrying fuel for the Afrika Korps.

Three days later the eighth Army entered Tripoli and deprived the Axis of another port for the receipt of supplies.

The effectiveness of the Squadron in its nomad existence was greatly dependent on three administrative officers and, of course, the men under them. These three were Flight Lieutenants Charlie Wall the Adjutant, 'Doc' Forbes the Medical Officer and 'Gibby' Gibbins the engineering officer.

Charlie Wall was an Australian veteran of the Great War, who had fought with the Anzacs at Gallipoli. He was a large avuncular man, who claimed to be in his forties, but it was suspected he had concealed his true age when he joined the Royal Australian Air Force in World War II. His influence was particular valuable in dealing with the younger and more hot-headed of the Australian aircrews, but everyone liked and respected him. He had a good rapport with the ground crews and a ready ear for any incipient discontent or trouble, so the CO was able to tackle the problem before it became serious. His philosophy was that the three M's - Meals, Mails and Money were key elements in morale. Corporal Lacey was his assistant in a well-run Orderly Room and together they dealt efficiently with all the paperwork.

Maydwell writes, 'Charlie Wall had plenty of common sense, and if he did not agree with anything he often said; "The whole idea is not worth a hat full of cold water", and then again, if some airman got himself into trouble he would say, "Well, he has certainly got himself into a rotten pozzy". Later, he was awarded an OBE. Unhappily, soon after the distinction, he received notification of his son's death in Burma. The Engineering Officer, 'Gibby' Gibbins was English and was a qualified pilot. This enabled him to fly as co-pilot on flights to decide how best to achieve the lowest fuel consumption and greatest distance possible or to solve some other problem connected with the Marauder's performance. 'Gibby' worked miracles in keeping the aircraft flying and the rate of serviceability under his control was exceptionally high.

'Doc' Forbes has been quoted already, but a further reminiscence is appropriate:

'We left Fayid and after many weeks on the road and in the air we arrived at Blida in Algeria. An incident comes to mind which occurred during the long journey. We were camped near a forward landing strip consisting of levelled ground with metal strips on top. I was on duty one dark night, when I was alerted as enemy planes began dropping magnesium flares. I jumped into a nearby slit trench and found the only occupant was an airman, who turned out to be a Squadron Leader Fighter Pilot, who had attended the same school as I had in Perth (Scotland), Perth Academy. Surely a million to one chance!'.

'Doc' flew on an operation with a crew to gain first hand experience. He was very popular with all ranks and treated everyone with the same care and attention.

On 4 February 1943, the Eighth Army crossed the border into Tunisia, and the Desert War was over. Two days later the Commanding Officer received a letter, written in Arabic from the Emir Abdullah of Transjordan, congratulating the Squadron on its achievements and expressing the hope that his long association with it would continue for many years.

On the 11th February, most of the Squadron's aircraft and personnel returned to Shallufa for further torpedo training.

Two days later Einsaar, Taylor and Clarke all received the award of a DFM as recognition of their distinguished service.

On St. Valentine's Day the 14th, the Commanding Officer led three Marauders on another mine-laying trip to the Burgi Channel. His No 2 had engine trouble and was obliged to return to base. The other two crews pressed on in appalling weather conditions - thick cloud low over the sea and heavy rain. The mountains surrounding the target made flying very hazardous and they were obliged to drop the mines from an extremely low level, so low that the splashes struck the undersides of the two aircraft. There was some light anti-aircraft fire, but it was inaccurate. Intelligence later reported that as a result of this operation, one ship was sunk and another severely damaged by these mines and the channel blocked for a considerable time. Maydwell was later awarded the DSO for this outstandingly successful operation.

The following day, 15th February, two Marauders armed with torpedoes, took off from Shallufa, to carry out an armed reconnaissance in the Aegean. The aircraft captains were a South African, Lieutenant 'Les' Jones, and an Australian, Carl Truman. All contact with Truman's aircraft was lost after take off, but Jones's wireless operator sent messages that they had attacked a ship, were flying on one engine, but losing height. It was learned later that Jones had landed safely in Turkey, where the crew were interned, but they were repatriated after a while.

The Squadron moved to Berka on the 17th after seven months based at Fayid; the longest period in one place since leaving Port Sudan in April 1941, almost two years earlier. Next day it was formally declared to be fully operational. The conversion and training of crews had been completed successfully without one flying accident either by day or night, apart from the crash on the bombing range due to metal fatigue. This record spoke very highly not only of the skill and aptitude shown by the pilots, but also of the outstanding reliability of the Marauder, which would continue to prove itself an excellent machine and which in no way deserved the disparaging epithets of 'The Flying Prostitute' and 'The Widow Maker' that had been applied to it before delivery to the Squadron.

The main ground party moved on to Berka on the 19th a day's journey over more than 255 miles of desert tracks damaged by war, scrub, and sand dunes. They drove past Wadi Natrun, Mersah Matruh and Burg el Arab.

1500 ton Merchant vessel torpedoed by Flg Off Elliott RAAF. (20 January 1943).

Ships on fire in Melos Harbour after Squadron attack.

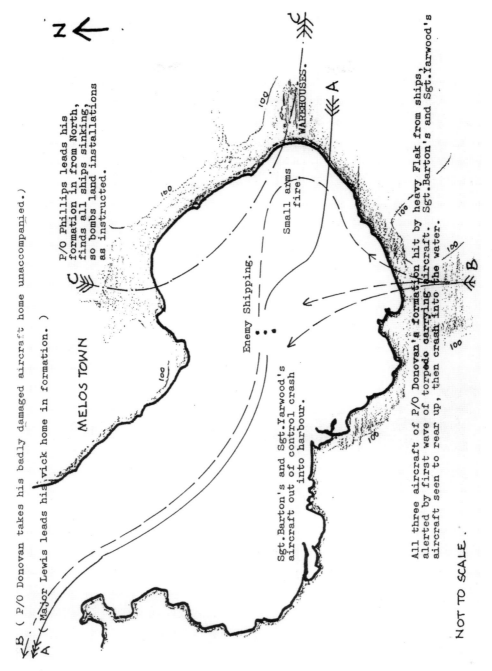

'Raid on Melos Harbour (21 February 1943)'.

THE RAID ON MELOS HARBOUR

On Sunday 21 February 1943, No 14 Squadron mounted its biggest Marauder operation yet. The target was the harbour in the horse-shoe shaped island of Melos about 80 miles north of Crete, which reconnaissance had shown to contain enemy shipping on its way to supply Axis Forces in Tunisia.

The Squadron was ordered to mount the raid at short notice. In 1989, Dick Maydwell recalled that, 'This operation was organised in a great hurry. Three torpedo Marauders and six bombing Marauders were needed. It was essential to attack the shipping in the enclosed harbour of Melos without delay. Major Lewis, a South African, who had already carried out many successful operational flights, was to lead the operation. The problem of briefing for the raid was complicated. The torpedo Marauders had to fly slow and low over the target before releasing the torpedoes, whereas the bombers had to fly low and fast so that they did not get hit by the explosion of their own bombs. Group HQ had provided a plaster model of Melos and the harbour, but no alternative targets were marked on it. No air photographs were given. It was the shipping or nothing, so that when the aircraft flew over Melos on the raid, there were two ships and they were sunk by torpedo. This did not leave much for the bombers to destroy but when they came in a minute later a third ship was seen, by then the AA defences were fully alerted and two bombers were lost'.

The nine aircraft that finally set course for the island were captained by:

Major Lewis, Flying Officer Lapthorne and Pilot Officer Clarke-Hall armed with torpedoes and forming 'A' formation.

Pilot Officer Ted Donovan, Sergeants Barton and Yarwood carrying four 500lb bombs fused for a three second delay. This was formation 'B'.

Pilot Officer Chris Phillips, Sergeants Egebjerg, a Dane serving in the RAF, and Bullock also armed with bombs. This was formation 'C'.

Plt Offs Donovan, Phillips, and Bertuch.

Wally Clarke-Hall recalls: 'The Plan was for the Torpedo planes to attack first from the south east, closely followed by three bombers, with the remainder flying round the island and coming in from the north with shore batteries and army barracks as their objective, and timed so that the first six would have just cleared the target areas.

'Major Lewis with Rod Lapthorne and myself flying the torpedo planes led us across the Mediterranean at nought feet in loose formation, through the Kasos Strait between Crete and Scarpanto Island and headed north-west for Melos, an island, whose main claim to fame was the discovery there of the beautiful statue of Venus de Milo.

'On arrival about an hour before sunset, we climbed slightly to clear the shore and there before us in the small landlocked harbour were the ships, one of about 3,000 tons fully-laden just getting under way, with the other of approximately 6,000 tons, anchored.

'We let down to dropping height of 100ft and made our run in. For the few seconds it took Jerry to wake up, all seemed to be too good to be true, but then the tracer from the ships began whipping past. Release distance of 800yrds quickly came up, and I fired my torpedo aimed at the larger ship and counted off the five seconds necessary for the piano wires holding the torpedo tail horizontal to run off, ensuring straight tracking. This was without doubt the longest five seconds of my life. Stuck there flying straight and level at 80ft, closing at 180mph. with more rapid firing guns joining in. Sitting ducks well aware that between the visible tracers were nasty solid stuff we couldn't see - wishing we were flying a smaller target and cursing the antiquated naval torpedoes we were using. I was the last to drop, and in turn followed the other two steeply left then right out through the narrow entrance channel, amazed that we appeared to have come through untouched. As we turned into the channel, my mid-upper gunner, Clarke, reported a strike on the 3,000 tonner, which had been the target of the other two. It was later reported sunk with my target down at the stern'.

'Immediately after Formation A had carried out its attack from due south, Formation B, led by Donovan attacked with the three bomb-loaded aircraft. The enemy AA was now fully alerted. Donovan takes up the story: 'At the right time, the signal was given to break. The torpedoes went on their way, I increased speed to 250mph, and turned to port with my two in line astern. The idea was that we would come to the island, then pull up over the hill into the harbour and pick off any targets we could see. We would spread out because, as there was only a three second delay on the bombs we had to keep apart otherwise we would be blowing each other up. As soon as I came over the hill into the harbour, I saw one ship on fire and another with a huge cloud of smoke pouring out of it, so with these gone, I was a bit non-plussed. Then a terrific barrage started hitting me. I pushed the stick forward and got as low as I could on the water and then spied another ship, still afloat, behind the smoke. I did a half circuit of the harbour, being hit continuously, and ran in on this remaining ship, I can well remember having to pull back my stick rather sharply after I had dropped my bombs because I thought I was going to hit the funnel. Bits of metal were flying in the cockpit and the aircraft was actually twice blown virtually out of my hands as I ran in. We got through the harbour entrance and on looking out I saw the aircraft was very badly damaged. The Turret gunner, John Stuart, said the other two in our formation had been shot down. In the turmoil, his own turret had suddenly rotated madly and he hadn't been able to see if our ship had been hit'.

Formation 'C' coming in from the north saw that all three ships had been struck, so attacked the shore targets of barracks and warehouses.

As his aircraft left the island, Ted Donovan saw the leading three torpedo aircraft were flying away south in formation, but his own Marauder was too badly damaged to catch them up, so a lonely course for home was set. He pulled up to 5,000ft and headed through the falling dusk towards Gambut. The aircraft felt very unstable and the temperature of one engine was rising ominously through loss of oil. Approaching Tobruk, Allied gunners opened up with their Bofors guns. The Marauder fired off the colours of the day and flashed its landing lights but to no avail, so Donovan had to turn out to sea again. He told the crew to don their parachutes and bale out as soon as they re-crossed the coast. At the second approach, the Allied gunners had apparently got the message and did not fire again. However, the overheating engine was on its last legs and now the other engine was overheating. Sighting a flarepath, Donovan flew over it, did a left hand circuit and came in high, because he feared having to do an engineless landing. He put the undercarriage down, throttled back and made his approach - very steeply, as one engine had stopped already and the other was likely to do so at any second. The landing was a bit heavy, but the aircraft was in one piece. As Donovan turned off the flarepath, the remaining engine seized.

Donovan then discovered that his crew had failed to comply with his order to bale out, because they had complete confidence in his ability to get down safely. For his outstanding airmanship and courage, Donovan was awarded the DFC and Lewis the DSO. Lewis' navigator, Flight Lieutenant Ridley was also awarded the DFC.

Donovan's co-pilot had behaved in exemplary fashion throughout the operation, remaining calm and efficient and was rewarded by being given his own crew. He took with him his navigator, so Donovan was left without a co-pilot or a navigator. His turret gunner knew that Teddy Meadwell's navigator was without a crew. Donovan was invited to the Sergeant's Mess to meet him. The three, Ted Donovan, John Stuart and Tony de Yarburgh-Bateson had a beer or two together and it was agreed that Bateson should join Donovan's crew.

NORTH AFRICA

While the Eighth Army was winning the Battle of Mareth and the First Army attacking from the West, March was a confused month for No 14 Squadron, while many aircraft, air and ground crews were in Algeria, carrying on with operations over the Mediterranean, the rest of the Squadron was still scattered about the Middle East, variously occupied with training of one sort or another.

On 1 March 1943, sixteen Marauders took off from Shallufa and flew west to Berka in four formations of three aircraft and one of four. The first, led by Major Lewis, was airborne at 0815hrs. The other four formations took off at regular intervals afterwards, the last being led by the CO. Lapthorne remained in charge of the rest of the Squadron at Shallufa to continue training. Flying Officer Parks was in charge of a detachment at Berka and Flying Officer Dunsmore of another one at Gambut.

The following day, the sixteen Marauders flew on to Castel Benito in Libya, where they were refuelled before proceeding to Telergma in Algeria. The airfield at Telergma, near the town of Constantine, was an American Air Force base. They accommodated the RAF Squadron personnel in billets and were helpful in every way. The party did not leave for Blida until 12 March. Back in the Western Desert, on Wednesday 3 March, the contingent at Berka were instructed to join up with those at Gambut, which they reached on the 6th.

Two Marauders piloted by Goode and Clarke Hall left Telergma, on Wednesday 10 March to fly to Blida. The weather forecasts predicted fine weather, but crossing the coast they ran into foul weather over the Mediterranean. This improved when approaching Algiers. The wireless operator in Clarke Hall's crew picked up a signal from Goode's aircraft at 1127hrs, but it gave no indication that the other Marauder was in trouble. However, it never reached Blida, crashing into the Bay of Algiers: an accident that was later attributed to tail fin failure. Everyone on board perished; Squadron Leader Peter Goode, Flight Lieutenant Beacham, Flight Sergeant Clapson, Sergeants Brown, Walkinshaw and Hunt. The passengers on the aircraft were Flight Lieutenant Sieward the Squadron Intelligence Officer, Taylor - NCO of A Flight, and Bullen. Many squadron records were also lost.

Two bodies were recovered on the 12th and identified as Sergeants Clapson and Hunt. They were buried in the British War Cemetery at Et Alia. Two more bodies were later found in the water of Algiers Harbour and these were buried at sea. The remaining aircraft left Telergma and landed at Blida.

Back at Shallufa, during a period of moonlight, the crews on the Torpedo Course practiced night flying. On 13 March 1943 the Gambut contingent returned to No 107 Maintenance Unit, and on the 15th joined up with the remaining members of the Squadron in the Middle East theatre.

In contrasting weather in Algeria there was snow on the Atlas Mountains, allowing personnel to ski and toboggan. All aircrew were given 48 hours leave after the long months in Egypt, the Western Desert and Libya.

It was soon decided that, since the runway at Blida was not long enough for fully laden and armed Marauders, the Squadron would operate from Maison Blanche a few miles nearer Algiers until a new runway at Blida was ready for use. Five aircraft and some ground crew were detached to Maison Blanche. Aircrews due to fly on operations left Blida at 0400hrs to travel to Maison Blanche, where armed and fuelled aircraft awaited them.

Meanwhile at Fayid, Sergeant Fletcher, who had been Donovan's co-pilot on the Melos raid, had been practising circuits and landings. In practice flying on one engine he was unable to restart the starboard engine and was forced to attempt a single-engine landing. In turning to line up with the runway, the Marauder stalled, and he tried to put the aircraft down on the sand, which was very soft. The nose wheel dug in and the undercarriage folded. Immediately on impact the aircraft burst into flames. Sergeant Fletcher, his spine fractured, and his badly injured air-gunner were extricated and taken to Hospital. A flight mechanic, Leading Aircraftman Lewis, who was acting as flight engineer, was killed instantly.

In the Middle East, confusion reigned. Firstly Flying Officer Lapthorne was informed by the powers-that-be that the Squadron had been transferred from the control of 201

Group to the control of 206 Group. No signal to this effect was received by Maydwell in Algeria. Then Lapthorne received a barrage of conflicting signals and instructions from 201 Group. It seemed to be a question of the 'right hand not knowing what the left hand was doing'. A request came for a party to proceed to Fayid to practice formation flying, so some Marauders could take part in a demonstration flight over Egypt. In addition, a request came for a party to return to Shallufa to continue training. Lapthorne with the wisdom of Solomon solved the dilemma by combining both operations at Shallufa.

On the 26th flying from Maison Blanche, three Marauders captained by Grimsey, Slade and Ken Dee flew offensive reconnaissances throughout the western basin of the Mediterranean. Dee's aircraft was airborne for nine hours and ten minutes.

The contingent in Algeria was now operating under the control of Mediterranean Allied Coastal Air Force (MACAF) commanded by Air Vice Marshal Sir Hugh Pugh Lloyd who on 27 March sent a message of congratulation to No 14 Squadron on the excellence of its work. A signal was received on the 28th from 201 Group to say that HM King George VI had approved the award of the DSO to Wing Commander Maydwell and the DFC to Flight Lieutenant Goodwin for his excellent work as the Squadron Navigation Officer and during many operational flights.

On the 30th March Warrant Officer Bob Francis's crew flew a reconnaissance. They intercepted an enemy convoy of six ships, escorted by 16 fighters (Messerschmitt Bf109s, Fw190s and Macchi 202s plus four Ju 88s). The Marauder was attacked by a Bf109 and Ju88, but managed to avoid being hit and no crewman was injured. Len Einsaar's crew flew a separate reconnaissance but reported few sightings.

Throughout April the Squadron was once more divided. The operational crews and supporting personnel were in Algeria, and the crews flying training and their supporting personnel remained in Egypt under the control of 201 Group.

In Algeria, the Squadron mounted daily sorties with anything from one to two Marauders taking off at intervals of between one and five hours. The aim of this surveillance of the Mediterranean was to deny the Axis powers unfettered use of Mussolini's boasted 'Mare nostrum'. Almost all these sorties reported the position of shipping. Information of great value to intelligence, but a large number, despite the risk of being attacked by enemy fighters or shot at by warships, were deemed unexciting by the crews. Indeed, one pilot described such a trip in his log book with the succinct word 'Boring'!

On April 1 a party of 70 groundcrews under Warrant Officer Young plus a mass of equipment and personal kit left Kasfareet in Egypt in five Dakotas bound for Blida, where the weather was cold and wet. Many aircrew members fell ill with colds and influenza, but to ensure regular surveillance, crews swapped personnel. On the 4th O'Connor and his crew took off from Maison Blanche in a Marauder armed with four 500lb bombs for an eight hour reconnaissance along the east coast of Sardinia. They had not been airborne for long, before RAF Hurricanes came in to attack the Marauder. It took ten long minutes of frantic signalling and cat-and-mouse manoeuvring to persuade the fighter pilots that they should take further lessons in aircraft recognition. O'Connor then continued the patrol. Eleven different enemy aircraft were sighted, but no shipping.

Two days later, four additional Marauders and crews arrived at Blida from the Middle East, and three sorties by Lewis, Law-Wright and Einsaar reported much aircraft and shipping activity by the enemy.

On the 7th, Clarke-Hall's crew reported the position, speed and direction of a large enemy convoy with an aerial escort, which did not attack the RAF aircraft. The next day, MACAF sent a signal of congratulation to the Squadron, saying the convoy sighted by Clarke-Hall's crew had been totally destroyed in consequence. Three more aircraft and crews arrived from the Middle East and four reconnaissance sorties were flown.

Three more Marauders flew on reconnaissance missions on Sunday, 11 April. Bates reported having 'an unfriendly brush with a Ju52, but no harm done'. A number of ships were sighted by the three aircraft.

The next day was a sad one for the Squadron, as Len Einsaar's aircraft did not return. Amongst the crew was John Buckland of O'Connor's crew. The others were Sergeants Kitkin, Cloway, Harrison and Goldsmith. Fortunately, they were all reported later to be Prisoners of War. (Their bizarre experiences following their capture are described in *Adriatic Adventure* by Squadron Leader John Buckland and published after the war by Robertson and Mullens of Melbourne).

A week after his 'unfriendly brush with a Ju52', Sergeant Bates' Marauder was attacked by two Bf 109s but evaded their attentions and safely returned to base.

Next day, 19 April. Francis attacked an He115 and inflicted some damage, but could not claim a 'kill'.

Sergeant Dee's crew sighted a convoy on Tuesday 20 April. An escorting Ju88 attacked the Marauder but was repulsed by the Australian gunners and broke off the engagement.

That day, at the other end of the Mediterranean, Donovan led a formation of four Marauders at the start of their flight to Algeria. All four aircraft took off from Shallufa heavily laden with equipment and spare personnel in addition to the regular aircrews. Donovan's own crew was, Sergeants Paddy Reid, Dickie Slatcher, Tony Bateson, John Stuart and George Collins. In addition the aircraft carried three passengers: Flight Lieutenant Cecil Goodwin the Squadron Navigation Officer, Flight Sergeant Rollins who had been Reid's Navigator and Leading Aircraftsman Walmsley, a fitter.

Shortly after take-off, Russell's aircraft had to return to base, but rejoined later. As the remaining three Marauders were approaching the Bay of Salum trouble struck Donovan's aircraft. The petrol transfer pump became unserviceable, so he landed at Gambut. It did not take very long for the pump trouble to be rectified, but in the afternoon, when an attempt was made to get airborne, the aircraft exhibited a violent swing to port. This happened twice and by the time the fault had been diagnosed and rectified, it was too late to fly on and the night was spent at Gambut. Next day, Donovan's heavily-laden Marauder took off, but within an hour it became evident the starboard engine was using too much oil, so a further landing at Berka, near Benghazi, was made. After a short delay, it was possible to proceed to Castel Benito, where the other three Marauders were waiting. Unfavourable weather at Castel Benito prevented the Marauders there from moving on.

Next morning, one of the main wheel tyres of Donovan's aircraft 'ballooned', so it was unable to accompany the other Marauders on their way westward. The crew and passengers were faced with the daunting task of fitting a new tyre without the proper tools. These were borrowed from the engineering officer of a USAAF Squadron, who regretted he was unable to offer the help of his technicians but advised: 'All you need is a little soap'.

The wheel was removed from the aircraft and work started on replacing the tyre. By great good fortune, Rollins had worked pre-war in the Canadian Goodyear tyre factory, so he was put in charge. Under his tutelage and encouraged by a flow of lurid language, the new tyre was fitted to the wheel, but perversely the valve hid itself inside the rim. The struggles of the Junior Service had been watched by an officer of the Royal Navy with wry amusement. Now, seeing the problem, he stepped forward, cried "The Navy's here!" and proceeded to lasso the recalcitrant valve with a short piece of string to retrieve it. Finally, after three hours of 'blood, sweat and tears' the wheel was in place and the dirty and exhausted crew were able to return to their billets and try to get clean with the limited amount of water available.

On Saturday 24 April, Slade's Marauder left Blida for a reconnaissance of the area between Tunisia and Sicily. Slade and his wireless operator Sergeant Lindschau, had survived three crashes in Blenheims. On this sortie, they were attacked by a FW190. To escape the fighter's attentions, Slade used full boost and shortly afterwards the port engine failed. Attempting a single-engined landing at Tingley, the starboard engine also cut out. The Marauder crashed and burst into flames. Slade, still strapped to his seat, was thrown clear, but his co-pilot Bedell was killed. Gil Lindschau suffered a broken leg and first and second degree burns to his face and hands. Macdonald, (the navigator) was also severely injured, but both turret and tail gunners were unharmed apart from the shock. Slade and Macdonald were taken to an RAF Hospital. Lindschau was treated excellently by the Americans, but it was three months before he was fit enough to return to the Squadron.

On the same day the gremlin in Donovan's aircraft discovered a new way of preventing it from reaching Blida. Flying over the Sahara, there was a sudden explosion in the starboard engine. The aircraft lurched before Donovan righted it and asked the turret gunner for a report on what he could see of the stricken engine. John Stuart, after a pensive pause, replied "Well, Ted. There's a lot of smoke and a reasonable amount of metal coming from it!". Bateson told Ted that there was a landing ground nearby, but the two pilots were unable to see it, so Donovan chose a seemingly flat piece of desert near the oasis village of Tozeur to make a reasonably smooth landing in 420yds. In Tozeur, which was some three miles from the site of the landing, was the Hotel Transatlantique which housed a number of French officers, but Madame made room for the stranded airman.

Two days later, Tony Bateson wrote in his diary: 'Cecil Goodwin falls ill today with stomach pains. I fetch the village doctor, an exotic figure in brown slacks and sandals on his bare feet. He assures us the water is all right, but says it contains a large percentage of 'sulphates of magnesium' - Epsom salts in fact! We wait for rescue. Ted has tried to phone Biskra every day but Gafsa exchange never put him through and presumably the others will have notified the Squadron of our plight. The flies are very numerous. They start annoying one at 0500hrs. and do not cease until very long after dark. The heat too is most oppressive'.

FORCED LANDING AT TOZEUR - 24 APR 1943

TOP: What do we do now?
Left to Right: LAC Walmsley, John Stuart, Paddy Reid, Dickie Slatcher

Below: This is what we will do
Right to Left: Flg Off Ted Donovon, Sgt Reid, Sgt Rawlins, Flt lt Cecil Goodwin behind, LAC Walmsley, Sgt Stuart, Sgt Dick Slatcher, Sgt George Collins, and French Officer.

On Sunday 25 April, the Squadron lost another aircraft which failed to return from a reconnaissance over the Tyrrhenian sea. It was never learned what misadventure befell Bullock, Trovillo, Patman, Bentham, Mouatt and Warburton, who were the crew.

On the 27th, three reconnaissances were flown by Clarke-Hall, Johnson and Francis, whose Wireless Operator Jack Canavan describes what happened on their trip: 'One of the most memorable operations of our crew comprising Pilot Officer Francis, Miles 2nd Pilot, Scott-Murphy, myself Wireless Operator, Carnie turret gunner and Slogett tail gunner was engaged in, occurred on 27 April when we were operating in daylight from Blida, through Maison Blanche on a normal anti-shipping offensive reconnaissance, doing a search pattern north of Sicily.

'On one of the early legs of our search pattern, we sighted a merchant vessel, a Destroyer escort and some smaller vessels, with four Messerschmitt Bf110s as air escort. They apparently did not see us approaching so Francis continued on course and flew at 50ft, right through the centre of the convoy. As we passed out of the convoy some heavy AA fire from the destroyer was too late and inaccurate. Francis suggested that they had not seen us the first time and stunned us all by saying we were going through the centre again. So, on completing a wide turn he increased his speed and continued on directly through the centre of the convoy again, making sure of our sightings for our reports. About half way through, we passed below the fighter escort, again being allowed to do so without challenge.

'We then continued on and completed our patrol, at the same time sending our sighting report with a couple of amplifying reports on the convoy, seeing that we had been allowed to make such a complete count of ships etc. On our way back to Tunis, we returned to the convoy's position to check any changes. By now the air escort was seven Bf 110s, and two Cant 506B Italian float planes, no doubt because of our earlier visit. About halfway past the convoy, we passed directly underneath one of the Cant seaplanes. Carnie opened fire with his two 0.5inch guns and caused the centre engine of the Cant to catch fire, while pieces were seen to fall off the fuselage of the aircraft - this surely added insult to injury and started a hornet's nest of activity.

'We were immediately attacked and chased by Bf 110s. Fortunately the speed of the B-26 Marauder was too much for them, for while one of them gave up the chase, after about five minutes, the other one fruitlessly tried to lob his cannon shells onto us by firing from behind, unable to catch us!

'While we were being chased by this Bf 110, we sighted another merchant ship of about 1,500 tons, and sent out a sighting report and further amplifying report on this one. The time for the whole operation was a little over eight hours and was surely one of our busiest, our most hectic and probably most effective - It certainly made Bob Francis smile.

A copy of a signal indicates the busy time we had from the first sighting report through to our request for a landing forecast.

From:-	Signals Officer, RAF Station, BLIDA
To:-	Officer Commanding RAF Station, BLIDA
	(Copy to:- Officer Commanding No 14 Squadron)
Ref:	BL/703/Sigs.

Date: 27th April, 1943.
Subject: SIGNALS EFFICIENCY

1. The following extract of the BLIDA wireless log for the afternoon of the 27th April 1943 is an example of very efficient Wireless Operating.
2. The Aircraft Operator in H/14 Squadron was F/Sgt. CANAVAN and throughout, his signalling was of a very high order.
3. During the period of the signalling the aircraft was flying between the coasts of ITALY and SICILY, a distance from BLIDA of over 450 miles, and at height of less than 50ft.

4.

TO	FROM	N.R.	G.R.	TEXT	T.O.O	.T.O.R
BLIDA	H/14	1	7	First Sighting Report	1320	1329
BLIDA	H/14	2	3	Amplifying Report	1330	1337
BLIDA	H/14	3	6	Amplifying Report	1342	1354
BLIDA	H/14	4	6	First Sighting Report	1550	1557
BLIDA	H/14	5	7	Amplifying Report	1605	1611
BLIDA	H/14	6	5	Request for landing Forecast	1615	1619
H/14	BLIDA	1	12	Landing Forecast	1634	1638

(Signed) D R R FAIR
Squadron Leader Signals Officer
RAF Station, BLIDA

On the 28th, three reconnaissance sorties were mounted. Flight Lieutenant Brown's crew attacked and damaged a Heinkel He 59 seaplane. They, in turn were assaulted by a Bf 110, which failed to score any hits. Hugh Bates', aircraft did a 'Creeping Line Ahead' patrol north east of Ustica and reported seeing an Me 323 and two barges.

Ted Donovan's crew and their passengers were still stranded at Touzeur. One by one they had suffered pains in the stomach and diarrhoea. Donovan was very badly affected on the 29th. The French Captain, who had arranged for the French Sergeants to control the Senegalese troops guarding the Marauder, announced regretfully that he could no longer spare his NCOs and suggested the RAF NCOs could take over the duty. When they did, one of the Senegalese soldiers on guard grinned and said: "Bomb-bomb pas bon-bon!".

On 30 April, O'Connor's aircraft was once again the target of what 50 years later would have been termed 'friendly fire'. The Marauder was engaged on a low-level reconnaissance North of Sicily, when four USAAF P-38 Lightning fighters attacked for eight minutes before their pilots recognised the colours of the day and letters being flashed by the RAF aircraft. Continuing on its patrol, the Marauder later was the target for 'unfriendly fire' from two Italian fighters, but they were unable to match the B-26's superior speed at ultra low level. The sortie lasted 6hrs 15mins.

At the beginning of May all aircraft inspections by the maintenance crews were being carried out at Blida, but all the operational flying was done from Bone, where the camp was within a few hundred yards of the beach. If it had not been for the vast quantities of mosquitoes, the site would have been ideal. Those crews that were not flying a reconnaissance were able to lie naked on the sand and bathe in the Mediterranean. The camp was several miles from the airstrip at Bone and crews were taken to their aircraft in open three-tonners, which some wit called 'Tumbrels'.

On 2 May, a USAF T-6 Texan, piloted by Captain Simms circled Touzeur and landed beside the stricken RAF Marauder. On board he had a master Sergeant and a stock of US Army rations, which were received with unbounded joy. Before leaving, he promised to arranged for a new engine, American technicians and all necessary equipment to effect an engine change to be brought to Touzeur in a C-47 the next day.

The next day, the Squadron at Blida moved in to permanent billets from the tented camp they had occupied, and at Touzeur, American get-up-and-go was being shown dramatically. As promised by Captain Simms, a C-47 arrived, bringing an engine, jeep, equipment and technicians prepared to replace the dud engine of the Marauder. When all had been unloaded, Goodwin, Slatcher, Bateson, Stuart, Collins and Walmsley, with such kit as they possessed, boarded the C-47 and were flown to Telergma. Ted Donovan and Paddy Reid stayed behind to undertake the daunting task of flying the Marauder from the crudest and shortest airstrip conceivable.

The Americans included a black Sergeant and a white Sergeant. The former saw the Sengalese soldiers were also black and went across to chat with them. After a very brief exchange, he came back and said to the white Sergeant, "Say, Sarge, those guys are black ain't they?" "Yea, I guess so". "Well, they're a funny kind of blacks, they don't speak English".

On a later occasion, a squadron group composed of Britons and Australians wearing bush hats were engaged in idle chit-chat. When the Aussies walked off, some US troops, who had been listening to the conversation asked, "What nationality were those guys in the funny hats?" "Australians, why do you ask?" "But they spoke English".

The Senegalese troops used their trenching tools to help level off humps in the runway that would be required for takeoff. The Americans and the two Britons, meanwhile, set about lightening the Marauder by removing everything possible. An aeronautical engineer sent by the manufacturers used his 'balancing stick' to ensure the stripped machine had the centre of gravity within the correct tolerances.

The Wireless Operator, Navigator, and two gunners of Donovan's crew were destined to stay at Telergma until 27 May. They were billeted in a large room at the end of a long hut, at the other end of which served as a club for American officers. One evening they had a great party to which they invited some very glamourous US Red Cross girls but omitted to provide lavatories for the ladies. That evening, Dickie Slatcher returned from Constantine and, approaching the blacked out billet, almost fell over one of these girls answering a call of nature. The poor girl cried out: "Say, have a heart fellah!"

It was on 7 May, that both Tunis and Bizerta were taken by the Allied armies, and six days later General Alexander sent this laconic despatch to Churchill in London: 'Sir, it is my duty to report that the campaign in Tunisia is over. All enemy resistance has ceased. We are masters of the North African shores'.

On 9 May, a Marauder crewed by Russell, Fennell, Dyson, Nicholas and Armstrong and Ayton was shot down north of Sicily. The wireless operator, Nicholas, sent out a message saying they were ditching and giving a map reference. At the time Flight

Sergeant O'Connor's crew were engaged in a reconnaissance, and his wireless operator received instructions to divert to the position given and search for survivors. Sadly none were found and the Marauder landed after a flight of nine and a half hours, only to be told they had been given the wrong position to search.

A few days later O'Connor carried out a low level 'creeping line ahead' patrol along the south west coast of Italy. In his own words, 'Chased by single-engined fighters for seven minutes. Sighted enemy hospital ship off Naples. Attacked three large six-engined transport aircraft (Me 323) and set an engine of one on fire'. We were to learn later that the Me 323 had a fully armour plated cockpit. The Commanding Officer and our crew had a look over a damaged one of these massive machines at Castle Vestrano in Sicily.'

Three reconnaissances were carried out on 13 May, by Brown's, Graham's and Phillips' crews. The latter aircraft was attacked by two Fw 190s, which chased it for fifteen minutes but scored no hits on the Marauder.

Two days later Rawlins flew one of the three sorties and his crew sighted several aircraft movements. His gunner scored strikes on a Ju 52, but the enemy aircraft escaped. Ted Donovan and Paddy Reid were able to fly the repaired Marauder away from Touzeur on May 15. Ted describes the take off: 'There was no sign of any wind, so Paddy and I and the crew chief got up before dawn. The reason for starting so early was that the early morning was much the coolest time of day and the air, therefore, denser, allowing us to take off more quickly than if we had waited for the heat of the day. We walked through the palm trees to the aircraft just as the first light was showing in the East that is the false dawn. I climbed into the aircraft, did my checks, and then got out again and inspected the aircraft for outside checks with the help of Paddy and the crew chief. I called him crew chief, which is an American phrase for master sergeant, who knows every part of the aircraft and has a gaggle of men working under him. This chap asked if he could come with me. I decided it was too dangerous as I reckoned we only had about a 50/50 chance of getting off. I promised him, however, that I would arrange for him to be picked up the minute we got back to base.

So I turned into the runway that we had made and opened the throttles steadily. The sand barrier that we had constructed worked beautifully, and the engines achieved their full power before we had used up very much distance. We fairly shot out after about 50yrds, had a very bumpy ride and then we were virtually thrown into the air after 500yrds'.

On the 16 May, Francis with characteristic daring flew his Marauder right into Spezia harbour and sighted a Littorio class cruiser and two other ships. Canavan, his wireless operator said no one seemed to notice their entry and exit!

ATTACKS AND ATTACKED

Squadron aircraft were engaged in more aggression on 17 May, when Brown's crew attacked a Me 323, but claimed no hits. Bates describes his encounter: 'We were in the vicinity of the bay of Naples, when we saw four aircraft (two in front and two following) in the classic positions of two fighters each with their No 2 gently weaving about behind them. I immediately assumed that the best place for us was directly underneath them, where they hopefully would not see us unless they decided to fly upside down! So we turned towards them (they were at 2,000 to 2,500ft) to close the gap as quickly as possible. It very soon became obvious that the gap was only closing very slowly, i.e. we were all heading in the same direction into the Bay of Naples but - not only that - it also became evident that they were not fighters but two aircraft, each towing a glider, so we immediately opened the taps and climbed hard and ended up with them as a formation of five aircraft with us a couple of hundred yards behind them and 150 - 200ft below them, though they were quite unaware of our presence. As soon as the turret gunner opened fire, there was a technical hitch, i.e. a jam, so we eventually quit. In any case, 2,000ft above the Bay of Naples was no place for a man, who had no head for heights!'

On 20 May, Joe Elliot and Ken Rawlins flew reconaissances and saw some shipping. Ken attacked an enemy motor torpedo boat with cannon fire and surprisingly was chased by a Savoia-Marchetti SM79, whose pilot must have been unaware of the superior speed of the B-26A.

Law-Wright attacked a formation of Me 323s and shot one of them into the sea. This was the Squadron's first successful attack against one of these giant machines, which had been designed originally as gliders, with six 1,140 hp. Gnome-Rhone engines having been added to make the powered version. The wing span was 180ft $5^1/2$ins. (The wing span of a Hercules is 132ft 7ins). Its maximum speed was 177mph, and it could carry up to 130 fully armed troops or up to 35,030lbs of military stores. The defensive armament consisted of five 13mm and ten 7,92mm machine guns,

On 27 May, Flight Sergeant Bates attacked an Italian SM79, which fled, and next day, Clarke-Hall's aircraft claimed strikes on a submarine during a reconnaissance. Three days later O'Connor's crew flew a creeping line ahead patrol between Corsica and Italy. They sighted a Ju 52 and later were chased by two Bf 110s, which they outpaced.

Fighter pilots, Flying Officer Crawford and Sergeant Campbell seconded to the Squadron claimed damage to a Ju 52. The German pilot must have been very skilled to escape from two Mustang aircraft.

After the surrender of the Axis forces in Tunisia in May, the Allies next move was to invade Sicily and from there move into Italy. On Wednesday 2 June, the main squadron ground party travelled east from Blida to Protville in Tunisia, but Gibbins, the Engineering Officer, and some maintenance staff stayed at Blida to work on the aircraft operating from there. The journey from Blida to Protville was of about the same distance as from Aberdeen to London, and involved crossing a mountain range and some rough and hilly roads. Cook Ron Haley recalls: 'Our next move was in convoy over the hill (sic) into Tunisia. Our first stop was on a landing ground on some mud flat, and where it was so dry the ground was creviced and cracked. Then, a few days after moving in, we had rain and up from the cracks came hordes of lizards about a foot in length. They were everywhere, so we moved onto a site with some sand where we were more at home'.

The cooks on No 14 Squadron throughout the war achieved miracles of improvisation and provided everyone with meals however impossible the conditions. Admittedly men sometimes grumbled at the monotony of corned beef, hard biscuits and margarine marked 'Unfit for human consumption after 1940' which the Army provided.

On 3 June a Marauder went out on a reconnaissance from Bone and failed to return. The all NCO crew was Rawlins, Austin. Burton. Liddle, Nuttall and Lumsden. Their fate was never known.

On the 5th, a road convoy set off at 0545hrs from Souk Ahras and travelled the mountainous route between Algeria and Tunisia. Approaching Medjerda, at 1900hrs, they had their first sight of Tunis in the distance. Since moving from the Middle East, the motor transport drivers had learned that the RAF Bedford trucks were inferior to the American Dodge trucks in that the British vehicles overheated on long mountainous ascents. This 13-hour journey was no picnic.

Flying Officer Johnson's and Flying Officer Donovan's crews flew two reconnaissances on Sunday 6 June. Donovan's navigator prepared for the flight with special diligence as it was to be his first operation in a Marauder: flying low over the sea throughout the six-hour sortie.

In the B-26A, the wireless operator and navigator occupied a cabin behind and lower than the cockpit, in which the two pilots sat. Each had a desk and equipment at hand. At the right of the navigator was an instrument known as the Bendix Drift Meter, a down-facing telescope through which he could observe the ground or sea. There was an adjustable graticule, lined with the direction of the surface beneath, then the angle of drift read off on a scale. Observation of the wind lanes on the surface of the sea and assessment of the strength of wind by the white caps and spume enabled the navigator to plot the aircraft's progress on his Admiralty chart.

The Marauder covered an area touching on Sardinia, Sicily, Naples and Stromboli Island. Two enemy aircraft were seen but, as Donovan recalled, 'They made us run away as we were not yet used to seeing hostile aircraft'.

The next day, in Tunisia, the road convoy moved to a new site that was devoid of lizards. All the vehicles were unloaded and the nomad Squadron created a new camp.

Back in Algeria, two of the No 14 Squadron Mustang pilots, Flight Lieutenant Blair and Pilot Officer Gildner shot down a twin engined float plane in the Gulf of Oristano on the west coast of Sardinia. That day, the two Marauder reconnaissances were flown by Bob Francis and Ken Dee.

The Allies planned to take the tiny island of Pantelleria, which lay between Tunisia and Sicily as a necessary step towards invading Europe from the south. In case Axis forces tried to prevent this, the Squadron was briefed to fly cross-over patrols between Pantelleria and Sicily. The first patrol was flown by Johnson's crew. When his aircraft was being attacked by 6 Bf l09s, his Wireless Operator, Sergeant Robinson, sent a coded message ,"Am being attacked by fighters. Will call you later" to which he added in plain language "Maybe", for which he was duly reprimanded!

Robinson was a short stocky Australian and very much his own man. He preferred not to share a tent with others, but had a small bivouac, into which he crawled at night. He appeared to think there was less chance of being hit by a bomb in the event of an enemy air raid because his tent was so small a target! This habit earned him the sobriquet, 'Bill the Beetle'.

The afternoon patrol by the CO took off from Bone at 1700hrs. He was on the easterly leg, when his tail gunner, Graham discerned two enemy aircraft attacking out of the sun. Alerted by him, Maydwell increased speed. The Bf 109s closed to 100yrds and split with the evident intention of attacking the Marauder from port and starboard quarters. Maydwell threw the B-26 into a steep 180-degree turn. It seemed as though a wing tip must have hit the water, but the manoeuvre was successful, forcing the German pilots to turn and fly into the sun.

Maydwell then took the Marauder up to 80ft, then down to deck level and skidded it from left to right and vice versa. Graham afterwards reported that on several occasions, there was a terrific 'whoosh' of cannon shells that boiled in the sea just where the Marauder had been seconds before. The turret gunner fired a burst before the fuse blew, rendering his guns useless.

Gil Graham, however, scored good hits on one of the Bf 109s, which departed the scene with glycol leaking and forming a stream of white smoke. The other one must have run out of ammunition and appreciating the Allied aircraft's turret guns were out of action, closed to within 60yrds and flew in formation on the port side of the B-26. Graham returned to see in Daily Routine Orders that he had been awarded the DFM.

On the 10th also, Hugh Bates and his crew were involved in action. Their reconnaissance route took them from Bone up the east coast of Sardinia and Corsica, then east to Montecristo Island and Civitavecchia. West again to the east coast of Sardinia and back to base. Between Corsica and Montecristo they sighted a tanker of 8,000 tons, escorted by 2 He IIIs, which, surprisingly, took no notice of the Marauder.

On the way from Civitavecchia to Sardinia, they caught up with a three engined bomber - an SM79 - heading west and about 1,450ft above them. Seeing that he was observed, the Italian pilot dived down to sea level with the idea of gaining sufficient speed to outrun the B-26A but the latter had a speed advantage of more than 40 knots at deck level. Bates was able to position the Marauder on the port side of the S.M.79 so that the turret gunner could follow the Italian aircraft easily. The Italian pilot's only possible defensive move would have been to turn to port and cut across the bows of the Marauder, causing it to break off the attack, if only temporarily. Instead, he turned to starboard and offered Bates' turret gunner a target he could not miss and he blasted it into the sea.

On 11 June the more recent additions to Donovans crew were blooded. The reconnaissance took them to the east coast of Sardinia, then across to Spezia, back to Corsica and past Sardinia to base. Sighted were two merchant ships, one of 5,000 tons and the other of 2,000 tons, and a motor launch, but the story is best recounted by Donovan himself: 'From the top of Sardinia we were chased by a Ju 88, which dived from about 1,500ft. We opened our throttles and went out to sea towards Italy. The Junkers couldn't catch us, although it put in one or two shots from its cannon, which went far too short, and we kept steaming along without it gaining on us. Stuart, of course, kept up a good commentary and shot off the odd tracer as a warning. Every time I tried to turn, the Ju would cut the corner and close in. This went on the whole way across the Tyrrhenian Sea, and the coast was coming up, so I edged towards the Aeolian Islands with Bateson's helpful navigational course and when we got there I did a steep turn around the northernmost island shot off back to sea again.

The enemy aircraft gave up the chase at this stage. We carried on then up the coast to Spezia, which was a base for the Italian navy. From there we went across to Corsica and down past Capraia Island. We carried on down the east coast of Sardinia and it was when we were about half way down we were suddenly attacked by two Bf 109s. The first I knew was a shout from John Stuart: "Turn right, GO!", which I duly did, to see some tracer flashing over the wing. He took over the direction and gave me a commentary, turning this way and that as the fighters came in. At one stage I saw splashes of their cannon fire in the water on the starboard side. In the end, after what seemed a long time, but was probably only five minutes, John said: "He's turned back with smoke coming out" I said rather crossly: "What happened to the other one?" George Collins, the rear gunner, replied: "John shot it down."'

The following day Graham's gunners claimed damage to a Ju 52 in the course of making a number of useful sightings. Chris Phillips noted three liners in different positions, which may have been troopships.

Major Eric Lewis SAAF, DSO, DFC, said farewell to the Squadron on 12 June, after two years and three months, flying some 74 operations both on Blenheims and Marauders. His luxurious 'Pilot Officer Prune' moustache was greatly admired and became something of a mascot. He was extremely popular with all ranks and returned to his native South Africa to take up flying training duties.

Two reconnaissances were flown on 17 June by Chris Phillips and Ted Donovan, whose navigator, Tony Bateson, had a bad cold. Travelling from camp to airstrip in 'the tumbrel', Donovan asked him how he felt. Much to the amusement of the Australians in the three-tonner with them, the 'whinging Pom' replied: " I feel much too ill to be killed today". Bateson wrote in his diary. 'The trip lasted 7hrs 10mins. I had a bad cold and had swallowed two aspirins before starting. The sea was very rough with a 35 knot wind. At 30' above the waves we had a very bumpy ride, which made me feel sick. We sighted a 1,600 ton merchant vessel and a Ju 88, which did not see us'.

The next day the CO came across a surfaced submarine and his gunners peppered the conning tower, but its commander decided to stay on the surface and shoot it out, so the Marauder reported the sighting and continued its primary duty of reconnaissance! Ken Dee's aircraft was chased for 15 minutes by an enemy fighter but he managed to escape undamaged. While these operations were being carried out, some members of No 14 Squadron were able to line the route, when HM King George VI passed near Bone during his tour of North Africa.

Bob Francis and Hugh Bates reconnoitred over the Tyrrhenian Sea and along the coasts of Sardinia, Corsica and Italy on 23 June. Bates' crew reported seeing two tankers, ten Me 323s and five escort vessels. One of the tankers was sunk later by Beaufighters as a result of his sighting report.

On 26 June four reconnaissances were mounted, two in the morning flown by Squadron Leader Law-Wright and Flying Officer Owen Phillips and in the afternoon by the CO. Near the north west tip of Sardinia, an Italian destroyer of the Navigatori class was seen and shot at the B-26 from about a mile with dangerously accurate aim. Next sighted were three Me 323s heading south east. Returning past the destroyer, the Marauder received further unwelcome hostility. Later, two ships escorted by four Ju 88s were seen. The enemy fighters made to attack, but Maydwell increased speed and escaped. The second afternoon reconnaissance was flown by Donovan who recalls: 'As we came round the end of Elba, we came very close to an Italian cruiser travelling at full speed. It was of the Condottieri class. As there was only one of these in service, it was undoubtedly the Guiseppi Garibaldi. They were so surprised that they did not even shoot at us until we were well out of range. I said to the navigator: 'It's a Condottieri six-inch cruiser'. It had a silhouette similar to a Roma class battleship, so it was vital we got our identification right, as there is a world of difference between a battleship and a six-inch cruiser!

Later, four more small ships and three landing barges were seen as well as three enemy aircraft. After 6hrs, 40mins, the aircraft landed at Bone and Paddy said to Ted, 'You have wonderful eyesight, I couldn't even see the guns!'

Sadly, the Squadron lost another Marauder crew on the 28th, when Francis, Murphy, Miles, Carnie, Jellis and Sloggett flew out on a reconnaissance from Bone and did not return.

Bates' crew during a reconnaissance on 30 June sighted a Dornier seaplane and two fighters escorting a 3000 ton merchant ship with four destroyers and one escort vessel. The two Bf 109s attacked the B-26 for 15 minutes in ten separate attacks. The Marauder gunners fired 650 rounds and damaged one Bf 109. None of the crew were injured and the aircraft suffered no damage, due to excellent crew co-operation and skilful flying and gunnery.

During June 1943, No 14 Squadron's operations resulted in the destruction of one SM79, one Bf 109 and damage to one twin-engined float plane, two Bf 109s, one Bf 110 and one Ju52. A tanker was also sunk as a result of Bates' sighting report.

INTO EUROPE

The Mediterranean war moved into a new phase in July. The Axis army in North Africa having been comprehensively defeated, the Germans and Italians were forced back to the mainland of Europe and the Allies were set to pursue them by first invading Sicily. The reconnaissance patrolling by the Squadron throughout the daylight hours provided up-to-date intelligence of Axis shipping movements. The Marauders were despatched singly at wide intervals. Sometimes two areas of sea and coast were surveyed by different aircraft at the same time.

On 1 July, Marauders flew two reconnaissances. One aircraft captained by Neil O'Connor made sightings without seeing any action, but the other, captained by Chris Phillips was chased for four minutes by a Bf 110 before the enemy fighter gave up.

On the following day, two reconnaissances were flown by John Hunter and Neville Freeman. The latter was attacked by a Ju 88 but evaded damage. Hunter's aircraft was attacked by a Bf 110, but speed and evasive action made the enemy pilot give up the chase.

Graham's crew made one sortie and the CO's the other on 3 July. The latter saw the Italian battleship Roma inside Spezia harbour and outside were two Parthenhope class destroyers with a number of torpedo boats, schooners and smaller craft. One of the destroyers opened fire at the Marauder but failed to hit it.

On the way back to base a serious petrol leak developed in the port engine, so Maydwell took the aircraft up to 100ft in case fire broke out but they got home safely.

The same day Pilot Officer Dolan was bringing a Marauder up from the Delta to

Tunisia. When landing at Castel Benito, the undercarriage folded and the aircraft crashed. It burst into flames immediately. The navigator died and all the rest of the crew were severely injured.

On 9 and 10 of July, the Allied Forces landed in Sicily. General Patton's US 7th Army attacked the west flank of the coast between Piano Lupo and Licata, defended by the Italian 6th Army under General Guzzoni. At Licata the Italians retreated without a fight. General Montgomery's 8th Army attacked the east flank of the coast from Piano Lupo to Syracuse, defended by the German Herman Goering Panzer Division.

The invasion was by sea and air. Unfortunately some of the drops from the air, both gliders and paratroops, were mistimed and soldiers and gliders fell into the sea. Over 200 British troops were drowned and even more Americans. The island was defended by 315,000 Italians and 90,000 Germans.

On 10 July, Chris Phillips tried to make a forced landing at Bou Fousha, near Bizerta. His aircraft crashed and burst into flames. The 2nd Pilot Jimmy Colyer had a miraculous escape, being thrown through the nose of the Marauder. He was injured only slightly and returned to the Squadron the same day. Sergeants Jones and Rise were killed instantly; Flying Officers Chris Phillips and Wally Bertuch and Flight Sergeants Park and Mason were very seriously burned and injured. They were sent to the 8th General Hospital, which had followed the 8th Army from Egypt.

On 11th July Flight Sergeant Ken Dee's crew (Warrant Officer Johnny Ring, Flight Sergeants Cyril Allingham, Jimmy Bolton and Bill Cavanagh and Sergeant Worthington) sighted enemy destroyers escorting two merchant ships, one of 9,000 tons, one escort vessel and two unidentified aircraft. Later they attacked a Me 323 and scored hits, but failed to bring it down.

Bateson recorded in his diary on 12 July: 'Worse news. In the afternoon Ted goes to see Chris and the others in hospital. While he is there, Chris dies. The others are still on the danger list, though Jimmy (Colyer) is hobbling about the camp and making the best of it. He is very plucky. The funeral is to be tomorrow.'

Bertuch and Parker died shortly after Phillips. They were all buried in the Military Cemetery at Tunis with full honours and members of the Squadron in attendance.

Orders for operations on 14 July nominated the crews of Dee, Graham and Donovan. The latter flew north of Sicily and west of Naples. Two enemy aircraft were sighted in the distance, then a Ju 52 was found. Donovan decided to attack it and his turret gunner Stuart disabled its port engine before the fuses of the turret blew. The German pilot was lucky to limp home on his two undamaged engines.

Four reconnaissances were flown on the 15th. The aircraft captains were Maydwell, Law-Wright, Freeman and Hunter. Gil Graham, gunner in Maydwell's crew, describes their flight: 'We took off from Protville with our usual crew, to carry out a low level reconnaissance at dusk in the Tyrrhenian Sea area. On the outward journey just off the coast of Sardinia we attacked and shot down an Italian SM 82 transport plane. It did however appear to us that the pilot deliberately ditched the aircraft before we did too much damage to it. We photographed the plane in the water as proof. (The 82 was a large 3-engined, transport aircraft, similar to, but larger than the SM 79). A little while later we came across an armed merchant vessel, which opened fire with some light and heavy anti-aircraft guns, but we sustained no damage. As we turned south just outside Genoa harbour we were attacked by two Ju 88s, but we headed away from the coast and got clear by sheer speed without having to open fire on them.'

The Allied ground forces were now firmly established on Sicily and ready to start their push up the long leg of Italy itself. The High Command had to come to a decision as to whether or not the City of Rome should be bombed. It was decided that it should, provided the Vatican and St. Peter's was not attacked or harmed. It was essential that the bomber force should be certain of a clear view of the city, unhampered by cloud cover. A weather report of conditions over the city was required immediately preceding the take off of the bombers. Two Marauders were despatched from Protville in the early hours of 19 July. Donovan's aircraft was airborne at 0300hrs and Maydwell's took off half an hour later.

The CO's aircraft crossed the Italian coast near Anzio at crack of dawn and flew directly over a German airfield, crammed with aircraft, including numbers of He lll bombers. Both the British airmen and the Germans on the ground were taken completely by surprise and neither fired at the other. There was no doubt, however, that the encounter had warned the enemy of the presence of Allied aircraft over the Italian mainland, so Maydwell hedge-hopped over the trees and houses until he reached Rome. Weather conditions were noted and transmitted in code. Flying north, he found a number of Cant 506 seaplanes moored on Lake Bracciano. Turret and tail gunners sprayed them with gunfire, damaging several. Next, the engine of a goods train was attacked, before Maydwell turned out to sea again.

Donovan flew by a different route, and reached the enemy coast just north of Rome as first light showed. There was some low-lying stratus cloud clinging to the coastline but he brought the Marauder down to 200ft to fly below the cloud layer. An Italian driving a cart along a road was seen to look up at the Allied aircraft in utter astonishment. Skimming low over the roofs of Rome, the Marauder then turned out to

Me 323 under attack by 14 Squadron Marauder.

SM79 about to ditch after attack by 14 Squadron Marauder.

Oberfeldwebel Walter Honig,
German Air Force

Honig with knee bandaged and some of the
crew of the Me 323

sea and passed directly over a convoy of ships, which opened up with anti-aircraft fire of some intensity. Donovan threw the Marauder about in a series of evasive manoeuvres, while Bateson coded the weather report for Slatcher to transmit. On the way back, they passed beneath the 600 strong Bomber Force flying high above it on route for Rome. Two of the escorting P-38 Lightning peeled off and came down to investigate. They must have seen the wake the low-flying Marauder was leaving on the surface of the sea.

Neither the Vatican nor St Peter's were harmed but the marshalling yards were severely damaged. Regrettably 2,000 Romans were killed and the Basilica of San Lorenzo was destroyed in the raid. Undoubtedly it contributed to Italy's decision to be rid of Il Duce and to surrender to the Allies.

Two days later, on 21 July, Neil O'Connor and his crew flew a low level reconnaissance of the Tyrrhenian Sea. They reported two men in a dinghy off the north east coast of Sardinia and an enemy hospital ship off Montecristo Island between the east coast of Corsica and the Italian mainland.

From Elba they flew a 'creeping line ahead' patrol of Leghorn and Spezia naval bases. The Marauder was fired upon by three enemy destroyers. It was heavy, intense and accurate, but they got clear without damage.

Next day, Maydwell took off from Protville at 0820hrs. This reconnaissance followed much the same pattern as that followed by O'Connor's aircraft two days earlier. Graham describes what happened: 'We reached the Isle of Elba without incident and were heading north west towards Corsica when we encountered a large 4 engined Ju 90 transport plane flying towards the town of Bastia at low level, probably preparing to land on an airfield near Bastia. We had no hesitation in attacking him from the rear port quarter and the first big burst got in some good hits around his port engines. He did exactly what must not be done in combat - he turned away from us and in so doing exposed the underside of his aircraft to us and also prevented the troops aboard from firing at us. This gave us a good chance to get in further bursts, but he was now very close to Bastia and we were being shot at by coastal defences, so we broke off the attack and headed away from the coast. From my rear turret I was able to watch the Junkers stagger on towards Bastia and then he disappeared and a blinding flash followed by a thick column of smoke rising from the town. There seemed little doubt that he had crashed in the town. We were able to secure some good photographs of the combat'.

Post-war German records confirmed that a Ju 90 was destroyed - shot down by their own flak, they said, over Bastia.

On Saturday the 24th July, the Squadron suffered the loss of another crew when John Hunter's aircraft failed to return (Hunter later reported as a POW) Donovan and O'Connor flew the other two reconnaissances on a day, that will live for ever in Neil O'Connor's memory: 'This was the day John Hunter went missing. We were out that day too, early take-off, flew up west coasts of Sardinia and Corsica, over to Genoa, down to Spezia, saw a hospital ship at Leghorn, past Elba and down east coast of Corsica, where we were chased by two Bf 109s, over to Naples, where we met Hunter and crew. They were going up and each thought the other an enemy aircraft but our WOp/AGs soon made contact with Aldis lamps and we passed quite close to each other. John had two Aussies in his crew, Dick Egan (Navigator) and Laurie Murphy (WOp/AG). They were jumped by two Fw 190s off Leghorn and had an engine shot up. Being a sitting duck, Johnny decided to ditch. All the crew managed to get into the dinghy but Johnny. 'Spud' Murphy dived down and was just able to release the roof panels above the cockpit. Johnny was slumped over the controls. Spud doesn't know how he got him out, but they propped him in Mae Wests, both nearly drowned. Johnny's scalp was ripped half off. He told me, after the war, that he woke up two days later in an Italian hospital, whilst they were still stitching his scalp down!' John Hunter suffered the rest of his life from his injuries and sadly died in 1987.

Ted Donovan recalls a patrol flown on 28 July: 'We sighted two merchant ships off the north coast of Elba, with two escort vessels, and a Ju 88 which promptly dived on us. I made off and Tony started to encode the sighting, while John and George fired at the Ju 88. We then found a destroyer by Capraia Island and two barges. As we came round the north of Capraia we bumped into 30 Ju 52s in loose formation. The Ju 88 had lost interest so I told John to have a go, while I flew in formation. He had just started scattering .50 bullets among them as we went down the west coast of Capraia, when Paddy, my co-pilot, saw a large ship. Tony said crossly that it would have to wait while he got the other messages off! The ship turned out to be a hospital ship and we also reported three schooners. This activity was probably the beginning of the evacuation of Corsica.'

On 30 July, two reconnaissances were flown by Elsey and Maydwell, who took off from Protville at 0815hrs but after 20 minutes flying, had to return to base due to generator failure. The crew changed aircraft and were again airborne at 0920hrs. Approaching the Isle of Elba, a large armada of enemy transport aircraft was seen coming from the opposite direction. There were some Me 323s and many Ju 52s as well as other unidentified aircraft. Escorting fighters swooped down on the lone Marauder and a high speed chase at low level amongst the islands of the Archipelago ensued. Eventually, the fighters gave up the hunt. Continuing the reconnaissance, just north of Corsica, Maydwell saw one of the Me 323 aircraft approaching at low level and, miraculously, unaccompanied. He decided to attack and positioned his aircraft so as to come in from the rear starboard quarter and fly fast across the front of the enemy aircraft only 60yrds ahead so as to give both turret and rear gunners a chance to fire.

The Me 323 was formidably armed with five 0.5 inch guns and seven 0.3 inch machine guns. It was heavily armour-plated in the cockpit area. Maydwell's navigator, Kennedy said it looked like a block of flats! The Marauder made more than one attack and the German gunners fought back without causing serious damage and after a while it was seen that the three engines in the starboard wing of the huge aircraft had stopped with the middle one on fire. The pilot was clearly having difficulty in flying with only the port engines effective. Before the Marauder could attack again, the Me 323 crash landed, on the coast of Corsica. The co-pilot took excellent photographs of the attack. An account of the battle (translated from the German) by Oberfeldwebel Walter Honig, the *Luftwaffe* pilot of the Me 323 follows:

'On 30 July 1943 we were ordered to fly from Istres to Rome. We were a formation of six Me 323s. My machine was carrying one towing vehicle for heavy anti-aircraft guns (tracked vehicle), three VW personnel carriers and six tons of ammunition. On the way we were to pick up fighter cover. I had difficulties starting one engine. The rest of the formation took off at about 1000hrs. After the engine had been repaired I took off alone about 30 minutes later and flew after the formation at a low altitude. Shortly before 1200hrs I sighted an aeroplane on an opposite course at a distance of about 6 km. It turned towards us and went into the attack position, coming at us from the front and to the right. I immediately altered course for the northern tip of Corsica to get as near to land as possible. My gunners were only able to fire briefly, as the enemy machine was flying in what was a blind spot as far as our guns were concerned. We were also having difficulties with our nose cannons as the battery installation had been shot away at the first enemy attack. The gunner had received a superficial wound in the head and was unconscious. Two engines were hit in further enemy attacks and gave up soon afterwards. A third engine was also giving off smoke and we were afraid of fire. Even the bullet-proof tanks were hit but no petrol escaped.

'Our flying speed got lower and lower and I was just able to hold the 'plane at about 130 km/h with the flaps at 10 degrees. The British machine flew past us so close at each attack that I could see the faces of the crew (with brown leather headgear and glasses). One shot hit the armoured window in front of my face and splintered it and the projectile was left sticking in it. I tried to find a suitable landing place on the rocky coast, as there would have been little chance of survival if we had had to land in the water. We made a rather bumpy landing near a small fishing village. Before we did so the wireless operator in the hold had ordered everybody to the rear and this helped to save our lives.

'On board was an eight man crew and the four drivers of the four vehicles. While we were freeing ourselves from the machine, all of us injured to some extent, the British machine flew quite low over us but did not shoot at us again. Corsican fisherman and later Italian soldiers did the best they could for us and later we were taken to the hospital at Bastia.'

Maydwell recalls: 'This encounter had a most interesting sequel, as 39 years later, the Luftwaffe pilot, Walter Honig, wrote a letter to *Flight magazine*, asking who was the pilot of the Beaufighter (sic) who had shot him down? A reply was soon forthcoming from my friends, who said it was a Wing Commander flying a Marauder. Walter was delighted to hear it was a senior pilot who had shot him down and not some 'sprog'. He further said that he had been serving on the Russian front for the past two years and his Me 323 had been attacked many times without effect by Russian fighters firing from 400yds. Then on his first trip in the Mediterranean he got shot down from 50yds by the RAF! He was most annoyed!'

On 11 September 1982, Maydwell met Walter Honig at Pforzheim in Baden Wurtenberg and presented him with a propellor tip from his crashed Me 323 He returned the gesture by giving the RAF pilot a pewter plate inscribed 'A memento of our meeting off Cape Corse 30 July 1943'. Later the *Luftwaffe* pilot took the RAF pilot for a flight in his glider, powered by a Volkswagen engine, over the Black Forest. On landing, they had a long talk in the open air, while drinking beer and eating frankfurters.

THE TURN OF THE TIDE

World War II was now moving in favour of the Allies. Already Italy was reeling from repeated blows. In the Pacific, the Japanese were beginning to retreat and the Germans had suffered severe reverses on the Easter Front and had been driven out of North Africa.

From Protville on 1 August 1943 two Marauders took off, one several hours after the other to maintain surveillance of the Mediterranean sea and its coasts throughout the daylight hours. Freeman came across the rare sight of a composite Heinkel aircraft, formed by joining two He llls, towing two Gotha gliders towards Sicily.

The Squadron was commended by HQ 328 Wing of MACAF for having the highest standard of aircraft recognition at its lectures above any other squadron in the Wing. No doubt the need to fly alone over hostile waters for up to nine and a half hours concentrated the minds of the Marauder aircrews most wonderfully.

On 5th August, Flying Officer Thomas' and Law-Wright's crew flew on separate reconnaissances. Three He IIIs were attacked and two were damaged. Flying Officer Elsey successfully located a dinghy containing seven crewmen from a USAAF B-17. A Catalina flying boat was sent out to rescue them, as a result of the signal from the reconnaissance plane.

At this time, some prisoners of war were attached to the Squadron to help in non-combatant tasks. One was a very smart Afrika Korps soldier, who struck up a friendship with 'Fritz', the German-Palestinian cook and they could often be heard talking German together. Most, however were Italians and all were addressed as 'Tony' regardless of who they were.

Squadron Leader Brown, a Flight Commander, had given one 'Tony' some clothes to wash. 'Tony' brought the wet garments back to him and Brown looked in vain for a line on which to hang them out to dry. Sudden inspiration caused him to use one of his tent guy ropes and tie it to his flight gharry. Then he went into his tent for a well-earned lie-down. Suddenly, a thought of a task not done struck him; he leapt from his camp bed and jumped into the driving seat of his gharry, started the engine, eased out the clutch and sped away - dragging his tent behind him!

On 6th August at 1630hrs, Flight Lieutenant Ted Donovan was summoned to the Operations Tent with his crew and briefed to do a special reconnaissance. The Wing Intelligence Officer instructed him to do a cross-over patrol to the north of Elba and remarked mysteriously: 'You'll probably see something'. He took off at 1735hrs and flew straight to the designated area. Close to the Italian coast they sighted five Ju 52s, which the Marauder attacked immediately. Stuart certainly damaged one with fire from his turret, but Donovan reminded the crew the purpose of the trip was reconnaissance and broke off the engagement. It is well that he did, as the two gunners were to need all the ammunition they could lay their hands on.

Dusk was near, as they approached the Corsican coast and suddenly encountered two Condottieri class cruisers, escorted by two destroyers and some smaller ships. While identifying these warships Stuart suddenly shouted over the intercom, "Fighters! Turn right!" Six Fw 190 fighters were bearing down on the lone Marauder. The gunners disabled one, but the other five came in, two on each side and one behind.

Collins, the tail gunner, kept the latter at bay, while Donovan followed Stuart's directions. Without banking the Marauder more than 10 degrees, he skidded the aircraft into the attack and forced the enemy to break off. Flat out, the B-26 was speeding low over the sea at 320mph. The battle lasted for ten minutes and covered over 50 miles. Reid was monitoring the engine revs, temperatures and pressures, while Slatcher and Bateson were fully occupied coding and sending out the sighting report. At the southern tip of Sardinia, the Focke-Wulf fighters gave up the chase. In his diary Bateson wrote: 'Got back very late (2235hrs), the Group Captain (Geoffrey Tuttle) gave us all a cup of tea, which was excellent'.

On the 7th, three reconnaissance flights were flown by the CO, Freeman, and Thompson, whose aircraft was attacked by two Bf 109s. The Marauder's gunners damaged one, causing the pilot to break off with smoke streaming from its engine, and the other decided discretion was the better part of valour.

On the 12th the crews involved were Squadron Leader Law-Wright's, Flying Officer

Donovan's, and Flight Sergeant Dee's. Reports of seeing 24 Ju 52s or Ju 88s, four schooners and a mine-sweeper were radioed to base. Separately Flight Sergeant Freeman's crew went on an air-sea-rescue mission and located three men clinging to a water-logged dinghy. The Marauder dropped two dinghies and the men were observed clambering into them. The wireless operator sent out a message giving their position.

Two days later, Graham was sent on an air-sea rescue search as the final sortie of his operation tour. Graham had been nicknamed 'Goofy' because his strangely uncoordinated gait, manner of speech and laughter was reminiscent of the Walt Disney character. He was a very popular member of the Squadron and earned a well-deserved DFC. When he left for South Africa, one of the flight mechanics was heard to remark: 'Funny thing about 'Goofy' - we all thought he was a bit of a joke when he joined the Squadron, but he turned out to be one of the best pilots.'

Squadron records noted that since August 1942, the Marauders had flown 8,100hrs with only two avoidable accidents.

Donovan's route on 16 August took him up the west coast of Sardinia to Toulon, Nice, Genoa, Spezia, Leghorn and home via the west coasts of Corsica and Sardinia. A large merchange ship was seen in Imperia harbour and this was later sunk at night by Wellingtons. Also seen were two motor boats and nine launches.

As they flew past Genoa harbour, Ted Donovan decided to photograph the shipping in it. He passed control to his co-pilot, who was a substitute for Paddy Reid and had very limited experience of flying a Marauder at such low level over the sea. Donovan suddenly sensed that the aircraft was getting dangerously close to the sea and quickly pulled back the stick to ensure the propeller tips did not dig into the waves. The tail of the Marauder slapped down into the water and the tail gunner, George Collins, let out an anguished cry: "What the hell is going on? I'm sitting in the bloody water!"

Gil Graham describes the CO's reconnaissance on 17 August: 'We took off from Protville at 1225hrs in 'Dominion Triumph'. When this flight was finished the Skipper was to be promoted to Group Captain and would leave the Squadron but we had first got to complete the operation....

'When flying on the easterly leg we went in very close to the coast near Imperia and Alassio to photograph what appeared to be a beached merchant vessel. We soon discovered it was armed and we came under some fairly heavy anti-aircraft fire, so having taken pictures, we departed hurriedly with no damage. A slight lapse in concentration in the area around Spezia naval base got us caught up in cross fire between some destroyers and E-boats of the Italian Navy, and that brought us very rapidly to our senses.

We noted that the giant battleship 'Littorio' was still in Spezia harbour. We then moved south and just off Leghorn we attacked a lone Junkers Ju 52, but their gunner hit back, and caused some damage to the nose of our aircraft. Once again the top turret gave problems and we had to break off the engagement, having inflicted considerable damage on the Ju 52. It was possible that he did not get back to base.

On the return journey we sighted two dinghies, each with four men in them. We reported their position. Only when we received a 'return to base' signal did we leave them. All eight were rescued the following day.'

On 18 August, two dinghy searches were carried out by O'Connor and Long, who had both been promoted to the rank of Warrant Officer. O'Connor's crew sighted a dinghy and circled it until a Catalina arrived. Long sighted a submarine making a crash dive. Three further air-sea rescue flights were mounted that day by Archer, Thomas, and Freeman. All three sighted a dinghy with seven men aboard and circled it in turn until a high speed launch arrived to take the men off. They were all USAAF crewmen from a shot down B-17.

Daily Routine Orders announced that Wing Commander Maydwell had been promoted to the rank of Group Captain and posted to take command of a station in Italy. Law-Wright was promoted to Wing Commander and 'posted' to No 14 Squadron to become Commanding Officer, although he was already serving with it,

On Thursday 19th August, Grimsey and Donovan flew the sorties. Grimsey's crew sighted four Ju 52s but left them in peace. Donovan's crew made no sightings in a six hour reconnaissance, but the Marauder was chased by four Macchi 200s, which failed to catch the B-26. Donovan recalls, 'Bateson said it was very un-British to run away from fighters. We were obviously getting cocky!'

In the last few days the Squadron had been responsible for the rescue of 32 American survivors from Flying Fortresses, who had baled out over the sea, after raiding Italian manufacturing centres and railway marshalling yards.

On the 22nd, the reconnaissances were flown by Harry Grimsey, Ted Donovan and Carl Long. Donovan's Marauder followed the well travelled route up the west coast of Sardinia, to Toulon, along the northern coast of the Gulf of Genoa round to Leghorn and back down the west coast of Corsica and Sardinia. The crew sighted two enemy aircraft, one 3,000 ton merchant ship, two coasters, one Aviere class destroyer, which opened fire at the Marauder, as did the shore batteries, but it was not hit. The weather was bad with thunderstorms.

On the 25th August, Grimsey, Thomson, Elsey and Long flew on four separate reconnaissance flights. Long's gunners attacked a Cant Z 1107 seaplane and were horrified to discover, when it landed on water, that there were Red Crosses on the top of the wings and the fuselage.

The same day, Wing Commander Law-Wright assumed command of the Squadron, and Group Captain Maydwell made his farewell address to the whole squadron, praising their morale and excellent performance. It was a moving occasion and everyone was sad to lose so fine a CO.

Reflecting in 1994 on his time in command, Maydwell comments:

'It still amazes me that so many aircrew were always keen to fly, when casualties were so high. Yet there was no LMF (lack of moral fibre) on No 14 Squadron.'

The risks were amply illustrated on the 26th, when Ted Archer's Marauder failed to return from a reconnaissance. Archer, a Canadian, was known to be somewhat rash, and it was assumed that he must have taken one risk too many. After the war, this assumption was proved to have been correct, as testified by the navigator and the wireless operator flying in his crew on that day. Kennedy was normally Maydwell's navigator and the Australian wireless operator, Gil Lindschau had only recently returned to the Squadron after being severely injured on Slade's crash on 24 April and he was standing in for Archer's sick wireless operator.

It seems that some five hours into the flight, Archer was tempted to attack an enemy Ju 52. He made two attacks. Lindschau recalls: 'I positioned myself in the Astrodome to direct the gunners.' Apparently, Archer turned away after attacking and exposed the unprotected belly of the Marauder to enemy fire. The Ju 52 was a transport aircraft, but carried some defensive armament. Kennedy took up the story: 'I had been beaten to the astrodome by the wireless operator and saw nothing of these activities, so when I heard the rat-tat-a-tat of machine gun fire, I wished him (Archer) luck, until I saw the partition between us and the fuel tanks in the bomb bay suddenly framed by a foot of fire jetting out in all directions. The wireless operator and I promptly moved to the pilots' cabin and tucked ourselves behind the seats of the pilots. I remember shouting "For Christ's sake, ditch!" I don't recollect any fear of ditching, but as I had begun to singe, I was scared stiff of being fried to death. After my shout the second pilot, Flight Sergeant Smith, looked back to be confronted with the fact that the whole body of the plane was a raging inferno and he promptly cut the throttles. Ted then checked the position, opened the throttles for five or ten seconds, then cut them again. By this time we were skimming the surface of the water, which looked as if it had been painted in streaks; then nothing until I regained consciousness about ten feet from the edge of the biggest bonfire I have ever seen with the fin and rudder visible for about five seconds as it sank into the flames, then, a few minutes later, as the flames died out there was no visible sign whatsoever of the Marauder'.

Lindschau resumes: 'We all survived except the tail gunner. We were bobbing up and down, our life jackets supporting us. It was some time before a flat bottomed boat appeared coming from the Italian mainland and pulled us out of the water. It was manned by German soldiers. The boat's crew told us that as Leghorn harbour was only four miles away, they had watched the tail end of the fight and that, when the Marauder hit the water and had blown up, they had decided that there would be nothing to rescue. However, the pilot of an Bf 109, which was circling, radioed that there were survivors. On the way back to Leghorn, the Germans took our wet clothes and hung them on a line so they were dry by the time harbour was reached'.

At Leghorn, the Allied airmen were met by the German Town Major. Lindschau records he had a punctured lung, broken ribs and damaged back. 'The second pilot and I were taken to a field hospital near the Leaning Tower of Pisa. After a few days in hospital we were transferred to Rome for interrogation, where we had some gruelling moments. The German interrogation officer said to me I was fighting on the wrong side with a name like that. I replied my father came from Flensburg, a town in Denmark and was a naturalised Australian.'

The unfortunate turret gunner had a fractured spine and was in hospital with the second pilot and wireless operator, who remember him scream with pain and the Germans administered morphia morning and night until he was repatriated by the Red Cross in Switzerland.

The following day, 27th August, Squadron Leader Donovan's crew reconnoitred a route via Rome, Corsica, Leghorn, Spezia and home by the West Coast of Corsica and Sardinia. They sighted two motor torpedo boats, six barges, one 800 ton merchant ship and one unidentified aircraft. Two Ju 88s chased the Marauder, but could not match its speed.

As a postscript to that trip, Ted Donovan later recalled: 'I came back in the middle of the afternoon. Everybody, of course, was asleep. I heard the telephone ringing in the Squadron's operations tent, which was not usually manned the whole time. I picked up the phone and said, "No 14 Squadron here" A voice replied,

"Sholto Douglas here, where is your CO?" " I don't know as I've only just landed". SD angrily, " What's happening there? I want to talk to your CO" Donovan, sternly, "I'm very sorry but I have just landed and I cannot see anyone about at the moment. You'll have to ring again." SD even more angrily, " Do you know who I am?" "No". "Well, I'm your Commander-in-Chief, WHO ARE YOU?"

I put the phone down. A few years later I met Air Chief Marshal Sholto Douglas and told him about this. With a smile he said, " You were a very wise young man".

On 31st August, Donovan did another trip taking off from Protville at noon. It was a cross-over patrol between Corsica and Italy to ensure that the Italian fleet did not sail out south and attack the Allied supply routes to Sicily and Italy. The Marauder landed at 1930hrs. Flight Sergeant Bateson noted in his diary, 'We did a 7 1/2 hour trip today, which brings me up to 61hrs 55mins, operational hours this month.'

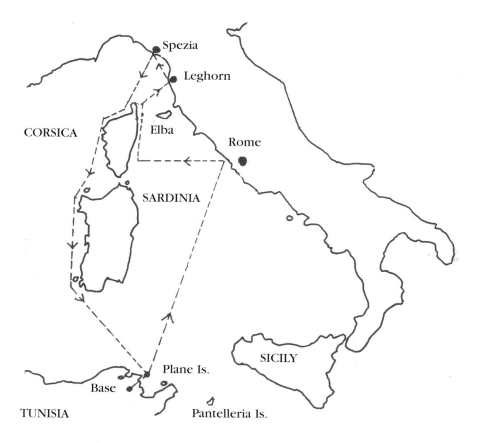

Navigator's Log of Reconnaissance Flight on 27 August 1943.

CHAPTER 7

THE MEDITERRANEAN AND SICILY

SEPTEMBER 1943 - OCTOBER 1944

'Admiral di Courten, (Chief of Staff of the Italian Navy since 25 July, when Mussolini resigned) was called in by Marshal Badoglio, head of the new Government that succeeded Mussolini's Fascists on 3 September 1943. The Admiral was told that Italy's plenipotentiary had signed an armistice that day. This was the first time that 'Supermarina' had been officially informed that Italy was extricating itself from the war, which had proved so unpopular and disastrous for the nation.'

Squadron group photograph with B-26, 1943.

ITALY CAPITULATES

The Italian fleet at this time was divided into two parts: the Tyrrhenian Sea had three battle ships, five cruisers, about ten destroyers, fifteen submarines, twenty-eight motor torpedo boats, a few of the 10th MAS assault units, plus about fifteen destroyer escorts and corvettes. They were to operate in the Tyrrhenian Sea should any attempt be made to land in the Naples area. Should landings take place in the Ionian/Adriatic sector, the naval headquarters at Taranto had at its disposal two smaller battleships, the *Doria* and *Guilio*, three light cruisers, one destroyer, nine submarines, six motor boats, ten destroyer escorts and corvettes'. (M A Bragadin, *The Italian Navy in WWII* (*USNI, Annopolis*))

The CO and Flight Commanders were warned on 3 September to be prepared for a major effort as there was likely to be much maritime activity around Southern Italy. No further information was vouchsafed, but that day the Allied invasion of mainland Italy took place. Known as Operation *Baytown*, Montgomery's army crossed the Strait of Messina and Allied Forces were on the mainland of

Europe for the first time since the evacuation from Greece in 1941.

On the 5th No 14 Squadron carried out five sorties and reported seeing three small ships. The following day, a Marauder sighted a small convoy, but for the most part three daily reconnaissances produced no major sightings until the 8th. During these early September days the only excitement was a rumour that parachutists had been dropped near Blida with a view to sabotaging aircraft. Extra guards were detailed for camp and aircraft duties and the armament officer gave a demonstration of the sort of plastic explosive likely to be used, but nothing in fact happened.

During the afternoon of 8 September, Donovan and his crew were briefed at short notice to take off and do a crossover patrol just south of Elba. They were informed of a rumour that the Italian Fleet was sailing south and told to maintain their patrol until last light and then proceed to Salerno Bay, report any gun fire and make contact with Force H. Force H consisted of the battleships *Nelson* and *Rodney* among other warships that were giving cover to an invasion force due to land at Salerno at dawn next morning. Donovan was told to make contact with Force H, making a special secret signal to ensure that he was recognised, and was then to pass by Aldis lamp the signal which gave the all clear that the Italian fleet was not at sea.

Having carried out the crossover patrol, the aircraft then went down to the position of Force H but on the way there flew alongside the beaches of Salerno. He did not close directly on to Force H and its battleships and cruisers without due care. Donovan showed the silhouette of their aircraft and Slatcher fired off the colours of the day and gave the secret signal by lamp. Needless to say the ships replied with gunfire and one can hardly blame them as they had an important duty to protect not only the convoy but indeed themselves. This barrage continued for some time and eventually large columns of water were seen coming up and the crew realised that the Nelson and Rodney were firing their main guns at them. Eventually the barrage closed down and the aircraft made contact with the flagship and passed its all clear message. When the aircraft returned to base Donovan said to Slatcher, 'It was good to get that message through'. The signaller replied that he got tired of flashing the secret signal and instead sent a message in plain language saying 'Dry your eyes', which caused the gunfire to stop! Subsequently it was found that the 16-inch guns of the battleships had indeed been used as a method of deterring low-flying aircraft.

Bateson's diary recorded the patrol:

'At 1700hrs we are called out on a trip. Another of these rush jobs which fall to the lot of Squadron Leaders and other important people! Base - Naples Bay - Sardinian coast Base. Grandstand seat at invasion of Italy. Saw the great Allied invasion fleets. HMS *Rodney* opened fire at us. Intercom failed and all was chaos. Dickie flashed 'Dry your eyes' on the Aldis. It was almost dark when we arrived at the Italian coast. Navigators Light failed. Was airsick - probably through taking off without food. Learnt that ITALY CAPITULATED at 1730hrs!'

Italian Fleet surrendering on 9 September 1943, escorted by 14 Squadron Marauder.

ITALIAN FLEET SURRENDERS

General Eisenhower announced that an armistice had been signed on the 8th, but Supermarina had not been informed and had been expecting to fight Force H. There was evidently much confusion as the Allies had informed the Italian Supreme Command that nothing would be announced until the 10th. This caused some chaos in the Supermarina, but nevertheless the fleet weighed anchor from Spezia and Genoa and followed a course down the west coast of Corsica and Sardinia. At first light on the morning of the 9th, Flight Lieutenant Owen Phillipps sighted the Italian fleet and shadowed it until he was relieved by Flight Sergeant Freeman. Freeman was relieved by the CO, who continued escorting the fleet on its journey southwards and was present during the German bombing and sinking of the battleship *Roma*. This flight was carried on until last light and set an endurance record for Marauders by flying for ten and a half hours. Law-Wright witnessed the strike on the battleship and saw it sink before his return back to base. Bateson wrote: 'Another great day for No 14 Squadron.' Phips', sighted the Italian Fleet - three Littorio class battleships - six Cruisers and some Destroyers - heading 190° down the West coast of Corsica. Freeman and Wing Commander Law-Wright continued shadowing the Fleet, which had left Spezia at 0230hrs that morning. The Fleet, continued South down the Sardinian coast, being covered at night by Wimpeys of No 458 Australian Squadron. The shadowing being taken up again at first light by Marauders of No 14 Squadron!'

The Fleet proceeded down the west coast of Corsica and at midday turned into the Strait of Bonifacio. The reason for this has never been cleared up. However, while they were there some aircraft came over which the Italian sailors assumed were allied aircraft to give them cover, but they were German aircraft which had flown down from Provence. The *Roma* was struck by a new wireless-controlled bomb and blew up. She was the flagship of Admiral Perganini, who was killed together with the majority of his crew.

In the meantime the rest of the fleet was at Taranto in the instep of Italy. This included the battleships *Doria* and *Guilio*. In the late afternoon of 9 September, a British Naval Force composed of the battleship *Howe*, five cruisers, and a convoy of the landing force reached Taranto. The Germans, after a few hours of disorientation, began to occupy Italian cities. They used numerous divisions which had been sent into Italy after the 25 July largely without the knowledge of the Italian Government. The Italian Navy could do little to prevent the occupation of the ports whose defence against ground attack was the responsibility of the army which had not been briefed to resist the Germans and like the navy, was taken by surprise. This delay in communications on the Allied side unfortunately resulted in many prisoners of war being transferred to Germany. However, on the 9th, Taranto was occupied by British airborne troops who held off German attacks.

The main fleet sailing from Spezia was continually shadowed by No 14 Squadron and was eventually handed over on the 10th to the Royal Navy who escorted it to Malta. They were joined by the fleet from Taranto and Admiral Cunningham sent his famous signal to the Admiralty saying, "The Italian Fleet is under the guns of the Fortress of Malta". The RAF thought he might have given some credit to the Air Force who had been escorting the fleet for the past two days. Between 8 - 10 September the Squadron carried out fourteen separate sorties. Graham recorded, 'We took off from Protville on 10 September 1943 but it was very soon clear that this was to be a flight of great significance as we came upon an extraordinary sight. Yes - an entire navy on the move. The Italian Fleet, which we had been shadowing and watching for many months, had at last capitulated and here it was sailing in line astern with a British escort heading towards Malta. It was, to put it mildly, a very stirring and emotional sight being able to fly alongside them without being fired upon was really marvellous!'

Soon after, 328 Wing Headquarters was visited by the Air Officer Commanding Mediterranean Allied Coastal Air Forces (MACAF) and was located in Algiers. This was Air Vice-Marshal Hugh Pugh Lloyd and he gave a congratulatory talk to the Wing which had five squadrons: 14 with Marauders, 39 and 47 with Beaufighters, 52 with Baltimores and No 458 (Australian) Squadron equipped with Wellingtons. He picked out No 14 Squadron particularly and announced the immediate award of the DSO to the CO, Wing Commander Law-Wright.

The Italian smaller ships abandoned their ports in the Adriatic and made their way south. Many did not have the range to get as far as Malta so it was agreed that they would assemble at Palermo in Sicily. It was soon clear that the Germans were evacuating Sardinia and Corsica as many barges, Ju52s and Me 323s were sighted by the Squadron.

Between 10 and 13 September, four aircraft took off on recces each day. Submarines heading south were sighted and numbers of barges, ferries, Ju 52s and Me 323s were seen evacuating Corsica and Sardinia. An air sea search aircraft found a dinghy containing three men and reported its position.

On the night of the 12th, Donovan gave some night instruction to a small number of crews. Evidently some crews owing to the number of moves had not been passed out for solo night flying but the state of the war meant that the Squadron was liable to be called on to fly sorties before dawn and after dusk.

On the 15th, Group Captain Maydwell visited the Squadron to say goodbye to Charlie Wall who had been adjutant with the Squadron for 1 $^1/_2$ years and was immensely popular. His place was taken by the one-time intelligence officer, Flying

Officer Dunsmore.

GERMANS EVACUATE SARDINIA AND CORSICA

Throughout September the Squadron mounted between three and four reconnaissance's every day. A large number of barges were reported which were obviously evacuating both Corsica and Sardinia. During these sorties, crews were involved in a number of combats often taking the initiative. For instance, on the 18th two of three aircraft on patrol, attacked and damaged two Ju 52s and one Ju 88. Next day they sighted a large number of Ju 52s and three Italian Reggiane Re 2001 fighters which attacked one of the Squadron's aircraft. Minor damage was done to the Marauder and one of the Re 2001s was set on fire. That solitary Marauders of No 14 Squadron were so often able to escape serious damage from attacks by fighters of the calibre of Messerschmitt Bf 109s, Fw 190s, Macchi MC200s and Re 2001s may surprise some readers, who do not know of the intensive training in evasive and fire-control tactics undertaken by the crews. Furthermore, the Axis fighters were designed for combat at higher altitudes and their pilots were not experienced in attacking so close to the sea as 50ft, where their manoeuvrability was severely restricted.

It was now reported that American and French forces had liberated northern Corsica. Some weeks later Squadron Leader Donovan was told to take a detachment up to North Corsica. To be sure of local ground transport an experiment was made of slinging a motor bike in the bomb bay which proved successful. In the past the Squadron had found itself with little or no transport on first arriving at a new station. In the middle of September, Seibel ferries were sighted. These carried a formidable armament of anti-aircraft guns and were not to be underestimated. In fact the barges presented a very difficult target even though Wing had both Beaufighter squadrons armed with torpedoes, bombs and forward firing guns, but these weapons were not very successful against shallow drawing barges, nor was thought given to carrying depth charges. On the 21st, squadron aircraft made attacks on seven Ju 52s and scored hits on two before being driven off by enemy fighters, while on 23 September, 50 Ju52s were sighted and some of the formations were attacked unsuccessfully.

On the 25th, few significant sightings were made but an air sea rescue search was successful and a dinghy with two occupants was located. The Marauder remained with the dinghy until No 52 Squadron relieved them. Most of the Squadron's effort had been concentrated on the Sardinian and Corsican coasts, but on 17 September Donovan went north into the gulf of Genoa where the crew sighted two four engined Piaggio P.108 bombers, four Ju52s, eight landing craft, some escort vessels and a merchant vessel of 5,000 tons, a schooner, and a dinghy with two corpses. The anti-aircraft fire was considerably heavier than usual particularly near Toulon, and from the escort vessels, so it was assumed that the Germans were occupying the whole coastline. It was now clear that the armistice with Italy was not going to produce the clean sweep hoped for and indeed, as we know, the Allied forces faced a long hard slog up the Italian peninsula, which lasted a year.

On 23 September, Flight Lieutenant Williams, arrived to take over the duties of

Squadron Adjutant from Dunsmore. On 27 September, one of our aircraft was attacked by Arados and Bf 109s, but the Marauder was able to destroy one Arado and damage one Bf 109. Owing to damage received in that combat, the Marauder crashed on return to base, but thanks to the skillful handling of the aircraft no injuries to the crew were sustained.

After the Italian surrender, the Germans were quick to take over. The USAAF, with its Liberators and Marauders, took great toll of the land supply routes, but the rugged Italian coast was not making it difficult for the inshore supply of troops from the coast. The assault force at Salerno had some difficulty holding out until the 8th Army was able to advance from Calabria to join it.

Luckily there had been no casualties during September, but the number of Marauders damaged beyond repair had now reached a point where No 14 Squadron had to look elsewhere for reinforcements. These turned out to be B-26Bs from American Squadrons. (The B-26B-10-MA was the result of a major redesign. The wing span was increased from 65ft to 71ft, which required a taller tail fin and rudder to maintain stability. The wing area increased from 602 to 659sq ft, and the gross weight rose to 38,200lbs. The maximum speed at 15,000ft fell to 282mph, and the take-off run was reduced by 300ft). Grimsey and Donovan did acceptance flights, using their own crews to test guns, radio and other equipment. (Some of the aircraft had colourful names such as *Daisy June Two, Flak Eater* and *Captain Blood*).

DETACHMENTS IN N. AFRICA, ITALY, SARDINIA, AND CORSICA

On the 1st October 1943 Grimsey took a detachment of 48 officers and men including the crews of Bates, Gellatley, Cameron and Spedding to a southern Italian airstrip not far from Taranto called Grottaglie. Their duty was to cover the Adriatic and the Ionian Islands; allied troops were now entering the suburbs of Naples and the Germans were said to be retreating to a new defence line. At Protville on the 2nd, Leadbetter and Mitchell successfully completed reconnaissance's and made several useful sightings. On 4 October, Donovan did a 7 $\frac{1}{2}$ hour sortie after which he and his crew were told to leave for England the next morning. They had to get their UK uniforms out and be ready to leave first thing for Tunis. Bateson decided not to return as he wanted to finish his tour.

Some 21 sorties were flown from Protville and Grottaglie between 5 and 12 October with few sightings of interest, but on the 14th Hugh Bates' log is worth quoting; '14 October 1943 Patrol - Grottaglie - Delagosa Island - Durazzo - Base. During this patrol we reported sightings of five vessels. One tanker (3,500), one merchant ship (2,000), two merchant ships (2,000) and one tug. Two of these vessels were very promptly caught by the Royal Navy.' The Squadron was advised by the Flag Officer Taranto. 'As a result of your excellent air reconnaissance's yesterday, one enemy ship has been sunk and one captured and towed into port. Please convey my hearty congratulations to all concerned.'

On the 19th, Flying Officers Gellatley and Cameron took off on patrols. Gellatley reported several sightings but Cameron sent no signal after take off and no replies were received from repeated calls to his aircraft. A search plan was worked out and next day two Hudsons went to search the central Adriatic and a Marauder flew on the tracks presumed to be flown by Cameron, whose crew were Sergeants Ritchie and Lesley, Flying Officer Ingram and Flight Sergeants Williams and Proud. Hugh Bates found a survivor clinging to a petrol tank. Dinghies were dropped and he was seen to climb into one. Further searches were made but with no results. The survivor was subsequently rescued by a Walrus amphibian and found to be the second pilot, Sergeant Ritchie, who was admitted to a field hospital near Foggia, suffering from exposure and shock. Squadron Leader Grimsey, in command of the Grottaglie detachment, visited Sergeant Ritchie in hospital, who seemed to be pulling round, though he was obviously very shaken and gave, as his opinion, that aileron failure had caused them to fly into the sea. This was never substantiated, and no other survivors were found despite further searches.

Despite appalling weather and sodden airfield conditions, the Squadron managed some 80 sorties during the month of October. However, the weather finally forced the Squadron away from Protville and Sidi Amor and Flight Lieutenant Lapthorne led a formation of six aircraft which included Flying Officer Mitchell back to Blida where the training flight and sufficient ground crew to service the aircraft were to be based. 'Mitch' Mitchell was a young Australian of slight stature. Returning from a flight, he stepped from the aircraft to be met by the Captain of a USAAF Marauder, who was understandably misled by Mitch's evident youthfulness and said, "Say, Junior, where's your Captain?". M: "I'm the Captain'. A: "Oh, may I see over your ship?" M: "Sure, carry on." Having examined the cockpit and navigation cabin, the American opened the door to the bomb-bay and was amazed to see the huge extra petrol tanks fitted there. With typical Yankee wit he said, "Well, what d'you know? It's nothing but a goddam flying gas-wagon!"

As 1943 drew to its close in November/December, the weather began to dictate the movements of the Squadron and force it once again into a nomadic existence. Protville began to deteriorate and sorties were flown from Sidi Amor at first on a day-to-day basis until Protville became so badly flooded that it was decided to move completely to Sidi Amor. This move however, did not last very long. Sidi Amor lay at the foot of a hill and the whole camp was flooded. Once more the Squadron moved its training flight ring flight and headquarters flight back to Blida in Algeria and a detachment moved to Corsica. This detachment set off to drive more than 400 miles from Tunisia to Algiers, which involved going over the Medjerda range in hail and snow. Having achieved this they then went by sea from Algiers to Ajaccio on the west coast of Corsica and then over a 2900ft pass to an airstrip at Ghisonaccia on the east coast about 48 miles by road. While all this was going on the Squadron remained operational, and flew 74 operations during the month of November, reflecting well on the ability of the ground crews and the maintenance engineering flight.

The detachment at Grottaglie was now being reinforced but they too had their difficulties, so an aircraft was kept permanently on standby at Brindisi on the Adriatic coast. This detachment, which had started off by having 45 men and four aircraft, was progressively reinforced, and there was a constant shuttle of aircraft

Johnson, RAAF, on left and Coath, RAAF, on right with Gracie Fields in centre.

Ron Haley (RAAF), a Squadron Cook.

Flt Sgt Shepherd, RAAF, and W/O de Yarburgh-Bateson. Bateson's uniform is largely of American origin given following forced landing at Touzeur in tropical gear.

returning to Blida for servicing, and crews who were tour expired leaving and new crews arriving.

Harry Lee was a despatch rider who recalls that: 'On the 28th October 1943 the Squadron left by convoy for Sidi Amor, not too pleasant. Rained quite a lot. Made getting about rather difficult. November 16th 1943 - Left for Algiers. Then move again - Left aboard Belgian *Seaman*. First day out OK, But afterwards it became rough. The ship did everything barring a somersault, eventually arriving at Ajaccio. After a few days it rained again. Left for Ghisonaccia. December 6th - After a difficult convoy journey arrived December 8th - Got our MT arranged, got settled in. Tents up, etc. but it was still a bit damp. A great change to see the greenery again. After a while all went well. December 25th - Another Christmas Day but a good day was had by all present.'

Only air crew and sufficient ground crew to service the aircraft remained at Blida to train crews and carry out major inspections until such times as conditions were suitable in Corsica. They reported as being settled in on the 28th November and training recommenced.

The Squadron's re-deployment in November and December 1943 reflected the military situation on the Italian mainland. The long and bitter struggle fought by the Allied forces up the leg of Italy and the stubborn German resistance has been described in many an account, but in this history of an RAF Squadron, it is necessary only to emphasise the importance of supply routes to the German Army. The Allies had air superiority and were able to disrupt use of the coast roads, but were less effective in the mountainous spine of the country. However, the routes available were not suited to carry more than a proportion of the supplies. The Germans were obliged to use coastal shipping for the rest and it was in order to detect this traffic that No 14 Squadron's reconnaissance's were flown.

Instead of covering the whole of the Tyrrhenian sea as hitherto, the Gulfs of Genoa and Venice received intensive surveillance as well as the eastern coast of Italy and the western coasts of Yugoslavia and Italy. In the Adriatic, small supply vessels could travel south from Trieste by a devious route amongst the many small islands west of Yugoslavia and across to Italy for the most part in darkness.

Flying at 170 knots for five or more hours, a single Marauder could cover 850 sea miles. Even a fast merchant vessel might be at sea for more than 24hrs and stood a very good chance of being discovered during daylight.

Naples was entered on 1 October 1943, a major step in the Allies long slog northward. The Germans formed a defence line along the Volturno river, thirty miles north of Naples. On the 13th, Italy formally declared war on Germany and joined the Allies, but apart from courageous resistance fighters, was unable to inflict much damage on German forces, who ensured the country was a battlefield for the rest of the European war. While these historic events were taking place, the Squadron maintained regular patrols over both the Tyrrhenian and Adriatic seas and it seemed sometimes to the crews that they were doing a vast amount of flying for very modest returns. However there were rewarding occasions such as the patrol by Flight Lieutenant Lapthorne on 2 November. Form 540 reads:

'2 November - Marauder - Captain. Flight Lieutenant Lapthorne:

0919hrs 4303N 0546E (off Toulon) sighted one D/D (destroyer) one funnel, one tanker, 6,000 tons rusty colours, one V/M (merchant vessel) 4,000 tons black, split superstructure, one funnel, two masts, flying two balloons, one V/M 3,000 tons camouflaged dark grey and white, composite superstructure, one funnel, two masts. All vessels riding high, presumably unladen, course 300 degrees - 6 knots. D/D challenged with white Aldis lamp, challenge unreadable. D/D then opened fire with heavy gun, believed 75mm shells burst 200yrds short. Marauder made a circuit going about five miles away and then returned for further investigation of the convoy. D/D again opened fire but fire was inaccurate. 0945hrs 4300N 0545E turned south, weather bad, wind 25 knots, cloud ten-tenths at sea level with rain-storms. Visibility nil in storms and ten miles outside. 1018hrs Levant Island coast-line to Toulon. Search for convoy but no results. 1040hrs 4300N 0610E (Iles d'Hyeres) set course south. Gunner saw one V/S 1000 tons stationary in position 4305N 0610E close inshore. Flown from Protville.'

'2 November - Marauder - Captain. Squadron Leader Grimsey:

A special fighter co-operation sortie. Twenty-four Spitfires were led by the Marauder to the Radar station north of Durazzo. The fighters strafed the station very effectively and the building was left blazing furiously. Photographs of the attack were taken by the Marauder which later proved beyond doubt the success of the operation. Flown from Grottaglie'.

On 27 November another patrol from Grottaglie reported sightings. Flight Sergeant Shepherd's navigator Warrant Officer Tony Bateson recorded in his log-book '0700hrs RECONNAISSANCE. Grottaglie-Paxos-Geroghambo-Sapienza-Corfu. Sighted one 8,000 ton hospital ship, one three masted schooner 500 ton MV wrecked. Bad weather at south end of Adriatic and heel of Italy. Rain and cloud down to deck. Flying time 5hrs 10mins.'

During November Bill Shepherd's crew flew 48hrs on operational sorties and throughout the month maintained a regular vigil for enemy shipping movements.

On 1 December the *Seaman* reached the harbour of Ajaccio. Personnel and stores were transported by squadron vehicles still in a serviceable condition and driven over the mountains to Ghisonaccia. This was to be the new detachment location and further personnel began arriving. On 5th December most of the per-sonnel moved to a tented area outside the town. The airfield was still unservice-able on the 7th and considered likely to remain so until mid-January. Quite apart from this, no operations were possible on account of the heavy rains. The adminis-trative offices had been accommodated in buildings in the village but on the 14th they were transferred to the tented area and the buildings vacated were taken on by the USAAF. Five days later it was decided that since the aerodrome at Ghisonaccia was not in operation, operations would be carried out from Blida to cover the area west of Italy, leaving the detachment at Grottaglie to patrol the Adriatic.

Despite the Squadron's dispersal and the inability to fly from Ghisonaccia dur-ing December, Grottaglie was able to carry on with single patrols without sight-ings on 2 December and again on the 5th and 6th. The first operational sortie from Blida was on the 9th and training started on the same day. On the 11th a recon-naissance to the Northern Adriatic was completed by Long and during that day Flight Sergeant Davis in charge of maintenance, flew to Naples from Grottaglie in a Dakota to collect spare parts. Four aircraft flew anti-submarine sorties on the 14th from Blida, and the following day Colyer and Croskell flew from Grottaglie.

Squadron Leader Donovan returned from England in a Marauder having taken ten weeks to collect the aircraft from Lyneham in Wiltshire. He landed at Rabat on the Moroccan coast where he was stranded with the weather making the take off impossible until 17 December. On arrival at Blida he was told that he was to leave almost immediately for Egypt and join 70 OTU in the Canal Zone which was start-ing an operational training flight of Marauders. Evidently they had had two runaway props and were in urgent need of an experienced Marauder pilot. Donovan and Flying Officer Leadbetter, who was now tour expired, both went to Egypt.

Wing Commander Law-Wright, accompanied by the Engineering Officer Gibbins flew to Grottaglie and brought a mass of mail on the 23rd to celebrate Christmas there, but was unable to leave until 3rd January 1944 as the airfield became unserviceable.

On Christmas Day Colyer and Shepherd did separate patrols over the Adriatic. That evening an excellent dinner was enjoyed by everyone on the detachment and a large number fell into bed far from sober.

Bateson wrote in his diary on the 27th: 'It is cold and the ground is wet, but an icy 30mph wind is blowing across the drome and will dry it out. Two Italian pilots landed Re 2001s last night. Bill (Shepherd) and I walk across to look at them. One pilot speaks a little English. He is a Lieutenant (2 stripes), fair-haired with grey eyes. His age may be 30 or 35. He has not shaved this morning. He is charming and shows us everything. He says Macchi MC.205 is a good fighter! Better than the Re 2001. The two have Mercedes-Benz motors. He likes the Spitfire and Forts and Lancs and Marauder, but thinks Kittyhawks, Lightnings and Airacobra fighters were poor. He was up at Spezia on Macchi MC.200s of which they had seven. He says it was useless against 200 Forts. etc.'

The following day, Gilroy's Marauder failed to return from a reconnaissance in the Toulon area. Searches were made on succeeding days but no trace was found.

Meanwhile the training flight had returned to Blida. Flight Lieutenant 'Chuff' Hornby with a crew trained on Wellingtons at an Operational Training Unit in England arrived in Algeria and was immediately sent to Protville to join No 14 Squadron, but the Squadron had already left, so Hornby's crew slept a night before being returned to Maison Blanche, near Algiers, and from there travelled by open truck in pouring rain to Blida. No 14 Squadron had not yet arrived and the unfortunate crew were obliged to doss down in the passages of already occupied billets. When the Squadron arrived the CO gave Hornby's crew an outline of their job. He told them they would do a four-week conversion course on to Marauders and then go to Corsica, which would be their base.

Hornby's wireless operator was Flight Sergeant Joe Lowder, who wrote in his diary: 'My job was to be the wireless operator and fire-controller for the whole tour. Geoffrey Unsworth was to be the upper gunner and Ken Williams the rear gunner although both were trained wireless operators. Although Blida was a permanent aerodrome built pre-war for the French, cooking facilities were non existent, but the RAF had installed a range of Sawyer stoves out in the open by the mess huts. Fuel was wood and paraffin, which was supplied by Arabs. One awkward thing was that the Arabs would call around the chalets to sell their goods, i.e. eggs etc, and anything left near the doorway or window would be lifted. One such case was so infuriating to an Aussie that he got out his revolver and shot off at every Arab he saw around about 0700hrs. Of course, the law stepped in and an irate Aussie was led off to the guard room between two service police. The Aussie, the next day, caught the thief walking through the camp and took him to the guard room. The lad in his teens, spent the day there until his mother and grandfather appeared. They managed to get George, the Aussie, to drop the charge and for days after that George was showered with fruit and eggs.'

Lowder recalled the airfield lay about two kilometres north of the town of Blida itself and was the usual quiet French Arab community and terrace buildings separated by narrow alleyways. There were the usual estaminets mainly run by the French; a plate of egg and chips could be had but there was nothing else to do for a bit of life, apart from the French brothel which was known as 'Madame Felix's'. There was a bar and chairs and tables, and one could buy wine and 'girl tokens'. Another break was for us to go into the hills of Chrea, the ridge of mountains south of Blida. Trucks would take us up most of the way to the ice and snow level then we walked. It was great to have snowball fights.'

There was no 'Madam Felix's' in Grottaglie, but Bateson in his diary entry for 2 January 1944 notes: 'A young Italian girl of 15 or 16 walks up from the village. After some bargaining, it is agreed she will give herself for 10 lira (six pence) a time. Three of the fellows go with her, one by one, in a nearby slit trench. It is very sordid.' At least one of the 'fellows' paid for his foolishness by catching a venereal disease.

On 28 December Hornby and crew were ordered on their first operation for. This is what Lowder records:

'Last evening - 27th. We were briefed in the Ops Room by the Controller, the Met man and the Intelligence Officer. Our patrol was pointed out to us on a large wall map with many tips on defence. All this we took in and then returned for a good night's sleep. There were just two kites flying out from our squadron, between us covering all the French and Italian coasts. At 0530hrs on the 28th, we were woken by the Police Guard, got together all our gear and went down to the mess for breakfast (special bacon and eggs and toast, etc). Here we drew our flying rations, then went back to our chalets to await the lorry to take us to our final briefing and to our kites. The other crew, Gilkey's, took off at 0830hrs, and we at 0900hrs. We set course for La Galite up to a new position 15 miles off the Italian coast at Imperia. Corsica could be seen, very mountainous, to our starboard. It was just about here we sighted an aircraft believed to be our fellow Marauder flying towards Corsica. This was the last time the aircraft was seen. To continue, we turned in towards the Riviera at about Monaco, then after about another four or five miles we turned south, coast crawling past Nice, Cannes, down to Levant Island and the Porquerolles. Just south of Cannes however, we came upon a fair sized enemy vessel of 1,000 tons. At the same time, red flashes appeared from the decks as it turned its head towards us, to lessen their target presumably. Flak came up at us, light and heavy fire as we zigzagged on. Then we saw that there was another ship of about 2000 tons two miles further on. This also sent up quite a barrage and at one time we were being fired upon by both. Then more heavy flak came, this time from the shore batteries of Levant. Here was the end of our patrol so we turned out to sea, heading homewards, still weaving for quite a few moments. My work then started in getting these sightings transmitted back to base on my radio. With no trouble, I carried this out and got back contented that this was my bit done.'

On landing they were met by the CO who told them that they had done well on their first job and asked them if they had seen their fellow aircraft. Apparently it had suffered engine failure and tried to get to Corsica but disappeared on the radio location screen about 15 miles from Ajaccio on the west coast. Air sea rescue patrols were sent out by the Squadron but after two days further searches were abandoned.

In the first week of January 1944, fourteen recces were carried out, equally divided between Grottaglie and Blida although in the case of Grottaglie, two sorties had to be carried out from Brindisi as the airfield was unfit for take off. Again on the 8th, two sorties were carried out from Brindisi by Collyer and Shepherd.

Meanwhile in Corsica on the same day, the new airmen's canteen was opened. The canteen, one of the old houses in the village of Ghisonaccia, had been redecorated and altered by the ground crew of the detachment which provided to be a great amenity. It was christened 'Get Some Inn'.

On 9 January Hornby took off on his crew's second operation from Blida on a seven and a half hour sortie covering the west coast of France and down to Genoa and Spezia in Italy. They reported a 1,500 ton tanker which opened fire as did the shore batteries. They cleared out of it weaving, twisting and corkscrewing. Later they came across five barges of 400 tons each, escorted by three vessels rather like our corvettes. The nearest one challenged by Aldis lamp, so Lowder, the signaller, replied with any old letter but before he had finished the first flak appeared by and beneath the tail spattering the sea all round. This was from the shore batteries, but quite soon the corvettes were also shooting at them so the Marauder made off. 'Chuff' Hornby carried out his usual evasive manoeuvres. He was called 'Chuff' as his name was synonymous with the famous model train sets. He was a very experienced pilot and had flown an operation from England on the first day of war in 1939. A total of 15 sorties were flown on the 9th, 10th, and 11th. This included a large number of air sea rescue sorties on the 11th.

As communication with Head Quarters, situated at Ghisonaccia, had proved difficult it was decided to return them to Blida, and that Ghisonaccia would be the second detachment. Two Dakotas transported about 30 personnel to Blida. On the 14th transport was provided to Chrea in the Atlas mountains behind Blida where there were facilities for skiing and tobogganing and turns were taken by different crews to rest there for 48hrs. On the 15th the first sorties were carried out from Ghisonaccia by Thomson and Coleman. A U-Boat hunt had been going on for three days since the 11th within the an area south of the Balearic Islands by Wellingtons and several engagements had taken place between them and Ju 88s. Two or three were shot down on either side and air sea rescue services were working at top speed. No 14 Squadron was called on to help the search but Thomson and Coleman saw nothing despite about 7hrs searching. However it was learned later that four airmen had been rescued. Ghisonaccia had now been reinforced and there were sufficient aircraft and crews to fly up to three sorties a day. This was most opportune as an Allied force was due to land at Anzio south of Rome on 22 January.

Flying from Ghisonaccia considerably reduced the number of hours spent on patrols. For instance, a patrol on 16 January, although they had no enemy sightings, managed to cover the arc from Spezia, westward to Levant Island twice in just under four hours, covering some 680 miles from base and back. The flying time from Ghisonaccia to Blida was about three and a half hours on average. On 24 January, Donovan's former co-pilot Paddy Reid went out on a recce and never returned. No signals were heard but as soon as he was overdue, searches were made. The next day Yelloly sighted three K-type dinghies (one man life rafts) lashed together about 8 miles off Cannes. He circled and saw there were three occupants, one laid out apparently as if injured, while the other two waved distress flags. The position was reported and Yelloly was told to continue on his patrol. This proved fatal as a half gale was blowing at the time and when the flight of Spitfires passed over the position some time later, they saw no dinghies. Later it was rumoured that they had drifted inshore and had been picked up by the enemy, but this was never confirmed.

With the opening of Ghisonaccia, flying had increased and in January some 97 sorties were carried out. Unfortunately, but perhaps not surprisingly, the number of crews and aircraft lost had also increased.

The Allied forces in Italy were held up at Monte Cassino, where three battles to take the mountain took place between January and May 18th. In Corsica, American medium bombers were stationed to interrupt German supplies and bomb targets standing in the way of the ground forces. No 14 Squadron's role, flying from Corsica, was to keep a close eye on such reinforcements as could be moved south by sea.

Winston Churchill and General Alexander met in Carthage and decided to land two Divisions at the small fishing port of Anzio a few miles due south of Rome. Before the landing took place early in the morning of 22 January 1944, the Squadron's patrols were especially vital to evaluate the strength of opposition, which the Divisions might encounter.

Although the Marauders reported a considerable amount of supply shipping, the Squadron was rarely told of any successful action by our naval forces, which had superiority following the surrender of the Italian fleet.

Throughout February the Squadron carried on with its patrols at the same rate of two, three and sometimes four a day, both in the Adriatic and along the west coast of Italy and south of France. The sightings followed the same pattern that had been established in the last three months. On 3 February, Lantinga showed remarkable skill in flying a circuit of the aerodrome at Ghisonaccia after a main wheel broke off during take off and rendered the ailerons and air speed indicator useless. Although he was unaware that the main wheel had gone, he landed the crippled aircraft without injury to the occupants. The aircraft was written off. The Air Officer Commanding directed that the captain's and second pilot's log books be endorsed to record the exceptional airmanship displayed. On the same day Squadron Leader Grimsey, the commander of the detachment at Grottaglie, was promoted to the rank of Wing Commander and went to command No 52 Squadron. Flight Lieutenant Elsey was promoted to the rank of Squadron Leader and given the command of the Grottaglie detachment. On 8 February Croskell took off from Grottaglie to fly to Blida; nothing else was heard of this aircraft but an aircraft was seen to crash into the sea at a position where he would have reached at that time. All the occupants of the aircraft were reported missing. They were Croskell, Milford, Irwin, Sims, Ellenbogen and Lussier but included in the aircraft was Climpson who, being tour expired, was returning to base as a passenger. By this date the number of sightings, both in the Adriatic and off the coast of Italy, were much fewer.

Flying Officer Wright of No 2 Film Production Unit, joined the detachment at Grottaglie on 20th February with the intention of remaining a few days to take some cine shots during patrols. Squadron Leader Elsey, commanding the Grottaglie detachment, had arranged to air test Aircraft F and took off at 0920hrs with Wright aboard but during the first circuit the port engine was observed to be cutting. The aircraft turned towards the aerodrome, the pilot's intention apparently was to make an immediate landing and the undercarriage was lowered and the aircraft lost height very rapidly and seemed to become out of control. Although the under-carriage was retracted the plane continued to lose height and crashed a short dis-tance from the aerodrome. Flying Officer Metcalfe described the disaster:

'We rushed from our hut when we saw the aircraft crash on a bomb dump not far from our billet (a wooden hut). We rushed to the scene and seeing a pair of legs protruding from the wreckage, I pulled, and out came Squadron Leader Elsey, the top of whose skull had been sliced off, Flying Officer Merkley sat dead in the co-pilot seat smoke coming from his knees and elbow. Flying Officer Campbell died later in the military hospital at Taranto. I was in the funeral party and stood at the head of the carriage carrying the three coffins. I was impressed by noticing that an old peasant standing nearby removed his cap as we went by.' Jim Wright survived the crash but was blinded and badly burned. He was one of Dr McIndoe's 'Guinea Pigs' and later became famous for his charity work for the war-disabled, and remarkably founded and managed a successful filming company.

'21 February 1944 - Op 13 (Recorded in Lowder's diary)

'The powers that be decided to try and catch Jerry napping by sending us off earlier than ever before, as they knew we were preventing his shipping from mov-ing freely by day so that he was slipping out at nights. Off we went at 0658hrs - still dark, for a 4hrs 30mins operation. As we reached Spezia we saw five E-boats which opened fire on us with cannon and machine gun. Green tracer whipped past us as we took violent evasive action. Then the shore batteries joined in and heavy flak appeared everywhere. However, we got out of range safely and went on down to Leghorn, where we saw a tug just off shore. Out to sea positions again (these legs out to sea were to confuse Jerry if he should be able to D/F us) and back to Genoa, where we went back to Spezia again - hoping to see our 'friends', the E-boats. But they must have gone into Spezia as we never saw a thing.

'Then off we set course to Monaco and down to Levant. This leg was quite a thrill for when we came to Cannes, we turned in and opened out to 300mph to go through the harbour behind Lerins Isle. It was strewn with row-boats, presumably fishermen who stood up and stared as we roared through just above their heads at 40ft. People were on the quays either side of us, streets and houses plain as any-thing. Not a shot was fired at us. We must have surprised the defences.

'However, there wasn't any shipping so that was that - 'phew!' Then on down past dear old Cap Agay, that well known place for heavy accurate flak - yes, and we got it! A terrific burst off our starboard wing tip was the start, then hell let loose. We weaved, climbed, turned, dived as we opened out to 300mph out to sea and were soon out of range. Then we came upon an 800 ton vessel going south. The next point of interest was the next flak Cape - Cape Camerat. Here we got it in the neck again with heavy flak showering the sea around us. So off we went again in mad gyrations over the sea till we were out of range. Then to Levant where we turned for home and I got to work on the radio. I got all the radio sighting reports through without any trouble and then sat back with a pipe thinking - 'another job done'!'

This description of a typical reconnaissance shows that these operations were not such easeful jobs as the word 'recce' might imply. During any one patrol, there was a constant risk of coming under fire from enemy aircraft, ships or shore batteries and at 50ft above the sea little chance of extricating the aircraft from damage to the controls or of the crew baling out.

Despite February being one of the worst months for bad weather, seventy patrols were flown.

The first half of March carried on with the usual routine of operational sorties being flown from Grottaglie and from Corsica, while the training flight at Blida was managing to do extremely well in replacing crews, who were tour-expired or missing. Early in March, Flight Lieutenant Gellatley was promoted to Squadron Leader and put in command of the detachment at Grottaglie. The weather was poor throughout this period and several patrols had to be curtailed due to the conditions.

From Blida, one of the training aircraft piloted by Flight Sergeant Jones was intercepted and shot up whilst on a navigation exercise and the gunner, Flight Sergeant Clifford, was wounded. The attack was made by an Airacobra of a French Squadron. A Court of Inquiry was held, but the result of its findings was not known. Clifford died some months afterwards from galloping consumption. 'Lou' Clifford had suffered from TB as a boy and had been educated in a French school in Switzerland, so was fluent in French, which caused much surprise amongst the local Algerians.

On 17 March the training flight at Blida was ordered to operate under the American Bombardment Centre at Telergma, about 180 miles east of Blida and south west of Constantine. Lapthorne left by air and reached the new location later in the day. Flight Lieutenant Jones, his navigation officer, was in charge of the road party and arrived at Telergma on the 18th. The Squadron was thus scattered far and wide with bases at Blida, Telergma, Ghisonaccia and Grottaglie, with subsidiary aircraft kept at Brindisi in case of bad weather at Grottaglie. It was some 900 miles from Blida to Brindisi, 540 to Ghisonaccia and 460 from Brindisi to Ghisonaccia, so members of the Squadron were rarely all together in one place for any jollification!

The Brindisi aircraft, at this time, took a member of the US Navy as a passenger in order to obtain photographs of parts of the Albanian and Greek coasts. By the 20th, the training flight at Telergma was already in action and commenced their training with five B-26Bs. News also arrived on that day that the base at Blida was to prepare to move on the 27th of the month to a new base in Sardinia. A road convoy consisting of 19 vehicles carrying personnel and equipment of the HQ and Engineering Flights, left Blida on route for Bizerta at 0800hrs. The officer in charge was the adjutant Flight Lieutenant Jones. The convoy reached the transit camp in Bizerta during the morning of the 30th where everyone would remain in camp until all the vehicles and equipment were loaded. A train party consisting of about 150 people who could not be accommodated in the road convoy had already arrived at the transit camp on the previous day, and the two parties were now amalgamated; waiting to be embarked on 4 April aboard the American Liberty ship *George W Lively* and taken to Sardinia.

Throughout the month a good rate of operations had been maintained and amounted in total to 85. A fine effort considering the dislocation caused by the Squadron's movements and the poor weather. Sightings continued to be few but the flak from the coast defences was steadily increasing particularly at Toulon, where the Germans obviously had radar-controlled shore batteries. On 29 March, however, an aircraft captained by Flying Officer McDonald failed to return. No messages were received after take-off but information was received much later that an aircraft had crashed near Barcelona and that three bodies had been identified as McDonald, Lampen and Woods and buried at Mataro. It seems likely the aircraft had been damaged by flak and the pilot made a desperate attempt to land on the Spanish shore.

Loading aboard the *George W Lively* was completed during the afternoon of 4th April. The ship left Bizerta harbour for the Bay of Tunis where she waited for the remainder of the convoy and then set sail for Sardinia at 1600hrs on the 6th. Next day the convoy arrived in the bay of Cagliari on the southern coast at 1900hrs and dropped anchor. A strong wind was encountered and the sea was rough in complete contrast to the conditions in North Africa. A small detachment of fitters and other maintenance people, which had flown from Blida in charge of the Engineer Officer on the 26th March, was carrying out inspections of aircraft flown in from Ghisonaccia. The road party left Cagliari at 0830hrs and arrived at Alghero on the west coast of the island, more than 100 miles away, during the afternoon and immediately began to organise the camp. The CO having supervised the loading at Bizerta on the 4th, had flown to Alghero to begin preparations for the Squadron's new base.

A few days later on, on 19 April, the convoy left Ghisonaccia bound for Alghero and arrived on the 21st. Over the next eight weeks the Squadron slowly gathered its forces from Corsica, transferring them to Alghero, but operations continued from Corsica while the Engineering and HQ flights (including 'Doc' Forbes and his staff) were preparing Alghero to be the main Squadron base. The Squadron HQ was established in the administrative block, a brick built building on the aerodrome itself. The main camp was three miles away by the sea.

The re-deployment of the Squadron had not affected the number of operations needed. Two were mounted from Italy and two from Corsica every day. There were not many sightings but on 6 April, Hornby, sighted and reported a merchant vessel of about 1,500 tons marked as belonging to the International Red Cross just off Marseilles. Later he saw nine aircraft coming straight towards the Marauder and then he and his crew saw tracer bullets coming at them. They fired back, turned 90 degrees and opened up to over 300mph and weaved. As they turned they noticed that the aircraft were Beaufighters with RAF markings. The B-26A got away safely, and were told the next day that the fighters had mistaken them for a German aircraft as they had been sent out to sink the Red Cross ship which had false markings, which they did, but one of the fighters was shot down by the ship during the attack.

The number of sorties was boosted between 10 and 12 of April by the mounting of two anti-submarine sorties, one from each base. However, on the 12th, Cornish was attacked by Spitfires flying from Corsica. This was apt to happen and was always a problem for the captain of the aircraft: whether to fire back at his own kind, which would only encourage them to attack further, or flee as fast as possible, hoping the fighter pilots would recognise their mistake,

Again on the 14th and 15th, U-Boat hunts were carried out both from Italy and Corsica. Weather interfered with any flying from Corsica on the 16th and on the 17th the CO flew back to Ghisonaccia, taking back with them the Doctor.

On the 19th, four recces took off from Corsica - Squadron Leader Yelloly, Warrant Officer Mailer, Flying Officers Cornish and Budge, who failed to return. It was learnt later that Budge had been shot down by enemy fighters having sent an emergency signal - FGQ, which meant, 'I am being attacked by enemy fighters'. Searches found no survivors or debris.

The following account, written by Joe Lowder, is typical of the hazards faced by the Squadron from enemy fighters:

'14 April

'Op 18 Marseilles to Sète we patrolled with our starboard generator u/s and the port one pretty shaky. So skipper decided that we would go back to base after this leg. We reached Sète and turned out to sea about five miles out. I had just got out of my search position in the astro hatch when Ken (Williams , the rear gunner) called out on the intercom. "Two Bf l09s dead astern 300yrds". They had 'jumped us' out of cloud. I jumped up into the hatch again as we opened out to 300mph corkscrewing out to open sea.

'I saw one bank off our tail about 200yrds and go off to port quarter about 7-8 o'clock and creep up. The other slewed round to five o'clock climbing to roughly 200ft. Both these were our 'blind spots' so they had us taped and were in their attack positions. Well, here it was at last. Serious business and with two Bf l09Gs, Jerry's latest fighters. I had no feeling of fear but just an acceptancy in my mind of, 'Here it is and make the best of it'.

'They kept their positions just for a few seconds and then started to come in at the same time. As we cork-screwed out, Ken and Geoff (Unsworth, the turret gunner) were able to blast at them. In they came and I shouted the evasive instructions to skipper. When they got in close with Ken and Geoff's tracer going right at them - they swung in on our stern and interchanged positions 5 o'clock and 9 o'clock. This went on for 12 minutes and they made 12 such-like attacks with their cannon and machine gun fire cutting through the water up past our tail underneath us and under our wings. The cannon fire was the fuse type which burst in the air above us like miniature flak.

'At one time, one Bf 109 out at 9 o'clock had a terrific pasting from both Ken and Geoff, who were able to fire at the same target owing to the cork-screwing. This aircraft broke off and made off back climbing as he went. The remaining Jerry kept up attacks for a further two minutes on our stern and he certainly did hang on to us. But then owing to us going way out to sea and the petrol going like hell at this speed he knew he couldn't chase us much further. So he made the last attempt to get us by coming right up close on our tail. Ken had run out of ammunition so his guns were silent, so the Jerry perhaps thought he had silenced our rear guns. However, it was his last, and off he went in the same direction the other had taken.

'We had informed all stations that we were being attacked by enemy aircraft so a complete radio silence was imposed everywhere so as to listen out for any more distress from us. So as I sat down again I sent out the OK message and a further one of our returning owing to mechanical trouble. Then the after-effects of this 'shaky do' came on me!'

This is an excellent account of fighter attack and is only too typical of what could have happened on many occasions when aircraft failed to return. In many cases pilots would not have been aware until it was too late that they were being attacked as fighters would come out of the sun. On the other hand of course, a hit by anti-aircraft fire from coastal battery or even a sudden engine failure would have the same result.

During April, Flying Officers J B MacDonald and Smith were both made first pilots and started their operations later in May. April drew to a close and on the 29th, Fletcher and Clark flew a recce from Grottaglie and strafed with machine-gun fire an armed trawler and also a schooner which had fired at them. Several neutral shipping sightings were made, which were becoming quite common along the coast of Spain. During the month a total of 118 operations were flown and only one aircraft lost.

The first week in May was taken up with the usual recces from both Italy and Corsica. Further reinforcements of aircraft and ground crew were arriving at Alghero from Telergma. There were a number of anti-submarine sorties, to protect our convoys reinforcing the army in Italy for its push towards Rome. On the 7th, Smith and his crew failed to return from a recce, which was his first operation as captain and particularly sad as he had become a father only two months previously. He had taken off from Ghisonaccia. On the same day, Flight Sergeant Jones had been forced to return from a similar mission owing to bad weather conditions. On 9 May, Herschell and Mailer were forced to abandon patrols, Ross and his crew failed to return from a similar mission. No signals had been received during the flight. Flying Officer Cornish and Flight Sergeant Clark flew a combined reconnaissance and search for the missing aircraft without success. Jones sighted a submarine in swell following a crash dive but could claim no result from his gunner's fire.

On the 11th, Johnson flew a patrol from Grottaglie and Lantinga flew one from Ghisonaccia. Lantinga's aircraft was attacked by three Bf 109Gs which were escorting an enemy motor ship and extensive minor damage was inflicted on the Marauder. Severe damage was done to one fighter and slight damage to the other two. On the 13th, three sorties were flown and MacDonald claimed damage to a Ju 88, scoring two bursts with machine guns.

Recces were continuing from both Italy and Corsica and on the 15th Squadron

Leader Haddingham arrived at Grottaglie in Italy to commence operational flying. On the same day, training of new crews commenced at Telergma and Group Captain Maydwell (the former CO) flew as a second pilot with Flying Officer Johnson on a recce from Italy. On 20 May, the CO flew to Corsica to supervise the move of the detachment to Sardinia and returned to Alghero the same day, and Glanville and Boyes flew aircraft to Alghero from Corsica. A small rear party was left at Ghisonaccia to service the remaining aircraft.

On 22 May Lieutenant Overed of the South African Air Force, crashed at Telergma whilst training. The aircraft caught fire but no one was injured. Next day, while further sorties were made both from Grottaglie and Alghero, the first part of the convoy from Ghisonaccia arrived at Alghero, having proceeded by ferry from Bonifacio to Santa Teresa in Sardinia, and then by road via Sassari to Alghero. On the 24th, Johnson strafed several barges and schooners while on a patrol from Grottaglie, striking most of them with machine gun fire. The remaining part of the road convoy from Corsica arrived during the night at Alghero.

At this time, news of the land fighting was much better. Polish troops captured the wrecked monastery at Mount Cassino on 18 May and the Allied force rolled forward. Field Marshal Kesselring was forced at last to withdraw from the Gustav Line on the 23rd and on the same day the Anzio garrison broke out of the beach-head. By 4 June, Rome was in Allied hands.

On 25 May no sorties were carried out because heavy rain rendered the airfield at Grottaglie unserviceable, but during the last days of May, sorties were flown from both Grottaglie and Alghero. These patrols were given the name 'Snatch'. The purpose was to throw a screen between the North African and French coasts to try to intercept torpedo aircraft which were being despatched by the Germans to attack the large convoys from the US and Britain to support the Italian front. During subsequent weeks this was to happen quite frequently. A total of 69 sorties were flown during May with the loss of two aircraft.

On 5 June, Wing Commander Law-Wright and the Engineer and Intelligence Officers went to Olbia on the north east coast of Sardinia to inspect the wreckage of two Me 323s. He was advised by an Italian Colonel who had been stationed there at the time, that they had crashed as a result of Law-Wright's Marauder attack on three of them on 22 May 1943. One had certainly been shot down but now the Squadron was able to claim destruction of the other two as well.

The CO was now posted to the No 63 Wing in North Corsica which was under the command of an American Brigadier General who also administered Alghero. No 63 Wing consisted of No 6 Squadron (equipped with Hurricanes) and three B-25 squadrons. Their role was to attack any ships which were reported by No 14 Squadron. He handed command of the Squadron to Wing Commander Donovan, now returned after converting 70 OTU in Egypt, to Marauders.

Donovan arrived on 8 June, having been briefed by the AOC in Algiers, who told him that the landing in Normandy was the major assault on Europe but it was important that the enemy was uncertain, whether the main invasion would come from the South. He wanted No 14 Squadron to reorganise the detachments and convert to night flying as soon as the runway at Alghero was finished. The Squadron was to maintain an aggressive stance to reinforce German doubts about the Allies intentions. This would enable aircraft to be on patrol from dawn to dusk in support of future operations in the South of France and Northern Italy.

On 8 June, Ted Donovan wrote: 'I was flown to Alghero, and was met by Law-Wright who was ready to hand the Squadron over to me. We went to the Squadron office in a big headquarters building of three storeys where I met the adjutant, Jones. We then drove some two miles down to the beach and there were all our old tents looking like home. The camp was in sand hills on a beautiful bay with excellent swimming. The town of Alghero was about two and a half miles away. I was introduced to the officers just before dinner and they seemed similar to the mixture we had had before. There were several Australians but more Canadians this time and two South Africans. After dinner we drove back to the airfield and I was introduced to our Group Commander, Group Captain McDonald and Bill Dunsmore, who of course I knew. The rest of the Wing consisted of 36 Wellington Squadron, 272 Beaufighter Squadron and 17 South African Squadron who had Venturas. I spent a few days there and then went around the detachments which still included Blida.'

On 12 June Donovan flew to Telergma to check the training flight which was still commanded by Lapthorne. The Americans at Telergma were doing the major inspections. On the next day, the 13th, he went to Blida to check the servicing being done there and met Gibbins again. They were doing the intermediate inspections. He went back to Mediterranean Allied Coastal Air Forces HQ to ask permission to move the Blida detachment to Telergma and then to move them all to Alghero. It was agreed, so on the 14th he flew back to Telergma to arrange this with the Americans.

While there, he found that the Americans had lost one of No 14 Squadron's B-26s. They seemed not very put out, and offered another aircraft instead! This turned out to be the later 'F' type, and was quite a new animal. Its wings were altered by some 10 degrees to the main fuselage. This meant that when bombing at medium-level, the fuselage was level, but when flat out at low level, the pilot was hanging on to his straps as the aircraft flew with its nose down and the speed had dropped to a maximum of about 250mph.'

Donovan flew back to Alghero on 14 June and took some of the pupil Canadian air crew who were ready to join the front line. He had no crew of his own and was using intercommunication flying to train one. On the 17th he flew to Grottaglie. The flight there was still commanded by Haddingham. They were sharing the airfield with a wing of USAAF B-24 Liberators. A non-commissioned RAF navigator was surprised to discover that non-commissioned Americans appeared to have less powers of decision and always referred them to their superior officer. This particular navigator was refused 'The Colours of the Day' by an American officer because he was an NCO and the USAAF regulations ruled that only commissioned officers could be trusted with such secrets!

On the 18th Hogg flew a reconnaissance in the Bete-Novelle area west of Marseilles and was attacked by two Bf 109s ten miles south of Agde. These aircraft gave chase and opened fire at 800yrds. The chase lasted 10 minutes and the Marauder took evasive action, but the fuselage was holed in the rear, and both gunners were slightly wounded. The Marauder's undercarriage was damaged but Hogg made an excellent emergency landing back at Alghero.

On the 24th June, a week later, Hornby arrived back with the aircraft which he had picked up from the UK. Next day, Holland avoided contact with two Bf 109s whilst flying a recce from Alghero. On the 26th, Robertson was attacked by two Arado 196s which fired several bursts without striking him. On the same day. Lieutenant Brumner of the South African Air Force, failed to return from his sortie. Later, eye witnesses reported that they had seen him crash into the sea just off the north coast of Sardinia. The dead crew members were all recovered by Italian fishermen, except for Brumner whose body was not found. They were subsequently buried on the 28th in the war cemetery at Cagliari in southern Sardinia. Yelloly and Hornby and their crews attended the burial.

On 26 June, Donovan picked up a B-26 at Blida and visited MACAF HQ, where he learned the whole Combined Headquarters was to be moved to Caserta Palace, near Naples. Flight Sergeant Clark sighted a 2000 ton MV during a recce from Nice to Barcelona on 29 June. On the same day the advance party of the training flight arrived at Alghero, and the main party arrived on the 30th.

Despite such dispersed deployment, a good operational rate was maintained. From Alghero at least two sorties a day were flown with one aircraft on stand-by. These sorties covered a huge area from the front in Italy, (north of Rome) round the Gulf of Genoa, across the Italian and French Rivieras, to Toulon and Marseilles and on to the Spanish border and lasted about 5-6hrs. At Alghero, the Squadron had about ten or twelve aircraft, and about six at Grottaglie with one at Foggia. They too were flying two sorties a day. The nominal strength of the Squadron was 18 aircraft plus two for training and there were about 18 fully-trained crews.

Small ships and schooners were the main sightings although two E-boats and a 1,500 ton coaster were seen in the Adriatic by Cornish. Flak was both light and heavy, and caused some damage to the Marauder.

A total of 87 operations sorties were flown during June. These were evenly divided between Italy and Sardinia.

SOUTHERN FRANCE INVADED

During July, while the Allied armies fought their way north of Rome through yet more German defensive lines, it was agreed that an invasion of the south of France was needed to support the Normandy landings by forcing the Germans to fight in the south as well as the north. Troops therefore were withdrawn gradually from the Italian front and made ready for this new campaign. This slowed down the advance in Italy, where the Germans had 21 Divisions as opposed to the 20 of the Allies, and destroyed any hope of getting into Germany through Trieste and the Balkans. It also made it imperative that supplies to the enemy in southern France be restricted as much as possible. The Squadron's long-standing task of reconnoitring the coasts of north-west Italy and southern France became even more important.

On 3 July, the CO called on the AOC of 242 Group at Taranto and was told to prepare to move 'A' Flight from Grottaglie to Foggia further north.

A level of two reconnaissance's per day was kept up from Algharo and

Grottaglie, sometimes increasing to a total of 13. Flying Officer Cornish failed to return from a flight north of Ancona into the Gulf of Venice on 1st July. Overed covered the same course but found no sign of the missing aircraft. The CO taking over Glanville's crew. flew a reconnaissance on the 4th with two Beaufighters in the Adriatic. The Beaufighters remained out at sea as they were more vulnerable to fighters (the Beaufighter MkX armed with rockets had a maximum speed of 303mph at 1,300ft and was without a tail gun so the Marauder went in close to look for targets for them.) Unfortunately there were no sightings.

On the 23rd July, the Grottaglie flight was instructed by HQ 242 Group to pre-pare to move to Foggia Main aerodrome by the 26th. On the 24th an advance party left for Foggia by road with Flight Lieutenant Ingham in charge of the trans-port convoy of 44 officers and men. On the 26th, Grottaglie was evacuated, the air-craft leaving at 0800hrs and a road party of the remaining 30 personnel under Flying Officer McDonald some two hours later. On the 27th the CO accompanied by the medical and engineering officers, flew to Foggia to inspect the new loca-tion for the flight.

On the 25th, notification was received of the award of the DFC to two former members of the squadron, Pilot Officer R K Francis and Flying Officer E B Scott-Murphy, who had been reported missing on a reconnaissance on 28 June 1943.

On 31 July, eight sorties were flown from Alghero (including Snatch Operations) and two from Foggia. This brought the total for the month to 105 operations.

The Squadron was able to start night flying on the 2nd August as the runway was now ready. This gave a 2,000-yard take-off on tarmac but entailed a starboard turn of some 10 to 15 degrees to fly down a valley. It was nine months since the Squadron had done any night flying. The CO dual instructed Warrant Officer Mailer and Flight Sergeant Clark, and on the same night the more experienced pilots 'soloed' themselves by taking-off at dusk and flying circuits and bumps as it got darker. On the 4th Flying Officer Holmes and Warrant Officer Holland flew solo at night, after dual instruction by Donovan. On the 5th August Donovan took Flying Officer Duncan on his first operational flight, taking off in the dark and arriving at the French coast at dawn. This was the first operation that had been flown by the Squadron at night for nine months. For the rest of the month, pre-dawn take-offs were made and two night landings at the end of each day.

On 10 August the CO flew Clark and his crew on another night operation to the French coast at Cape Camarat then continued east to Antibes, Nice, San Remo, Imperia, Vado and finally Savona, where they encountered plenty of flak and two merchant vessels in Savona harbour, one of about 3,000 and the other 2,000 tons. Donovan flew Pilot Officer Herschell and his crew to the same stretch of coast on the 12th, this time starting at Savona. Changing tactics, they flew along the beach before reaching the harbour, sheltering in the shadow of the land to the west. The CO had been asked to take a good look at the harbour to see if the ships were still there and got closer than intended. He actually flew over the harbour wall, and could see and reported the ships, which were then bombed by No 17 Squadron Venturas later that night. There was plenty of flak, but it was wild as surprise had been achieved. There was another ship in Imperia, and on leaving two Fw 190s appeared; but did not attack.

To supplement single photographs of coastal targets it was decided to build a complete line overlap of the coast, and these were taken all the way from the Italian front to Marseilles, some 70 miles. Every sortie brought back pieces of the mosaic. The co-pilot held the camera, the navigator, or the wireless operator turned the film. The co-pilot counted the photographs, whilst the handle kept turning. A rough and ready method but practical, which produced good results. The runs were about 2 miles, height at 50ft, which drew flak but was avoided either by increasing speed with the flak falling behind, or by decreasing speed with the flak falling in front. Most chose to accelerate, and when the tail gunner began to get worried at the proximity of the flak, the aircraft would break off and fly out to sea. The Squadron managed to complete the line overlap well before Operation Anvil (the invasion of southern France)began.

One day at the beginning of August, the Squadron commanders were told to be at the Ops Room in the morning. Air Vice-Marshal Lloyd joined the gathering consisting of Group Captain MacDonald, Wing Commander Garton, the CO of No 36 Squadron, Wing Commander Williams, the CO of No 17 South African Air Force Squadron, Lieutenant Colonel McKenzie, Wing Commander Innes commanding No 272 Squadron flying Beaufighters, and Donovan, CO of No 14 Squadron. The AOC told them to gather around him and he wrote down a date, 15 August, on a piece of perspex and then immediately rubbed it out. He went on to say that the invasion would take place at this date and that the squadrons were to be prepared for a maximum effort. Then he saw each CO individually. When he came to Donovan, he told him that after the invasion was established ashore there would be very little to do west of Italy. Therefore, given a fortnight's training in formation flying and bombing, No 14 Squadron could become a medium-level bomber squadron. The invasion was to be centred on St Tropez and would cover a twenty mile front. The outer limits of the landings were from east of Toulon to west of Cannes. The squadron's duty would be to cover the whole coastline either side from dawn to dusk.

Before dawn on 13 August the CO took off on patrol with Elliott and his crew. They went up the east coast of Corsica and let down to near sea level aiming to make a landfall at Toulon. As they reached the coast there was a considerable amount of mist obscuring the land. When they were a few miles off Toulon they were straddled by heavy gun fire, which came obviously from coastal batteries and augured ill for the invasion force due to land on the 15th. The coastal fog lifted and they flew westward to Marseilles. The only sighting was two enemy aircraft over land and there was the usual flak around that great port. Elliott flew very well at night and was detached to Grottaglie to help the night conversion of 'A' Flight.

The Squadron was at this time flying four sorties a day, covering the coast for the whole of daylight. On D-Day, 15 August, Squadron Leader Yelloly and Flying Officer Hornby covered each side of the invasion area, their take off delayed an hour by fog.

Lowder wrote:' We were briefed with another crew, Squadron Leader Yelloly's, for this special trip to cover the landing of the invasion forces. We were to patrol from Cannes to Genoa, the others from Marseilles to Levant.

'There was a very low, thick land mist in the early hours delaying our take off until 0855hrs. The zero landing hour was 0600hrs. Not a single E-boat or human torpedo could be seen. Everything went off as smooth as could be in brilliant sunshine with a little haze over the sea. The landings were made on the Porquerolles, from Levant up to Cannes. This spot was where our patrol ended, so we did see quite a lot of transports and destroyers of which we took photographs. These areas were a safety lane for the shipping, so strictly forbidden to any land-based aircraft. This was to ease the duties of the carrier-borne planes and the identifying of single aircraft. So all the bombers, softening up the various airfields and concentrations, kept strictly out of this great safety lane from Ajaccio, the jumping off port on the west coast of Corsica, to the south of France.'

On 19th August the CO took Flying Officer MacDonald and his crew with him for a patrol that lasted until after dark. They flew from Sète eastward to Porquerolles Island and sighted and shadowed two merchant vessels of 2,000 and 1,500 tons. The heavy and medium flak was accurate, but it was later heard that they had both been sunk by 17 (SAAF) Squadron. They flew to Fort St Louis and there met even heavier flak and more accurate than usual. The coast line erupted in bomb bursts and explosions, as the battle raged for the French troops advancing on Marseilles.

Donovan recalled:

'Soon after the invasion, one of the Squadron NCOs Alghero came and said that the French were demanding spare parts for their Marauders. My ground crew were upset because they thought they were being bullied but I assured them that the verb 'demander' in French was not as forceful as it is in English. I went along and found a French Squadron commander. Eventually I understood they needed spares and help in preparing their aircraft to fly the next morning into France itself. I quickly said that we would help them all we could and congratulated the Squadron commander on liberating his country. I said, "My squadron is yours, ask for anything you want". He then kissed me on both cheeks.'

'A' Flight at Foggia continued with its two sorties a day with the Squadron now averaging six sorties a day. On 5 August, Flying Officer Johnson sighted a U-boat despite the fact that the Squadron had no special search equipment. However, it crash dived and managed to escape.

The squadron's operational record says that on 7 August it was a quiet day for Alghero and Foggia, but went on to say that the Squadron flew seven sorties. The record paid a great deal of attention over the weeks to football, cricket, swimming and the rifle range. Sporting facilities at Alghero were excellent and little doubt that the exercise and games against other squadrons greatly enhanced the morale of the squadrons.

242 Group HQ ordered 'A' Flight at Foggia to return to Grottaglie and between 15-17 August the move was carried out and operations resumed from there. Personnel were housed mostly in farm buildings and wooden huts. On the 27th a reconnaissance was flown in the south Adriatic amongst the islands. Off Levkas, near the Greek coast, barges were strafed. Flak and rockets with cables attached were fired at the aircraft in reply.

The routine of six sorties per day continued until the end of the month, amounting to a total of 154 operations for August.

Wing Commander Donovan composed a general review of events in August. He wrote:'It had been a notable month for the Squadron in many ways. The number of sorties flown namely 154 was, so far as is known, a record for the squadron. There had been only one accident - a tribute to both the air and ground crews. Moreover, during the month the whole Squadron had converted to night flying, and at least four sorties a day involved either a night landing or take-off. Having no crew of my own at the beginning of the month, I took the opportunity of flying with five crews on their first night sortie. I found the general standard high. Fighter control was well done. Flak was met but no aircraft was damaged. The comparative scarcity of sightings on both sides of Italy is a tribute to the efficiency of past daylight strikes. It is remarkable that the coast had become hazardous to the enemy simply by the presence of the squadron's constant surveillance backed up by limited daylight strikes. Furthermore a major invasion of seven divisions was mounted with no loss to Allied shipping due to enemy action at sea.'

The land battles in northern Italy and southern France were now progressing so successfully that it was obvious that there would be few coasts for the Squadron to patrol. The AOC at Caserta Palace said MACAF was to close and that the CO was to make a survey of two airfields on the mainland of Italy; one at Tarquinia, 45 miles north of Rome, and the other at Ancona on the Adriatic coast. He also said that Alghero would be closing down. The headquarters, the engineering flight, and aircraft of 'B' Flight were to move down to Cagliari on the south coast of Sardinia where they would then be taken by sea to Naples.

Meanwhile as many as five sorties a day were still being flown by the whole Squadron from Italy and Sardinia. There were more sightings in the Adriatic, where many schooners and other small craft were seen and strafed. Occasionally the Marauder would be accompanied by Beaufighters, and in one case they left a large schooner on fire. Flying Officer Holmes, sighted a ship on 4th September flying some balloons and his gunners fired on these and succeeded in hitting them. Two days later Squadron Leader Haddingham sighted the Italian transatlantic liner, the *Rex*, a ship of over 50,000 tons sailing from the southern Adriatic aiming, according to intelligence reports, to reach Trieste and there to block the harbour by scuttling herself. The Squadron shadowed the *Rex* during daylight. On the 8th, Flying Officer Robertson sighted the *Rex* and landed at Ancona and briefed the Beaufighter crews, who then attacked the big liner with rocket fire while Robertson observed damage. Photographs were taken before and after the attack, but the bad weather made the pictures disappointing. Flight Lieutenant Gibbs, on 9th September reported the *Rex* as listing heavily to starboard and smouldering. The controversy over the sinking of this ship, remains to this day.

About this time, Group Captain McDonald said that the American General commanding No 63 Wing in Corsica wanted to decorate some members of No 14 Squadron for the excellent work they had done in finding targets for them. Evidently the General was thinking of four Air Medals. The CO wrote four citations. Later he was told the one for Warrant Officer Stout was to be upgraded to an American DFC, but nothing ever materialised.

The Squadron had become used to the small number of awards made for reconnaissance work; apparently the case in all theatres.

On the 12th several flights were made to Tarquinia with stores and tentage and on the same day the CO, Flying Officer Hogg and Flying Officer Jordan reconnoitred the Gulf of Genoa for human torpedoes, without sighting anything.

On 13 September the following signal was received: PERSONAL WING COMMANDER DONOVAN FROM AIR VICE MARSHAL LLOYD. YOUR SQUADRON HAS ESTABLISHED A REPUTATION IN THE MEDITERRANEAN WHICH WOULD BE HARD TO BEAT AND ONE WHICH WILL NOT TARNISH WITH THE PASSING OF TIME. I AM PROUD PERSONALLY OF THE ACHIEVEMENTS OF NO 14 SQUADRON AND HAVE WATCHED IT NOW FOR OVER 2 YEARS. I WISH TO CONVEY TO THE SQUADRON MY DEEP APPRECIATION OF THE EXCELLENT AND RELIABLE WORK WHICH HAS RESULTED IN SO MUCH DAMAGE TO THE ENEMY.

The euphoria engendered by such was quickly dissipated by a tragedy on the same day, Flying Officer Holmes and his crew, took-off from Alghero and crashed into the hill immediately ahead. All were killed. On the 14th, the CO was called to MACAF HQ in Naples, where Air Vice Marshal Lloyd told him that No 14 Squadron was to join the Balkan Air Force. The plan was to move 'A' Flight up to Foggia, and then to form an advance base of six aircraft at Ancona. Donovan was told to start packing up 'B' Flight at Alghero and assemble his aircraft at Grottaglie before moving to Foggia, Ancona and Tarquinia. The AOC said he would like to make some awards to the Squadron to mark its departure from his command, and Donovan wrote out citations, but nothing came of this either, nor to the BEMs recommended for some of the long-serving ground crew. A disappointing outcome.

The CO flew back to Alghero on the same day and spent the 15th putting in train the move from Sardinia.

On the 16th, the CO flew to Grottaglie and briefed Haddingham. Next, he flew to Ancona on the 18th, which he found capable of taking six aircraft. As he was about to take off, he was asked to take two German prisoners to Rome on his way to Naples. He agreed to this unwillingly because, as had happened before, there was nobody at the airfield to take the prisoners off his hands. He took them into Rome and by the time they were handed over, it was dark and there were no night flying facilities. The next day on take-off a tyre burst at 130mph, and wrecked the aircraft.

As soon as possible, Donovan sent signals to MACAF HQ, Grottaglie and Alghero saying what had happened and asking to be picked up as soon as possible. He recorded: 'I was depressed when told by the airfield that the weather was closing down and the outlook for the next few days was very poor for any type of flying. At last, on the morning of 22 September, there was a message to go to the airfield where we would be picked up. In the late morning Flying Officer Hogg turned up in a Marauder and as soon as he jumped out he said: "Have you heard the wonderful news, we are going home". I asked what he meant, and he said the Squadron was being posted back to England. I was thunderstruck by this and got him to take me to Naples. Sure enough, when I got to Caserta I was told that indeed the Squadron was posted back to England to fly Wellington Leigh Light aircraft. MACAF was virtually disbanded and we were now under the direct command of Air Marshal Slessor, the AOC-in-C Mediterranean. I was instructed to go back to Grottaglie where all the aircraft and personnel were assembling. The Sardinian main party including the HQ Flight at Alghero, were already on their way by sea to Naples.

On the 21st Elliott and his crew crashed into a hill on take-off at Grottaglie. They were all killed and were subsequently buried at the British Military Cemetery near Taranto. On the same day, Leading Aircraftsman E G W Hall was awarded the BEM for his gallantry on the ground trying to rescue the occupants from Squadron Leader Elsey's crashed aircraft.

On 17th September, the CO and Yelloly decided to travel to Naples, to No 3 Base Personnel Depot, where they could have some contact with the HQ in Naples and find out why the Squadron was not being moved into the Balkan Air Force for medium bombing. They were told that MACAF had been disbanded and that representations to the combined HQ would be fruitless.

'This month', recorded Donovan, 'has seen the end of the squadron's work in the Mediterranean and brings to a close the 'Marauder' period of the squadron's life. This had started in August 1942 when the enemy was at the gates of Cairo and finished with the Allies on the threshold of Germany. There was not a man on the Squadron who did not regret the departure of the Marauders, as they rightly felt they had been pioneers in the RAF with these fine aircraft. It was fitting however, that though No 14 was the first RAF Squadron to operate the Marauder they left them still in general service.

The operations during September had been coastal reconnaissance with a moderate number of sightings, dominated by the shadowing and destruction of the *Rex*. Aircraft had watched that liner for four days and finally briefed Beaufighters for their strike. Night flying continued to be the rule rather than the exception again; but two crews were lost in B-26 Marauders. As during take-off at night. These accidents, occurring as they did some six weeks after the Squadron started to operate consistently at night, underlined the very small margin of safety for the B-26 Marauder in a night take-off. Operations closed on 21st September 1944. This ended a period of two years continuous operating and covered more than a dozen major moves and some 2,000 miles advance'.

The Squadron had flown 69 operations during that month and the rest of September was spent in reducing the Squadron to a personnel basis in preparation for embarkation. The Squadron then ended a period of overseas service which began in November 1915 and was only broken when the Squadron temporarily returned to England in 1919 for disbanding, until it was reformed at Ramleh in Palestine in 1920.

TRANSFER TO THE UK

On 1 October 1944, orders came through for all personnel at Grottaglie to prepare to move to Naples to join the main body of the squadron. The next day all personnel entrained at Grottaglie at 1400hrs into cattle trucks. They arrived at No 3 BPD, Naples, at approximately midnight.

On the 5th, all ground staff personnel who had not completed their overseas tour were taken off squadron strength and replaced by tour expired personnel. Only 10% of its original ground staff remained.

Joe Lowder recorded the squadron's departure on 12 October: 'We stepped off the soil of Italy onto the ship, the *Capetown Castle*, a fine ship of about 27,000 tons. With two squadrons of RAF personnel, a few hundred others, the Manchester regiment, a Canadian regiment, a large ENSA party, and parties of nurses and Maltese wives of British servicemen, we were a fairly crowded lot. But the quarters were airy and comfortable, the food was good and there was a variety of entertainments'.

After a week at sea he recalled: 'On 21st October there was cheer upon cheer as we sailed up the Mersey to dock at the Liverpool pierhead. Crowds lined the dock side and a brass band played loudly with which we all joined in singing. A welcome speech was relayed over loudspeakers and then the band played again for our amusement. Many, including myself were silent for a while with lumps in our throats, for it was with a feeling of thankfulness to be back safely, remembering many of our pals we had left behind never to return'.

While the Squadron embarked for England, the CO was ordered to proceed by air as a passenger in a Stirling, landing at Lyneham, and went on to HQ Coastal Command HQ at Northwood, where he was introduced to the Commander-in-Chief, Air Marshal Sholto Douglas. Donovan recalled that, 'the Commander-in-Chief gave me a flattering welcome and said that he had been told that we were the best Maritime squadron in the Mediterranean and he knew that we would really pitch in as there was a big job to do'. This work was to involve searching for new types of German submarines operating in the English Channel and the seas off the British Isles. Donovan assured Sholto Douglas that every effort would be made to accelerate the training programme and enable the Squadron 'to get into the line quickly'. Sholto Douglas said, 'I am very glad to hear you say that because I know your squadron with their team spirit will not mind missing their disembarkation leave'. He was then sent to Plymouth, the Headquarters of No 19 Group. where the AOC, as Donovan recalled 'rather reiterated what Sholto Douglas had said and told me that I must do the best I could regarding disembarkation leave'. The next few days were spent there being shown around the headquarters and being initiated into its workings. Donovan says that he was given 'a brief in depth on the anti-submarine war'. By breaking a few rules Donovan contrived to grant unofficial leave to the unhappy squadron members.

As Lowder recalled in his diary, 'On 23 October at 0530hrs we dis-embarked and entrained for Chivenor in N Devon. The NAAFI issued tea and sandwiches with papers and cigarettes to enjoy during our long journey home. We went on leave, but it was not granted easily, and we had been told we had to be operational and ready as soon as possible, and there were bad feelings among us, but Ted Donovan at last won his way with Group HQ at Plymouth. I spent the happiest and most restful leave of all continuing our honeymoon from last June. Half I spent in St Helens, Marjorie's home, the rest in London at my place, throughout which we were constantly worried by the doodle bugs and rockets, V1s and V2s. On return to Chivenor we got down to our training for anti-sub patrols, the old job our crew were first trained for before we went overseas. This was a little different in some ways as the enemy are using the 'Schnorkel' tube apparatus now, making it harder for visual and radar sighting. So to start, Geoff, Ken and myself found ourselves on the Radar Training flight, for a 9 days course on special radar equipment. We flew 14hrs 30mins, before we were qualified and rejoined the general training, over the Bristol Channel area. Then came flying training, as a crew in the old familiar 'Wimpey'. Yelloly's crew and ours, being old stagers on Wimpeys got well ahead of all the other crews so as to get the Squadron on operations early'.

Donovan recalls this period of training: 'Many squadron members had never seen radar before so had to learn from the beginning. At least the three signallers were required to carry out radar, wireless and gunnery during the many long hours. A new jargon came to be bandied about when 'talking shop'. Phrases like 'automatic homing and controlled diversion' came into use as understanding progressively grew'.

The pilots had to learn to fly a new type of aircraft but a substantial number of the Squadron members had had some experience on Wellingtons. Indeed, a significant number of the pilots had done OTU Wellington training before they were posted to Marauders. Donovan found the Wellington a simple aircraft to fly, but a great deal of team work for the crew needed to be practised and practised again to perfect the illumination of a designated night-time target by the aircraft's powerful Leigh Light. The amount of time needed for the training programme and administration did not leave Donovan much time to 'work up' a crew of his own.

The Squadron had had twenty Marauder crews in the Mediterranean, but this increased to thirty Wellington crews. Donovan recalled 'I fell in with the custom of the other squadrons of giving each crew a number even though this seemed impersonal. I had a picture of each captain with his crew in my office and slowly learnt to recognise each name, but remembering two hundred was tough'. In addition to the 180 names allocated to crews (that is thirty crews of six members), there were always about 20 other men without crews which meant that the strength of the aircrew establishment was in fact two hundred'.

The stations at Coastal Command were organised in what was called the 'three prong system'. There was a Flying Wing, a Technical Wing and an Administrative Wing. The Technical Wing had overall responsibility for all technical trade airmen, and the Squadron simply had a handling party for seeing the aircraft to and from the daily inspections.

There were two other squadrons on the station: No 36 Squadron, which had been flying anti-submarine operations from Sardinia, and a Canadian squadron equipped with Vickers Warwicks which had been flying Leigh Light anti-submarine patrols for some months. For No 14 Squadron it was to be a new way of life. After so many years of operating from foreign lands, it was good to be based in the Homeland, but squadron members from the CO down to the humblest AC2 were faced with a testing challenge. The aircrews were well accustomed to flying over water for long hours, but they had to accustom themselves to the use of new technical equipment, as did the maintenance crews. There was more night flying and the weather was more severe.

CHAPTER EIGHT

OPERATIONS IN UK

NOVEMBER 1944 - MAY 1945

After hard training in November on anti-submarine work, the Squadron started flying in December. Squadron Leader Yelloly and Flight Lieutenant Hornby and their crews had completed an operational training course on Wellingtons and were a great help in converting other crews to the new aircraft.

Squadron group photograph with Wellington.

CONVERSION TO WELLINGTONS

The Wellington was fairly straightforward compared to the high-performance Marauder, but pilots had to get used to accurate instrument flying over long night periods. They also had to learn to descend at night, on bearings given by the radar operator, down to a height of 250ft. To avoid ditching in the sea a radio altimeter activated at 400ft with three lights, amber green and red - to indicate critical heights. On a bumpy night it was wearing and tense work going down to such a low level and then at a distance of half a mile to the target to switch on the Leigh Light. Crews had to learn low level straddle bombing techniques in daylight as well as in darkness.

Wellington Mark XIV Leigh Light.

Wellingtons were the first aircraft to be fitted with lights and were first operational in 1942. The light consisted of a 24 inch naval searchlight of 15 million candle power mounted in a retractable 'dustbin' under the rear fuselage. Movement of the light was made by the operator lying on his belly in the nose of the aircraft, under the front gun turret, by remote control handles in the vertical and horizontal planes. It had a range of 2,500 yards for a small target in average clear weather.

By the time No 14 Squadron started operating with Mk VIA Radar, the U-boats were fitted with the French designed Metox, which allowed the U-boat to detect the radar transmissions. This meant that sightings were few but that U-boats were reduced to a speed of 6 knots when submerged, which restricted their ability to attack.

The navigators had a difficult task in that the plan of Coastal Command was to smother the whole of the South Western approaches to the British Isles with radar patrols overlapping each other. They had to follow a strict drill, well illustrated by quoting from Wing Commander Donovan's former navigator, Tony de Yarburgh-Bateson, who had now returned to the Squadron as a Flight Lieutenant after a spell as an Instructor at a No 2 Operational Training Unit, where B-25 Mitchells were flown. He wrote: 'I had to do a navigation course to fit me for the high navigation standard required by Coastal Command who insisted that only the best DR methods would do for the long flights over the sea when accuracy and position fixing were vital both to avoid losing an aircraft, and to ensure reliable reports.

To this end, the Headquarters Wallahs had devised a form of drill which laid down that all navigators must follow set procedures, doing certain tasks at fixed times in the hour. For example, I remember that every 15 minutes a check on the wind direction and velocity had to be made by one or other of the recognised methods of wind finding. So demanding had become the drill that every second of every hour was occupied with work of one sort or another. To cap it all, some efficiency enthusiast at Group Headquarters demanded that all station navigation officers should submit a return from the navigators stating the time taken to perform individual items of drill. I well remember that not one of the No 14 Squadron navigators calculated the full drill specified for 60 minutes could be done in less than 75 minutes!'

The signallers had all been wireless operators/air gunners. Many had seen radar before though not as sophisticated as the Mark VIA which, in theory, was able to detect submarine Schnorkels. This meant that one could take it in turn for a radar watch while the second could man the radio, listen or send signals if any sightings came, and the third man would be in the rear turret. The Schnorkel was a pre-war Dutch device, as the historian John Terraine explains: 'This was an air-pipe which could be extended above the surface when the U-boat was at periscope depth; it meant that 'the air inside the boat could be kept fresh even though the rest of the craft was submerged; more important, a submarine could run virtually submerged on the diesel engines indefinitely, without the need to expend precious current from the batteries'. It had disadvantages: it limited the U-boat's speed to six knots; it caused much discomfort to the crew in rough weather; it could still be detected, both by eye and radar, but obviously with much more difficulty than a fully surfaced boat or even a conning tower.' (Page 454, *The Right of the Line*, Hodder &

Stoughton London, 1985).

The length of sorties was always over ten hours. There were two pilots but only one navigator and he had the toughest task of all. Keeping warm was difficult. The weather over the Atlantic was much colder and all aircrew wore woollen vests and long-johns with fur lined jackets, trousers and boots.

Aircraft icing was a serious problem for the de-icing process at this time was rudimentary, being merely a paste spread on the wings. Carburettor icing was more dangerous, and could result in a sudden loss of power. Squadrons had the occasional loss which would involve simply an emergency call and then nothing, just a failure to return.

Wing Commander Donovan had still not been able to find time to gather his own crew to develop any teamwork, so he repeated what he had done on Marauders, when he first took command, and flew with different crews for training and then on operations. He found the low level bombing exercises easy as he had experienced them before - first on Blenheims and then on Marauders - but the intense concentration needed for ten hours instrument flying was extremely exhausting. The constant bearing approach involved flying a bearing, say of 090° degrees reported by the radar operator on a contact, then if the next bearing came up at 095°, allowance had to be made for wind drift to ensure that when the target was eventually met the aircraft was flying on a constant bearing to allow a successful straight bomb run. This took a deal of practice teamwork between the radar operator and the pilot, who at the same time had to let down to 250ft and, call for the Leigh Light to be switched on at the right time. The pilot then had to adjust from instrument to visual flight.

Training went on right through January 1945 and the first operations were not flown until February. The aircraft nevertheless were loaded with depth charges during flying exercises, in case a U-boat was sighted.

OPERATIONS: UK WESTERN APPROACHES

Operations began on 2 February and the Squadron's task was to fly six aircraft every night with two aircraft on stand by reserve, and with two aircraft on training flights. Coastal Command had planned a detailed routine of training and the drills for operational flying were very precise. They introduced an engineering pattern called 'Plan Flying and Plan Maintenance'. The system worked very well, but was soulless, turning out sorties like a factory line. Each sortie lasted about ten hours and was flown on box patrols in the Channel and out into the Western Approaches. It took some weeks for the Squadron to reach its target of six operations a day, as the training of new crews took priority.

Donovan recalls: 'One day we were given a fright when one of our aircraft was overdue from a sortie over the Western Approaches. We eventually received a phone call from the crew who thought they had landed in Devon and were as surprised as we were to find they were in Northern Ireland. Their master compass had precessed so badly that they had been flying in circles; luckily when daylight came they saw land and chose the nearest airfield'.

Flt Lt Hornby's crew at Chivenor. L to R: Lionel Copp (Nav),
Geoffrey Unsworth (WOp/AG RADAR), Joe Lowder (WOp/AG RADAR),
'Chuff' Hornby AFM (Captain), K J Williams (WOp/AG RADAR), Fred Hoyle (2nd
Pilot).

Lowder recorded in his diary: 'On the 20 February, we had to get ready for our first op on the new job tomorrow. The CO is to fly with us too so we shall have to be on our toes. Take off time was brought forward to this evening at 1805 and off we went with the CO and settled down to the full night's flying off the south-east rn coast of Southern Ireland. Actually our flying time was to be $10^1/2$hrs, but bad weather cropped up back at base and was spilling over Wales, so we were diverted to Brawdy in South Wales. We had plenty of contacts on the radar screen but they were all ships. Our rest to sleep was not to be because the beds were damp. The next day we flew back to Chivenor.

'On 27 February, we carried out an anti-submarine patrol. This patrol was called a box patrol which meant the trip covered a square area of sea decreasing in size as each box was flown. There were no radar contacts and it was an uneventful trip of 10hrs 20mins. This length of time in the air certainly knocks everyone up. In fact, when we got out of the kite I had something like a sailor's roll, the ground seemed to weave up and down. Also, having to stare into the radar screen to search for possible contacts gave we three WOps bad headaches.'

The Squadron's navigators had the use of a device called Gee. From separate land based stations, radar beams spread out to sea. The aircraft set gave the position from intersecting beams. Late in the spring of 1945 it was supplemented by another system called Loran, which had a much longer range, but it added to the electronic work which crews had to learn to use. Hornby did the first trial in February which was very successful, but the aircraft were not fitted with the new equipment until months later.

'These anti-submarine patrols', recalled Bateson, 'were flown at an average of 1500ft and, if one had flown slightly off course and lost height, the greatest danger was flying into a cliff in the darkness. The trips were singularly boring and unrewarding as the Germans and their Schnorkels were extremely difficult to contact since our radar screens could not distinguish a seagull from a U-boat. Once only did Mac's crew go to action stations. (Bateson had been crewed up with Flight Lieutenant MacDonald, formerly a Marauder pilot). While the radar operator kept an eye on the enemy blips and the Captain prepared to attack, the navigator had to lower the Leigh Light, a large 15 million candle power searchlight, which then projected below the aircraft. On this occasion our disappointment can be imagined when the searchlight illuminated a fishing boat filled with a lot of very frightened Irishmen!'

'On some trips further over the Atlantic' continued Bateson, 'it was difficult to

Painting by Arthur Deramore of Leigh Light operation.

keep on track when darkness fell and the sky was overcast hiding all stars. Out of range of radar land contacts, and committed to radio silence there was no help to be had from flares as they would give away the aircraft's presence to any Schnorkelling U-boat. Under these circumstances, the instructions stated that the navigator was to report to his captain that he was no longer certain of his position. Could anything have been designed better to destroy the confidence of the wretched crew listening on the intercom? Most navigators would rather have died than confess their ignorance of the aircraft's exact position.'

He further recalled an occasion when MacDonald was patrolling an area around 14° west (of the prime meridian through Greenwich). 'Suddenly Mac asked me, over the intercom, if I was sure of our position. It was about 0300hrs and I was not certain of our position within 50 miles or so! I affected great indignation and asked him why he wanted to know. He replied that the Sunderland flying boat which was supposed to be patrolling the area to the west of us had just passed by to the east. I said, "Well they must be off track", with a supreme self-confidence which I did not feel. When we got home I was interrogated by the Duty Navigation Officer, and had a very sticky time, as he insisted on asking me how I could have been sure that I had patrolled exactly the area on which we had been briefed. I replied that under the conditions nobody could be sure to cover the exact area, but as our final course had brought us exactly over Lundy Isle, within a minute of our estimated time of arrival, I could not see that we had been very far off our correct track. I don't think he was entirely satisfied even then.'

Another trip that Bateson remembers with rueful clarity was flown over the English Channel. 'I was desperately air-sick and after five hours of vomiting could hardly think. Mac offered to return to base but I suggested that we continued flying by the flight plan prepared before take-off but using the latest wind factor. This we did and I let the drill go hang for the remaining five and a half hours. I must have looked like the wreck of the Hesperus. One of the toughest-looking WAAF cooks was so filled with compassion at my appearance that she volunteered to cook me something special instead of the usual baked beans on toast. However I was past wanting to eat and sat miserably drinking warm, sweet tea. Even the Intelligence and Navigation Officers let me off lightly for my log was a disgrace.'

The CO flew with 16 different crews on training and operations and had been able to get to know the crews as well as the captains. This gave him an insight into the navigators and wireless operators suitability for commissioning.

On one of the early operations in March, a contact was made which the radar operator claimed to be very small. There was great elation as the aircraft homed in and then when the signal came to put the light on, what was seen was a large frigate! The light was switched off, and the aircraft hurried back into the dark, lucky not to have been blown out of the sky.

On 11 March, Lowder records one flight 'On a patrol of areas of the Western Approaches and Scillies, it was at about 0830hrs that we sighted a Liberator of No 103 Squadron US Navy flying parallel with us on a patrol at 8 miles distance. About 5 miles from Bishop's Rock it turned sharply away diving. We turned too and saw a surfaced sub sitting nice and pretty. The Liberator dropped its depth charges and as we drew near the sea heaved and swallowed the submarine completely. We turned and opened up both bomb doors and took up action stations as we went into attack. As we drew nearer we saw the sub sinking stern first and the crew milling about in the water. Some were floating lifeless, some wallowed in the waves and some were on collapsible rubber rafts waving like hell, presumably to draw attention to the fact that they were helpless, and didn't want another stick of explosives'. That was the end of Unterseeboot U-681. Hornby's wireless operator reported the sinking in code, but made no radio contact with the American aircraft. Continuing the patrol the crew of the Wellington saw the convoy, which had been spared one attack. Many of the German crew were rescued and it was learned that the submarine had run aground and, being badly holed, was heading for Ireland, when found and sunk.

A month later, on 12 April, Lowder's diary states: 'My commission came through yesterday so I am now a Pilot Officer. We patrolled the usual area off Cornwall for ten hours and ten minutes. On return, whilst circling base, we found the hydraulics were U/S. This meant landing without brakes and flaps - a tricky business - especially as the runway drops off into the river. However, we made a very good landing, and by using the starboard engine we slewed ourselves round on to the grass not too far from the river's edge.'

CHANGE OF COMMAND

At the beginning of April 1945, Wing Commander Pawson was posted to the Squadron. He had just completed a Wellington OTU course but had not flown on operations. Donovan was told to give him operational experience before handing over command. On 20 April, Donovan was then posted to Headquarters No 18 Group in Scotland. He was disappointed not to finish the war with the Squadron, but he said it was probably his own fault as he had volunteered to go to the Far East with Tiger Force on B-29s, under the command of Air Marshal Lloyd who had been his AOC in the Mediterranean. Wing Commander Ted Donovan had been with No 14 since the autumn of 1942, apart from a few months in 1944, when he was instructing at an OTU in Egypt.

Leaving was made harder to bear because on the night of 18/19 April, Flight Lieutenant Hogg flew into a cliff at St Eval. Donovan flew down to see the wreckage. Hogg was a very experienced Canadian pilot and had evidently called up St Eval to say that he was in trouble and making an emergency landing. He was homed towards the airfield but crashed into the cliff about two miles short of it. One theory for the cause of the crash was that the Wellington may have had an internal petrol leak and Hogg became overcome by the fumes and lost consciousness. The last words the controller heard from him was that he could not see. The CO went back to Chivenor to be given more bad news: Lieutenant Overed was overdue. No word was heard and he was posted as missing over the Western Approaches. Donovan spent his last evening with No 14 Squadron writing twelve letters of condolence to the relatives of the killed and missing, and was denied the farewell party which would have given his fellow airmen the opportunity to express their respect and affection for the commander who had led them through so many trials and tribulations. After he had gone, the new CO, Wing Commander Pawson, received a letter from Air Vice-Marshal Maynard expressing his regret and sympathy to the Squadron for these losses.

When he arrived in Scotland to take up the post of Wing Commander Training at 18 Group, Donovan had the satisfaction of noticing in a staff paper a report on all the Squadrons in the Command, in which No 14 Squadron came top of the list for navigation.

On 20 April, Pawson was duly inducted with a litre of beer in one of the two silver tankards, which had been presented to the Squadron by the Emir Abdullah of Transjordan. These, and a dozen or so pewter pint pots, were last seen in the Officer's Mess at Chivenor.

Next day, a search was made for Overed's aircraft but nothing was found. Operations and training continued until after VE Day on 8th May 1945. The last entry in Lowder's diary was for 10th May: 'Op No 50. Good news from all European war fronts. Things look like finishing any day now. U-boats seem to be still active though. Two or three ships have been attacked in the last few days in the Irish Sea. Some U-boat commanders, although radioed, would not cease fire.

Today's trip is our last to complete a full tour of operations. It was 0510hrs when we took off for convoy escort duty off the east coast of Ireland. The weather was very bad and dense fog enveloped the convoy almost all the time we were up. Of course we could see the whole lot by radar. Conditions worsened so we were compelled to return to base for the last time. You could tell from the way we looked and talked that all six of us had the thought in our hearts, 'Thank God I've come through safely'.'

Not long after VE Day, the Squadron was closed down and the number 14 was transferred to No 143 Squadron at Banff, which was in 18 Group, so Donovan was able to ring up the CO of No 143 Squadron, sympathise with him over the loss of his old number but congratulate him on having the number 14 instead. He emphasised that No 14 Squadron was one of the very first squadrons to be awarded a standard in 1943, and had a string of battle honours

One of the Squadron's diarists wrote: 'Thus we played out the last remaining months of the War in Europe. We lost a few crews in accidents of one sort or another and assisted in the surrender of one or two U-boats after Germany threw her hand in, but it was dull stuff compared to earlier days, and one felt almost ashamed not to be doing more for the War Effort!'

EPILOGUE

Ted Donovan was mentioned in dispatches shortly after leaving Chivenor The others, who have featured in this chapter, were posted to many different duties. Lowder went to a transport squadron as an instructor. Several, including de Yarburgh-Bateson and Hornby joined No 179 Squadron equipped with Warwicks, which were a more powerful version of the Wellington, at St Eval in Cornwall. Others went to Transport Command to fly Liberators, but still others were classified as redundant aircrew.

Since 3rd September 1939, the squadron had travelled many thousands of miles from Transjordan to the Red Sea in the Sudan. Then to Egypt, Syria and Iraq, again to Egypt and the Western Desert and from there to Algeria, Tunisia, Italy, Corsica and Sardinia. Finally the squadron returned to England after twenty nine years of overseas service. It was not to stay in its homeland for long, and was soon moved to Germany, where it still serves in 1996. Maintaining its honourable record, No 14 Squadron Tornados flew with the Coalition Air Forces in the Gulf War of 1991, now recorded as the most recent battle honour on their Standard.

APPENDIX A

No 14 SQN RAF 3 FEBRUARY 1915 - 31 MARCH 1946

SQN COMMANDERS, AIRCRAFT TYPES, BASES & DETACHMENTS

WHEN	WHO	WHAT (until)	WHERE
3 Feb 15	Major G E Todd	M Farman Longhorn (Aug 15)	Formed at Shoreham UK
May 15		Caudron (Aug 15)	Hounslow
Aug-Nov 15			Gosport, en route Egypt
Nov 15		BE2C (Sep 18)	
Dec 15		Martinsyde (Jan 16)	Alexandria-Ismailia Dets Mersa Matruh Heliopolis, Dets Abu Ghandir Qantara
20 Jan 16	Major W R Freeman		To Ismailia Dets Sidi Barrani, Sollum Mersa Matruh Suez Rabieh, Mustabiq
16 Jun 16		Martinsyde G100 (17) DHIA (Mar 17)	
1 Jul 16	Major E J Bannatyne		
20 Jan 17			Kilo 143/Ujret el Zol Dets Yenbo,el Wejh
Mar/Apr 17			Dier el Ballah, Sinai, dets Suez Kilo 143,Aqaba(TJ)
6 May 17	Major A C Boddam-Whetham		

Appendix A

WHEN	WHO	WHAT (until)	WHERE
Jul 17		Vickers FB19 MkII (Aug 17)	
4 Oct 17	Major C E Medhurst		
Oct 17		RE8 (Nov 18)	
Nov 17			Julis Junction Stn, Jericho, Jerusalem
Feb 18		Nieuport (Oct 18)	
24 Oct 18			Kantara (Egypt)
6 Nov 18			To Mikra Bay (Greece)
1 Jan 19			To Tangmere(UK) as a Cadre
4 Feb 19			Disbanded
1 Feb 20			Reformed from 111 Sqn at Ramleh
Feb 20		Bristol Fighter (Feb 26)	Dets Amman, Damascus, Aleppo, Mafraq (TJ) Beersheba (Pal)
10 Apr 20	Sqn Ldr W L Welsh		
1 Dec 21	Sqn Ldr J S Bradley		
Jun 22		DH.9A (Mar 30)	
21 Sep 23	Sqn Ldr W H Dolphin		To Amman(TJ) dets Ramleh
6 Jun 24	Sqn Ldr A N Gallehawk		Det Ramleh

WHEN	WHO	WHAT (until)	WHERE
26 Jun 26	Sqn Ldr J Everidge		
2 Dec 26	Sqn Ldr A N Gallehawk		
8 Oct 27	Sqn Ldr Hopcraft		
Nov 29		Fairey IIIF (Sep 32)	
3 Dec 29	Sqn Ldr F O Soden		
Jul 32		Fairey Gordon (Apr 38)	
29 Oct 32	Sqn Ldr L H Cockey		
16 Aug 35	Sqn Ldr T C Traill		Palestine Arab Revolt
Mar 38		Vickers Wellesley (Dec 40)	
4 May 38	Sqn Ldr A D Selway		
24 Aug 39			To Ismailia dets Qasaba
19 Dec 39			To Amman det Port Sudan (May 40)
24 May 40			To Port Sudan
Jun 40			War against Italy
Jun 40		Gladiator I & II (Mar 41)	
28 Sep 40	Sqn Ldr D C Stapleton		Det from 112 Sqn Port Sudan

258

Appendix A

WHEN	WHO	WHAT (until)	WHERE
			WHERE
Oct 40		Walrus (Apr 41)	ASR duties Port Sudan
Oct/Nov 40		Blenheim IV (Aug 42)	
12 Apr 41			To Heliopolis
May 41			LG21 Western Des
7 Jul 41			Petah Tiqva (Palestine)
10 Aug 41			To Habbaniyah (Iraq)
24 Aug 41			To Gaiyara (Iraq) Iran War
8 Oct 41	Wg Cdr J N Buchanan		To Habbaniyah
26 Oct 41			Lydda (Pal)
4 Nov 41			LG15, LG75, Gambut, Bu Amud, LG16,116
1 May 42			Dets Gambut, Baheira, Elfirdan
10 May 42	Wg Cdr W S Maydwell		El Firdan det Kabrit LG176
28 Jun 42			To Qassassin, dets LG97,98,88
Aug 42		Marauder B26A (Sep 44)	
10 Aug 42			To LG224
25 Aug 42			Fayid dets Berka, Gambut

259

Sqn Commanders, Aircraft Types, Bases & Detachments

WHEN	WHO	WHAT (until)	WHERE
23 Feb 43			To Gambut dets Berka, Shallufa
1 Mar 43			To Telergma
10 Mar 43			To Blida, dets Gambut, Shallufa, Bone, Kasfareet
May 43		Mustang I (Jun 43)	I Flt Bone, Protville dets Grottaglie
25 Aug 43	Wg Cdr A H Law-Wright		
27 Oct 43			To Sidi Amor, dets Bone, Ghisonaccia Grottaglia
5 Dec 43			To Ghisonaccia
13 Jan 44			To Blida. dets Grottaglie, Ghisonaccia, Telergma
11 Apr 44			To Alghero dets Foggia
8 Jun 44	Wg Cdr E Donovan	Marauder B26B (Aug 44) Marauder B26C (Sep 44)	
Sep/Oct 44			To Grottaglie then Naples
24 Oct 44			To Chivenor (UK)
Nov 44		MK XIV Wellington (Leigh Light) (May 45)	
24 Mar 45	Wg Cdr G I Pawson		
25 May 45			Disbanded

Appendix A

WHEN	WHO	WHAT (until)	WHERE
25 May 45	Wg Cdr C N Foxley-Norris	Mosquito VI (Mar 46)	Reformed @ Banff from 143 Sqn
25 May 45			
Oct 45			Camarai/Eponoy, Sylt
31 Mar 46			Disbanded
1 Apr 46	Wg Cdr R I Jones		Reformed Sylt Germany

APPENDIX B

Translation of a diary found on BARRA MUSA KEBIR Island
19° 14' N. 38°11' E...written by a member of the crew of the Italian submarine
(Macalle) which foundered there on 14/6/40.

(With acknowledgements for the translation from the Italian to English by a member of
the Worcester Regiment then detached to Port Sudan).

We proceeded on our voyage after having cleaned the accumulators as best we could.
The sea is rough and the submarine is rolling. I am not feeling well. Tonight we arrive
at the Port of our intended ambush. Tomorrow we shall be awaiting for our prey. The
immersion apparatus is damaged and we had to recourse to an auxiliary system with
Naptha Houley rendering an unpleasant smell in the room where this auxiliary system
is situated.

13 JUNE

We submerged at daylight; submarine was low. We came up from time to time to have
our periscope above the water to explore our surroundings. Fore all the crew were ill.
We do not know the cause, some are feverish, some have pains and are vomiting,
others have diarrhoea. I have been there this morning to examine a motor. The plan is
in disorder, with a Napthanal bad smell. Last night the sea was rough and a few were
seasick. There has been vomiting. A real disaster. A few of the crew are alarmed. Aft, we
are alright. I am a bit constipated since we left and have not been to the WC once.
Now with the new system that we have adopted I dare not go to the WC. Tonight the
sea will be rough again. The submarine is 80m under the water and is rolling as though
she was on the surface. We will come to the surface in about an hour. Thermometer
points to 130F degrees. Breathing is difficult. We came to the surface at 22:15hrs and
the sea was rough. Having got the motors going we proceeded on our course. I went
to my cabin in the hope of finding sleep, but my bunk was going from one side to the
other and I was compelled to tie it. At midnight I got up feeling very bad and ten
minutes after taking over my duty I was vomiting. Afterwards I felt a bit better; I went
on deck and smoked a cigarette. Afterwards I returned to my post and felt very sleepy.
At 04:00hrs I was relieved from my watch. I was homesick and hope to return to Port
soon to get some news.

14 JUNE

Immersion at the usual hour. At 07:00hrs the submarine suffered a terrific crash to the
Fore, but I do not know the cause. At noon I was informed that the crew placed Fore
of the submarine were not feeling well, due to a gas of Methyl Chloride from the
compressor of the submarine air conditioning system. As a result of this they are all
vomiting and seem to be terribly drunk. They cannot utter a word and behave foolishly.
About five or six are effected in this way. We were under water for a longer time and

consumption has been more than usual. Tonight we shall have to ? for some time. I went to bed at 20:20hrs but was not sleepy, it is impossible for me to go to sleep. My watch begins at midnight. At 02:00hrs the motor on the right side was not working well from where I stood, I instructed one of the crew to transfer motor to Acc. At 02:15hrs I reload the motor. I was just regulating the intensity of loading when I felt a strong blow which sent all the hull of the submarine vibrating. Successively and within a short time there was a succession of blows. I was under the impression that the hull was being taken away from under my feet and I grabbed something to keep my balance. The submarine took a list. The crew, who with the exception of those on duty were asleep, got up and in their eyes there was bewilderment. To put an end to our astonishment we heard the Captain through the megaphone communicating with the Second Officer, who was inside the submarine. I remained at the Poop trying to calm the crew but they are perturbed not knowing if we are on the surface.

A few metres under water we prepare the gas-masks which are not sufficient for the members of the crew in the Poop. The partition is open and we can see as far as the manoeuvring room, where a number of people are gathered but cannot see what they are doing. The megaphone from the manoeuvring room informs us that we are at the surface and to remain calm at our posts. I reply that it is essential that mechanics be sent to close the Port holes tightly as I noticed that water was passing through and falling on the Thermic Motors in such important quantities which may pass in the auxiliary room and thence to the battery room. I saw a stoker closing some valves. An SC Eletto coming towards the Poop gives me some idea of the situation. Some of the crew are already on the deck and others are proceeding there. He also tells me that one of the batteries is emitting smoke and vapour with slight smells of chloride. On being informed of this I withdrew to go into the situation. I order the crew to stand by at their posts and they will be told what to do later on using the basin of the conning tower; the Chief Engineer is directing operations. The crew continues to get out and I have sent up two SC electricians from the manoeuvring room. I returned to the Poop and go to the manoeuvring chamber. The same instructions were to the crew aft of the submarine. At this moment I found that there was nobody to go up so I went up myself with the number of the crew in charge of the Poop complement. On deck I see the Macalle with a heavy list on her Port and I am under the impression that she will not be able to go to sea again. From her launching to her end.

15 JUNE

There was a roll call on deck, all were present including those who had suffered from the effects of the chloride. It was not easy to bring these on deck. Action was taken for the salvage of foodstuffs etc. The deck is full on account of low tide, and it was decided to stop bringing up further supplies until what was on deck was transferred ashore. I jump in the sea and swim ashore. The distance is not great and with four strokes I reach the beach. The bottom is rocky. I reach shore after having fallen many times and hurting my leg in the same place where I was hit when the submarine hit a submerged rock. It is dawn and the situation is clear before us. The submarine has such a list that it was impossible to open the conning tower without flooding. Efforts are being made to recover further foodstuffs but the smell of chloride is increasing and gas-masks were put into use. We could not have acted otherwise. We take stock of liqueurs and mineral waters, two cases of hard biscuits, lard, 3 tins of caviar, 3 tins of marmalade. Ashore we are 45 persons all in good health. All what we have is just sufficient for a complete meal per man. I went around the island to see where we are.

The circumference of the reef is about 500m. Part of the island is sandy and part is covered with thorny bushes. We found a sign reading as follows:-

'INTREP .....', We have stones uniformly laid out and we understand that in 1936 the island was surveyed. It is completely deserted. I return on board in the hope of being useful, nothing however can be done. I return ashore and go for a swim. I am sleepy but do not lie down. I return on board to have another try. I fail. The last man who returned from the submarine informed us that the light had gone off as the batteries have gone dry through one of the carburettors. A last expedition is made to the submarine at 17:00hrs to bring back foodstuffs. The plan was to flood the Aft chambers then allowing us to proceed to the Fore part of the submarine and recover the greater part of the foodstuffs which were lying there. On opening this door only some water got to the chambers and only after forming bubbles which is proof that the chambers were already nearly full of water.

Some of the crew were withdrawn from the submarine in boats others threw themselves in the water. The submarine goes up slowly, Fore first, goes backwards, takes a vertical position, and founders.

My old submarine the 'Macalle' in which I spent 3 1/2 years, is no more, but before she foundered she left us on a lonely reef but safe. A few seconds after disappearance a patch of oil appeared on the sea and then some electrical material were floating. Far away something which I could make out was floating. The current very soon swept all before it. It is 17:00hrs, the submarine has ceased to exist; an inglorious end, but before she went down she helped all the members of the crew to be safe. On the shore we are all working feverishly and we are now facing the only hope left to us namely rescue. From the charts we are 30 miles away from Suakin a port in the Anglo-Egyptian Sudan.

The commander has decided to try and reach the Eritrea coast which is 15 miles further on. The departure which was fixed for the next day was anticipated and it was decided to leave that afternoon. We are doing all we can to make ourselves useful. The expedition is supplied with foodstuffs, compass, sail, etc. At 21:35hrs the expedition is in the charge of a sub-lieut which consists of three men in all: a steersman, a sailor, and the Lieut. Our hopes lie with them.

After bidding them goodbye and good luck we returned to our improvised huts, bushes covered with pieces of wood. After such a hard day we were given no food, only a drop of water. This is all for today. I go to sleep.

16 JUNE

I have slept profoundly. When I got up I tried to distil water but I was not successful. I tried by means of two bottles and a filter. I was not able to obtain a single drop of water. I went round the island in search of food, hunger was upon me. I found some crabs which I ate later. With a bed sheet, I caught some small fish which I ate. This food, crab and fish which are salty, increased my thirst. The breakfast served consisted of one crab per person. That was all and the day was Sunday. The most impressive picture are those members of the crew who are ill. Three of the unfortunates go from hut to hut quoting numbers and making ridiculous speeches. It seems to me that we are living in a mad house. One of these is in a pitiful condition. On Saturday, this man who is not very strong, was running about the island until final exhaustion. He speaks with great difficulty. His eyes are wide open and he stares vacantly. His lips are cut through thirst and he can hardly stand up. These three wretched men are the desperation of others. Nobody can help them. They are laughed at by all. It is a heartrending sight. At 10:00hrs we had our first breakfast; one hard biscuit, some lard (not more than 20 grams), a drop of water (mineral) mixed with a drop of cognac. Whilst eating, my mouth was paining me. After this breakfast, I was successful in distilling water. I distilled a small quantity and will try again tomorrow. I went to bed at 22:30hrs. I was very restless in my sleep.

17 JUNE

I woke up. The first complaint came from one of the three who were sick. He was insisting on seeing the Captain saying that he was going to die that day or the next. He wishes to be buried according to the Christian rites. All this opens my days work. An electrician who drank salt water yesterday came to me stating that he felt very ill.

He is better this morning. During the day, I suffered terribly from thirst, to such an extent, that I felt my tongue as a scale of fish. I could not move my tongue. I was looking for the aeroplane which according to my calculations, should have been looking for us by now. Vain hope. I was in the sea for a considerable time because by doing so, I did not feel so thirsty. On the other hand, a long stay in the sea weakens one so terribly.

When I came out of the water yesterday evening, I was so weak that I could not walk. I dragged on with great difficulty, I was greatly impressed with my weakness. My lunch consisted of a crab. A live crab which I wholly ate with the exception of the legs. I was sorry to kill it, but I could not do otherwise. In the evening I had a hard biscuit and some marmalade, a drop of water, not mineral, but water distilled by me. My experiments for distilling water were successful. It is possible that during a whole day and night I can make distilled water in larger quantities than what we are at present consuming. A false alarm. One of us said that he had seen a funnel sending out coloured lights. He transmitted his imagination to us and we all believed. We light a fire on the highest point of the island, but so far, no one has come. Tomorrow, I am on duty distilling water.

18 JUNE

One of the three who are ill is worse. The other two are very much better. I drank two eggs (seagull and some ?), after which I was feeling better. At noon I had an egg punch, with eggs, sugar, coffee, wine and ?. This was very good and nourishing.

Plans for the Afternoon

Bathing - at 13:00hrs disillusionment, I was expecting to find a hard biscuit, but there was nothing. I was greatly disappointed. The quantity of water has increased, but its quality has diminished. Distilled water now has a strong taste of gum. We mixed the distilled water with Orange squash, but the taste of gum was still there. At 15:30hrs, we heard the roar of guns from the North. It is said that this a good augury. The gunfire seemed to come from shore batteries and not from Naval units.

19 JUNE

We are waiting and waiting. We are full of expectation, but nothing has happened. For breakfast I had roast Seagulls. I could not eat them owing to stomach troubles. At 08:00hrs I went for a bathe and having swallowed some salt water, I vomited. I vomited so much that I felt weak, I fell and fainted. They had to carry me and brought me to life again by pouring drops of fresh water into my mouth and slapping my face. My meal was an egg punch as yesterday, also a crab which made me feel very bad in the stomach. In the afternoon I went for another swim, afterwards, I was vomiting but not as much as in the morning. At 14:30hrs SC died. He is better where he is for he suffers no more.

Life out here is unbearable.

Swimming lessons........

APPENDIX C

AIRCRAFT OPERATED

BY 14 SQN 1920 - 1945

	Bristol Fighter	DH. 9A	Fairey Gordon	Wellesley	Blenheim IV	Marauder B26A, C, & G	MK XIV Wellington Leigh Light
Engine (s)	280 HP RR Falcon	400 HP Liberty	525 HP AS Panther IIA	925 HP Pegasus XX	2 x 920 HP Bristol Mercury XV	2 x 2000 HP Double Wasp PW	2 x 1735 HP Hercules XV11
All Up Weight	2590 lbs	4645 lbs	5906 lbs	11,100 lbs	13,500 lbs	37,000 lbs	26,325 lbs
Ceiling	20,000 ft	16,500 ft	22,000 ft	33,000 ft	22,000 ft	28,000 ft	24,000 ft
Max Speed	125 mph @ Sea Level	114 mph @ 10,000 ft	145 mph @ 3,000 ft	228 mph @ 19,000 ft	266 mph @ 11,000 ft	305 kts @ 15,000 ft	250 mph @ 600 ft
Range		500 nm	600 nm	1500 nm Nrml Tnks Note: This ac held world long distance non stop record at 7,162 miles at just under 48 hours.	1460 (UK) nm 1200 (ME) nm	1550 - 1800 nm depending on load	1325 nm
Bomb Load	2 x 112 lbs Bmbs Wg	450 lbs	460 lbs	2000 lbs	1040 lbs	4000 lbs	4950 lbs
Armaments	1 Vickers (Fwd) 1 Lewis (Aft)	1 Vickers (Fwd) 1 Lewis (Aft)	1 Vickers (Fwd) 1 Lewis (Aft)	1 Vickers (Fwd) 1 K (Aft)	2 x Browning Fwd 2 x Trrt	1 x .3 Nose 2 x .5 Dorsal 2 x .5 Tail	2 x Vickers Frnt Trrt 2 x Browning Tail Trrt
Cruise Speed	108 mph @ 13,000 ft	90 mph @ 5,000 ft	110 mph	188 mph	210 mph	280 kts	180 mph

267

APPENDIX D

This appendix records extracts from a number of publications and responses from ex-members of the Squadron to requests for articles and reminiscences about their times with the Squadron. Some extracts from the responders already appear in the main body of the History, but these that follow are selected mainly to illustrate conditions or to convey the flavour and atmosphere under which the Squadron operated. The extracts, except for minor factual corrections, are as written.

Flt Lt COLIN FALCONER (1922-28)

From Cranwell I was posted to No 14 Squadron in Palestine. I was out there with them from 1922 until 1928. First we were at Ramleh, and then we transferred in 1926 to Amman in Transjordan. It was a very interesting place to be. I tried to fly around the Holy Land with a Bible but got completely lost!

In Ramleh we were using First World War aircraft, Bristol Fighters. At Amman we moved on to DH.9As. That was a delightful aeroplane, a real old gentlemens aircraft.

It was not an eventful life, for the most part. The only thing that happened of real interest, as far as I was concerned, was that I got wounded in 1924. Ibn Saud and the Wahabis had decided that they didn't like King Abdullah any longer. Ibn Saud sent a raiding party on camels up to Amman, and they were scattered by armoured cars. But there was a shortage of aircraft, and they called on us at Ramleh for a flight to help them out. So we spent the whole afternoon chasing the Wahabis away from Amman. And I got hit! I remember seeing two men up on a camel, and one hanging on by the tail. And one of them was a jolly good shot, because he had a crack at me, and the bullet broke one of the hinges on the elevator, went straight on through my arm, through the cockpit, and out through the engine cowling. My air-gunner produced a very oily handkerchief, which I think he'd been cleaning plugs with, and asked whether he could tie my wound up with that. I said "no". We got back safely without crashing, but I was bleeding hard.

In the early days at Ramleh we used to send a flight around various villages and black-tented camps, where the Arabs had their sort of parties. But it was purely a show-piece. So apart from those very few sorties over the villages the RAF didn't do a great deal. We had to go around to inspect landing-grounds, and check up that the petrol hadn't been stolen by the Arabs; and there was a certain amount of co-operation with the Palestine Gendarmerie.

There was some very good flying. Messages were picked up in a most interesting way. The Arab soldiers would stand with their backs to us, holding the message up on their lances while we flew over and plucked them off with the pick-up hook - not always an easy trick.

The Palestine Gendarmerie was spread all over Palestine, a company or so in each place near a landing-ground, and we used to go round to visit them and drop their letters and anything that they wanted. Once I had a fortnight's tour south of Palestine, looking for landing-grounds. That was all on camels, escorted by a nice lot of Palestine

Gendarmerie.

We thoroughly enjoyed the life; it was a very nice climate there. We had an Officers' Club in Sarafand. Once a week there was a dance. The families were living in quarters which had been condemned by the Army in 1914. I met my wife when she was four, when her father was posted to Palestine HQ. I knew him quite well. I didn't meet her again until she was an Air Force widow already with a little boy, and within six weeks we were married. My future wife's family had been the first children to arrive, but once they were out there, quite a lot of other families came out as well.

The countryside in Palestine was very beautiful. All around Sarafand there were lovely orange groves and almond groves. It was very hot in the summer. It was very beautiful looking down on this country whilst flying, but you tended to see the scenery once and then you took it for granted.

After Ramleh I was posted to Amman. I was out there for a long time because I kept on volunteering. I had a horse there, though in Amman there was no hunting, just exercising.

We did the first single-engine night flight from Amman to Baghdad. The leader of our three was Flt Lt Wigglesworth, who later went very high in the Air Force.

Once in Amman we were sent to rescue a Spanish fellow who was trying to fly around the world. He was following the track from Baghdad to Ziza, and he ran out of petrol. Instead of sitting by the aeroplane, he went walking. And of course we had to search for a couple of days to find him. He was alive and very angry. He didn't like being found.

Another task the Squadron had there was to fly Peake Pasha, the GOC of the Trans-Jordan Army. He was with Lawrence in the Arab uprising, and we used to take him down to places like Aqaba. In fact I took him to one of the railway stations which he'd blown up. He went straight to one place and cleared away some sand, and there was a box of ammunition, which must have been there for ten years. It looked brand new.

SQN LDR GIBBS (1925)

My next job was in No 14 Squadron in Palestine and Trans-Jordan - a far better climate and an easier life. Palestine even then was a land of quick contrasts. Could anything have been much more different than the old Arab city and port of Jaffa - cheek by jowl with the new Jewish town of Tel Aviv? In the former the Muslim past with its mosques, its culture, its treasures, the picturesque East and the rags - in Tel Aviv a suburban type of modern town, spacious and comparatively clean, but lacking character and having many of the tawdry and less desirable features of the West.

Contrasts persisted inland, where in the fertile coastal strip were found model Jewish farming settlements, such as Balfouria, where a fine class of progressive settlers were improving their land and their homes out of all recognition - while nearby were the old Arab villages with a biblical flavour where nothing had changed for centuries. Further inland in Jerusalem one met the orthodox Jew with long ringlets and his quaint black hat, and then as one approached Trans-Jordan typical desert country began. Personally I love a nice desert. Pure sweet air, even if it is very hot in the day, very few people - and they with good manners even if they don't want your company.

Little water, some game and lots of space and it's all yours to use wisely. There is nothing 'enclosed' but the little camps of travellers - and they are usually hospitable with the camaraderie of the of the desert.

We had some very fine swimming in the Mediterranean at Jaffa, and some very amusing swimming in the waters of the Dead Sea. It is, of course, impossible to sink in those waters, but the effort of keeping right end up is almost as great as that of ordinary swimming. Moreover, any sensitive skin area such as a shaved face is severely punished by the salt and other chemicals in the water. We used to take some cans of fresh water from the River Jordan to wash with after our Dead Sea swim. In my day I regret to say that religion there was somewhat exploited commercially. I remember a sign in the Jordan Valley which said 'To Isaiah's Pool, Cafe and Bar'!

R HALEY. (Cook with No 14 Sqn in ME, N Africa, and Corsica 1940-43), PORT SUDAN

I joined the Squadron (14) at Port Sudan, after a ship and train journey up the Nile. My impression of the camp was that it was well laid out and orderly, it would have to be, as it was a peace time station. Actually after a couple of weeks when we were used to the Sudanese doing most of the cleaning and keeping the water jars filled, also our laundry taken and returned for a slight remuneration, the trousers, jack tailored to the extent they only slightly resembled the originals, we started to feel that if we had to spend the war anywhere, it would be quite acceptable there. After all we had the Pelican Club and swimming pool, plus a few bars in the towns, where I was first introduced to a John Collins, a better drink for a hot climate would be hard to find.

The following comes to my mind:

The great interest of the exploits of fixing 2 x 250lb bombs together, in the hope that they would knock a road, on the side of a hill, into the valley below.(It didn't work).

The Savoy 79 (SM 79) on its Postal run, how it tossed out the odd personnel bomb, as it went over every week. It did on one occasion do some damage to the Fuzzy Wuzzies. I can remember a couple of Hurricanes arriving by surprise, but the Savoys weren't seen while they were there.

After a few weeks dysentery hit the camp and I was one of the unfortunate victims, so spent a few days in the native Maternity Ward, with just a screen partitioning the ward, so if anyone tells you the natives just have their babies and go on their way, don't believe them, as I can still hear their screams now.

After a few days at the Hospital, a serum arrived from England, and the Sister came round with a darned great syringe, the biggest I had ever seen, and pushed the lot into my thigh, and then did an encore on the other leg. Then in minutes I had a horrible oily taste in my mouth, it did the trick, and two days later I was having my first chicken soup, then I was soon up and walking about.

Back to Butlins, the MO decided no cooking for me for six months, I wasn't doing a lot before. The powers to be decided I should become an MP complete with red arm band and whistle. Two things are vivid in my mind, whilst I was thus employed. Firstly, on one night duty as the feast ending Rhamadan, how the screaming and drums under full moon, literally made my hair stand on end. Secondly, another night the Duty Officer and a couple of Sergeants, brought a Flight Sergeant aircrew over and told us to lock him up for the night. All hell let loose in the cell and there was our prisoner, running his head against the wall. We went in and between us managed to get hold of him, as he seemed to have the strength of nine men. After a time he gave in and, while I sat on him, my colleague got assistance, then the MO gave him an injection, after which he was moved away.

The billet we were in was the usual type, beds down each side, opposite me was another Cook. Every night he read his Bible for an hour or two, Sundays was spent at Churches. He was picked for the advanced party to Cairo, where the next time I saw him, he had discovered the delights of Shara El Barker and was never the same again.

An experiment by one of the airmen in the hut resulted in a spectacular show, between the walls of the hut and the roof was a gap, along the top of the wall a rat used to make its track. Two metal plates connected to the electricity supply and we were set for a rat electrocution. It worked in the middle of the night, there was a vivid flash and a very singed rat landed on some unlucky one's mosquito net.

BURGH EL ARAB

We paused in Heliopolis just long enough to pick up transport, then on to Burgh El Arab, where we first got our taste of things to come and I don't have to describe to anyone who was on the Western Desert its moods and changes.

When we first arrived, we received fresh supplies from the Nile area, hard biscuits and axle-grease was an immediate substitute for butter and bread. Although the tins it came in were labelled 'Butter for hot climates', the airmen seemed to prefer their biscuits dry, so we used it for other things especially cakes and pastry, in fact I learned to make Puff Pastry with it from 'Fritz' Mathanson (a German Palestinian) and he maintained it was the best Puff Pastry he had ever made.

We received bags of potatoes, that were in fact good, but what they had been grown in I hate to think. Tomatoes, onions and particularly bananas were plentiful. Meat was mostly sheep, I nearly said lamb, the types with great lumps of fat for a tail and see-through carcass. One day we received a large load of cat fish, black ugly things with whiskers. The word must have got around, because no one turned up for dinner. Actually it was obvious that what we were getting certainly wasn't the cream of Egypt's produce.

It would be about this time that dehydrated foods started to come in. The well-known ones came first, instant mash, peas, and of course egg. You may not know there were many different kinds of dried egg, and one or two of them could be made quite palatable. The more unusual dehydrated vegetables, including cabbage, beetroot, mixed veg, onions, carrots, beans and parsnips. Some were more successful than others, onions were particularly good and could even be fried if treated properly.

It was here that someone came up with the idea of using oil and water for heat. The method was so simple, a piece of iron underneath the tea boiler we brewed the tea in, a piece of rag with paraffin, lit on the top of the iron and then adjust the drops of oil and water. The heat generated was terrific, it could buckle boilers and bend iron plate

271

an inch thick. When we extended our cooking to an open trench, we were always brewing up tea this way and the aircrews reckoned they could see our air strip twenty miles away and didn't need a wind sock. It's a good job the Luftwaffe weren't around.

My outstanding memory of Burgh El Arab was our last few weeks, when virtually more of our aircraft sent out failed to return than returned.

Pat and I had arrived at a landing ground one afternoon there was plenty of bell tents spread over holes, perhaps 2 to 3 deep. We went to throw our kit in and found someone had used it as a toilet, so we had to move to another place. Next morning, there was a bigger hole in the first tent - from a bomb during the night. We were at a couple of places, where we got it a bit rough at night. One of the cooks, he was perhaps three or four years older than I - Ron Redwood by name. In about two weeks his black wavy hair had turned white.

I travelled up to forward LG one day in the gun turret of a Bleinheim, two other aircraft formed up on either side as we circled to go West. In our aircraft we had bottles of gas for welding and a couple of tents. We were the first to land. On getting out, the second aircraft was on the runway and the third was burning just at the end of the runway and a Bf110 was going away in the distance. I believe this was one of the first attacks by a 110 in the Desert.

I really think I should have been given the Purple Heart for this episode: I got into bed with a scorpion. He got me twice before getting squashed, a sandstorm was in full blow, but I tottered over to the medical corporal, who was full of sympathy. His exact words to me were, "Take these two Aspros and if you're still alive in the morning, come back."

The same medic: When I was putting something through a mincer (and certainly I couldn't claim distraction from the fairer sex) I took the top of my finger almost off, it was just hanging. Again I looked the medic up, but lo and behold he had no thread to stitch it back on again, so he just tied it up tightly and said, "we will hope for the best."

SGT E MEADER (W/Op/Elec Mech 1942)

A Reminiscence - Night out in Ismalia
This was No 14 Squadron's last retreat from the Western Desert and we were pulled back to just outside Cairo. We were to lose our Blenheims and be re-equipped with an American Aircraft, as yet non-specified. Therefore - as a Squadron - we were in a state of limbo. This being so, certain tradesmen were to be seconded to other units to be re-called when new aircraft arrived and the Squadron was operational again.

Being a WOP/Mech myself, Sgt Horace and Jock were sent to the main Middle East Transmitting Station at Ismalia. Slinging our kit in the back of a truck we started our journey and eventually reached our destination late afternoon. This station was well guarded by manned outer and inner stockades - the first by Egyptian civilians and the second and most important by soldiers of the Indian Army.

Sgt Horace and ourselves duly reported to the Senior Warrant Officer and this was our first contact with the 'free English' as base types were referred to by the Squadrons and in their quiet havens I do not think they realised there was a war going on. So just imagine their reaction when three khaki-clad types presented themselves - they were not at all keen at having us in their midst!

There was about eight staff, all of NCO ranks. They all messed together with servants waiting on table. The mess bill was about 50 'akkers' a week and myself, a Corporal, and Jock, an AC/2 were allowed the same facilities at the same price.

Personnel here were all regulars and very well looked after; most had their own boats on Lake Timsah, their sleeping quarters were good but we were relegated to the verandah.

A small road separated our quarters from the transmitters and to negotiate this obstacle before being on watch it was 'compulsory' to wear a 'pith helmet' - ye gods, we nearly died laughing - shades of Kipling!

For all this bull-shit the station was well run; the transmitters which carried very important traffic were kept spot on and once a week we had to go over to auxiliary power by means of a petrol driven generator; working was not disturbed - everything ran superbly. I found it an interesting break from normal Squadron work, but it was monotonous - a really cushy number for some.

Major E LEWIS (SAAF 1941-1943)

I joined No 14 Squadron at Port Sudan on 10 March 1941 after travelling from Habbeniya (after we did our conversion to twins in Oxfords) by service bus to Haifa, then train to Ismailia (where we did our OTU on short nose Blenheims). Then by rail to Aswan, river steamer to Wadi Halfa and train again to Port Sudan. Stan Forrester and I were the only two SAAF pilots to join at this time but another S African, Sgt Jeudwine, a RAF pilot joined at the same time.

It was quite an experience joining what was virtually a peace time squadron. I recall the Squadron silver was laid on the table at meals. This wasn't such a surprise as we had come from Habbeniya where the officers dressed for dinner in dress uniforms and the hunt went out on Sundays in pink coats chasing jackals!! I only realised when the old faces went and new ones came in, what an honour it had been.

Port Sudan. I remember heat, sharks in the harbour. I had my first go of 'gyppo' guts there - sleeping naked on 'anganiya' (a string bed with an overhead fan on). We had a dysentery scare on while we were there, with some fatalities. Buck Buchanan's epitaph for them was 'He fought on every front, surviving every blitz but wretched man, in Port Sudan, passed out with the shitz.'

George Hill was my flight commander and I did my first operational raid on Keren.

There was great excitement when the Italian destroyers left Massawa and made a break for it. Some Fleet Air arm types with Swordfish arrived to help. It was they who stopped the destroyer on which I managed to get a hit. Stan Forrester caught the other two beached on the Saudi Coast and damaged both.

Rejoined Squadron at Heliopolis.

Then to western Desert for various ops.

I forgot to mention Crete. We took a beating over there so lost a good number of old faces including my opo Stan Forrester. I was lucky in that after being briefed for a Crete raid I threw stones for our flight dog to chase and put my back out. I could hardly walk - let alone fly. No one came back from that raid, I think! I was damn lucky. I had to go to hospital in Alex for treatment. I naturally got dressed up in uniform but had a bad time at the hospital as it was full of wounded from Crete who have a poor view of the Air Force through lack of air cover. I tried to explain but it did no good. I was pleased to get back to the Squadron.

Then to Peta Tiqva in Palestine to reform - we couldn't believe our eyes when we saw all the greenery in Palestine. Our 'drome was cut out of a wheat field but had two HT lines at our end of a runway. They had been diverted to make one approach slanted, tho' not enough, as Cookie Leon collected them one day, and had the plastic blister next to his head cut off. He was lucky.

Another new pilot from UK didn't realise that in the Desert we only had 100 octane fuel in our outer tanks which we used for take off. He took off on inners and had a rather hair raising take off, actually cutting two swathes of corn with his props!

The Cyprus trip was the only time I had had engine trouble during my whole air force career - damn lucky.

From Peta Tiqva to Habbeniya again - but what a difference this time. They had withstood the Iraqi Rebellion and still showed the wounds. Saw my first Bf110 in the hangar there. It had been left by the Jerries but had been repaired and flown by Deryck (CO).

Then to Gaiyara - S of Mosul - to drop leaflets on Persia who were playing up apparently. The second one over Kasvin, gave me a fright when an intact bundle of leaflets came out of the CO's plane and hit my port leading edge of wing, bending the aileron control rod. Had a hell of a time keeping straight and level.

We were at Gaiyara some time - it was really hot there. A runway of rotted oil and sand. We couldn't fly after + 0930hrs as the mechanics could hardly touch the planes. We were guarded by an Indian mob with only one white officer - a major who we often invited to our mess (they had built us a lovely new mess that time). When he heard I was South African, he asked me whether I'd like some curry (which I love). I accepted gladly and had dinner one night. The curry was lovely and hot as I like it. No tools to eat with - just fingers. The major had briefed me to show appreciation by burping which I did, much to the delight of the Indian officers, none of whom spoke English. It was a lovely night.

We were invited to dinner at the local sheikh's place. Lovely setting on a roof top in moonlight. Usual food mutton on a mound of rice. Very interesting night. We used to fly just after dawn when possible to escape the heat and took much pleasure in beating up the locals' houses, most of whom had been on the rebel side during the rising.

It was a boring time and when we heard we were returned to the Western Desert there was a hell of a party - we nearly burnt our brand new mess down. At this stage, Deryck Stapleton handed over, and Buck Buchanan became our CO.

Then back to Habbeniya where we waited while the ground crews went by road to our new 'drome. There follows a long blank in my log book caused by our flight dog which had saved my bacon during Crete. A signal came back that it had contracted rabies and had been destroyed.

The local quacks then wanted to know which of the aircrew had been in contact with the dog. There were no volunteers and so to show the flag I said I had, together with my crew. God what a bad move it was. I expected one injection perhaps, but we ended up by having an injection a day for fourteen days in our stomachs. Each injection left a lump the size of a cricket ball which had to be rubbed down and hurt like hell - after the first the stomach was so bruised that you couldn't tell where the injection had been, so they made a chart dividing our guts into seven, and then ticking them off so they wouldn't give two in the same place. It was hell, especially as we weren't allowed to drink!! When it was over we asked the doc if we could drink and he said "Yes, I'll join you!" We got full on Bristol cream sherry at lunch time and woke up for dinner hanging over terribly. To this day I can't look sherry in the face!!

We had to take this land route back to Egypt. Eventually caught a train to the Western Desert. I laughed to note the Gyppo crew gave way to Kiwis when it got a bit close to the front! I think it was at Daba that we got off and I phoned the Squadron for transport. The CO answered and when I said Lieut Lewis, he said, "You mean Capt Lewis" - the first intimation I had of promotion. Naturally we celebrated when I got to the Squadron. I had no spare pips to put up but worse was to come. A few days later I was bumped up to Major and naturally had no crown available to put up. My Flight Sgt - Harry Hawkins, however, came to light with a couple of his crowns which were the first insignia I had. It turned out to be a bit embarrassing. As I'd no chance to put up my third pip, with my crown up, there was only one set of vacant holes showing on my shoulder tabs so. Instead of promotion, it looked as tho' I'd been reduced from a Lt Colonel!!!

I don't want to shoot a line but, as I was commissioned on 30 September 1940, this meant I'd gone from pupil pilot to major in 14 months. Again not wanting to shoot a line, I had another unique experience in that after leaving No 14 Squadron I was only in operational squadrons till the end of the war - No 25 Squadron SAAF as OC Coastal Waters (Venturas and Ansons) No 262 Squadron RAF (Catalinas) Coastal and finally 15 Squadron SAAF Rocket Beau fighters (10 RPs) in Balkan Air Force. A further coincidence was that my first CO, Deryck Stapleton, was also my last as he commanded the Wing to which No 16 Squadron belonged at the end of the war. He also gave me the only 'exceptional' assessment I ever received!!

I had settled down with a grand crew. Sgt Johnston (NAV) P/O Cooke (WOP/AG). Cookie was a real character and an old timer from the Squadrons pre-war Wellesley days who had shot down a couple of CR32s or 42s from the back of a Wellesley!! He was a damn good WOP too. One horrible sight I witnessed was two flights of 3 ac taking off from opposite ends of the same runway at the same time - none of them hit each other but two pulled up too steeply, stalled, crashed and blew up. The Free French Squadron. it was a shocking sight, especially as we were waiting behind the one 3 to take off after them.

8.1.42. Cookie's 100th raid!! I let him fly us back from Halfaya Pass - I think he enjoyed that. We told him to go on one more raid so that he could say he had done more than 100 trips, but he wouldn't tempt fate, although we were on a daily milk run to Halfaya.

8.2.42. The Derna LG raid was to catch fighters refuelling. We were to have a top cover of 12 Hurricanes, another 12 as medium cover and 6 Kittyhawks of Killer Caldwell's crowd (Aussie Squadron) as close cover. It was a mess, as when the medium cover took off from their 'drome they were jumped by Bf109's. Our top cover came down to help them, but when the shemozzle was over, they couldn't find us, so we went over the target with just our 6 Kittys close cover and got jumped on the way out. Apparently, they got 3 Bf109's but lost 3 Kitty. I heard that Killer Caldwell was furious about the whole thing.

A nasty experience - one of our a/c was accidentally shot down by a SAAF Squadron and the CO (who happened to have been one of my instructors!!) brought the 2 pilots involved to apologise. It was obvious which one had done the shooting. Being the only S African I had to try and make things as comfortable as possible, which as I said was not a pleasant experience.

When I saw my first Marauder I was scared as I thought I'd never be able to fly (to me) such a huge aircraft. However I was lucky with my instructor, Captain Marrs, a civilian pilot who'd ferried a Marauder out. He made me feel confident and after about 11/2 hours duo I went solo.

I retained my Blenheim navigator Ridley (now a P/O) but Payne my WOP/Gunner went home. I found the Marauder a lovely ac to fly in spite of sometimes being called the 'flying prostitute' as she had no visible means of support! (short wings).

About this time I managed to get Bruce Young posted to the Squadron and into my flight. We had trained together and were great friends.

I had a lovely Marauder FK143 - the best ac in the Squadron I maintained. On inspections I used to make the aircrew help the 'erks' by changing engines, cowlings, etc. 'They' didn't like it but I think it encouraged the erks to do their best as they saw we were interested in the servicing of our plane.

On the way back from Malta saw an incredible squall stretching from horizon to horizon across our course with so many water spouts that it looked like a collade of pillars. We had to fly along it for some time before we could find a gap to go through. Unfortunately, we didn't have a camera in this aircraft, otherwise it would have been a wonderful illustration for a 'Met' text book.

Bruce Young got shot down over the Aegean but was taken POW. We often flew together and on losing him I paired up with Wally Clarke-Hall and we flew together for a long time.

21.2.43. This was the first raid I had had in which I lost 2 a/c in this case. Everything seemed to go right - navigation spot on. Going over the hills into the harbour I recall doing a turn which foxed Wally Clarke-Hall a bit and he had to break formation as he was unsighted. I also recalled seeing a Jerry soldier come out of a hut, on our way into the harbour, stretching his arms over his head, and his reaction when he looked up and saw 3 Marauders bearing down on him was ludicrous. Having done all our training on a 10 knot deflection I suddenly realised my target was barely moving and had to adjust my approach accordingly. The 3 torpedo bombers got through the harbour OK but 2 of the 3 following bombers were shot down. Just as we were bolting through the Kythra Channel for home, I heard some garbled German over the radio in which "torpedo bommenwerfer" was mentioned!! I often wondered how this happened, but it made us head as fast as possible out to sea until we were out of fighter range from Crete. On my approach to Gambut that night, I saw a night fighter Beau pass between me and this flarepath. It gave me a turn as I presumed we had been expected!

(Author's note: Lewis was awarded the DSO for this raid. See Chapter 6).

SQUADRON LEADER J. BUCKLAND, RAAF (1942-43)

The following is an extract from his book Adriatic Adventure published by Robertson and Mullens of Melbourne. It describes an incident that happened to Einsaar's crew, when they were POWs at the time of the Italian Armistice.

'Two days after the news of the armistice was made public an astounding request was made us. Together with Tom, Len and I were requested to appear at the Commandant's Office. Rather puzzled, we nevertheless appeared in his doorway on time and were told to sit down in front of his desk while he proceeded to question us:

"Can any of you fly a plane?" Len said - "Yes, of course."

"Well then, I am offering you your safety in return for a slight favour. Several Fascist planes have landed in a nearby field and the crews have deserted. I have here an official of the Italian Air Force who wishes to fly with secret documents to the British lines. You will be taken off under escort tonight to test the plane, and tomorrow morning you will leave." He looked at each one of us. "I wish you good luck!"

I was so astounded at our good fortune that I have no recollection of leaving his office or of walking out to the truck.

What would the Squadron think of us returning complete with aircraft?

We took off under escort in the truck, together with an important looking Italian gentleman in dark civilian clothes, and carrying a black attaché case. We tested the plane, a Savoia, similar to an Oxford, and found it in working order so that we could have flown away then, but as the Commandant had treated us fairly, we decided to 'play ball' with him. We returned quietly to camp and all spent an excitedly sleepless night planning the things we would do after hitting British lines.

How many times in the succeeding days were we to chew on our stupidity in not leaving in the plane that first afternoon. For, next morning, we were greeted with the sad news that Fascists, during the night, had killed our would-be passenger and sabotaged the plane. So much for our glorious chance.'

BIBLIOGRAPHY

CHAPTER 1

1.   F M Cutlack, foreword to Aces and Kings, an account of that campaign written by L W Sutherland MC DCM, an Australian observer in No 1 Squadron, Australian Flying Corps. First published 1929, reprinted Greenhill Books, London, 1985.

2.   Public Record Office (PRO), London, AIR 1/1660/204/97/7 & 11: a list of the machines allotted to No 14 Squadron at Hounslow Heath and Gosport, 22 May-31 October 1915. PRO AIR 1/1660/204/97/5 & 12 list Squadron officers, 25 February-4 November 1915.

3.   Sholto Douglas, Years of Combat (Collins, London, 1963) pp91-3.

4.   J C Watson's unpublished History of No 14 Squadron, Royal Flying Corps and Royal Air Force, composed 1921-2 is in PRO AIR 1/689/21/20/14. The work of t his former Squadron pilot (and later a lawyer in Edinburgh) gives backbone to this chapter and is the source of most unattributed points below.

5.   Squadron Leader R M Drummond DSO OBE MC, Air Work on the Sinai-Palestine Front (June 1916-November 1918), an essay written in 1922 at the RAF Staff College, Andover, and published with other essays by the Air Ministry in December 1923 (Air Publication 956).

6.   Drummond, pp133.

7.   Raymond Vann, Palestine: The Forgotten War in Cross & Cockade GB, vol 3, no 2 (Summer 1972) pp78-85; Drummond, pp134.

8.   Peter F G Wright, Skies over the Holy Land in Cross & Cockade pp13-30.

9.   P T Mallahan, The Hassana Raid in Over the Front, vol 4 no 2 (Summer 1989) pp148-154.

10.   His amazing experiences in captivity are vividly recounted both in his own memoirs, The Spook and the Commandant (William Kimber, London, 1975) and in those of Lieutenant E H Jones, The Road to En-dor (Bodley Head, London, 1919).

11.   Air Marshal Sir Richard Williams, These are Facts (Canberra, 1977) pp42-3; Australian War Memorial (AWM), Canberra, AWM 224, Mss. 515 (Report on Work of 1 Squadron, 16 March 1916 to 31 December 1917); L W Sutherland, Aces and Kings, pp1.

12.   Leonard Bridgman, The Clouds Remember: The Aeroplanes of World War 1, with a commentary by Oliver Stewart, MC AFC (Arms and Armour Press, London, 1972) pp19; PRO, London, AIR 1/2389/ 228/11/118: Squadron Leader H I Hanmer, RFC and RAF War Experiences, 1914-1918 (RAF Staff College, Andover, December 1928) pp2-3. See also his lecture Aircraft in the Palestine Campaign, also written at Andover in 1928 in AIR 1/2397/264/1.

13.   AWM, Canberra, AWM 25, 81/3/1 (AFC).

14. Drummond, pp115.

15. Williams, pp43-6.

16. Charles Schaedel, Men and Machines of the Australian Flying Corps 1914-1919 (Kookaburra Technical Publications, Dandenong, Victoria, 1972) pp12-22.

17. Hilary St. George Saunders, Per Ardua: The Rise of British Air Power 1911-1939 (Oxford University Press, 1944) pp176-7.

18. In Charles Anthony, The Winged Crusaders in Airmail 1952.

19. PRO, London, AIR 1/408/15/240/2: History of Training of Pilots in Egypt.

20. Bridgman, pp74-6.

21. Drummond, pp118-119.

22. Drummond, pp119-121

23. Their names, and those of subsequent reinforcements, are recorded in PRO, London, AIR/689/21/20/14 after Watson's narrative and discussion of it.

24. PRO, London: C Flight records, AIR 1/2383/226/16/1 & 2.

25. Saunders, pp245; Lawrence, pp342; H A Jones, The War in the Air, vol vi (Oxford, Clarendon Press, 1937) pp184.

26. Bridgman, pp23; Jones, vi, pp184; Wright, pp15-17: Williams, pp56-7.

27. Jones, vi, pp183-5; AWM, Canberra, AWM 224, Mss. 515 pp1; Wright, pp19.

28. Jones, vi, pp193-4.

29. Jones, vi, pp204-5.

30. Lawrence, pp585; Jones, vi, pp212-3.

31. Lawrence, pp596; Jones, vi, pp213-4.

32. Jones, vi, pp228-234.

33. AWM, Canberra, AWM 224, Mss 515, pp2.

34. As well as Watson's account, see also Guy Slater (ed.), My Warrior Sons: The Borton Family Diary 1914-1918 (Peter Davies, London, 1973), pp100-101.

35. AWM, Canberra, AWM 224, Mss. 515, pp1& 4.

36. AWM, Canberra, AWM 224, Mss 515, pp3.

37. AWM, Canberra, AWM 224, Mss. 515, pp3.

38. Drummond, pp121; Williams, pp71-2.

39. Williams, pp70-71; Sutherland, pp140-56 (a photograph of Floyer, Palmer and Felmy with other German airmen appears after pp148); Wright, pp25.

40. Raymond Vann, 'CO in the Sideshows: The Flying Career of Major F A Bates, MC AFC DL in Palestine and Salonica in Cross and Cockade International, vol 24, no 1 (Spring 1993) pp38.

41. Drummond, pp137-8.

42. Anonymous instructor on Allenby's Campaign in Palestine at the Air Corps Tactical School, Maxwell Field, Alabama, 1938 (microfilm A.1927, Bolling AFB, Washington DC) pp7-8.

43. Williams, pp63-4; Cecil Manson, A World Away pp92; Drummond, pp122.

44. Diary of 1st Class Air Mechanic Joe Bull, 1 Squadron, AFC: currently (1995) being edited for publication by Squadron Leader Mark Lax, RAAF, Air Power Studies Centre, RAAF Base Fairbairn, Canberra.

45. AWM, Canberra, AWM 224, Mss. 515, pp6; Schaedel, pp18.

46. Williams, pp69; AWM, Canberra, AWM 224, Mss. 515, pp7.

47. Williams, pp71-2; AWM, Canberra, AWM 224, Mss. 515, pp8-9.

48. Williams, pp70-1, 73 & 79; AWM, Canberra, AWM 224, Mss. 515, pp1.

49. Manson, pp94.

50. Manson, pp100.

51. Vann, CO in the Sideshows, pp38.

52. Hanmer, pp11-12.

53. Alec McNeur Letters, National Archives, Wellington, MS 4108, Folder 5.

54. Sutherland, pp273. A nominal roll of No 14 Squadron pilots and observers 'employed in Artillery Co-operation' during October 1917 appears in PRO, London, AIR 1/1759/204/141/39; pilots and observers on strength in November are listed in AIR 1/1214/204/5/ 2630 and those on strength between 1 November and 29 January 1918 in AIR 1/1752/204/141/1. See also Wright, pp26-7.

55. Leonard T. Towers, Mr Valiant: The Story of Arthur G Hopkins M C (The Epworth Press, London, 1926), pp41-5.

56. Vann, CO in the Sideshows, pp39.

57. Hanmer, pp13-15.

58. Bridgman, pp27; Hanmer, pp23; Manson, pp99.

59. Personal correspondence with Kevin Kelly, aviation historian.

60. Hanmer, pp17-18; Manson, pp97.

61. Hanmer, pp21-2; Vann, CO in the Sideshows pp40.

62. Alec McNeur Letters, National Archives, Wellington, MS Folder 6.

63. Vann, CO in the Sideshows, pp40.

64. Jones, vi, pp175.

65. Jones, vi, pp177-8.

66. Hanmer, pp25.

67.   Wright, pp19; Manson, 97-8.

68.   AWM, Canberra, AWM 25, 81/3/1 (AFC).

69.   Hanmer, pp24a.

70.   Hanmer, pp28 & 29.

71.   Jones, vi, pp180-182, 185-90 & 194n.

72.   Jones, vi, pp190.

73.   AWM, Canberra, AWM 25, 81/3/1 (AFC).

74.   Sutherland, pp236-7.

75.   Slater (ed.), My Warrior Sons. Biffy claimed to have christened German anti-aircraft fire 'Archibald', later abbreviated to 'Archie', while serving as a pilot on the Western Front with No 5 Squadron in November 1914: while evading fire, he and his observer sang the chorus of a popular music-hall song of the day, 'Archibald - Certainly Not!' (pp15).

76.   Jones, vi, pp202 & 209. The Handley Page bomber, flown by Brigadier General Borton and Major Archie MacLaren, formerly of No 14 Squadron (who took along his dog, Tiny) had left Manston in Kent on 28 July for Heliopolis, arriving on 8 August. Its great size and low speed made it suitable only for night operations and the fact that it was equipped with Rolls-Royce engines, similar to those in Bristol Fighters, caused it to be assigned to the Australian squadron. Captain Ross Smith flew it on all its operations in Palestine. In 1919, Ross and his brother Keith would fly an even bigger machine, a Vickers Vimy, from England to Australia, thereby earning £10,000 and a knighthood (Wright, pp30; Williams, pp91-2; Slater, pp175-195).

77.   Jones, vi, pp207-8; Drummond, pp125 & 138.

78.   Jones, vi, pp206, 210-2; Sutherland, pp237-9; Drummond, pp25.

79.   Jones, vi, pp214-6; Drummond, pp126-31.

80.   Sutherland, pp253.

81.   Williams, pp95-6; Jones, vi, pp216, 222-8; Sutherland, pp36, 253-9.

82.   Jones, vi, pp230-8; Williams, pp98-9; Drummond, pp139.

83.   PRO London, AIR 1/689/21/20/14, following Watson's narrative; according to AIR 27/191, the Squadron suffered 31 casualties in action (6 killed or died of wounds, 3 reported dead or presumed dead, 19 wounded, 3 prisoners of war) and 12 in accidents (4 killed or died of injuries, 8 injured). The latest figures are in Chris Hobson (Compiler), Airman died in the Great War, 1914-1918. (J B Hayward & Son, Suffolk 1995) pp331 & 361.

84.   Towers, pp47.

85.   Alec McNeur Letters, National Archives, Wellington, MS 4108, Folder 8; Robin Higham, Air Power: A Concise History (St. Martin's Press, New York, 1972) pp41.

PERSONNEL INDEX

Blair, J, Dr, 76
Board, A, Air Cdre, 62, 63, 65
Boddam-Whetham, A C, Maj, 24, 25, 256
Bolitho, H, (Author), 69
Bolton, J H, FSgt (RAAF), 207
Bonetti, ADM (Italian Navy), 137
Borton, A, BrigGen, 37
Bosworth, Sgt, 170
Bower, R C, Plt Off (RCAF), 80
Bowyer, C, (Historian), 47, 173
Boyes, FSgt, 237
Bradley, J, Fg Off, 75
Bradley, J S, Sqn Ldr, 46, 257
Broadhurst, Sgt, 97
Brooke-Popham, R Sir, (AVM), 57
Brooks, C A, Capt, 22
Brooks, Flt Lt, 176
Brown (Bingo), Air Cdre, 149
Brown, F F, Fg Off (RAAF), 181, 182, 199
Brown, Sgt, 112, 193
Brown, Sqn Ldr, 213
Brown, Plt Off, 145
Brown, J, 2Lt, 11
Bruce, Fg Off, 50
Brummer, Lt (SAAF), 239
Buchanan, J N, Wg Cdr, 145, 147, 153, 156, 164, 171, 172, 259
Buckland, J, FSgt, 182, 183, 195
Buckland, J, Sqn Ldr, 277
Budge, Fg Off, 235
Bulfin, LtGen, 25
Bullen, LAC, 193
Bullock, FSgt, 181, 186, 190, 198
Burnett, C, LCol, 37
Burcher, Sgt, 119
Burton, FSgt, 203
Bury, Sgt, 145
By, Sgt, 171

Calver, Sgt, 144
Cameron, Fg Off, 223
Campbell, Fg Off (RAAF), 202, 232
Campbell, Sgt (RAF) Mustang Pilot, 159
Canavan, J, FSgt, 198, 201
Card, H, Flt Lt (Canada), 81, 94, 97
Cavalier Le, Fg Off (Canada), 97, 123, 145

Cavanagh, L W, FSgt (RAAF), 207
Carnie, W L, FSgt (RAAF), 198, 206
Carr, Sgt, 182
Cecil, Lord, 84
Chaplin, Sgt, 172
Chappit, 2Lt (SAAF), 172
Chaytor, E W C, BrigGen, 10, 11
Chauvel, H G, MajGen, 10, 38
Chetwode, P, Sir, LtGen, 22, 38
Chick, Sgt, 97
Chubb, Sgt, 159
Churchill, W, Sir, 44, 98, 155, 200, 231
Clapson, FSgt, 193
Clark, FSgt, 236, 239, 240
Clarke, Sgt, 179, 185, 187
Clarke-Hall, G W, Flt Lt, 181, 190, 191, 193, 195, 198, 202
Clifford, L, FSgt, 233
Climpson, FSgt, 232
Cloway, T P, Sqn Ldr, 195
Coath, (RAAF), 225
Cockey, L H, Sqn Ldr, 76, 258
Cockington, Sgt, 182
Coleman, D H, Flt Lt, 230
Collins, G, FSgt, 195, 197, 205, 213
Colyer, J, FSgt, 207, 227, 230
Coningham, M, AVM, 13, 153, 157
Cooke, W, Fg Off, 54, 57, 97, 275
Copp, L, Sgt (RAAF), 251
Cornish, Fg Off, 235, 236, 239, 240
Cornwall, Sgt, 172
Corsegio, Sgt, 176
Cox, H Sir, LCol (Brit.Res), 45, 49, 50, 56, 84
Cranchini, Capt (IT), 121
Crawford, Fg Off, 202
Croskell, Sgt, 227, 231, 232
Crouch, E, WOff, 109, 110, 128
Crowe, H, Flt Lt (Ref also Crowe Air Cdre), 51
Cruishank, H, Fg Off, 81
Culham, Sgt, 144
Culley, 50
Cunningham, Admiral RN, 221
Curtis, Sgt, 171

D'Albiac, J, Sqn Ldr, 49, 151
d'Arcy, Sgt, 109, 120

Dawnay, A G C, LCol, 17
Davies, N G N, Sgt, 62
Davis, FSgt, 185, 227
Dee, K M, FSgt (RAAF), 181, 194, 195, 203, 207
Dennis, Fg Off, 159
de Yarburgh-Bateson, A, Flt Lt, 192, 225, 249
di Courton, Admiral (Italian), 218
Dickson, Sgt, 145
Dill, J, MajGen, 93, 94
Dixon, Sgt (RAAF), 119, 182
Dixon-Spain, J, Maj, 12
Dobbie, W, Brig, 59, 60
Dolan, Plt Off, 207
Dolphin, W H, Sqn Ldr, 47, 257
Donovan, E, Plt Off, 178, 180, 182, 185, 190, 197, 199, 200, 203, 205, 216, 219, 228, 238, 239, 242, 250, 260
Douglas Sholto, Sir, AVM, 2, 217, 246
Dowding, H, AVM, 60
Drummond, P, Capt, 3, 9, 13, 21
Dube, Sgt (RCAF), 184
Duncan, Fg Off, 240
Dunsmore, W, Fg Off, 192, 221, 238
Dyson, FSgt (RAAF), 178, 200

Eaton, Sgt, 144
Edwards, E W, 2Lt, 11
Egan, R, FSgt (RAAF), 210
Egebjerg, Sgt (Danish), 190
Einsaar, L, FSgt (RAAF), 181, 182, 187, 194, 195
Eisenhower, D, Gen (US Army), 220
Ellenbogan, Sgt, 232
Elliot, Plt Off, 97
Elliot, W, Flt Lt, 47
Elliot, J H, Fg Off (RAAF), 161, 176, 179, 181, 185, 188, 202, 241, 245
Ellis, Plt Off (RAAF), 176
Ellis, Sgt, 159
Elsey, Flt Lt, 211, 212, 231, 232, 245
Elton, J, Sqn Ldr, 108, 128
Everidge, J, Sqn Ldr, 50, 258
Exell, T E, Sgt (RAAF), 182

Fadin, Capt, (Italian Navy), 134
Fair, D R R, Sqn Ldr, 199
Falconer, C, Flt Lt, 268
Farrell, Sgt, 109, 119

Fearn, Sgt, 145
Feisal, HRH Emir, 16, 17, 42, 44, 71
Felix, Madame, 229
Fellowes, C, Capt, 25
Felmy, G, Ober Lt (German), 21
Fennel, Sgt, 200
Fenwick-Wilson, R, Flt Lt, 97
Ferguson, Plt Off, 97
Fletcher, Sgt, 193, 236
Floyer, E A, Lt, 21
Foli-Brickley, Plt Off, 184
Forbes, A, Flt Lt (Dr), 185, 186, 234
Forrester, S, Lt (SAAF), 136, 145, 273
Foxley-Norris, C N, Wg Cdr, 261
Francis, WO (BLAF), 181, 194, 198, 201, 203, 205, 206, 240
Franks, Plt Off, 159
Freeman, N, WO (RNZAF), 180, 206, 207, 213, 215, 220
Freeman, R H, Capt, 24
Freeman, W R, Maj, 3, 256
Fretwell, Sgt, 145
Freyberg, Gen, 146
Friel, LAC, 176
"Fritz", (Cook), 174, 213
Fuller, Sgt, 144
Furness-William, F H, Capt, 17

Gallehawk, A N, Sqn Ldr, 47, 58, 257
Gannan, G H, WO (RAAF), 182, 183
Garrison, Col (USAF), 178
Garside, Plt Off, 97
Garton, Wg Cdr, 241
Gasparini, Capt, (Italian Navy), 131, 133, 137
Gellatley, Flt Lt, 223, 230
George V, HM King, 71
George VI, HM King, 1, 79, 91, 194, 205
Gibbins, Flt Lt, 186, 202, 228, 238
Gibbon, D, Fg Off, 62, 67
Gibbs, Sqn Ldr, 269
Gibbs, G, Flt Lt, 243
Gilkey, Fg Off, 229
Gilmour, Sgt, 144
Gildner, Plt Off (Mustang pilot), 203
Gilroy, (Pilot), 228
Glanville, FSgt, 237, 240
Glubb, J Sir, MajGen, 44, 46, 73, 90

Godfrey, Plt Off, 97
Godly, A, Sgt, 171
Golding, J F W, Mr, 12
Goldsmith, Sgt, 195
Gomm, C, Flt Lt, 97
Good, A, Sgt, 171
Goode, P, Plt Off, 164, 172, 180, 181, 193
Goodwin, C K, Flt Lt (RAAF), 194-196
Grace, E, Flt Lt, 70
Graham, C, Cdre, 151
Graham, Lt (SAAF), 180
Graham, G, Sgt, 179, 185, 204, 207
Grant-Dalton, S, Capt, 8
Green, Flt Lt, 145
Greenhill, Plt Off, 97
Greet, C, Flt Lt, 62, 65, 66
Grimsey, D, Sqn Ldr, 159, 176, 181, 223, 227, 231
Grimsey, H, Plt Off, 185
Grinnell-Milne, D, 46
Gubbins, Cpl, 177
Guts, (Dog), 85, 88
Guzzoni, Gen (Italian), 207

Haddingham, Sqn Ldr, 237, 238, 243
Halahan, P, Fg Off, 71
Haley, R, Cpl (RAAF), 152, 176, 184, 202, 225, 270
Hall, E G W, LAC, 144, 145, 245
Hanmer, H, Lt, 28-30, 34
Hanson, Cpl, 157
Harris, A, Sir, 61
Harrison, Plt Off, 97, 195
Harvie, Plt Off (RAAF), 171
Hedges, FSgt, 160
Helsby, Fg Off, 97
Hepworth, Plt Off, 180
Herschell, Fg Off, 236, 240
Hibbert, FSgt, 171
Higham, R, (US Historian), 40
Highman, G F, Sgt, 176
Hill, C W, Lt, 5, 6, 46
Hill, R, Air Cdre, 61, 79, 85
Hitchin, Sgt, 129
Hitler, Adolf, 91, 97, 106
Hogg, Fg Off (RCAF), 238, 244, 254
Holland, WO, 239, 240

MacDonald, J M F, Flt Lt (RCAF), 236, 251
MacDonald, S D, Gp Capt, 108, 238, 241
MacDonald, W C, Fg Off, 234, 242
Mack, B J, Sgt, 184
MacLaren, A, 2Lt, 8
MacLean, C, AVM, 1, 79
MacLeod, Cpl, 150
MacNab, (SA), 97
Main, Plt Off, 159
Mailer, WO, 235, 236, 240
Manesch von Baron, (Austrian),154
Manning, J, Flt Lt, 103, 105
Manson, C, Capt, 23, 25, 30, 31, 34
Marsden, Fg Off, 50
Martin, Fg Off (Padre), 128
Martin, V A, Dr, 128
Martino, C, Capt (Italian Navy), 120
Mason, FSgt, 207
Matthews, Plt Off (Canadian), 97
Maynard, AVM, 254
Maydwell, W S G, Wg Cdr, 172, 181, 190, 193, 204, 207, 210, 215, 221, 259
McConnell, Sgt, 128, 145
McConnell, H, Lt, 28, 29
McDiarmid, G, 2Lt, 11
McDonald, E H, FSgt, 62
McIndoe, Dr, 232
McKenzie, LCol (SAAF), 241
McKenzie, M, Fg Off (NZ), 97, 115, 123, 129, 145
McNeur, A, Pte, 26, 32, 40
Meader, E, Sgt, 272
Meadwell, E, Sgt, 177, 284
Medhurst, C E, Maj, 25, 257
Merkley, Fg Off, 232
Metatich, Fg Off, 144
Metcalfe, Fg Off, 232
Miles, Sgt (RNZAF), 198, 206
Milford, Sgt, 232
Mildren, Sgt, 109, 112
Miller, Sgt, 159
Mills, Sqn Ldr, 170, 171
Minter, M, 2Lt, 8
Mitchell, Fg Off (RAAF), 223, 224
Montgomery, B, Gen, 178, 207
Moore, Sqn Ldr, 176
Moorehead, A, War Coord (Australian), 106 - 118

Moretti, Capt (Italian Navy), 134
Morris, Sgt, 75
Morrison, Sgt, 97, 144
Moulton, L, Sgt, 97, 123, 147
Murphy, L, FSgt (RAAF), 206, 210
Mouatt, Plt Off (RAAF), 198
Muir, S K, Lt, 24
Murray, A Sir, Gen, 2, 20

Nicholas, Sgt, 200
Nicholls, FSgt (RAAF), 178
Norris, Sgt, 97, 120, 128
Nuttall, Sgt, 203

O'Connor, N, WO (RAAF), 174, 181-183, 194, 201, 206, 210, 215
O'Laughlin, Plt Off, 159
Omissi, D, (Historian), 60, 91, 93
Overed, Lt (SAAF), 237, 240, 254

Page, Sgt, 145
Palmer, C B, Lt, 21
Paris, D R, 2Lt, 8
Park, Sgt, 207
Parker, Sgt, 144
Parker, H, Fg Off, 141, 149
Parks, Fg Off, 192
Patey, L A, Sgt, 96, 97, 112
Patman, Sgt, 198
Patton, Gen (US Army), 207
Paulus von, F, Gen (German Army), 142
Pawson, J I, Wg Cdr, 254, 260
Payne, A G, Sgt, 176
Peake Pasha, F G, Col (Arab Legion), 46, 48, 84
Peppino, Capt, (Italian Navy), 133
Perganini, ADM (Italian Navy), 220
Pettit, S, Capt, 30
Philby, H, St John, (BR Advisor), 49, 50
Phillips, C, Plt Off, 180, 190, 201, 205-207
Phillips, O A, Fg Off (RAAF), 181, 205, 220
Pirie, Sqn Ldr, 176, 177
Platt, FSgt, 182, 183
Platt, W Sir, LGen, 129
Playfair, P Gp Capt, 59
Ploskin, Sgt, 182
Plumer, Lord, Fd Mar (High Com), 57

GENERAL INDEX

Aircraft, Italian:
   CANT 506B, 198, 208
   CANT Z 1107, 215
   Fiat CR 32, 109
   Fiat CR 42, 109, 116, 120, 122, 129, 142, 144
   Macchi 200/202/205, 194, 215, 222, 228
   Piaggio P 108, 222
   Reggiane Re 2001, 222, 228
   Savoia - Marchetti SM 79, 202, 204, 206, 207, 209
   Savoia - Marchetti SM 81, 125, 129
   Savoia - Marchetti SM 82, 121, 122, 207
Engines:
   Beardmore, 4
   Hispano-Suiza, 4
   Liberty, 60
   Mercury XV, 127, 152
   Napier Lion, 62
   Panther, 70
   Pegasus XX, 89, 103, 115, 122
   Royal Aircraft Factory 90 Hp, 4
   Royal Aircraft Factory 140 Hp, 29
Airfields & Landing Grounds (See also Appendix A 256-261):
   Aboukir, 90, 91, 154
   Abu Sueir, 57, 64, 103, 150, 175, 180
   Adi Ugri, 120
   Agedabia, 141, 159, 161, 166
   Agheila, 141, 164, 166
   Ahwaz, 151
   Alghero, 234, 236, 237, 240, 243, 245
   Aleppo, 43, 44, 149
   Amman, 17, 43, 46, 47, 50, 54, 57, 59-61, 64, 67, 70, 74, 76, 85, 86, 88, 91, 96-98,
         147, 268
   Amriya, 172
   Ancona, 243
   Antelat, 161, 166, 170
   Aqaba, 17, 68, 70, 83, 256, 269
   Asmara, 108, 110, 120, 122, 125, 126, 129
   Azrak, 18, 38, 50, 55, 56, 68, 70, 71, 74, 81
   Bair, 74, 90
   Banff, 255
   Barce Megrun, 159
   Beersheba, 19, 20, 26, 43, 58
   Beirut, 149
   Benghazi, 130, 141, 145, 166, 171, 183
   Benina, 166

Australian Mounted Division, 8, 35
    Armament:
    Bombs: 20lb Cooper, 4, 6, 8, 17, 72, 95, 110, 169
          40lb, 110
          250lb, 6, 8, 16, 96, 100, 110, 113, 134, 161
          500lb, 125, 165, 169, 194
          Torpedo, 181, 182, 185, 187
    Guns: Lewis, 11, 29, 46, 81, 98, 109, 121, 169
          Browning, 98, 116, 121, 169
          K, 169
          20mm Cannon, 120, 128, 169
          Vickers, 89
Armoured Cars RAF No 2 Company, 46, 55, 59, 81, 86
Army Liaison Officer System, 143
Austrian AA Battery, 26

Baghdad, 68, 70, 71, 76, 91
Balfour Declaration, 44, 58
Balkan Air Force, 244
Bandershah, 151
Bara Marsa Kebir, 115, 262-266
Bardia, 160, 162
Bastia, 212
Bedouin, 3, 68, 154
Beirut, 39
Bethlehem, 31
Bir El Baheira, 158
Bir El Gobi, 159
Bir Hacheim, 177
Bir Hassana, 5, 6
Bir Magdhaba, 13
Bizerta, 200, 207, 234
Bomba, 159
Bou Fousha, 207
Bulawayo, 67

Cairo Conference 1922, 45
Cape (SA) Flights, 62, 64-66
Capraia Island, 211
Caspian, 151
Constantinople, 31
Convoys:
    B.N.1, 117
    B.N.2, 117
    B.N.3, 117

LRDG

Tehran, 151, 152
Tel Es Sham, 17
Teneib, 49
Tiger Force, 254
Transjordan Frontier Force, 46, 55, 60, 67, 69, 71, 73, 74, 76, 81, 92, 95, 96
Trieste, 226, 239, 243
Trinkitat, 106
Tubeiq, 74
Tulkarm, 92, 94
Tunis, 182, 183, 200, 203, 207, 234
Tunisia, 183, 184, 187, 202

Umbrella Hill, 27
Umbria: (Italian Steam Ship), 108
Ur, 91
Ustica, 199

SS Velho, 134
Venice, 226, 240

Wadis:
        Bair, 54
        El Fara, 38, 39
        Guzzeh, 19
        Hauran, 75
        Muksheib, 8
        Natrun, 187
        Rhum, 83, 84, 90
        Sheikh Nuran, 19
        Sirhan, 48, 50, 73
        Surar, 28, 30
        Ziglab, 96
Wejh, 15
Wings:
        1 Bomber, 97
        3 (SAAF), 165
        5 Wing, 2, 25
        40 Wing, 25
        63 Wing, 237
        254 Wing, 104, 107, 110, 117
        270 Wing, 160, 161, 163, 166
        328 Wing, 212, 221

Yaduda, 49, 76
Yehudad, 48

INVASION AREA

Marseille

Toulon
St Tropez
Nice
Genoa
Spezia
Belgrad
YUGOSLA
Sara

Barcelona
CORSICA
Elba
Ghisonaccia
Leghorn
ROME
ITALY
ADRIATIC SEA

Alghero
SARDINIA
Naples

Grottaglie

ALGIERS
M E D I T E R R .
Palermo
SICILY

Blida
Setif
Telergma
Bone
Constantine
Bizerte
Protville
TUNIS
Sousse
Malta

Biskra
Gafsa
Stax

Tozeur
Djerba
Gulf of Sirte

Touggourt
TRIPOLI
Misurata
BENGHA
Castel Benito
Sirte

A L G E R I A

T U N I S I A

L I B Y